Alastair Campbell

To Kay and Arthur

Alastair Campbell

Peter Oborne and Simon Walters

First published in Great Britain
2004 by Aurum Press Ltd
25 Bedford Avenue, London WC1B 3AT

ISBN 1 84513 001 4

1 3 5 7 9 8 6 4 2
2004 2006 2008 2007 2005

Designed and typeset in Haarlemmer by Geoff Green Book Design

Printed in Britain by Bookmarque, Croydon, Surrey

Contents

The article from the *Daily Mirror* of 3 October 1991 on page 67 is reproduced by kind permission of mirrorpix.com.

part one

part one

Prologue

Don't call me a liar.
Alastair Campbell, 30 January 2004

HE CUT A CONSPICUOUS FIGURE: a tall man with a confident stride, taut physique, a gaunt face and hair cut jagged and short. Observers seeing him for the first time might have guessed that he was a professional athlete in hard training. He carried an air of authority and command, and a whiff of menace. He did not, like so many visitors to 10 Downing Street, stop to ask directions. He walked straight in, and was suddenly among welcoming friends. During the months he had been away the atmosphere inside Downing Street had changed. It had become easier, less tense, some said less professional. Upon his return, electricity ran through the building again.

He had always known how to confront any problem. Now the Prime Minister was facing the greatest crisis in his career and wanted his old ally there to guide him. No one else had the panache, the certainty, the sheer contemptuous arrogance of Alastair Campbell – back now at the heart of government.

Five months earlier Campbell had had no choice but to announce his resignation. He had become the focus for all the suspicion and disgust directed at Tony Blair's government in the wake of the Iraq war. After the invasion the Prime Minister stood accused of making exaggerated claims about Iraq's military capacity, and also of being complicit in the death of the government scientist Dr David Kelly, who had killed himself after being revealed as the source for an allegation reported by the BBC's *Today* programme that the government deliberately exaggerated the case for war. Both Campbell and Blair knew that these charges could destroy the government.

The following day, 28 January 2004, would see Lord Hutton publish his long-awaited findings. A few copies of the Hutton report had arrived in Downing Street, twenty-four hours ahead of publication. It was a bulky document: including appendices it stretched to more than 700 pages. On the stroke of midday, after signing a heavy confidentiality clause, Campbell had it in his hands. Ever since Dr Kelly had slit his wrist in an Oxfordshire wood, the scientist's suicide had hung over Campbell and Blair. Neither man had been able to sleep without one thought nagging away at them: that Brian Hutton had the power to destroy them.

Campbell leafed through the report frantically, his eyes scanning each page. Slowly, as he read each gentle, redeeming phrase and judgement, relief began to overwhelm him. He kept re-reading, to check he had not missed a paragraph that condemned or criticized him. He had not. It was, he later proclaimed to his Downing Street friends, 'better than my best-case scenario'[1]. He felt relief, then gratitude, and exultation. This would quickly turn into a desire for revenge and retribution.

Campbell spent the night at Number 10 – partly to avoid the cameramen and reporters outside the front door of his home at Gospel Oak in north London. It was the most relaxed and jovial evening he had spent at Downing Street for many years. All the problems of the previous nine months, all the fears for the future, seemed to have washed away. Campbell rose early and had a thirty-minute work-out in the small gymnasium the Prime Minister had installed in his flat. Then he went downstairs and started work on his response. Few of the thousands of speeches, resignations letters, statements, newspaper articles and press releases he had written for others in nearly ten years as a spin-doctor gave him as much pleasure as this one. This was Campbell's personal document, just as the war against the BBC, to demand a retraction of the *Today* programme's allegation that he had personally 'sexed up' the Iraq intelligence dossier, had been his personal war. He demanded the right to make a personal response.

Campbell had no access to parliament, so he sought a comparably grandiose backdrop for his words. On the afternoon of 28 January, hours after the report was made public, and amid widespread disbelief at its clean bill of health for the government and coruscating criticism of the BBC, he prepared his victory dance. He went to the headquarters of the Foreign Press Association at 11 Carlton House Terrace, once the town house of the great Liberal Prime Minister William Ewart Gladstone, now used for Downing Street briefings to lobby journalists. A phalanx of TV cameras was in place when Campbell strode to the dais with the sweeping balustrade behind him. He used the full array of presentational skills he had perfected for Tony Blair to strike the right pose. Dressed in a sober dark suit, white shirt and plain dark tie, he looked more like an American president giving a press conference at the White House than a former *Daily Mirror* journalist turned political hack. Campbell wasted no time in getting to what, for him, was the heart of the matter.

'What the report shows very clearly is this,' he said. 'The Prime Minister told the truth, the government told the truth, and I told the truth. The BBC from the chairman and director-general down did not. Today a stain on the integrity of the Prime Minister and the government has been removed.'

He cited the BBC's chairman Gavyn Davies, its director-general Greg Dyke, the head of news Richard Sambrook and *Today* presenter John Humphrys all by name, accusing them of falsely claiming to have investigated his complaints. Their behaviour was 'unforgivable', and could only be exculpated with 'resignations at several levels'. Hutton was right to say, he continued, measuring each word, that '"the media has responsibilities to seek to broadcast and publish the truth". I was a tough, politically committed journalist and not alone in that. But I did not make up stories. I sought to check facts and did not believe politicians were all in it for venal or self-serving reasons. All we ever wanted was an acknowledgement that the allegations broadcast on the BBC were false.' Humphrys, who had been targeted by Campbell ever since his devastating interview of Blair at the height of the Bernie Ecclestone affair in 1997, said watching Campbell's performance that day felt 'like lying in the gutter while your head's kicked in'.[2]

Later that night, Campbell put his feelings rather more succinctly when he bumped into another senior BBC journalist: 'Your fucking organization has had it.'[3]

The following evening, Campbell hosted an auction at London's

Park Lane Hilton Hotel to mark his latest charity venture for Leukaemia Research, a triathlon event made up of distance running, swimming and cycling. The organizers advised Campbell, as a newcomer to the event, against attempting all three disciplines at his first attempt. Campbell ignored their advice and insisted on doing all three. But even on this night of giving, feted by celebrities, anger was still surging through him when he was interviewed in a private room at the Hilton, by ITN political editor Nick Robinson. Robinson did not give Campbell the easy interview he hoped for. 'Are you proud of the fact that you have done to the BBC what Margaret Thatcher and Norman Tebbit failed to do: decapitate its leadership?' he asked. After dodging the question several times, Campbell snapped: 'I didn't decapitate the BBC, they did it themselves.' When Robinson asked him to say sorry to the Kelly family, Campbell angrily rebuked Robinson for implying he had not already done so. The moment the interview finished, Campbell lowered his voice and scowled slowly and coldly at the ITN man: 'That is the last time you interview me. Just leave the room.' Robinson met fire with fire. 'What gives you the audacity to think you can tell me which room I should be in?' he replied. And with that Campbell returned to the charity reception and auctioned a signed copy of the Hutton Report into the death of David Kelly for £10,000.

On 30 January, Campbell took his story to the country. On stage in a theatre in South Shields, he was happy to answer questions from the public in the first of a series of solo appearances entitled 'An Audience with Alastair Campbell'. By then Gavyn Davies and Greg Dyke had resigned. News of the resignation of BBC defence correspondent Andrew Gilligan, who had originally reported the 'sexing-up' allegation, came through while Campbell was on stage. He put on a characteristic display of charm, wit and bluster, spiced with venom. There was praise for Tony Blair and savage criticism of the media. But his affability was punctured when a member of the audience queried whether he had told the truth over the death of Dr Kelly. 'I attended the Hutton inquiry,' said the questioner, an earnest-looking, slim, bearded man, 'and I do not believe that you did not personally try to influence the Joint Intelligence Committee assessment and presentation of intelligence, and I also do not believe that Blair was not involved in the naming of Dr David Kelly.' Campbell, seated in a *Mastermind*-style chair under a spotlight, adopted the belligerence so familiar to ministers, officials and journalists who had challenged his word. 'A week ago I defended myself, I defended myself at the Foreign Affairs Committee, and the Hutton inquiry and what's more – and maybe that's why I sometimes get a bit angry about it – this has had a big impact on me and my family and a lot more other people,' he said. 'So don't call me a liar. Please don't sit there when I have been cleared by a law lord, and call me a liar.'

chapter one

Fair and False like a Campbell

Much may be made of a Scotsman, if he be caught young.
Samuel Johnson on Lord Mansfield
[educated, like Campbell, in England]

THE NAME IS ALL IMPORTANT. To an Englishman the name Campbell is merely an indication that its possessor hails from a nation which has been in turn invaded, plundered, pacified and neglected but never quite absorbed in the course of a thousand years of frequently bloody encounters. To a Scot, and in particular a Highland Scot, the name Campbell is pregnant with a different kind of significance.

All Scottish Highland clans have a history of treachery. But the clan of Campbell, led for centuries by the dukes of Argyll, has a uniquely traitorous past. Their defining moment came on the morning of 13 February 1692 when, acting on the orders of the king, they massacred the Macdonalds of Glencoe, their hosts throughout the previous two weeks. The crime counted, under Scottish law, as 'murder under trust', an extreme form of murder on a level with treason. No Campbell was ever prosecuted, however, because the clan enjoyed the protection of the hated King William III. The story has all the Campbell hallmarks – betrayal, barbarity, a careful determination to keep in with the government of the day, and an enviable capacity to end up on the winning side. These characteristics have stood Campbells in good stead ever since.

In 1707 the English government turned to the Campbell clan to enforce the Act of Union between the two countries. The dukes of Argyll, as ever, were happy to barter their support. The second duke hastened home from the battlefield – he was serving under the Duke of

Marlborough in the War of the Spanish Succession – and demanded instant promotion to major-general, an English peerage, and command of the scrappy militia that passed for a government army. As petitions flooded in from Scottish boroughs and shires against the Union, Argyll ignored them: he suggested they should be turned into paper kites.

In the course of the eighteenth century most Highland clans joined the doomed Jacobite rebellions of 1715 and 1745. The Campbells ensured that they remained in good standing with the Hanoverian dynasty. The dukes of Argyll and their followers were well rewarded with honours and land, often at the expense of Highland rivals who had sided with the Jacobites. They stood apart from the other Scottish clans: wholly without scruple, and guiding all with a cold-hearted eye fixed only on the calculation of their own interests. In the terms of *1066 and All That*, they had a settled policy of being Right but Repulsive rather than, like most of their Highland fellows, Wrong but Wromantic. Perhaps Macaulay, in his *History of England*, best illustrates the widespread view of the Campbell character: 'A peculiar dexterity, a peculiar plausibility of address, a peculiar contempt for all the obligations of good faith were ascribed, with or without reason, to the dreaded race. "Fair and False like a Campbell" became a proverb.'

There are certain traits in Alastair Campbell that would have been instantly recognized, and richly approved, by the dukes of Argyll as they ensured their survival in the shifting sands of Scottish politics: a capacity for barbarism; a profound clannish instinct and ruthless loyalty to his family and those he has chosen to be his friends; an ability to enter into the most unlikely alliances. Most of all, however, they would have noted a strong vein of worldly pragmatism. All appearances to the contrary, Campbell is a man who found government congenial. He has possessed from a relatively young age the gift of ending up on the winning side. He is a talented politician, in large matters as in small, with the true politician's gift for making friends. Only in one part of the United Kingdom is Campbell disliked with any real violence – Scotland. Before the Scottish Assembly elections of summer 1999 he was obliged to make, alongside the Prime Minister, a series of trips north of the border to advance the case for devolution. The visits were marred by unseemly scenes and verbal abuse as the Scots turned against Tony

Blair. They saw him – for all his education at an Edinburgh public school – as an English impostor. They resented Campbell, the Prime Minister's hatchet-man, as a turncoat. Who can say that John Campbell, the second duke of Argyll who sold out so profitably to the English in 1707, was not chuckling to himself from whatever resting place Highland chieftains go to when they die, and smiling sardonically at the characteristic actions of his distant kinsman?

Campbells today are scattered all over Scotland as well as further afield. But Alastair Campbell's own line traces easily and directly back to the very Argyll heartland. For generations his family lived on Tiree, a Hebridean island of heart-stopping beauty whose inhabitants for centuries owed their fealty to the dukes of Argyll. It is sometimes known as 'the land below the waves', on account of the fact that it is almost entirely flat and treeless. It is a simple matter, using the archive in the General Records Office in Edinburgh, to trace Alastair Campbell's direct line back to the early 1800s. Hector Campbell, a farm labourer, was born in Tiree around 1820. His son Donald, a crofter, was born, also in Tiree, in 1853. He married Mary Macdonald in January 1878. Lachlan Campbell, Alastair's grandfather, was born six years later. They were all simple farming folk, but there is perhaps a sense of quiet ambition and steady progression through the generations: farm labourer, crofter, farmer. Today Alastair Campbell must have scores of cousins on the island. Though he has never lived there, Tiree is a central part of his blood and his heritage.

It was Campbell's father Donald who broke away from the Hebrides. Like so many Highland Scots, he benefited from a superb education system to abandon the hard life of his forefathers and find his way to the Glasgow Veterinary College. There he made firm friends with a fellow Scot, Murdo Ferguson, and this friendship was to prove decisive in the life of the young vet.

A vet's life in Keighley

Not long after the war, Ferguson was offered the position of assistant in a veterinary practice based around the mill town of Keighley in the West Riding of Yorkshire. He happily made the journey south and took up employment at the Aireworth Veterinary Centre. Very shortly afterwards

Hubert Holland, the owner of the practice, decided to retire. Unable to purchase Aireworth on his own, Ferguson appealed to his old friend Donald Campbell to join forces with him. They bought the practice together and for a few years they were partners.

It was a happy and fulfilling time all round in the life of Donald Campbell. Not only was he experiencing the rewarding sensation of building up his own business, he brought with him to Keighley his bride Elizabeth. She fitted in easily with the local Yorkshire folk. George Crabtree, who soon joined Donald Cameron in the veterinary practice, remembers her as a 'great lass, charming and very lovely'. (During the 1997 general election campaign Tony Blair was introduced to Betty Campbell. 'You can't be Alastair Campbell's mother,' he said. 'You're nice.') There is no question that the Campbells were an attractive and popular couple in the Keighley area. They threw themselves into local life. 'Donald worked hard and he played hard,' recalls Crabtree. 'If the work was done and he was off-duty he would go out partying with Elizabeth or enjoy a few drinks with his male friends.'

Donald Campbell, as befitted a man of professional standing in the community, was an active member of the local Conservative Club. You did not have to be political to belong to the Tory party of the 1950s. It was more a state of mind, a statement about the kind of person you were. In a decade when there was little else available in the way of entertainment, Conservative Clubs provided an important social hub for the communities they served. They were places to drink, to meet members of the opposite sex, to do business, to go when there was nothing else in particular to do. They were emphatically not places where people went to discuss politics. George Crabtree says of his partner: 'Donald was a member of the Conservative Club, but he was not particularly interested in politics. We would go there once every fortnight to play snooker and chat to the other members. It was a good social scene. Neither of us was particularly good at it.'

There were hundreds of Conservative Clubs in Britain in the postwar period. They flourished because professional men like Donald Campbell and his partner George Crabtree found them congenial to go to, even if it was only for the snooker and the beer. They were an important part of the hold that the Tory party had over the British people in the era of Churchill, Eden and Macmillan. It is just one symptom of

Conservative decline that for the last decade they have been closing down all around the country.

It is possible that young Alastair's earliest memory of the Conservative party was of a mysterious place where his father went after work and from which he occasionally returned reeking of alcohol, late for dinner and in disgrace. It is very doubtful whether Elizabeth Campbell approved of the Keighley Conservative Club as much as Donald Campbell did. Alastair may have noted that, and taken heed.

Not long after arriving at Keighley the young couple set about rearing a family. For several years the children came thick and fast. To friends it seemed as if Elizabeth gave birth every year. Donald, Graham, Alastair and Elizabeth – the only daughter – were all born about eighteen months apart. Alastair was born on 25 May 1957, at the Victoria Hospital, Keighley.

The West Riding was a stimulating, in some ways an ideal, place for a young child to grow up. Alastair's parents lived in Oakworth, a small industrial town outside Keighley. The family had a stone-built house called 'Lydstep' at the end of Station Road. The house has long since been demolished, but the railway line at the bottom of the road remains and is now in the hands of the Keighley and Worth Valley Railway, whose preserved steam trains still lumber up and down the valleys of the West Riding and form an inevitable part of any holiday taken in the region. In 1974 the station at the bottom of the road gained a modest kind of fame when *The Railway Children* was filmed there.

Just as important as the town itself were the Pennine Hills which surrounded it. The hill farms of the area provided much of the work for Donald Campbell's veterinary practice. Anyone wishing to gain some insight into Alastair Campbell's early life should study James Herriot's sequence of novels about the life of a peripatetic vet on the Yorkshire Dales, which paint a gripping and surprisingly unsentimental picture of the daily dramas facing any veterinary practice: the battles for payment with impecunious smallholders, the sudden midnight calls, the difficulties of access in winter to snow-bound hill farmers, the tedious but profitable triviality of dealing with domestic pets.

James Herriot himself, a veterinary surgeon whose real name was Alf Wight, was an acquaintance of the Campbell family. His books are based on the very post-war years during which Donald Campbell served the isolated communities of farming people in the north of England, and draw on experience which must have been very similar to Campbell's. The successful television series made from the Herriot stories have fostered a delusion that life in the Dales was some rustic idyll. But for Donald Campbell and his partners, it was hard and sometimes dangerous work. George Crabtree recalls seven-day weeks and nineteen-hour days. Even though theirs was a successful and well-run practice, it was difficult to break even because of missed payments. 'I used to dread the annual book-keeping,' recalls Crabtree. 'We would be depressed for days after the annual accounts.' There is some evidence that the Campbells were occasionally forced to take in lodgers to help make ends meet: when Alastair was born, one Wilfred Waterhouse is recorded as living at their address.

All this took an undoubted toll on the members of the Aireworth practice – as indeed it did on Alf Wight in Thirsk, who suffered from a debilitating form of depression all his life. A short history of the practice recently disclosed that a former partner took his own life by cutting his throat. Murdo Ferguson, Donald Campbell's friend from college days, was struck down by a heart attack while returning from a house call five miles away. He died in 1956. In due course it all became too much for Donald Campbell as well. Ironically, the event that caused the Campbells to leave Keighley – and which nearly cost Donald his life – took place while he was doing his beloved farm work.

It was a routine job. After a sow has given birth to piglets, the vet is called to castrate the males. Donald had carried out the task thousands of times. On this occasion it went horribly wrong. It is vital, when performing the operation, to keep the sow well away from the litter. Unforgivably, she was allowed to escape. The furious beast charged at Donald, and smashed him to the ground before sinking her teeth deep into his leg. As the vet lay on the ground, blood gushing from his wound, the farmer's young daughter bravely intervened to pull the angry animal away.

Donald was obliged to spend six weeks in hospital, and at least as much again recovering at home before he could go back to work. He was never again quite fit enough to cope with the demands of his arduous practice: he retired in 1969 and the family moved south to Leicester where Donald Campbell managed to secure a much less physically demanding administrative job with the Ministry of Agriculture.

The accident must have had a traumatic effect on the young Alastair Campbell. It happened at an age when any young boy is very dependent on his father, regarding him as a hero figure. The prostration of Donald Campbell would have smashed through the comfortable certainties of a happy childhood. At an almost identical age, Tony Blair suffered a similar though far more traumatic affliction when his own father – a man of high talent who was poised on the verge of a possible parliamentary career – was struck down by a massive stroke. Happily Donald Campbell needed just three months to recover. It took Leo Blair three years to regain the power of speech: the effect on the future Prime Minister cannot be overestimated. The two men share a common awareness of tragedy, gained at too young an age; it is one of the things that bind them together.

Keighley gave Alastair Campbell much. His early years were spent among solid northern country folk. For a man whose professional life has been devoted to the cultivation and conquest of a rootless metropolitan élite, this has been no bad thing. Keighley plays a role in Campbell's personal mythology similar to that of Hebden Bridge for Sir Bernard Ingham when he was Margaret Thatcher's press secretary. Sir Bernard felt that the lessons Hebden Bridge (which lies in the Pennine Hills, and near enough to form an outlying part of Donald Campbell's practice) had to offer were so profound that to celebrate his ten years in Downing Street he invited thirty valued colleagues to join him there for the weekend. Alastair Campbell's acknowledgement to the town of his childhood is – thus far – less demonstrative. His single tribute is to have accepted the presidency of the Keighley branch of the Burnley Football Club supporters' club, an honour that has been duly noted in his otherwise sparse *Who's Who* entry.

Burnley Football Club

The most tangible legacy of Alastair Campbell's Keighley years is his enduring devotion to Burnley FC. Anybody brought up in Keighley in the early 1960s had a choice of several football teams to support – Leeds, Bradford City or Burnley, to name three. Leeds lies twenty-five miles away to the east; Bradford is the nearest big city; while Burnley is more romantically positioned, twenty miles across the wilds of Keigh-ley Moor to the west. In the early 1960s, when Alastair was a young boy – the age when decisive choices are made in these matters – there was not a great deal to choose between the two teams of Leeds and Burnley. With the benefit of hindsight it is possible to see that Burnley was the declining force, its years of greatness behind it. Tucked away in a hidden corner of England, what had once been an important Victorian town was going nowhere much, neither commercially nor in footballing terms. Leeds by contrast was a bustling place. Great things were about to happen: the town was on the point of producing one of the finest League teams of all time: Don Revie's ensemble, which dominated English football in the late 1960s and early 1970s.

It seems unlikely that the Alastair Campbell of the Downing Street years would have made the choice the youthful Campbell made forty years ago. Assessing matters with his customary pragmatic and unsen-timental eye, he would have plumped for Leeds and Revie, the Alex Fer-guson of his day. New Labour is ruthless with losers. But as a small boy, he did not make these calculations. And family loyalty lay with Burnley – friends remember that his elder brothers already supported the club. Thus Alastair Campbell's long association with the little East Lan-cashire football club was forged.

Even during the most stressful times in Downing Street, Campbell would go to extreme lengths to attend a Burnley home game. Burnley games take precedence over practically everything else. It was natural, for instance, for Campbell to cite the necessity to watch his favourite team play as the reason why he could not attend Peter Mandelson's for-tieth birthday celebration. 'Alastair will drive the 240 miles up to Burn-ley,' observes political columnist and fellow Burnley supporter Chris Buckland, 'watch them get beat and then drive all the way back.'

Campbell is nowadays a revered figure on the Burnley terraces, where he normally chooses to sit in the Bob Lord stand, opened by Edward Heath when he was prime minister and, according to Buck-land, 'a Tory stand through and through'. He is beloved of all Burnley supporters, and, after four decades supporting the club, known to most of them personally. And the Burnley directors have become friends and some get invited down to Campbell's rare parties in London. Campbell takes a close and active interest in team affairs. From time to time the

Prime Minister's press secretary, having dealt with some important matter of state, would pick up the phone in his Downing Street office, dial the number of Burnley Football Club, and issue lucid instructions about 'who to put in the team and important insights into tactics'. Campbell's views are listened to with respect, even if they are not always acted on with the same promptness and thoroughness he has come to regard as normal in other areas of his life.

However, his credentials as an ordinary fan took something of a knock when Millwall Football Club chairman Theo Paphitis claimed Campbell asked him for a helicopter to get to a match and enjoyed the comforts of the director's box. 'Campbell's appetite for corporate hospitality is quite remarkable,' said Mr Paphitis. 'He knows that a quick call to the chairman of whatever club his beloved Burnley are playing will secure him a free seat, unlimited refreshments and, on occasion, even more than this. Last season, for example, he asked me for a helicopter.'[1]

He enjoyed no such luxuries in his student days, vast tracts of which were spent in making the lengthy and absurdly inconvenient train journey across central England from Cambridge to watch Burnley play – usually a depressing experience, since the team of his dreams had already embarked upon that melancholy gyration among the lower league divisions which has been their characteristic movement over the past three decades. Nick Hornby describes in *Fever Pitch* how he found his redemption when a goal deep in extra time against Liverpool secured Arsenal a famous league championship win in 1989. He suddenly realized football didn't matter quite so much after all. For Campbell, a supporter of lowly Burnley, salvation through his club's sporting success was never an option. For him it would come in a different way, by finding alternative objects of adulation: through the Labour party and tabloid journalism.

Leicester Highlanders

The Campbell family moved south to Leicester in the late 1960s and settled into a house in 11 Welland Vale Road. This was just half a mile away from the City of Leicester Boys' School, which Alastair entered half-way through the 1968/9 academic year. As at Keighley, Alastair's parents quickly made themselves popular in the neighbourhood. There is a pub at Thurnby, the Rose and Crown, which is no more than three miles from the Campbell family home. Even today, though it is more than ten years since the family left the area, the mere mention of Donald Campbell raises a roar of approbation among the locals. To say that he is vividly remembered would be an understatement.

It seems that the further south Donald Campbell – 'Old Man Donald' as he was coming to be known – went, the more Scottish he became. He never lost his links with his native Tiree and for many years he and Betty Campbell would load the four children – and their pet West Highland Terrier – into the back of their Morris Traveller and trundle all the way back up to the remote Scottish isle for the annual two-week holiday every August. Old Man Donald was a Gaelic speaker and for a number of years he contributed a column, discussing the latest developments in the language, to the *Oban Times*. At the Rose and Crown he is still remembered for the way that, dressed in the correct manner, he would pipe in the haggis on New Year's Day. On Sunday afternoons he would teach his sons the bagpipes. Neighbours still recall the colossal din that would emerge from the back garden of Welland Vale Road as the practice sessions got underway. But complaints were rare, and once they got used to the noise, locals came to quite look forward to their weekly entertainment. The eldest son, Donald, showed such facility with the bagpipes that he eventually joined the Scots Guards as a piper. Alastair, too, was an accomplished player. It is still remembered how he once took the pipes with him to school and amazed everybody with his dexterity on the instrument during break. Later in life, the instrument became his trademark and has been unveiled at the most unlikely times in the most unlikely places. The ability to play the pipes was one of the gifts that Old Man Donald bequeathed to his son. But there was much else besides that Alastair inherited: the capacity for hard work, a warmth and depth of character, a deep-seated enjoyment of life, an easy, conspiratorial charm. In short, Campbell inherited numerous amiable characteristics from his esteemed father; the barbarism, brutality and worship of power are his own.

Campbell was not happy in Leicester. Writing about the town in his early twenties, he took his revenge on the place. 'Leicester, like its

people, is dull,' he announced. 'To sit in a Leicester bus, listening
to incomprehensible conversations trundled out in an accent that
makes David Bellamy and Lorraine Chase sound delectable, is to be
nauseated'.

It probably wasn't quite as bad as that. The young Campbell was an
apt pupil. 'As a small boy he was fairly enthusiastic about whatever he
did,' recalls Bill Mann, his physics teacher. Mann says that Campbell
was an eager rugby player, and mentions the day when he had to drive
the boy to hospital with a broken arm. Once again, the episode shows
the innate good manners of the Campbell parents. 'About two or three
days later,' as Bill Mann recalls, 'during my physics lesson, Alastair
handed me a package from his dad, Donald. It was a packet of fine pipe-
smoking tobacco.'

Whatever his subsequent complaints about the city, Campbell flourished at the City of Leicester Boys' School. Talented academically, he
was one of the relatively few boys at the school to gain a place at Cambridge University: it was a formidable achievement and justly celebrated in the family home. But Alastair Campbell's four years at
Cambridge, reading modern and medieval languages (French and
German), were to be some of the most miserable of his life.

Cambridge party pooper

There were a number of brilliant undergraduates up at Cambridge with
Alastair Campbell in the mid to late 1970s who – it was obvious even at
the time – were destined to become distinguished national figures. At
Trinity College, a select coterie congregated around Charles Moore,
who already bore the air of high moral seriousness and Christian virtue
that subsequently made him such an anomalous figure in Fleet Street. It
was perfectly obvious that he would one day be a distinguished editor
of the *Daily Telegraph*. There were admirers who thought him a natural
candidate for the premiership as well: Moore disappointed them by
turning up his nose at the prospect of such a worldly distraction.

Moore consorted with men like Oliver Letwin and Noel Malcolm.
Letwin emerged after the 1997 general election as the MP for West
Dorset and a brilliant member of the rising generation of Tory MPs.
But most brilliant of all in this extraordinary troika was Noel Malcolm,

educated like Letwin and Moore at Eton. Malcolm learnt languages with the ease with which some men attract women. Two decades later he was to try the patience of his friends by writing a long and prodigiously learned work about a faraway place no one was interested in: Kosovo. His diagnosis – that Kosovo should become an independent or at least autonomous state – guided the strategy of NATO's high command during the ten-week conflict in the spring of 1999.

Alastair knew none of this glittering circle at Cambridge. It is just as well that he did not. He would have hated them with the bitter and venomous hatred a state-educated lad from Leicester at odds with the world would naturally reserve for the gilded youth of his generation.

At Selwyn College Robert Harris, who became one of Campbell's closest allies in the fetid lobby politics of the 1980s before converting himself into an accomplished thriller-writer, was feeling his way. Harris, from as modest a background as Campbell, coped better. He edited the university paper and became president of the Union. Another contemporary of Campbell's who managed the leaden progression to Union president was Andrew Mitchell. A decade later, in a celebrated article, Campbell was to pluck Mitchell – by then a Tory MP – out of the hat as one of six hand-picked rising political stars destined for greatness. Mitchell was the one dog that did not bark: the other five were Tony Blair, Gordon Brown, Mo Mowlam, Michael Portillo and John Major.

On the Footlights scene a brilliant generation of comedy stars was being formed: Stephen Fry and Hugh Laurie arrived at the university while Campbell was there, and so did a promising young actress called Emma Thompson. A bearded youth, Andrew Marr, appeared at Trinity Hall. Soon he plunged into student politics, taking up a post selling left-wing literature to baffled locals.

Campbell did not know any of these people. They, in turn, remained unaware of him. Adair Turner, an ambitious Cambridge Union member who later staged an inevitable, well-planned ascent to the director-generalship of the CBI, was for two years at Gonville and Caius College with Campbell. Despite the cheek by jowl physical proximity, he cannot conjure up the faintest recollection of his college contemporary. Keith Vaz, briefly a member of the government in which Campbell played such a luminous, if non-elected, role, was also at

Caius at the time. He has only the haziest memories of Campbell.

Campbell confined himself to the narrower sphere of college life. Gonville and Caius was a modest establishment in the centre of town with powerful links to midland schools. Kenneth Clarke, the former Tory chancellor, went on to Caius from Nottingham High School. Socially undistinguished, the college had a reputation for turning out brilliant history scholars. Fellow undergraduates recall Campbell vividly, some with a shudder of horror. In their minds he is irrevocably associated with the college late night bar – the LNB as the place was colloquially known.

At an Oxford or Cambridge college there is something almost shameful about too frequent attendance at the college bar. The brightest of each generation are to be found elsewhere. It is the plodders, the nonentities, the socially inept, the terminally dull – in short, the losers – who drink at college bars with regularity. Campbell made it his daily pastime. Though he made no measurable impact in any other area of university life, he became a legend at the college bar. 'I avoided Campbell like the plague because he was pissed out of his mind. By 11 p.m. he was on the floor of the LNB,' recalls one Caius contemporary. 'He was a loud, drunken, football-playing thug,' he adds.

Laudably perhaps, Campbell made no attempt to conform to the conventions of university life. He was the only student of Gonville and Caius to turn up for the matriculation ceremony for first-year students without a tie. Later, when Campbell had risen to prominence, an aggrieved former fellow student wrote to the *Daily Mail* to complain about this act of subversion: 'This tieless rebellion, together with the conspicuous positioning, constituted an unwelcome blot on a unique academic memento for myself and around 120 other undergraduates.'

Campbell's sartorial approach was highly distinctive. 'He was smartly dressed, after the style of the football hooligan of the day,' recalls John Morrish, a Caius contemporary. 'It was after the era of the skinheads and the suedeheads. His Burnley scarf would be done up very tightly at the neck so as to look like a cravat. He wore straight, stay-pressed trousers. His hair was cut like Rod Stewart's – high on top and cut close into the neck. This, remember, was the era that fashion forgot. Alastair didn't look like the rest of us. He looked like a football hooligan, a lad from the town. He spent all his time at the Caius late night bar and played football for the college football team. That was all he did.'

Not quite all. Fellow students recall a girlfriend, who came up at weekends from Leicester and produced a mellowing effect on Campbell's character. There are no reports of romantic affairs with fellow students. Indeed, the shortage of female undergraduates at the university was one of those subjects about which Campbell felt particularly strongly. He would ruminate angrily about it when, as was so often the case, he was in his cups at the college bar. A few years later, writing for *Forum* magazine, he would address the subject in tones of aggrieved frustration. 'Sex at Cambridge,' he announced,

> is like sex in no other place on earth, thank God, because two Cambridges would be too much for anyone, especially for anyone who wants to use some of his student years to learn a few things about sex. The main problem, put in unromantic terms, is one of supply and demand.
>
> Those who go to university to stave off the rat-race for a few years find another rat-race awaiting their arrival – the race for sexual conquest. I dropped out after a term, happy that I could go home every weekend to a girlfriend free of the pretensions that belong to a beautiful woman in a man's world. Any pretty woman in Cambridge is likely to have scores of men itching to get inside her, and she knows it, so she can lie back and take her pick. Parties in Cambridge are more like rugby scrums than jovial social events, and it's usually the same men that are picked – the rich, the handsome, and the intelligent and, unfortunately for Mr Average Student, there are still a few who are all three. Others turn to excessive working, excessive sport, or heavy drinking.

This sounds like a belated attitude-statement of the student Campbell: angry, baffled and resentful that he's not part of the glamorous university scene. Later in life, looking back on his university career, Campbell happily acknowledges that he made a mess of things. 'I could not hack it,' he admits. 'I hated first year. I was too young and too chippy. I drank too much and stayed away – going to football matches to see Burnley play. I didn't work hard enough.' Occasionally Campbell and a few cronies might sally forth into the town, on the look-out for a fight, preferably with an Old Etonian. There is ample testimony to his hatred of Old Etonians, who symbolized in Campbell's eyes much that was wrong not only with Cambridge, but with the world in general. This generalized loathing continues to the present day. Campbell was quite capable of interrupting a Downing Street meeting with a sudden, outspoken tirade against the pernicious influence of OEs in British public life, though by then there was less likelihood that this prejudice would express itself through a violent physical manifestation. There is no question, however, that as a young man Campbell was prepared, and perhaps at times eager, to use his fists. Upper-class accents and military uniforms in particular inflamed him. When Campbell was at Cambridge there was a boisterous group of officer trainees with generous army scholarships and an ample supply of money, flash cars and pretty women, who, speaking in loud, braying voices, would wander round Cambridge as if they owned the town. Campbell would from time to time lay down his glass, look dispassionately around the bar, and announce that he was off to beat up 'an upper-class twit'.

Nevertheless, he does not emerge as an unattractive figure at this time. There is a certain raw humanity about the undergraduate Campbell that marks him out as worthy of respect. This life of a lost soul, unhappy at Cambridge, has an uncertain, existential quality. Once, heavily hung-over, Campbell was shaken out of his drunken stupor by a friend. 'What is it?', groaned Campbell. 'I've got it!' replied the friend, who had been reading the works of Samuel Beckett for the last three days, and after two sleepless nights had finally mastered them. 'I understand Beckett! I understand Beckett!' he announced. 'Excellent,' replied Campbell. 'Now I want to go back to sleep.'

Campbell took his final-year exams in May 1979. It was the month Thatcher led the Conservative party back to power in a general election whose seismic importance few realized at the time. It is doubtful whether Campbell bothered to vote. He took no interest in politics, student or national. He has this in common with Tony Blair, who was up at Oxford five years before. Both of them had other ways of spending their time. It is only obsessives who get drawn deeply into politics while still students: people like Gordon Brown and Peter Mandelson. Arguably, the primary reason why Tony Blair became Prime Minister, rather than Gordon Brown, is that Blair has an understanding of what it takes to be an ordinary voter with aspirations to lead a reasonable life. Blair and Campbell possess this; Brown and Mandelson, for all their brains and phenomenal political expertise, do not.

Campbell's 2:1 was a minor miracle, an indication that if he had worked at all hard he could easily have achieved first-class honours. Needless to say, he had made no plans and barely given any thought to what to do with the rest of his life.

chapter two

Riviera Gigolo

He rather hated the ruling few more than he loved the suffering many.

Caroline Fox on James Mill

THE TYPE OF AIMLESS DRIFTING TO which Campbell devoted the next year and a half had gone out of fashion a few years before. In the 1960s and the first half of the 1970s it was customary for undergraduates to take a detached view of future prospects. Jobs were plentiful, and in any case, in the decade of flower power and fun-revolution there were deemed to be more important things than careers.

By 1979 the Keynesian post-war economic spurt which had made all this self-indulgence possible was over. A new gravity descended on the student population that made it both more boring and more amenable to adult employment. Most of Campbell's college contemporaries scuttled off into safe jobs in the professions. This trend horrified and baffled Campbell. He set off on a life of Rabelaisian adventure. For the next eighteen months or so, until he joined the Mirror Group trainee scheme, Campbell was without a regular job. It is not easy to establish exactly how he spent his time. Nine years later, when *Sunday Mirror* editor Eve Pollard was trying to convert her talented reporter into a star, she allowed a brief account of his life and times to be published in her newspaper. This version does not skirt round the fact that he 'first worked for a year as a busker after leaving Cambridge University,' but it is by no means the full story. A complete account of Campbell's eighteen months out would also have had to include a failed attempt to become a professional croupier. Most significant of all, Campbell took his first faltering steps as a professional writer.

On assignment with *Forum* magazine

Nowadays Campbell, when questioned about his career as a contributor to the pornographic *Forum* magazine, dismisses the matter as little more than a joke. In September 1994 he told a reporter from the *News of the World* – which, with characteristic speed and professionalism, was chasing the story within hours of his appointment as press adviser to Tony Blair – that it was down to 'youthful exuberance'. Campbell went on: 'It was partly a way to make some cash. The whole thing started as a laugh with a bloke I knew when I was living in France. We had this bet about who could first get into print. He was going to write for sports magazines and I thought there would be an insatiable market for this kind of tripe.'

The fact is that *Forum*'s importance in the life of the young Alastair Campbell can hardly be overestimated. It not only gave him his first experience of paid journalism, it enhanced his battered self-confidence and gave him some sort of mission in life. For the best part of two years it partly provided him with a living. When the time came to move onto a broader stage with Mirror Group newspapers, it was the experience with *Forum* that helped convince his next employers that he was capable of doing the job.

All of us can look back to two or three moments that changed our lives and set us on a new course. Alastair Campbell, whose life has been crowded with far more drama than most, can look back on six or seven or even more. One of them came when, as a third-year undergraduate idly leafing through *Forum* magazine, he spotted the world COMPETITION in an advertisement inviting readers to submit articles, luring them with the prospect of a cash prize. Alastair duly submitted his entry, forgot about it, and was amazed, a few months later, to learn that he had won. His submitted work was duly published under the catchy title of 'Inter-City Ditties'.

Campbell's first articles were introduced with some fanfare. 'These two stories have been written by a young man from the Midlands,' proclaimed the standfirst. 'He is still only 21 – and we believe they show great promise.'

The future tabloid man still had a lot to learn about the need for a grabby 'intro'. 'Train journeys are rarely very interesting,' he began.

'Any survey of how most people spend their time on trains would undoubtedly reveal that the vast majority of passengers in transit pass a large period gazing out of the window.' After this, however, the action moves on rapidly, culminating in a sexual encounter between two complete strangers in the train lavatory. Campbell takes twenty short paragraphs to get them ready for action. This first published piece carries some of the hallmarks of his later journalism. It is clear, unpretentious, has a sense of humour, and gets to the point in a thoroughly businesslike and professional manner.

'Inter-City Ditties' was the foundation for a long and successful association between Alastair Campbell and *Forum* which took off in the first months after he left university. During this period few editions of the monthly magazine were without one of Campbell's sharp and snappy contributions. For a brief time he was one of the magazine's most prolific and valued contributors. There is no question that *Forum* set him on his career in journalism.

It was Phillip Hodson who talent-spotted Alastair Campbell. Today he lives in Hampstead and works as a psychotherapist and management consultant. He is still fiercely proud of the paper he edited, arguing that it stood at the cutting edge of the sexual revolution and was far more than a mere pornographic rag.

Shortly after Campbell came down from Cambridge, Hodson sent him on his first journalistic assignment. He was told to travel round Britain reporting on sex at various universities. These articles are an uneasy mixture of ribald personal anecdote and austere sociological research. They alternate between interviews with solemn figures such as members of student counselling services and lusty accounts of Campbell's own more personal investigations.

Posing with Richard Gere

Campbell wrote two types of piece for *Forum*: short fictional pieces and factual accounts based on his own experiences. At first glance, his most controversial piece for *Forum*, 'The Riviera Gigolo', falls squarely into the factual category. It is written under Campbell's name, in the first person. Anyone perusing the piece was given every reason to assume that it was either true or a deception on the reader. It tells how, as a young *assistant d'anglais* teaching English in a French school, he developed a profitable and enjoyable sideline selling his services to mature French women of independent means.

One half of the story is clearly accurate. Campbell had indeed worked as an assistant in a French school, as many modern-language students do during their third year of university studies. It is the accuracy of the second half of Campbell's account that is open to question. Campbell describes how Madame Rinaudo, 'a forty year old attractive Mediterranean' type, meets him at a reception and invites him to dinner, 'an offer I accepted with pleasure for my interest in older women was a lively one and in any case, I was still finding my feet in a strange country. We were halfway through a bowl of marinated mussels when it became transparent that Mme Rinaudo had a more than purely personal interest in me.'

Campbell describes how he comes to perform stud duties for a wide circle of women, 'the majority of whom were rich, beautiful and in love with sex'. One such from Beaulieu paid him 1,000 francs – more than a week's salary at his school – and 'held my testicles firmly from behind, a slight pain preventing ejaculation, then let go as her orgasm approached'. The '37 year old wife of a fat and pompous German financier … paid me 2,000 of his easily earned francs to spend three days on one of her husband's yachts, moored on the harbour at Saint-Jean-Cap-Ferrat.' There was a 'lady lecturer at the University of Nice, who, in return for a handful of orgasms, helped me to write my thesis on Racine and Corneille'. And so forth.

Campbell today insists that 'Riviera Gigolo' was a work of fiction. He told a *Times* reporter that it was all 'totally in the imagination'. But that is not how his editor saw it at the time. 'We were very keen on realistic and fact-based copy,' Phillip Hodson insists. 'He told me that everything was true and I believed him. I still do. He had no motivation to lie to me.' Hodson insists that he discussed all Campbell's pieces with him before they were written, and that it was clear to all concerned they were based on his real life experiences. And it is not only Hodson who was taken in by Campbell if, indeed, his piece was not what it claimed to be. So was the *Sun*.

Campbell's article on being a gigolo was straight up the *Sun*'s street. It is likely that Hodson, who was alive to the commercial possibilities of the articles which appeared in *Forum*, played some part in introducing Campbell to the newspaper. On Friday, 9 May 1980, a photograph of Campbell appeared in the *Sun* alongside the headline: 'Wanted – Men for Hire'.

The *Sun* article was inspired by the 1980 film, *American Gigolo*, starring Richard Gere, about a high-class male escort who has sex with older women for money. Below a photograph of a naked Gere in a scene from the film, appears one of a youthful (and clothed) Campbell with the caption 'Campbell … he fitted the bill'.

He was quoted at length. 'One evening at a recreation for the English students,' Campbell told the *Sun*,

> a woman came up to me and asked me out to dinner with her. At the dinner she asked whether I would be interested in becoming a gigolo. The way it worked, she said, was that she gave parties in the afternoon, which women attended for a fee. At these parties, there would be a selection of young men, all available for hire, so to speak. Your job was to entertain them and put yourself at their disposal. You would talk, have dinner, make love. In return they would give you money or gifts. The women I met were mainly between 35 and 50 and wanted a young man who would make them feel good. It was all done very discreetly. It was completely civilised and there were very few risks. Only once did a husband turn up unexpectedly. Often these women didn't even want to have sex. More than anything they wanted an intimate companion – for pillow talk, for affection, to make them feel desirable. The most I got paid was £250 for one night. The least was £12.

Campbell claimed that

> there are men in the South of France who turn it into a profession and become very rich. You can be successful between the ages of 20 and 28. After that, you are less in demand. But think of the advantages – you choose your own hours, have a high standard of living, no ties, and all your clients are upper class, rich and civilised. It's never hard work, but the women do expect a high standard of performance.

The story about Campbell the gigolo was filed by a *Sun* reporter called Liz Hodgkinson. Hodgkinson still writes regularly for newspapers, but devotes the greater part of her energy to her career as an author and has had nearly forty books published. Scarcely older than Campbell himself, she vividly remembers the evening they spent together at the Orange

Tree pub in Richmond. 'He told me that he had acted as a gigolo in the south of France,' she recalls, 'and that all those middle-aged women down there were gagging for it and he was providing it. He was having a wonderful time and they paid for everything. I had no reason to disbelieve him.'

Hodgkinson is also happy to admit that she had every incentive to trust what he was telling her. She had been dispatched to write a story about gigolos, and gigolos were hard to come by, at any rate ones prepared to spill the beans to the *Sun*. Here was a gigolo, talkative and large as life. It would have been perverse to have questioned Campbell's credentials too closely. 'I wanted to believe him,' she admits, 'because we were doing a story about him.' Campbell, too, had every motive to spin Hodgkinson along, if that was what he was doing. He was being paid handsomely – one or two hundred pounds was the going rate. Either way, everyone was happy.

Croupier

Long ago, over a leisurely, drink-sodden summer lunch in the south of France, Campbell explained to an entranced group of friends that it really was possible to make a profit playing roulette. He set out in detail a complex system that tilted the odds very slightly in favour of the punter and against the casino. 'How do you know all this?' he was asked. 'Because I was once a croupier,' came the instant reply.

Campbell's brief stint as a croupier was his first serious attempt to get anything resembling a real job after leaving Cambridge. All the signs are that he would have persevered with it, for a while at least, had he not fallen out with the casino management. He was certainly committed enough to endure six weeks' training at the Golden Nugget casino in the West End. But he survived for only four days dealing American roulette on the tables as a professional croupier; according to the records at the Golden Nugget, he was dismissed because of 'failure to meet the required standards'.

John Galvani, now a senior executive with the casino group London Clubs, which owns the Nugget, remembers Campbell reasonably well. He says that he responded to an advertisement in the *Evening Standard* that the casino placed each week. According to Galvani, the Nugget was – and remains – 'a training casino where people go and learn their skills. Going out on the casino floor is a bit like going out on stage and some people freeze. There are subtleties in dealing with customers that you can't replicate in training and obviously if there are going to be mistakes then we'd prefer to see them at that end of the market. The supervisory staff are used to seeing people struggle. Alastair struck me as being pretty confident but not cocky. He didn't suffer from stage fright and beyond the reason listed in our records I honestly don't know what went wrong.'

Shortly after he left the casino Campbell wrote an account of his experiences for *Forum*. It is interesting to compare his own version with Galvani's and indeed the company records. Campbell's *Forum* article is perhaps the weakest of the pieces that he wrote for the magazine. It is embittered and filled with venom against the company management. 'From the moment one spots the gaudy advert in the *Evening Standard*,' he records, 'it's evident that the growing casino chains in London and elsewhere are trying to sell a false mystique based on the quasi-erotic aura of illicit gaming, enticing those of us who drift and thrive on excitement to become croupiers, entering a world where, with any luck, Al Capone and his merry band of psychopaths might suddenly burst onto the premises to profit from a business as sordid as their own.'

Campbell records that 'I answered the advert for various reasons. Chronic insomnia was one of them, another the desire to work through the night and use the day for a modicum of sleep and a maximum of writing.' He also says: 'I had been hoping to get some good quality gigolo work to supplement my other earnings.'

Campbell claims that he started work on 20 March 1980, and that 'twenty-nine hours later, I was sacked by a gaming executive'. This account is at variance with the company record which states that he started dealing on 10 March and lasted four days on the casino floor. Campbell was clearly baffled and angered by his expulsion. He writes, 'I was told by a fellow dealer that I was very good indeed.' His own speculation, and it may not be far from the truth, is that the management got nervous about employing a part-time writer. But, as he pointed out, he had informed the management that he wrote before he joined.

Busking with bagpipes

It is doubtful whether Alastair Campbell would have had anything to learn from Laurie Lee's *As I Walked Out One Midsummer Morning*, one of the most illuminating texts on the busking business ever written. From all reports, he knew every trick. 'I think he discovered, during the time that he was teaching at Nice, that any time he needed money he only had to play the bagpipes,' recalls Mike Molloy, an old friend who once saw him in action. 'It was almost like Picasso, paying for his dinner by sketching on a napkin.'

Something about this tall young man, in his Campbell of Argyll tartan, captured the imagination of the peoples of Europe. During this period he became a fabled figure. British holiday-makers brought back stories, from the south of France and elsewhere, of a strange piping Scotsman. They compared notes at dinner parties. Some of them recall him even today. A photograph survives of Campbell playing the bagpipes. Dating from 1980, it shows him – still with that Rod Stewart haircut – playing his pipes in the centre of a crowd of good-humoured shoppers. A sexy girl in jeans and tight-fitting T-shirt is collecting the money. Campbell was never again to be at the centre of so much concentrated attention until he addressed lobby briefings in the seclusion of Downing Street two decades on.

'Busking with Bagpipes' is Campbell's most accomplished work for *Forum*. This is partly because it is his third piece for the magazine: there is a growing assurance about his style. He is also writing about a subject he knows off by heart. 'I won't bore you with finance,' he proclaims in his preamble. 'Suffice it to say that during 10 months as a busker, I have lived comfortably, indeed very comfortably. Nor will I give details of busking techniques. I'm good at it, that's all you need to know.'

He travelled all round Europe. Campbell hated Italy, where he fell victim to predatory advances from homosexuals. 'Never, ever go to Italy,' he advised. 'The Catholic Church is viciously strong, the Italian lira pitifully weak. The women are virginal and coy, their men frustrated and obscene. Riding in a busy tram in Milan, the kilted busker realises that Italian men really do fancy anything in a skirt.'

Holland was highly satisfactory ('If Dutch women want something they ask for it. Her impeccable English told me to keep my kilt on. She gave me a leather belt. Her head disappeared and the next I knew of her was a gentle lick along my penis, which responded and rose. "Tie me in," she ordered … '). So was France, where a Parisian businessman paid Campbell 400 francs to play his pipes naked for a night outside his new restaurant in the nudist town of Cap d'Agde. Sweden, however, was a severe disappointment. 'The men were long and thin, the women insipid and straight-laced. Sweden, like Amsterdam, has far too many sex shops and not enough sex.' Best of the lot, to Campbell's mind, was Norway. In Oslo he met 'a very nice Norwegian man', who offered him food, lodging and unlimited access to his sixteen-year-old daughter Marit for a week. 'Our love-making seemed to last forever,' recorded Campbell. 'We were fast asleep when Marit's mother came in with a cup of tea and an old copy of the *Daily Telegraph*.'

The words and phrases are beginning to flow in 'Busking with Bagpipes'. Furthermore, Campbell is starting to get savvy about the press. He gives details of his first ever spin-doctoring operation. 'Even a busker needs public relations backing him,' reveals Campbell. 'I let the press do mine. Go to a town, find a busy bar, find a journalist, preferably pissed. Buy him a Bloody Mary, tell him you love his town; the morning paper does a nice article and for a day or two you're a local celebrity.'

Campbell was growing up. Something was telling him that it was time to drop his free-wheeling, easy-riding life and get serious. In a moment of clarity, he applied for a traineeship with the *Mirror*, then as now one of the great newspaper groups with a chain of local papers as well as the flagship *Daily Mirror*, *Sunday Mirror* and *Scottish Daily Record*. Every year nearly 5,000 ambitious young journalists would apply for the dozen or so places that were made available on the *Mirror* course. It was recognized by everyone in the trade as the best training any young aspiring journalist could possibly get.

Cub reporter

Campbell has had many pieces of good fortune in his life, but none greater than the fact that James Dalrymple was director of Mirror Training when he made his application. Dalrymple is a tough, working-class Scot, proud of his roots, who has worked for most Fleet Street papers at one time or another. It was Dalrymple who weeded Campbell's job application from the thousands that flooded into the *Mirror* offices. Applicants were asked to give a 500-word feature describing themselves. 'The thing that hit me about Alastair's,' says Dalrymple today, 'was that it was a well-written vignette, full of humour. It intrigued me.' Nothing was held back. It told how he had busked around Europe and written for *Forum* magazine. It was enough to ensure that Campbell's name was among the élite group summoned down to London for the interview process. Although there were thousands of other eager applicants for the course, the interview confirmed Dalrymple's hunch that, despite his unconventional CV, there was something exceptional in Campbell.

The scheme he joined had been founded in 1966 when the legendary Hugh Cudlipp still ran the *Mirror*. The paper acquired its group of regional papers in the south west partly in order to use them as a training ground for young journalists. When Campbell emerged two years later, he was an almost fully fledged reporter. After a short induction course lasting two months, the trainees were thrown in at the deep end on local papers. Campbell was seconded first, in the autumn of 1981, to the *Tavistock Times*, where he stayed for about a year before being moved to the *Sunday Independent* in Plymouth. Later Campbell enthused: 'It was absolutely fantastic. You went on to local papers and within days you're sports editor, columnist, chief interviewer.

It was during this period that he started to make friends, in a way that he never had at Cambridge. He met many of the people who were going to mean most to him for the rest of his life. For the first time since childhood, in a way that he never had been at university, he was at ease in his own skin. He had found an occupation that engaged him intellectually and emotionally. He was a born journalist, as James Dalrymple had spotted back in London. He was tough, arrogant, oozing confidence and charm: the ideal personality for a reporter. It had taken courage and bombast to travel all alone round Europe for months on end with just the bagpipes for company, and that courage and bombast would do just as well for the foot-in-the-door reporting the *Mirror* was crying out for. Add to that an ease with words and a gift for a phrase, and he made something close to the perfect package.

What, though, made him absolutely right for the *Mirror* was the chip on his shoulder. He was anti-establishment, an outsider with every-thing to prove. Campbell must have felt somewhere in his bones, as he joined his fellow trainees for their two-year stint in the West Country, a part of the world he hardly knew, that in some strange way he was coming home.

He was already wearing the heavy trench-coat that he made his trade-mark when he joined the *Daily Mirror* as a young reporter a few years later. Sometimes, for a joke, he would turn his head to one side and downwards and engage in imaginary conversations in the manner of an American secret-service agent murmuring into his walkie-talkie. He was beginning to develop the poise and urbanity that would stand him in such good stead when he moved into political reporting five years later. He also had a gift of which he was probably not yet aware: he could make people, even very important people, feel honoured that he should choose to confer his presence upon them. He was still very dangerous when drunk, and would remain so for some years.

On the training scheme Campbell made the closest friendship of his life. John Merritt was the most brilliant journalist on the course, ginger-haired and, like many talented reporters, quiet and softly spoken. A Roman Catholic, he was a journalist who felt the need to do good as well as sell newspapers. Some colleagues saw him as 'almost saintly'. He seemed destined to go to the very top.

Campbell not only met his best friend that first day in Plymouth: he also met Fiona Millar, the daughter of *Express* journalist Bob Millar and a fellow Plymouth trainee. Cedric Pulford, who was running the *Mirror* scheme at the time, remembers taking the new recruits on an induction tour of Plymouth. As part of the tour he took them to the roof-top viewing platform of the civic centre. He still vividly remembers one moment: 'I was just looking around making sure nobody was falling off the balcony or something and I caught a look between Alastair and Fiona which was totally electric. I've never seen such a look of mutual attraction between two people before or since. Alastair was in those days certainly classically handsome. He really was like the Grecian ideal of male beauty. He's over six foot, she's verging on the petite. Whether they were seeing each other for the first time I don't know. I would not describe the look as lascivious. I did not think that on either part it was

a look of lust, it was more what they call a cow-eyed look of dumb ado-
ration.' Pulford recalls that 'there was never any question from that
moment onwards it was Alastair and Fiona'.

By a striking coincidence, John Merritt also met the love of his life
on the first day of that training scheme. She was Lindsay Nicholson,
who is now the editor of the magazine *Good Housekeeping*. The two
couples became inseparable. They went on holiday together. When they
all moved to London a few years later, they were so close that they chose
to live in the same street in north London. They started up families at
the same time in the late 1980s.

It was around that time that things started to go terribly wrong for
John Merritt and Lindsay Nicholson, who has been obliged to cope
with the most unimaginable tragedy. When their daughter Ellie was
just eighteen months old, Lindsay learnt that her husband, at the very
height of his powers as a reporter, and aged only thirty-two, had
contracted leukaemia. John Merritt died of a haemorrhage in August
1992. Five years later she learnt that their little daughter Ellie had the
disease too: she died in June 1998.

Today Lindsay Nicholson can barely find words to describe the way
that Alastair Campbell and Fiona Millar rallied round. When Ellie was
ill Alastair Campbell, already under huge strain in Downing Street,
took on as much of the burden as he could. He visited the little girl, who
adored him, at least once a week as she lay in Great Ormond Street
Hospital. He threw his weight behind a national campaign to find a
matching donor for a bone-marrow transplant. As all this was going on
Lindsay Nicholson made a public pronouncement of sorts about Alastair Campbell. She told Roy Hattersley, who was doing a profile of the
Number 10 press secretary for the *Observer*: 'In times of trouble there
are those who will be there and those who won't. Alastair is always
there. Doing anything. Twice a week at the hospital. Driving me home.
Talking to Ellie about her father as only he can.'

In June 1999, in an interview with Catherine O'Brien of the *Daily
Telegraph*, Lindsay Nicholson poured out her heart even further. She
described how Alastair Campbell and Fiona Millar had drawn her deep
into their circle of friends: 'They call themselves "the Team"', she said,
'and they really are the most well-oiled machine. When John became ill
and died, they worked out who did what best and swung into action.

Ever since, they have coordinated between themselves to make sure there is always someone there for me.' Besides Campbell and Millar, the 'team' includes Cherie Blair and government minister Tessa Jowell. Some time before Ellie died, she was allowed home for Christmas: Tony and Cherie Blair immediately invited her up to Chequers.

If being interviewed by James Dalrymple was a huge stroke of luck, meeting Fiona Millar at this juncture was an even bigger one. Fiona has been the solid rock in Campbell's life ever since, giving him a loyalty that he has returned.

There have been many temptations, but he has resisted them. At a Conservative party conference in Brighton more than ten years ago, Campbell discovered that a young female Scandinavian journalist of striking good looks and intelligence was unable to afford accommodation in Brighton, but was travelling down daily from London, where she had secured temporary lodgings. Campbell, then political editor of the *Mirror*, soon secured her free use of one of the many rooms booked in the Metropole Hotel for the use of *Mirror* executives. Deeply grateful, the girl found it hard to believe that such generosity came without a corresponding obligation – an obligation, it was intimated, that she would not be averse to fulfilling. Several weeks later a postcard arrived at the *Mirror* offices thanking Campbell for his kindness. 'You know a great deal about British politics,' it read, 'but very little about Scandinavian morals.'

Tory spin-doctor

On the *Tavistock Times* Campbell did all the things that local reporters are supposed to do. He reported council meetings, flower shows and court cases. He developed an accurate shorthand note. He learnt how to file clean copy to a tight deadline. He knocked on the doors of grieving relatives who had just suffered a newsworthy bereavement. He gradually mastered the weird, convoluted craft of writing news stories. It is an ugly, soulless and mechanical job which demands the total abandonment of literary pretensions. A good, precise reporter has far more in common with a competent neighbourhood plumber or a reliable carpenter than with a flowery weekly essayist.

As Campbell made all these discoveries, he was also practising how to be a spin-doctor, although the phrase had not then become current. Still more surprising, the man he practised on – the prototype for Tony Blair two decades on – was a Tory. Robin Fenner is the sort of man who used to join the Conservative party as a matter of course – but rarely does today. He is founder and senior partner in Fenners, one of the leading West Country auctioneers. He is one of the most respected members of the Tavistock commercial community, for two decades served part-time as a local councillor, and was mayor of the town in 1984. Like Alastair Campbell's father, Fenner used to be a member of the local Conservative Club and like him he went along at least partly for the snooker. Fenner saw himself as a 'one-nation Tory': he was a member of the left-leaning Bow Group. He was never to be more at ease in the Tory party than in the 1960s, when Edward Heath was party leader and the local MP for Tavistock was Michael Heseltine; he left the party in the 1980s.

In 1980 Fenner, in his role as local councillor, played a prominent part in launching the Tavistock community recycling scheme. It was an innovative idea, the first ever to be sponsored by a local council. In the wake of the launch, the auctioneer was surprised to be rung up by a local reporter: the reporter expressed his admiration for Fenner's brainwave and asked if he could come and see him. Fenner readily agreed. That is how he met Alastair Campbell for the first time.

In Fenner's office the future press secretary to the Prime Minister got straight down to business. The basic idea for a community recycling scheme – called Tavistock Wastesavers – was good, he said. But the presentation had been poor. Fenner, he said, needed a good press officer. And Campbell was volunteering for the position. The auctioneer was enthusiastic. The two men shook hands. For the next few months Fenner had the benefit of the advice of a man who, he became ever more convinced, was a brilliant manipulator of the press. Campbell, in return, was in the place where he always wanted to be: at the centre of events. He was not just a journalist observing the passing scene from the outside. He was also on the inside of Tavistock politics, with privileged access to information and the key personalities who ran the West Country town. 'He had his finger on the button within a few days of arriving in Tavistock,' Fenner says. 'He became very well aware of what made the place tick.' It was an almost obsessive pattern of behaviour that would repeat itself again and again during Alastair Campbell's remarkable rise to power.

'He acted as my spin-doctor for one and a half years,' Fenner now recalls. Together the ambitious young reporter and the Tory politician wrote speeches, arranged press conferences and devised stunts designed to promote Wastesavers. For a brief period Fenner's star, under this mesmerizing new influence, shone brightly on the West Country scene. A press release drafted by Campbell grabbed the attention of the *Grapevine* programme on BBC2. They came down and made a programme about Wastesavers. Thanks to Campbell, Fenner was invited to lecture on environmental projects in the United States. But today he has no doubt who was the most important member of the team. 'I was the mouthpiece. He was planting the ideas.' Many of the ideas were planted at the bar of the Tavistock Conservative Club, where the two men went to play snooker.

'He never took no for an answer,' says Fenner. 'It was obvious who and what he would become. I have never known any journalist who could pen any story as quickly. He wanted to hit it on the head. If you look at his Fleet Street journalism, that was his trademark: he gets to the point.' Fenner claims that many of the techniques Campbell used in Downing Street were first tried out on him. 'I am convinced,' he remarked well before Campbell left Number 10, 'that two-thirds of every major speech by Tony Blair is Alastair's. He would help me put together speeches. I can still see Alastair saying to me: "We should put emphasis on this." There are certain terms I have heard coming from the Prime Minister's lips which I would have used in my speeches after talking to Alastair.'

There was one further trait that Campbell has kept from that day to this. He has always been prepared to fall out, if need be savagely, with his boss. On one occasion Fenner, outraged by some local vandals, called for the return of the stocks. 'It rankled with his nibs,' Fenner now recalls. 'Alastair was totally opposed. I said: "I've had people calling me all through the night." And he just said it served me right. I've never forgotten that.'

Punching above his weight

At the end of the two-year course, all the trainees wanted a job with one of the Mirror Group titles. It came as no surprise that the first to get a job with the flagship title – the *Daily Mirror* – was John Merritt. Campbell followed him shortly afterwards. As ever with Campbell, the circumstances surrounding his appointment were far from simple and even now remain shrouded in a certain amount of mystery. What is certain is that Campbell took it into his head to publicly abuse and, according to some versions, physically manhandle one of the most senior and powerful Mirror Group executives.

The incident took place at the Green Lanterns restaurant in Plymouth at a dinner hosted by Colin Harrow. Harrow had recently taken over from James Dalrymple as training manager; today he is the managing editor of the *Sunday Mirror*. Guest of honour at this occasion was Bob Edwards, a celebrated Fleet Street hand who had edited some of Britain's finest papers, and was currently nearing the end of a record-breaking thirteen-year spell with the *Sunday Mirror*. Edwards had come down to Plymouth to address the trainees. After such occasions it was Harrow's custom to use the Mirror Group's famously lavish expenses to invite the guest and a few others to dinner. On this occasion he suggested that Alastair Campbell and Fiona Millar – by now an established couple – should attend the event, mainly because Fiona's father Bob Millar was an old friend of Edwards.

Campbell and Edwards did not hit it off, and it is easy to imagine why not. Campbell was young, hot-headed and arrogant. He felt no automatic respect for title or rank, if anything rather the reverse. By this stage of his career Edwards had perhaps become slightly pompous. He had a splendid record in newspaper journalism, and felt that he deserved to be listened to with respect and even reverence, a feeling that Campbell did not share. It is possible, though at this distance of time difficult to say for sure, that sexual friction may have played some role in the incident. As an old friend of her family Edwards may have felt entitled to take a proprietorial or even gently flirtatious attitude towards Fiona. Drink played its full part in the dénouement, which was sparked by an argument over a *Mirror* story about the Afghanistan war; the piece had been hidden away at the back of the paper, and Campbell believed it should have had greater prominence. Whatever the rights and wrongs of it all – and Edwards was surely right to insist that Afghanistan was of little or no interest to the vast bulk of *Mirror* readers – Campbell was needlessly and brutally offensive to one of the most eminent men in Fleet Street. When he woke up the following morning, he had every reason to assume that his career as a *Mirror* reporter was over before it had even begun.

But Campbell had chosen exactly the right person to pick a fight with. Bob Edwards was not a popular man in the *Mirror* empire. Fundamentally, he was an *Express* man, reared in the Beaverbrook empire. More important, he was no longer the power in the land he had once been. It may even have been that Campbell, whose nose has always been highly attuned to the tiniest nuances of power, could sense some of this and that there was an element of calculation in his savage attack. So the following day, when news reached Holborn Circus of a fracas involving the editor of the *Sunday Mirror* and a young, unknown reporter, there was considerable interest in that young reporter. Opinion at the 'Stab-in-the-Back', the disgusting pub standing at the foot of the imposing *Mirror* building (its real name was the White Hart, but no *Mirror* journalist ever called it that), was firmly on his side, and the new generation of *Mirror* executives, impatient with the existing hierarchies, remembered Campbell's name with warm approval.

Whether or not the Bob Edwards incident can be held responsible, Campbell was not invited to apply for a job at the *Mirror* at the end of the course. Fiona Millar, however, was. Several months later Campbell accompanied Fiona to London when she went for her interview. While he waited for her to return from the interview, he dropped in at the Stab-in-the-Back for a few pints. Word spread rapidly round the *Mirror* building that 'the man who had thumped Bob Edwards' was to be found in the vicinity. *Mirror* journalists never needed much of an excuse to go to the pub, especially during working hours. After the paper had been put to bed Richard Stott, then an assistant editor on the *Daily Mirror* and a rising star who was in due course to assume the editor's chair, dropped down to the Stab. He liked what he saw, and asked Campbell why he had not been called up for interview. Campbell shrugged his shoulders. Stott told him: 'Give me a ring tomorrow and I'll fix you up with a shift.'

This was an amazing stroke of luck. Even so Campbell made an effort to evade his destiny. He did not call the following morning. Stott, furious about this, tracked him down and effectively ordered him in. Campbell, just twenty-five years old, was launched.

In Which Our Hero's Fortunes Sink Very Low

I always say that if you've seen one Gentleman of the Press having delirium tremens, you've seen them all.

P. G. Wodehouse, Bachelors Anonymous *(1973)*

THE FLEET STREET ALASTAIR CAMPBELL joined as a *Daily Mirror* reporter in the early months of 1983 was irretrievably squalid: lecherous, boozy, back-stabbing and brilliant. It fitted Campbell like a glove. He arrived in the dying days of the hot-metal era. The characteristic sound of a news-room was the clatter of typewriters as reporters spewed out their stories, to be grabbed by copy-boys and raced to the sub-editors, who would mark them up before dropping them down a chute to the compositors, who would expertly but laboriously set up the type. Fleet Street newspapers in those days were like ocean liners. From deep in the bowels of the building came the roar and hum of heavy machinery as the newspapers were produced. It was the last surviving centre of manufacturing industry in central London. Late at night articulated lorries would make their way as best they could through the narrow lanes round the great newspaper buildings, to be loaded up and set free to hurtle up the nation's motorways bearing their load of sensational stories to an apathetic nation. It was a hopelessly antiquated nineteenth-century system which modern computerized technology had made redundant. But nobody had yet found a means of overcoming the resistance of the printers' unions, which were corrupt, complacent and all-powerful. The slightest infringement of the rules they dictated to terrified newspaper management led to an instantaneous strike and the consequential loss of a day's revenue. When

Campbell arrived at the *Mirror*, reporters were not allowed to change their typewriter ribbons. A union man had to be called to carry out the task. He would invariably take hours if not days to arrive. Any protest at his procrastination caused offence: he performed his derisory function with the air of a man bestowing a huge favour, which in a sense he was. Salvation was round the corner in the shape of Tory employment legislation, then being roundly denounced as oppressive by – among others – Tony Blair, the promising young MP for Sedgefield. Undeterred by Labour threats of retaliation, Rupert Murdoch and Eddie Shah were poised to take advantage.

For the moment, however, the *ancien régime* survived – and prospered. Thanks to their massive circulations, Fleet Street papers could be hugely profitable. Journalists' salaries, compared to today's, were meagre. But they were rewarded liberally in kind. Expense accounts were prodigious. Senior management provided itself with large cars, expenses-paid holidays, first-class travel and lavish lunches. Of nowhere was this more true than the *Mirror*. In 1984 Clive Thornton, formerly the chief executive of Abbey National, was appointed Mirror Group chairman. It was not to be a long-lived appointment. The first thing he did was to bury his head in the *Mirror* accounts. Several days later he emerged. 'Do you know,' he declared in his nasal northern whine, 'the annual profits of this company are less than the sum *Mirror* journalists spend taking each other out to lunch. Not contacts out to lunch. Not people who could possibly give them stories or be of use. Taking *each other* out to lunch.' Thornton had lost a leg – in the war, it was thought. Inevitably the cry went round Fleet Street: 'In the land of the legless, the one-legged man is king.'

It was a cocksure, macho, boozy culture. *Mirror* men lived high on the hog. They felt themselves, with less justification than they realized, to be the governors of Fleet Street. They were a close-knit lot. They stuck together, drank together, ate together and conspired together. When they went to parties *Mirror* men tended to form themselves into little huddles as if it was lowering to mingle. As time went on, the paper began to read like that too. It had got stuck at a fixed point in the 1960s. Unlike its wide-awake mass-market competitor the *Sun*, the *Mirror* failed to spot that the world was moving on. This was the paper that took Alastair Campbell to its heart.

Doorstepping celebrities and rooting through dustbins

When he arrived at the Mirror Campbell was greeted with rapture by John Merritt, by now well on his way to becoming an established reporter. Merritt gave him two pieces of advice: always sit within earshot of the newsdesk so that you know what they are talking about; and always keep something up your sleeve so that 'if the bastards give you some boring rubbish to work on you can trump them with something better'.

Campbell proved himself very quickly indeed as a reliable, accurate and lively reporter. After becoming press secretary to Tony Blair, he frequently enjoyed contrasting the rancid triviality of today's newspapers to the serious, idealistic *Mirror* of his own day. There is a small measure of truth in this. Back in 1983, there were a number of names on the *Mirror*, such as Paul Foot and John Pilger, who were there to inform rather than entertain. Writers like Keith Waterhouse gave the paper style and class. But none of this had anything to do with Alastair Campbell. Nothing he contributed in the early days at the *Mirror* was ever likely to be a submission for the Pulitzer prize.

Early on he established a monopoly on the Miss World competition: 'Twenty year old Frédérique Leroy from Bordeaux has attracted heavy betting. Brown-haired and brown-eyed, she's been charming all week with a typically French, cute, sexy smile …'; 'Barnarda, Miss Yugoslavia, has been photographed in a variety of erotic poses, including topless shots.' Another Campbell staple during his days as a tabloid reporter was small animals. These, accompanied by an affecting picture, were perhaps a tribute to his early days trundling around the Yorkshire Dales in the back of his father's Morris Traveller. It would be possible to fill a small zoo with the animals Campbell wrote stories about during his time at the *Mirror*: they included swans, badgers, rooks, frogs, golden Labradors, foxes and mink. He has never lost his eye for an animal story. One of the memorable images of the Blair years in Downing Street, published in practically every paper, was of a mallard duck taking her ducklings for a walk in front of the steps of Number 10 Downing Street.

There were the inevitable celebrity stories. A gallant Campbell lent newsreader Selina Scott his Wellington boots ('this was sophisticated

Selina as you'd never seen her before') on a day out on the beach at Southend. Royal stories were important in Campbell's early career. Prince Andrew's girlfriends served him well. He made a splash with a story about 'glamour girl Vicki Hodge' and her affair with the prince, and he was one of the team which doorstepped 'beautiful Katie Rabett' as she left home the day after her romance with Prince Andrew had become public knowledge. Campbell and his fellow reporter Christian Gysin reported the birth of Sara Keays' baby daughter to Conservative MP Cecil Parkinson. It was probably Campbell who doorstepped the MP outside his Potter's Bar home the following day. Parkinson, who has always been civil to reporters and liked in return, paused on the way out to apologise for inclement weather conditions. 'I advise you to find some more interesting news,' he said to the assembled journalists, and was on his way. Campbell developed a line in gangsters and earned himself a rare front-page exclusive with a story about how the 'the notorious Kray twins were secretly reunited for their 51st birthday yesterday'.

Campbell also went through what he later described as a 'phase of rooting through dustbins and hanging around outside celebrities' homes, during which he raked over the sex lives of the rich and famous. He secured a page-five lead story about Cliff Richard, using the pop star's denial that he was having an affair with another man as an opportunity to imply he was gay. 'The man who has lived with pop star Cliff Richard for 19 years,' reported Campbell, 'denied yesterday that they are lovers.' He showed considerable ingenuity in pursuit of lesbian tennis player Martina Navratilova. Campbell was a member of the *Mirror* team that harassed Navratilova during Wimbledon 1984 over rumours about her relationship with her friend Judy Nelson. Having failed to get into the tournament by conventional means, he resorted to a typical piece of tabloid trickery. 'I had neither tickets nor accreditation,' he recalls. 'So I put on a tracksuit with lots of logos on it, carried a few rackets under my arm, signed a few autographs for queuing students who hadn't the faintest idea who I was, and the chap on the gate let me in.' Navratilova and Nelson hit back by calling him 'scum' – the very word he threw in the faces of tabloid reporters when he had exchanged Fleet Street for Downing Street. But he was not immune to the great pressures of the job. He was a junior member of the reporting team that dealt with the aftermath of the Brighton bomb. It was not one of his successes. He promised the *Mirror* newsdesk that he had secured a set of photographs of the inside of the wrecked hotel, but they were taken from under his nose by rivals from the *Sun*. Campbell was so distraught that he was reduced to tears.

But he had talent – and courage. At the start of the 1983 football season, he was commissioned to write a special report on soccer hooliganism. He infiltrated West Ham's feared Inter City Firm to produce a piece that revealed how apparently chance encounters between rival groups of supporters were actually engineered well in advance. He was made for tabloid reporting of this type. 'He was great fun to work with,' records Rupert Morris, who worked with Campbell two or three years later when he was on *Today*. 'He had this fantastic enthusiasm and dynamism. He was really passionate about his work. Almost like a boy scout.' From the very start his pieces for the *Mirror* communicate a directness and confidence. He clearly had no difficulty getting his copy into the paper and was accepted within a short space of time into the beery *Mirror* culture.

During the relatively few years that he was a drinker – he gave up around his twenty-ninth birthday – he turned drunkenness into an art form. Until the very latest stages of the evening he remained hypnotically funny or, when he wasn't being amusing, dangerous. The prospect of physical violence was never far away. He was anarchic, clever, witty and an accomplished mimic: a gift which could be used mercilessly against those whom he and his friends wanted to destroy. But there was nothing feigned about his graveyard humour, the brooding sense of violence, his sudden bursts of furious outrage. Campbell was beginning to suffer from the illness that would culminate in his nervous breakdown. But having Alastair Campbell as a member of your party in a pub or drinking establishment was an unmistakable badge of honour. There was only one reciprocal obligation. That was to stay with him to the end, and make sure that he returned home safe and sound. Many were the evenings when a kindly fellow drinker at the Stab-in-the-Back shovelled Campbell into the back of a cab, muttered an address, and put a fiver into the cabbie's hand, never failing to demand a receipt to claim back on *Mirror* expenses.

The real drinking geniuses – the Dylan Thomases and the Jeffrey

Bernards – create an alternative reality, a more amusing and arguably saner version of everyday life. Over the years Fleet Street has produced some world-class drinkers, though less so nowadays. For a brief five-year period, Campbell was to be classed among them. 'Alastair was a great drinker,' recalls Rupert Morris. 'He was absolutely the life and soul. He was a tremendous person to have around. He communicated an electricity that made you want to be part of it all. You had a feeling that no way was life going to be dull. He was a star but completely without any kind of vanity. You couldn't turn down a drink with Alastair because you knew anything might happen.'

The demands of his job were gruelling. There were some dangerous signs from a very early stage that drinking was beginning to intrude upon his effectiveness. One of his colleagues, Paul Callan, was then a well-regarded writer on the *Mirror*. His job was to furnish 'colour' while one of the reporters would perform the more onerous, but less enjoyable and prestigious, task of providing hard facts. On one occasion, Callan recalls, he and Campbell were sent to report on a visit by Prince Charles to a London hospital. 'Alastair was extremely pissed,' says Callan. 'He wanted to go into one of the wards with the Prince. He wanted to speak with the Prince personally. I said: I wouldn't do that if I were you. I propped him up against a wall and said: stay here. Then I went in to see the Prince. Fifteen or twenty minutes later I came out. He'd slid down the wall. He was a little muddle of limbs on the floor. Alastair was a good journalist,' concludes Callan, 'especially when he was sober'.

Bob and Audrey Millar

The one solid point in Campbell's world was Fiona. And not merely Fiona. As often happens, Campbell had fallen in love not simply with the girl herself but with all her family. Like the Campbells, the Millars were originally from Scotland. But they had embedded themselves in the heart of English metropolitan culture in a way his own parents, with a deeper Scottish identity and their provincial roots in Yorkshire and Leicester, had not. The Millars were a distinctive Labour type: civilized, decent, politically active in north London. The existence of people like them was one of the primary reasons that Labour survived as a political party during the convulsions of the early 1980s. They had nothing to do with the arid and destructive infighting of the period, belonging to an older, wiser, more profound and warmer version of socialism.

Audrey Millar, Fiona's mother, still works most days for the Labour party. She is a living link back to Labour's heroic period, when it was still establishing itself as a mass political party. Frank Field, the Liverpool MP who is a family friend, says of her: 'She is the last of that generation of women who would now have become doctors, lawyers or accountants. But the world was different then and she has devoted herself to voluntary work.'

As a young girl she was a secretary to G. D. H. Cole, the great Labour-party thinker and historian. She worked for a while in the House of Commons and for the Cooperative Movement. According to Bob Edwards – another family friend: the Edwardses and the Millars once took a holiday together in Spain, chugging down to Barcelona together in an aged Triumph Mayflower – she met her husband Bob Millar at Ruskin, the progressive Oxford college which has been responsible for the education of so many trade unionists and Labour politicians. Everyone who knows them says that it was a happy and successful marriage. When Bob Millar died, Alastair Campbell wrote a passionate tribute to him for *Tribune*.

Bob Millar was one of those extremely rare people for whom no one has a bad word. A very brave man, he served in the RAF during the war. His close friend Wilfred Greatorex, the television scriptwriter, recalls: 'He was a bomber pilot and as a sergeant he had a flight lieutenant as a co-pilot. In the air he was supposed to give him orders and on the ground he was supposed to salute him. I asked him if he did salute him on the ground and he said he'd be buggered if he did.' Upon his return to civilian life, he was a member of that idealistic and confident generation of political activists that rebuilt Britain along socialist lines. For a number of years Millar worked for *Tribune*. Like many *Tribune* writers – Bob Edwards and Michael Foot are prominent examples – he was in due course snapped up by Lord Beaverbrook, the legendary proprietor of Express Newspapers. Beaverbrook took a peculiar and specific pleasure in capturing leading writers on the left and moulding them for his own purposes.

Millar may have gone to work for a right-wing newspaper empire, but he never lost his Labour principles. He and Audrey, members of the close-knit north London Labour squirearchy, knew everyone who was anyone in the movement, and were particularly close to Michael Foot, a near neighbour, and the visionary Aneurin Bevan, founder of the National Health Service. For the young, raw, drunken Alastair Campbell the Millars were a revelation. Meeting them was a salutary reminder of something that he had at least partly forgotten since leaving his parents' home six years before: that there was more to life than sex, football, pubs, bagpipes and tabloid stitch-ups.

Millar was suspicious, as fathers of pretty girls tend to be, when Fiona first brought her boyfriend home. A number of Fleet Street journalists first became familiar with the name Alastair Campbell in the Bell public house, just across the road from the old *Express* building in Fleet Street. At around eleven most mornings Millar was inclined to drop into the Bell, often in company with the film critic Ian Christie, for many years a close friend and colleague. There was a brief period, in the very early 1980s, when Bob Millar was prone to confide to fellow drinkers at the Bell his disquiet about 'this strange man who was seeing his daughter, who played the bagpipes'.

This period soon passed, and suspicion was replaced by the warmest of friendships. Wilfred Greatorex recalls: 'Bob talked endlessly and Alastair just sat at his feet and learnt.' Campbell could not have hoped for a better teacher. The future Number 10 press secretary became so devoted to Fiona's father that he actually took up bowls, the sport to which Millar devoted his declining years, in order to see even more of him.

Campbell came to politics at a very late age. He did not have a political thought of any consequence whatever until he was approaching the age of thirty, when he came across the Millar family. He stood on the left, but in an ill-defined way. His political philosophy was pitiful: a kind of incoherent, inchoate, anti-establishment, half-formed anarchism. This is extraordinary for a man with such an intuitive sense of how power works and which levers need to be pulled. Meeting the Millars when and in the way he did was remarkable good fortune. It meant when he finally did learn about politics, it was not the half-baked, hardleft nonsense that was fashionable in the student halls and constituency

parties at the time. He learnt about the Labour party over the dinner
tables of Hampstead, with companions of the calibre of Bob and
Audrey Millar or Michael Foot and his wife Jill Craigie. He could not
have had a more privileged introduction to the Labour party.

Since that time in the early 1980s, a number of famous and powerful
men have loomed large in Campbell's life and helped to form his character. Among them can be counted Neil Kinnock, Robert Maxwell and
Tony Blair. None of them was half as important for Campbell as Bob
Millar.

Political correspondent

It was partly the influence of Bob Millar that caused Campbell to take
his first steps towards political journalism. But Campbell would probably have made the move anyway. He would have become aware soon
after arriving at the *Mirror* that lobby journalists are an élite. The political editor of a national newspaper is a powerful figure. He has direct
access to his editor, and very often to the proprietor as well. On many
papers he can, and frequently does, pull rank on the news editor. His
relationship with the other sections of his paper is very similar to
Downing Street's relationship with the rest of Whitehall. An effective
political editor has the capacity to move in on practically any story he
likes, on the grounds that it has entered the realm of national politics,
often to the intense resentment of specialist staff and ordinary
reporters. All of this would have been quite enough to draw Campbell, with his acute antennae for power, towards the lobby even if he
were not belatedly beginning to take an intelligent interest in national politics.

After his first eighteen months as a general reporter, it began to be
obvious to anyone who knew Campbell that his inclinations lay in that
direction. He started to visit the Commons and cultivate political correspondents. Colleagues remember him hanging round the press
gallery in the Commons, getting drunk at the press bar, always with a
Marlboro cigarette in his mouth. He started to travel up to party conferences as a news reporter and get to know politicians as best he could.
Wilfred Greatorex remembers being surprised when Campbell turned
up at a private lunch at County Hall hosted by Illtyd Harrington, then

deputy leader of the Labour group on the GLC. The episode shows how eager he was to get onto the political scene around this time.

Gradually Campbell was managing to get more Westminster-based stories into the papers. For a period the Tory MP Harry Greenway was Campbell's best – or at any rate most visible – contact. He was one of the few MPs who would give the unknown young reporter the time of day. 'We had an easy relationship,' remembers the former Ealing North MP. 'In his early days he was interested in people who had some character. He was very friendly. I was helpful. It would be wrong to say I took him under my wing because he wasn't the sort of chap who needed that.' Greenway, a popular back-bencher who lost his seat in the 1997 landslide, was renowned as much for the quantity as for the quality of his public pronouncements. His unfailingly populist observations formed useful ballast in Campbell copy. On one glorious occasion the obscure Tory MP even provided him with a coveted front-page story. When it was announced in October 1985 that the Princess of Wales's second son was to be christened Henry, Greenway weighed in with a ringing call for the baby prince to be known as Harry. 'Henry is too turgid a name for a prince with such exciting parents,' proclaimed the MP. 'Harry is a dashing, robust name which is in tune with the 1980s.' The *Mirror*/Greenway campaign met with instant success. Later on, Harry Greenway was puzzled when Campbell dropped him like a stone. 'I suppose he had more important fish to fry,' he now says, with perfect accuracy and not an ounce of resentment.

He did indeed. It is absolutely typical of Alastair Campbell that within months of setting out to become a political journalist he hooked one of the biggest fish in the sea – Neil Kinnock. The two men met properly for the first time at a *Mirror*-sponsored event. The editor, Mike Molloy, had the idea of inviting the extended Kinnock family – uncles, aunts, nephews, nieces, grandparents, second cousins, the lot – to central London for a family photograph. Molloy hoped that its publication would give the Labour leader a more homely and family-friendly image. He even planned to run a series on the Kinnock extended family around the theme of 'people like us'. The project was a logistical nightmare and a number of reporters were ordered to act as minders for the seventy or so Kinnocks who turned up for this unique occasion. One of them was Campbell. By the end of it all he was firm friends with every single one of the Kinnock clan, and above all Neil and Glenys.

In the words of Julia Langdon, then the political editor of the *Daily Mirror*: 'He was immediately entranced. It was like watching someone fall in love. Head over heels. Bowled over. Besotted. It was also the first indication of his obsessive streak. He followed them everywhere for years.' Campbell soon supplanted Langdon as the Kinnocks' favourite *Mirror* journalist. 'He ingratiated himself with them by proving such an effective propagandist for them. I was a journalist not a script writer, but they preferred Alastair's approach,' remembers Langdon, adding that 'Fiona Millar told me how I was a role model for Alastair but when I left the *Mirror* and Alastair succeeded me, she cut me dead and he barely spoke to me.' Later, when Campbell became press spokesman to Blair, an unflattering anonymous profile of him appeared in the *Spectator* magazine. Campbell accused Langdon of being the author. 'When I pointed out there were several errors which I would have known were inaccurate,' recalls Langdon, 'he said, ah, but I had included them deliberately to disguise my identity. He finished the conversation by saying: "I'll get you."' It was not the last time he was to make such a threat.

It speaks volumes for the sheer conviction of Campbell's personality that it imprinted itself so quickly on the Labour leader, an important man whose time was heavily in demand. Campbell was a junior reporter of some talent but no standing, with no real political knowledge or experience, not even a member of the parliamentary lobby.

For Campbell the benefits from the association were immense. In any newspaper the establishment of a direct, personal link to the leader of the opposition is a valuable commodity. At the *Mirror*, the flagship of the British left, it was priceless. Campbell's status within the paper doubled overnight: the road that would take him to the political editorship had suddenly become clear. Campbell made the switch from Holborn Circus to work out of the cramped *Mirror* office in the press gallery.

Breakdown

Campbell's decision to accept a job offer from *Today* newspaper in the autumn of 1985 now looks like the first indication of his impending mental breakdown. The move was partly attributable to his frustration at Robert Maxwell's method of running the *Mirror*. He and Merritt were both disturbed by the way the tycoon continually thrust his views and personality onto the pages; they thought he was turning the paper into a joke. Even so, the move was in no sense rational. Campbell was one of the most highly valued young reporters on the *Mirror*. He had just been given one of the most prized jobs on the paper. His prospects were assured. Eddie Shah's *Today* was a bold venture which, though a failure, has an honourable place in Fleet Street history. It brought desperately needed new technology to the newspaper industry and smashed through the labour practices that had hobbled it since the war. And yet it required no great insight to perceive, even at the time, that *Today* was fatally flawed by inadequate management and shortage of capital and that it was at best a highly uncertain prospect. Campbell was jumping off the first-class compartment of an ocean-going liner and choosing instead to bunk down with the crew on a leaky tramp steamer. His readiness to leave the Labour-backing *Mirror* to join the anti-union *Today* is an interesting commentary on the strength of his left-wing views at the time.

Many of his friends tried to dissuade him. Richard Stott, his patron at the *Mirror*, did his best. Joe Haines, press secretary to Harold Wilson, despite his initial reluctance to take Campbell on board, went to extreme lengths to keep him. 'He came into the office in the evening,' recalls Haines, 'and said that he had been offered a job on *Today*. I didn't want to lose him. When I asked him why he was going he said he was worried whether he would keep his job under Maxwell. So I went over to see Maxwell who said: "You can assure him his job is safe." By the time I got back Alastair told me he had resigned. I was not pleased. Nor was Richard Stott. I told him that he was not ready to undertake any executive job on any paper, particularly not a new paper, with the stresses and tensions that involves.' There is some confusion now – it may very well be that this reflects confusion at the time – about exactly what role Campbell performed at *Today*. One of the attractions for the ambitious young reporter may have been the prospect of an executive position and the chance to boss subordinates around. Doubtless he was flattered to be heavily wooed by another paper for the first time. It is certain that a large salary increase would have formed part of the attraction. Even so, his decision to leave the *Mirror* for such a flaky outfit strongly suggests that his judgement had entirely deserted him.

The paper was a shambles. Nobody knew who was doing what. The launch date was frequently put back. Just opposite the *Today* offices in the Vauxhall Bridge Road was a pub called the Lord High Admiral. It was gloomy, with a painted wood panel ceiling and heavily stained black panelling. It was very dark inside, and the enormous block of flats directly above it added to the strong sense of oppression. Not surprisingly, very few people visited the place. Campbell promptly colonized the pub, surrounding himself with boon companions. He started going there early in the day, and would return to top up at regular intervals. Once Fiona Millar stormed into the pub, seized Campbell by the scruff of the neck, and dragged him away.

On his desk in the office, which he visited from time to time, carefully placed in a position of honour, was a photograph of Neil Kinnock. He would often admire it ostentatiously. In the absence of a newspaper, there was nothing much to do. There was a limit to the number of dummy copies that could be brought out. For most journalists this was merely an irritant. It gave them extra time to write novels, conduct love affairs, above all drink in pubs. For Campbell, however, the lack of structure in his day was a problem. He insisted on inventing meaningless little tasks for himself. At one point he developed an obsession with Dean Reed, a mysterious American pop star who had failed in his own country but thanks to some peculiar chemistry turned into a celebrity in the Soviet Union. Campbell would bang on endlessly about Dean Reed in the Lord High Admiral, where fellow drinkers tolerantly viewed his latest enthusiasm as a sign of originality. 'I would have thought that this Dean Reed was a bit of a sad bloke but Alastair was really passionate about him in an almost boy-scoutish sort of way,' recalls a colleague. 'He wanted to know everything about him. Were the KGB after him? Did the CIA want to bump him off? He was planning to take flights to all sorts of weird places to track him down.' Close friends say that he came to believe that British intelligence – thought to have an office in the vicinity – was spying on him and drilling radio waves into his head.

Not surprisingly, things were starting to degenerate in the office, especially after Campbell was given the task of news editor for the Sunday edition. Reporters remember him wandering round with a large notepad issuing incoherent instructions. 'You didn't know if he was telling you what to do or just talking to himself. He would come over, mutter something, then wander away. He was absolutely useless,' remembers one *Today* journalist. 'He was positively the most incompetent newspaper executive that I have ever come across. And he obviously knew it.'[1]

The end of this distressing phase in Campbell's life finally came around the time when he travelled up to Scotland to cover the Labour Spring conference in March 1986. By this stage it was becoming increasingly difficult to dismiss his behaviour as eccentric: it had become downright peculiar. Julia Langdon recalls walking through Perth on the eve of the conference with her husband Geoffrey Parkhouse, the political editor of the *Glasgow Daily Herald*. In due course they reached the Conference Centre.

> I encountered him on the street, immediately outside the City Halls in Perth, where Kinnock was about to address the Scottish Labour party conference. Campbell was arguing with a policeman, but broke off when he saw my husband and I approaching, saying angrily that at least we would help him. 'He wouldn't tell me where the City Halls are!' he complained. We explained why and had a laugh and then as we all had some time in hand, we took him to the pub. It wasn't his first visit of the day. I remember my husband made him eat a sandwich and then we watched him dash across the road to sort out his press pass. 'I've never seen anyone who looks more likely to be heading for a breakdown,' my perceptive husband remarked when he had gone. He bitterly regretted his foresight afterwards because he guiltily felt he should have acted on his instinct. Later that night in Glasgow, still tracking the Kinnocks, Campbell did indeed break down. He was picking another unnecessary fight with a policeman and I seem to remember was arrested and nearly caused a serious political embarrassment to his hero.

The three journalists went off to a wine bar to eat some lunch, Campbell talking obsessively about Neil Kinnock. He was in Scotland, he told Langdon and Parkhouse, to write an account of a week in the life of the Labour leader. (Here is a clear sign of the shambles that *Today* had already become even before a copy had been sold. At the time Campbell was a news editor. The job of a news editor is to stay at his desk making decisions and handing out instructions, never to set out on jaunts of his own.) Several bottles later the three returned to the conference centre. Campbell was not allowed in. It became apparent that he had failed, once again, to provide himself with press accreditation.

Only a very few people know exactly what happened to Alastair Campbell in Scotland – his own family, Fiona Millar and some members of the Kinnock entourage.[2] A decade and a half later there are various accounts of where the catastrophe occurred: a hotel foyer in Glasgow, a shipyard on the Clyde, and the banks of a Scottish loch have all been cited as the scene of the dénouement. There appears to have been a function involving the Labour leader from which officialdom endeavoured to exclude Campbell, on the grounds either that he was not invited or that he was drunk, or very possibly both. Campbell said he was in a car when he was struck by a pain which felt 'like a piece of glass cracking into thousands of pieces inside your head.'[3] He said he abandoned the car in a lay-by and later, after taking all his clothes off, was picked up and put in a cell by police, who only agreed to release him after he agreed to seek hospital treatment. Describing his breakdown as a '24-carat crack-up', he added: 'I hit the bottle pretty hard, got completely manic and cracked.'[4] In hospital, he was told to write down how much he had been drinking each day. 'It dawned on me: I was drinking vast amounts and had been kidding myself that I did not have a problem. I was taken to the limit, really close to losing everything, at absolute breaking point, and I think that turned me into a stronger person.'[5] 'Coming out of the breakdown was slow, very hard, I was crushed by a numbing depression and unless you've experienced it, it's almost impossible to communicate. I couldn't physically open my eyes or lift myself out of bed. The phone would ring and I'd just look at it, unable to answer.'[6]

One colleague remembers the reaction among fellow journalists as the news filtered back to London. After brief initial obligatory expressions of sympathy and concern, Campbell's prospects were swiftly written off. 'We all thought: That's it. He's nothing in this business anymore, unemployable. We all thought that he would never work again.' There was nothing personal or vengeful in this assessment; they had seen the same thing happen to colleagues many times before.

Weeks later, by which time Campbell had resolved to become teetotal, Fiona Millar mentioned to a friend that he had stopped drinking. 'Why?' inquired the friend. 'Was he getting drunk a lot?' Millar replied: 'No. He used to go mad.'[7]

chapter four

Serving Kinnock and Maxwell

The whole world's against me. People are out to destroy me.
Robert Maxwell to Alastair Campbell, Brighton, 1991

CAMPBELL WAS OFF WORK for about six months. After a spell in hospital he spent some time recuperating, part of it at the quiet and pleasant country home of Sid Young, a former *Mirror* colleague. His friends rallied round. Years later, at his friend John Merritt's memorial service in St Bride's, Fleet Street, he recalled Merritt coming to visit him while he was still in hospital. Merritt was clutching a handful of marbles. He handed them to Campbell with the words: 'Here are your marbles back. Now don't lose them again.' There are those who still shake their head and wonder how Campbell got to the end of that address.

Today seems to have looked after him in exemplary fashion, making sure that he got proper medical treatment, that he remained on the staff, and that he was put under no special pressure to return to work. But when Campbell was finally fit enough to cope, he chose to go back to the *Mirror*. It is easy to see why. The *Mirror* was his real home and he returned to Holborn Circus in the same spirit that a wounded animal returns to its lair in order to lick its wounds. He asked a friend to make a discreet approach to Richard Stott, by now *Mirror* editor, to see if he would be welcome back. When a positive reply came Campbell jumped at the chance. No one at *Today* ever expressed resentment that the employee it nursed so generously and well while he was distressed should have abandoned the paper the moment he was fit to return to work.

The first thing that colleagues noticed was that Campbell had changed physically. Gone was the large, confident presence of his first few years in Fleet Street. He had shrunk. He no longer drank. He was thinner, paler, more self-effacing in manner. One old drinking friend remembers meeting up with Campbell and Fiona Millar shortly after he returned to Fleet Street. He recalls: 'Ali had those staring eyes and a hunted look. He was desperately on edge. One feared for him. He knew he had come within an ace of losing it. I looked at Fiona and thought: thank God nurse is there.' It would take him more than a year to regain the dominant, abundant personality that had been so attractive before the breakdown. But it did return. Those who knew him in his early days say that he has become very much the same imposing figure as before. This suggests that the brilliant figure at the Stab-in-the-Back was the genuine Campbell, not some artificial, drink-driven invention.

Campbell threw himself into teetotalism with the same manic enthusiasm that he had once devoted to alcohol. This made him very boring indeed. His old drinking companions recall with distaste how he would take them aside and lecture them about the dangers of strong drink. One reporter remembers Campbell trying – unsuccessfully – to wrestle his pint of beer out of his hand. Paul Callan says that Campbell wandered round the Stab-in-the-Back distributing temperance literature. It is clear that Campbell believed alcohol was the cause of his breakdown, and was endeavouring to save others from the same fate. It may have been important for Campbell to believe that alcohol was the primary cause of his troubles, but it was not entirely true. No one who knew Campbell well before the episode in Scotland thinks that he was an alcoholic. He drank heavily, but there was nothing exceptional about it and no suggestion that he was addicted. Merrritt's wife, Lindsay Nicholson, who was as close to him as anybody, states that he drank 'no more than any other young journalist with an expense account'. Others say the same. There is no evidence that he used the secret tricks and devices that real alcoholics are forced to resort to. Campbell was certainly a binge drinker, and giving up drink was the crucial step in helping him get to grips with his problem. But drink was only a part of the problem itself. Campbell's nervous breakdown was brought about as much by his inability to cope with the demands of his new job at *Today* as by alcohol.

Many people who undergo the kind of calamity Campbell suffered in the spring and summer of 1986 never fully recover. They remain haunted, torn in two, in some cases almost literally a shadow of their former selves. With Campbell the opposite was the case. It is as if the breakdown enabled him to solve a mysterious conundrum in his nature, some personal roadblock that prevented him from making headway with his life. From the moment that Campbell returned to work in late 1986, the course of his life became very different. It was no longer the story of a charming, unsettled, itinerant rogue. There was a new steel in his character. It would be entirely wrong to state that before 1986 Campbell was without personal ambition. But it was unfocussed. The fights, the boozing, the pornography, those long railway journeys to Burnley Football Club – all spoke of a desperate and almost suicidal lack of direction. From the end of 1986 there was a cool and precise sense of purpose about the man. He knew exactly where he wanted to go and who he wanted to become. His breakdown turned out in the end to be the springboard for one of the most meteoric rises that Fleet Street has ever seen.

One happy development gave Campbell a new stability. In the late 1980s he and Fiona Millar set about starting a family. The birth of their eldest son Rory was followed two years later by Calum, and, a few years on, by a daughter, Grace.

Fiona Millar to some extent put her career on hold when the children started to arrive. She had gone straight to the *Daily Express* at the end of the Mirror training scheme in 1982. Four years later Paul Potts, then political editor and today editor of the Press Association, had picked her out to join his team of Westminster reporters. He remembers her as 'hard-working and committed'. There is no doubt in Potts' mind that she would have become a political editor herself if she had wanted to. Potts says that Fiona, though known to be a socialist, was 'professional about the *Express* agenda' at a time when it was trumpeting Thatcherite opinions. Fiona continued to do frequent work for the *Express* on a freelance basis after handing in her notice in 1988. She also profiled MPs for *The House* magazine.

Political editor

Joe Haines wanted Campbell back on the political desk. But he says that Stott insisted that Campbell must work his passage back and gave him a general reporting job. It cannot have lasted very long. Within a few weeks Campbell had been found a safe billet as deputy to Victor Knight, the veteran political editor of the *Sunday Mirror*. Knight, a respected and knowledgeable political correspondent of the old school, took Campbell under his wing. But he was distracted by domestic tragedy. His wife was ill, and his own health was beginning to fail. Within a year of Campbell's arrival Knight had taken early retirement, prelude to an early death, and Campbell was formally appointed political editor of the *Sunday Mirror*, rather sooner than anyone intended, in the autumn of 1987. It was a job that he used as a stepping-stone on the way to the cherished and far more important position of political editor of the *Daily Mirror* only two years later. He was regarded as an outstanding success. Judged by any conventional measure of political journalism, this success cannot be explained.

The political editor of a Sunday newspaper has two primary functions. First is the provision of fresh, exciting, tasty political exclusives. Any political editor who fails to provide a worthy candidate for a front-page splash by the close of play on Friday evening is likely to receive a frosty glance from his editor. If he fails to do so for three or four weeks in a row the atmosphere is likely to turn icy. Any further dereliction of duty and he is in danger of being invited to an 'interview without coffee'.

During the full eighteen-month period that Campbell was political reporter or political editor at the *Sunday Mirror* he provided not one story of any note. Not only was his presence on page one negligible but his page-two offerings were also paltry things, effectively the dressed-up press releases that Gordon Brown, the latest rising star on the Labour benches, was already beginning to hawk around town with fatiguing regularity. The second – and subsidiary – function of a political editor is the provision of crisp, well-informed analysis about the week in Westminster. Campbell was provided with the ideal vehicle. His still-youthful features beamed out from above a weekly column, given plenty of space, a prominent position on page six in the paper, and the imposing heading of 'People, Politics and Power'. Admittedly, few political columns improve when they are re-read years later, but Campbell's column in the *Sunday Mirror* was unusually poor. It was almost entirely lacking in insight or information, the jokes were weak: it can only be classified as vinegary Labour propaganda.

The reasons for Campbell's failure as a story-getter are not hard to find. He knew hardly any Tories, an omission he was later to remedy but which at this stage of his career prevented him from delivering hard-hitting scoops about the government of the day. His contacts with the Labour party, by contrast, were good – too good. There is every reason to believe that Campbell knew a great deal that was going on in the Kinnock camp. Making use of such information, however, would have killed off the access that enabled him to obtain it in the first place. Campbell had allowed himself to become too close to the subject he was writing about: an age-old danger in any kind of journalism.

His failure as a columnist is more complex and more interesting. He had already proved himself as a capable tabloid reporter, and in years to come he would prove himself as a speech-writer. Cabinet ministers would marvel at Campbell's facility for turning a complex argument that had baffled Whitehall's finest brains into a form of words that even the meanest intelligence could understand. His speed of delivery is equally impressive. During the long prelude to the 1997 general election he would often dash off a thousand-word leading article on behalf of Tony Blair in an hour or, if the need was urgent, even less. The copy would be flawless, the message exact, the style precisely tailored to the intended audience.

Not so with Campbell the columnist. Columnists must possess a sense of mischief, a relish in the play of ideas, and a mastery of the texture and the rhythms of the English language. It was asking too much of Campbell, at the age of thirty, to possess all these qualities. What is so striking is that he possessed none of them. He possesses an unmistakable genius for the compelling tabloid phrase, as he proved years later when he conjured up the memorable 'People's Princess' in the wake of Princess Diana's death. But he has no real feel for the English language. His range of reference is hopelessly limited. He displays no knowledge of history, ideas or literature. Metaphors are drawn, to a monotonous extent, from the football field. What is most puzzling of all is that

Campbell's massive, complicated personality fails to communicate itself to the reader.

Something strange is at work here. Campbell the writer is most effective when he adopts an idiom, whether it is the arid formulae of tabloid news-reporting or the shrill platitudes of the press release. He is happiest of all when he surrenders his identity and allows it to be absorbed into that of someone else: converts himself into his political master of the moment for the purposes of a speech or a newspaper piece. If Campbell had been a painter and not a writer, he would have been an adequate but unoriginal artist. But he would have been a master forger.

Given Campbell's failure to provide a single decent front-page story in the entire period that he was political editor of the *Sunday Mirror*, it is worth asking how he survived at all, let alone achieved promotion so quickly to a bigger job on the *Daily Mirror*. Part of the answer lies in the fact that Campbell was an office politician of rare talent. By now Bob Edwards had finally been dispatched as editor of the *Sunday Mirror*. His replacement, Eve Pollard, doted on Campbell, luxuriating in the urbane charm he was quite capable of laying on when circumstances demanded it. When Campbell gave up being political editor he was succeeded by Peter MacMahon, who found handling Pollard a fraught affair. After one particularly sticky session, he retreated to the Stab-in-the-Back with the paper's chief sub-editor, a man called Andy Howell. MacMahon asked Howell what quality Campbell had possessed that he lacked. Back came the reply from the chief sub: 'Alastair always gave Eve the impression that he wanted to slip her one but was too busy at just that particular moment. You didn't do that.'

From journalist to propagandist

Dealing with a temperamental female editor was child's play as far as Alastair Campbell was concerned. He was playing a far bigger game. Well before the end of 1987 he had renounced the trade of journalism, at any rate as it is commonly understood by those who practise it, and turned to something which he found much more exhilarating: power politics.

It is impossible to exaggerate the closeness of the friendship that developed between Alastair Campbell and Neil Kinnock during this period. They had struck up a warm friendship before Campbell's breakdown. It was twice as close afterwards. It would be reasonable to imagine that the victim of the kind of crisis that Campbell had endured would feel a strong reciprocal obligation to those who had bailed him out. And Campbell did feel a sense of gratitude. But his benefactors were even more strongly tied to him. The Labour leader had got emotionally drawn into the drama, and liked to imagine that he had played some part in salvaging Campbell from the wreckage. The tale still goes the rounds of how Kinnock came across a drunken Campbell, seized him by the scruff of the neck, and gave him a dramatic warning about the perils of drinking. Neil Kinnock's leadership of Labour was spent veering between the depths of despair and the heights of elation. He was adored by his party. But every speech he made, every decision he took, was systematically and as a matter of course distorted by the parts of the Tory-controlled press. The deeply emotional Kinnock felt it personally, and was therefore open to a new member of his inner circle, a journalist who was ready to offer unconditional loyalty and adulation.

Campbell would do anything for the Kinnocks. He was a mixture of adviser, minder, speech-writer, family friend and manservant. Along with Fiona Millar, he would babysit the children, pick up the shopping, draft a press release, give a view on the handling of a sensitive political problem. The two families went on holiday together.

Writing about politics for the Kinnock-baiting *Express* was no easy task for Millar. She told one of her *Express* colleagues, the right-wing commentator Peter Hitchens, that she needed her daily early-morning swim to get rid of the frustration of listening to his constant criticism of Kinnock in the *Express'* Commons office. Like Campbell, she did not join the herd in the Commons press gallery. 'She was always rather grand,' remembers one of her fellow *Express* reporters, 'and she did not allow her political views to affect her work.' Years later, Campbell would travel to Wales for the funeral of Glenys' mother, while Neil Kinnock went to visit Bob Millar while he was dying in hospital.

The moment that established Campbell's new role as bruiser for the Labour leader came in March 1987, just over a year after his breakdown. Campbell was part of the team of political correspondents that accompanied Neil Kinnock on an ill-starred visit to Ronald Reagan at the White House. It was a highly charged time, with only months to go before the general election. Kinnock was endeavouring to project himself as a statesman on the world stage. Anyone could have told him that this particular attempt was doomed. Denis Healey, the Shadow Foreign Secretary who came with him on this visit, had strongly urged him not to go. Kinnock ignored this sensible and kindly meant advice.

The lobby pack were, as ever, after Kinnock's blood. As Robert Gibson, then the deputy political editor of the *Daily Express*, notes: 'The Tory Press went on trips with Neil Kinnock for one reason only: to watch him fall flat on his arse.' During this journey the Labour leader was doing his best to make their job easy for them. His meeting with the President, unwisely billed beforehand by the Kinnock camp as a weighty discussion between two prominent figures on the world stage, was vanishingly brief. Afterwards, Reagan's press secretary, Marlin Fitzwater, emerged to brief the waiting newsmen. His account of events gave the strong impression that the hapless Kinnock had been hauled over the coals by the US President over Labour's defence policy and his proposals for unilateral nuclear disarmament. It was more than enough. The boys had their story. The travelling party rushed to the phone booths to file their accounts of Kinnock's latest humiliation.

According to some of the pressmen who were on this trip, Campbell at first joined the rush. One reporter claims to have heard him filing the same line as everybody else. Later that night, Campbell pulled out at the last moment from a prearranged flight with the rest of the party to New York. Fellow lobby correspondents gained the impression that he had either been told, or decided on his own accord, to refile a more Kinnock-friendly account of the day's events. Certainly Campbell's story which appeared in the next day's *Mirror* was more measured, and appeared under a neutral headline: 'Kinnock and Reagan Clash on Defence'.

In the following week's *New Statesman* Campbell published his own version of events. This compelling article amounted to an extraordinary denunciation of his colleagues in the parliamentary lobby. He called them 'cynical, cowardly and corrupt' and accused them of colluding with the White House in a bid to 'stitch up' Kinnock. Ignoring the rights and wrongs of the matter – and there is a respectable case that the lobby in this instance was doing no more than reporting the facts –

it was a commendably bold thing to do. The lobby hunts as a pack, never more so than on overseas trips. For a reporter as junior as Campbell to place himself at odds with such a powerful institution showed a certain presumption, not to say foolhardiness. But Campbell had already made his decision. He would happily continue to make use of the privileges of the lobby and the access it provided. But in most essential respects he was from that moment on a member of Neil Kinnock's private office. Campbell's career as a Labour spin-doctor did not begin in 1993 when Tony Blair asked him to become his press spokesman. It really started seven years earlier when – to all intents and purposes – he went to work for Neil Kinnock.

Liz Lightfoot, later the education correspondent of the *Daily Telegraph*, remembers being abused by Campbell after she filed an anti-Kinnock story for the *Mail on Sunday* during the 1987 general election. The campaign bus had been following Kinnock on a trip to Wales. The day was carefully arranged by the Kinnock machine so that nothing could go wrong. Nothing did, until Kinnock lost his cool when questioned by the Press Association about some verbal atrocity that Ken Livingstone had recently committed. So Lightfoot – then going out with a Labour candidate and by no stretch of the imagination a Tory stooge – sent a story about how Labour's careful stage management was ruffled when Kinnock lost his temper. It was mild stuff by the standards of the day. Nevertheless, Campbell started to scream at Lightfoot: 'That's complete rubbish and totally untrue. You shouldn't be filing that.'

Campbell did not merely appoint himself Neil Kinnock's press enforcer. His reporting no longer sought to establish anything resembling the truth. It was dedicated instead to serving a political purpose. A notorious example was his story about Jill Morrell, the girlfriend of Beirut hostage John McCarthy. Morrell devoted herself to securing McCarthy's release, and became a darling of the tabloid press. On 3 October 1991, shortly after McCarthy's release, the *Daily Mirror* published a front-page article written by Campbell, headlined 'Exclusive: Labour want brave Jill to stand as MP.' Campbell wrote: 'Labour are to ask brave Jill Morrell to stand for Parliament, the *Mirror* can reveal.' He added that Labour planned to ask Morrell to stand as its candidate in the forthcoming Hemsworth parliamentary by-election. The story

Labour want brave Jill to stand as MP

By ALASTAIR CAMPBELL
Political Editor

LABOUR are to ask brave Jill Morrell to stand for Parliament, the Mirror can reveal.

They want the girl-friend of freed hostage John McCarthy to fight a crucial by-election.

One insider said last night: "Jill would be absolutely perfect.

"She is eloquent, articulate, committed – and people like her.

"I can think of nobody with a better image and profile to put our case at such a crucial time."

TV journalist Jill is being pencilled in to stand at Hemsworth, a safe Labour seat in West Yorkshire with a 20,700 majority.

It has traditionally been represented by a miner, but she comes from a mining family in nearby Doncaster.

Jill joined the party four years ago as her campaign to keep John's name in the headlines took off.

Since then she has met

IMAGE: Jill Morrell

Neil Kinnock several times – both publicly and privately.

And he admits being a great admirer of her.

It is not known whether Jill would be interested in fighting the by-election.

But the insider said: "It's worth a try."

The plan to approach her was revealed as Mr Kinnock and Prime Minister John Major stood together at a thanksgiving service for 34-year-old McCarthy.

It was held at the journalists' church of St

quoted 'an insider' as saying: 'Jill would be absolutely perfect. She is eloquent, articulate and people like her. I can think of nobody with a better profile to put our case at such a crucial time.' Hemsworth was a Labour stronghold. If Morrell was picked by Labour, she would automatically become an MP. But if readers had known how Campbell operated that night, they would have been shocked. Campbell later told friends that he made it up. The 'insider' was Campbell and a chum. A former *Mirror* colleague recalled: 'During the evening Alastair was with someone who had been drinking heavily. Alastair then filed the story about Jill Morrell. It was filed pretty late.'

When the first edition was printed, other political editors were contacted urgently and asked to follow up Campbell's scoop. Knowing Campbell's contacts with Kinnock, some were so confident it must be true, they filed it to their own papers straightaway. Seasoned political reporter Jon Craig, of the *Daily Express* and later Sky TV, tracked down Campbell late in the evening and was surprised by the response. 'I asked him if the Morrell story was accurate and he said: "No, it's bollocks, I wouldn't touch it if I were you."'[1] Campbell later told a *Mirror* colleague: 'The only story I ever made up was the one about Jill Morrell.'[2] The *Mirror* colleague explained: 'Kinnock had been getting a hammering from the Tory papers all week and Alastair was pissed off about it. He wanted to give Labour some good publicity and make all the other political editors abandon their dinners and follow it up.' Neil Kinnock was not amused. Earlier that day he had met Morrell at a service at St Bride's Church, Fleet Street to celebrate McCarthy's freedom and was embarrassed by Campbell's stunt.

Campbell struck up a strong friendship with Glenys Kinnock. The two would flirt openly – though innocently – in public places. The relationship between the two couples was so close that Fiona Millar and Glenys Kinnock agreed to write a book together, an endeavour which led to an acrimonious falling-out. The book, published by Virago Press in 1993, was largely made up of a series of interviews with prominent women. Much of the work – according to some accounts, the majority of it – was carried out by Fiona Millar. Glenys Kinnock's own connection with the enterprise was most visibly confined to a lengthy introduction. When proofs came from the publishers, Fiona felt that her role was not fully acknowledged. Campbell, in turn, passed on his own indignation to Neil Kinnock. Kinnock declined to become involved. 'Leave aside the justice of what you are saying,' he told Campbell. 'Glenys is my wife.' The dispute was replayed twenty years later when Millar became adviser and confidante to Cherie Blair, only to fall out with her when she felt Cherie mistreated her. On that occasion, as he had done with Neil Kinnock, Campbell complained to the Labour leader, Blair. And Blair responded in the same way as Kinnock, by siding with his wife.

There is something striking, indeed verging on the pathological, about the way the Campbell-Millars served two successive generations of Labour leaders. They are rather like those devoted couples who attach themselves to grand families and get passed on from generation to generation. In time they can come to embody the tradition of the great house to which they are attached more closely than the actual owners. There were Campbell-Millars in attendance upon Labour party leaders and their consorts for almost two decades, with the exception of the two-year John Smith interregnum. It was an arrangement that suited all sides. The leader and wife got unrivalled service, while the Campbell-Millars got unrivalled access. With the Kinnocks, the unrivalled access was never translated into unrivalled power. When it did, through their attachment to the Blairs, it led to much greater strains.

Getting to know Cap'n Bob

The intimacy of the connection between the Kinnocks and the Campbell-Millars could not fail to attract the attention of Robert Maxwell, the chairman of Mirror Group Newspapers. Maxwell, as a former Labour MP, took a profound interest in British politics. And as proprietor of the *Daily Mirror*, he took the very reasonable view that he was a force to be reckoned with in the Labour party. It was an opinion with which Neil Kinnock could not readily demur, but the Maxwell influence was one which he vigorously sought to resist. The extraordinary figure of Maxwell tended to inspire two powerful but opposing emotions: warmth and distrust. The two forces pitted themselves against each other in Neil Kinnock's breast. It is a tribute to his good judgement that distrust won the day.

Still, Maxwell could not be entirely ignored. His lavish hospitality could be spurned, the munificence of the proffered financial assistance viewed with the deepest suspicion, but it was an uncomfortable fact of life that he controlled the largest Labour-supporting newspaper group in Britain. It was here that Campbell came into his own. In Kinnock's eyes, he became the acceptable face of Robert Maxwell. This was politics of the most dangerous sort. This bracing period of Campbell's life was to last the best part of five years.

Today Maxwell is remembered as a fraudster and a conman. Those who had close dealings with the man are in danger of being contaminated by association. Campbell knew Maxwell as well as any present or past members of Tony Blair's government who were associated with him, but thanks to his instinct for survival he has been damaged the least. Campbell had been a junior reporter when Maxwell, in a spectacular City coup, obtained control of the Mirror Group in the summer of 1983. It is likely that he had shared the prevailing dismay at the news of Maxwell's arrival; indeed, as we have seen, he cited his suspicion of the tycoon as a reason for joining *Today* a year later. By the time Campbell returned to the *Mirror* after recovering from his illness, in autumn 1986, the new editor, his friend Richard Stott, had moderated the worst of Maxwell's abrasive behaviour and to some extent quelled the tycoon's instinct for embarrassing self-publicity.

As ever with Campbell, he made it his business to establish a personal relationship with the boss. Fellow reporters remember him accompanying Maxwell to Ethiopia during the famine on a mission of mercy to relieve the starving. Maxwell set out to the worst-affected area. Upon arrival, the scenes were so shocking that the publisher broke down in tears. No one knew quite how to react until Alastair Campbell strode across to the boss. 'He went up to Maxwell and put his arm round his shoulders as if he was a child,' says one witness. 'He said, "Don't get upset. You are one of those people who can really make a difference." That is the moment when Campbell and Maxwell really bonded.' When Maxwell had stopped crying, he barked orders at Campbell to make sure his philanthropic efforts received wide TV coverage. Campbell obliged. Later, at a Mirror Group Christmas party, to which wives and families were invited, a Campbell infant was brought into the presence of the publisher. Campbell's colleagues recollect how Maxwell held up the baby and boomed: 'This is another future *Mirror* worker here.'

Campbell's relationship with the Mirror Group chairman is another example of his skill at building a friendship with the individual at the peak of whatever organization he happens to be working for at the time. With Maxwell especially, there were hazards in such a frontal approach. Maxwell did have a generous side, and yet he felt an instinctive need to humiliate those close to him, diminish them, establish their total dependence upon him. The most notable victim was Peter Jay, the former British ambassador in Washington and once hailed as the most brilliant man of his generation. Jay made the mistake of accepting the title of Maxwell's chief of staff, a grand-sounding title with salary to match. Maxwell immediately relegated him to a drudge, taking a sadistic pleasure in drawing public attention to Jay's subservient role. Campbell avoided a similar fate, always making clear to Maxwell that he was to a certain extent an independent power who deserved to be treated with respect.

He was, nevertheless, happy enough on occasion to perform humiliating personal favours for his boss. In April 1989, when still *Sunday Mirror* political editor, Campbell went to Washington to interview Republican senator John Tower. Earlier that month, Tower's nomination by President George Bush as US defence secretary had been rejected after accusations of drinking, womanizing and conflicts of interest arising from his commercial links to the defence industry.

The story made big headlines in America, but received less coverage in Britain. At a time when the Labour party, and Campbell, were firmly on the left wing, Tower, a wealthy Republican businessman who had made a fortune out of the arms industry, was an unlikely object of admiration. It was rare enough for a *Sunday Mirror* journalist to fly to the USA to interview any politician, let alone an old-timer like Tower on the way out. Nevertheless the result was two full-page features in the paper in successive weeks. The articles gush with sympathy and paint their subject as a hard-working, down-to-earth victim of a political and moral injustice, and moreover, one who would soon be more influential than ever. The first was headlined 'Tower Power' under a 'World Exclusive' tag and datelined: 'from Alastair Campbell in Washington'. It blamed the Democrats and 'the media' for Tower's downfall.[3] Campbell was so impressed with Tower that he ran another article about him the following week, headlined 'Old Friend'. This phrase was meant to refer to Tower's friendship with George Bush senior: it had more to do with his being Maxwell's 'old friend'. A second headline stated: 'A key power broker rises in the West.'[4] Tower was indeed a power broker – on behalf of Maxwell.

In these unctuous articles, Campbell omitted to point out to *Mirror* readers that Tower was a Maxwell crony, paid £100,000 a year by the *Mirror* tycoon as a consultant, and a board member of Maxwell's US magazine, *Armed Forces Journal International*. Nor did the articles state that Maxwell had just given Tower a place on the board of his £1.5 billion New York-based Macmillan publishing group.

Roy Greenslade, editor of the *Daily Mirror* for a brief period in the dying days of the Maxwell regime, tells a story that rebounds more to Campbell's credit, involving a difficult encounter between Alastair Campbell and Robert Maxwell at the height of the crisis that brought down Margaret Thatcher. It was the night of the first ballot after Michael Heseltine's leadership challenge. As politicians mulled over the meaning of the prime minister's slender majority, Maxwell rang Campbell to inform him that he had an exclusive story of the highest importance. It was a story, the press baron intimated, which he would expect to see all over the front page of the following day's *Mirror*. Maxwell asserted that he had impeccable information to the effect that six Cabinet ministers were ready to resign unless Margaret Thatcher stood down with immediate effect. Maxwell was right: it was a story with colossal ramifications. Such was the fear-infected culture Maxwell encouraged in his sprawling empire that nine out of ten Maxwell employees would instantly have done his bidding and agreed to put the story wherever the publisher wished. There was, after all, no percentage in failing to do so. If the story turned out to be wrong, then Maxwell was unlikely to return to the matter again. If, on the other hand, it turned out to be correct, then retribution on a giant scale could befall anyone who had failed to be dazzled by it.

Campbell told Maxwell he would not run with the story unless he knew the source. Maxwell could hardly believe such impudence. His roars of rage that anyone could doubt his sources of information echoed round the *Daily Mirror*'s Holborn Circus headquarters. Of course, he boomed, he would never breach a personal trust at the whim of a mere employee. But Campbell stood by his guns, and a furious Maxwell threatened to fire him. Somewhat shaken, Campbell spoke to his editor, Roy Greenslade, and Joe Haines, the *Mirror* leader-writer who carried considerable sway in the Maxwell camp. Both stood up for him.

This was by no means the only occasion when Campbell defied the *Mirror* chairman. The author and journalist Andy McSmith, who worked for many years on the political desk at the *Daily Mirror*, recalls that the tycoon once imperiously summoned Campbell to join him on a trip. Campbell refused to go, citing the funeral of Sean Hughes, the little-known Labour MP for Knowsley South. 'Not a lot of *Mirror* functionaries would have dared to do that,' records McSmith.

Batting for Kinnock

When Julia Langdon stepped down as political editor of the *Daily Mirror* in the autumn of 1989, there was some surprise that Campbell was asked to succeed her. Those who did not keep their eyes wide open saw only a low-ranking Sunday political editor with no special understanding and not much track record: a tabloid journalist who had only recently become interested in politics. But there was no doubt in the mind of anybody capable of reading the signs that Campbell would get the job. Becoming political editor of the *Daily Mirror* was a formal recognition that he was well on the way to becoming a man of power and substance at Westminster. Campbell, at the early age of thirty-two, had reached the top of his profession. He had used a singularly unconventional route to do so. The cultivation of powerful men, rather than a series of hard-hitting scoops, was the key to his success. Fellow lobby correspondents have on occasion speculated that, had Campbell been a woman, he would inevitably have been accused of sleeping his way to the top.

Most young men and women making their way in the world, if they have any sense, concentrate on getting on with the job in hand. They keep their head down, steer clear of office politics, allow their achievements to speak for themselves. The opposite approach, of ingratiating oneself with one's superiors, is, as a general rule, pitifully transparent, even to the very people being wooed and flattered. Even if it works, short-term gain is the best that can be achieved. In the medium to long term office crawlers are held in derision and contempt.

From the day he started work in Fleet Street, Campbell made it his business to go for the very top. Intermediate levels of seniority seem to have had little or no attraction for him. Within months of going to work for the *Daily Mirror* he had become one of the closest friends of Mike Molloy, the editor and – though in private a quiet and unassuming man – a mighty figure in Fleet Street. An apparently chance encounter lay behind the association. Molloy was on holiday in the south of France, and he and his family were in the habit of eating out at a particular restaurant in Villefranche. Emerging onto the street at the end of the meal one evening, Molloy heard the sound of bagpipes, as surprising a sound in the south of France then as it is today. Investigating further, he and his wife witnessed the splendid figure of Campbell playing the pipes to an admiring crowd, with Fiona by his side to ensure it contributed financially to the evening's entertainment. Vastly amused by this spectacle, Molloy did not fail to offer his ten francs, muttering that he did not realize that he paid Campbell as badly as all that. An invitation to dinner was soon forthcoming, and the following year Campbell and Millar were invited to join the Molloys on holiday.

The Villefranche meeting was a happy coincidence as far as Campbell was concerned – if it really was a coincidence, something fellow reporters are inclined to doubt. It would have been an easy matter, they observe, to discover where the editor was staying and position oneself strategically for a 'chance' meeting. Most junior journalists, of course, would have tended towards an opposite course of action: found out where the editor was staying and ensured that they were nowhere in the vicinity. Among these may have been Fiona Millar. There are reports that Millar, then a *Daily Express* reporter and lacking Campbell's appetite for self-promotion, had already banned her boyfriend from busking in a nearby town where her own editor, Larry Lamb, was reputed to be staying. Like most normal people, she felt no desire to ruin her holiday by meeting the boss.

'Alastair was never interested in employer-employee relationships,' says Roy Greenslade. 'He always wanted to change the "for" to working "with". He feels he is the equal of anyone.' Greenslade's remark goes a long way towards explaining the nature of the Campbell technique. His behaviour, although possessing many of the outward signs of the syco-phant, has never been sycophantic. Greenslade further recalls: 'When he was political editor, he would come into my office, put his feet on my desk and tell me the splash was trivial crap.'[5] There is no reason to sup-pose that Campbell took a different approach with any of his other edi-tors, or with Neil Kinnock.

It is Campbell's readiness to tell the truth and take risks with even his most powerful patrons that marks him out as much more than an office crawler. In anyone else, such huge self-esteem would have mani-fested itself as an intolerable bumptiousness. But in his case, others are ready to take him at his own assessment. The most powerful in the land have always been ready to admit Alastair Campbell as one of them. And this partnership of equals is, more than anything else, what has defined his relationship with Tony Blair.

There is something extremely unusual, almost disturbing, about Campbell's attraction to very powerful men. It is the most noteworthy and characteristic feature of his personality. His worship of power manages to coexist with a subsidiary tendency towards anarchism, though there is no doubt which is the dominant characteristic. Politi-cians are typically driven by three separate and competing motivations: power, money and the advancement of their social position. Campbell is interested in power only for its own sake: its incidental benefits appear to have no attraction for him. This is one of the things that made him such a formidable operator. It distinguished him sharply, for instance, from Peter Mandelson, for many years his principal rival for the ear of the Prime Minister. But Campbell is not happy within him-self until his light is refracted through someone he has deemed to be an even larger figure than himself.

From the moment Campbell was appointed political editor of the *Daily Mirror* in 1989, before the Labour conference with Neil Kin-nock's heady slogan 'Meet the Challenge, Make the Change', Campbell never had the slightest doubt what the job was all about. His predeces-sor Julia Langdon, though standing on the left, was journalist first and propagandist second. Campbell perceived with a Leninist clarity that his job was about advancing the interests of Neil Kinnock and the Labour party. Journalism, in the sense that it is commonly understood, had nothing to do with it. Trevor Kavanagh, who was political editor of the *Sun* throughout Campbell's time as political editor of the *Mirror*, had to chase up a political story in his mass-market competitor on only one occasion during the four years that they were direct rivals. The only scoops that Campbell got on a regular basis were his interviews with Neil Kinnock. These were always billed 'exclusive' and came round regular as clockwork.

Labour hagiographer

With inner fanaticism, Alastair Campbell dedicated himself to boosting Kinnock and his allies while laying into his enemies. This process had already begun at the *Sunday Mirror*, for which Campbell continued to write his column while political editor of the *Daily Mirror*. During the late 1980s Alastair Campbell and Fiona Millar set about writing a series of hagiographies of approved members of the Kinnock team. It was a heroic project, undertaken with the same dedication and selflessness with which Beatrice and Sidney Webb set about their famous investigations into the deserving poor in the 1930s. The prose style is a strange mixture of the gushing platitudes of *Hello!* magazine and those steely tributes to heroes of the Russian working class that used to appear in *Soviet Weekly* during the Stalinist years. It would be pleasing to record that this journalistic style has since died out; but nothing could be further from the truth. Those Campbell-Millar *Sunday Mirror* profiles contained the first stirrings of what would in due course become a literary horror: New Labour English. Already present in them is the stark use of words, the absence of humour, the poverty of language, the lack of interest in ideas, the impatience with other points of view, the bustling determination to make everything appear in the best possible light. In due course, after a number of modifications, and given a generous evangelical injection by Tony Blair, it would emerge in the form we know today. New Labour English, as it manifests itself in conference speeches, party literature, Tony Blair's annual speech to the Labour party conference, and in the hundreds of articles ostensibly written each year by the Prime Minister, was above all the creation of Alastair Campbell. He started it, and it spread like a disease. When this arid subject becomes, as it undoubtedly will, the subject for a PhD in the history of the English language, the aspiring doctor must not omit to pay tribute to the source of it all: Alastair Campbell's *Sunday Mirror* column and his profiles of leading Labour figures.

Needless to say, the first profile was on Neil Kinnock. Campbell, along with his photographer Fritz von der Schulenburg, was granted privileged admittance to the Labour leader's 'detached three-bedder' in Ealing. Schulenburg produced lavish pictures of Neil Kinnock looking statesmanlike in the kitchen, and cuddling up with his wife on the sofa. Campbell complemented these with observations like: 'When it comes to cooking, the kitchen is very much Glenys-territory.'

Fiona Millar visited Gordon Brown at his Edinburgh flat. There she discovered Labour's newly promoted trade spokesman and latest rising star living in a state of incomparable squalor. It was clear, she informed colleagues upon her return to civilization, that the Brown establishment had been neither cleaned nor tidied since he moved in several years before. This presented difficulties for a writer determined to present the subject in a homely and domestic light. 'Brimming with character' is the form of words Millar finally settled on to describe Brown's domestic arrangements. 'The overall impression is very much a bachelor pad.'

A second problem presented itself when the moment came for photographs to be taken. Brown was wearing a dark suit, not ideal for a piece that was designed to highlight the softer side of his personality. It was indicated that it would be helpful if he changed into something more casual. Brown slipped into his bedroom and swiftly re-emerged, having changed his tie. It became clear, to the incredulity of both Millar and the photographer, that this strange, brilliant man did not possess any form of leisure wear at all or indeed any form of garment apart from his daily working suits.

Campbell wrote the profile of Peter Mandelson. He visited the Labour party director of communications in a Herefordshire village. Some misty dream of rustic peace and tranquillity had driven Mandelson to purchase a farm worker's cottage. 'With every mile I drive from London, my mood lifts,' he told Campbell, implausibly. Mandelson still had his moustache in those days. He was photographed pruning the roses in his tiny garden, unmistakably ill at ease in the rural setting. The cottage itself was disposed of soon afterwards.

The Blair article was turgid. It is a testament to Campbell's growing influence within the Mirror Group that he was able to get it into the paper at all. It was not an interview with Blair himself, then a moderately glamorous figure who might well have been acceptable to a magazine editor short of an idea. It was a breathy account of an evening with the general management committee of the Sedgefield constituency Labour party. Campbell dutifully recorded that the 'three to one representation of the sexes was fairly accurately represented in the mixed lounge' and other such information. No self-respecting journalist would have had anything to do with such a dire piece of writing, least of all in a Sunday colour supplement. What was going on here, of course, had nothing to do with journalism. Campbell was quite deliberately using his position at the *Mirror* to build alliances and strengthen his own position.

What is striking is how clinically and accurately Campbell, in the late 1980s, had identified the generation that would emerge as the dominant force in the second half of the 1990s. There was no *Sunday Mirror* interview with John Smith, John Prescott, Robin Cook, Roy Hattersley or Bryan Gould – all senior members of Neil Kinnock's Shadow Cabinet. Campbell, with his immaculately tuned antennae, understood that it was better to buy shares that were still available cheaply rather than trade in established reputations. He picked out Gordon Brown, Tony Blair and Peter Mandelson: the very three men who would build New Labour. Each was a bullseye. At this stage, like everyone else, he saw Gordon Brown as the future prime minister, 'with Blair a likely chancellor'.

Hagiography was not the only activity into which Campbell threw himself with enthusiasm. It was his duty to stick the boot in on behalf of Neil Kinnock, and he carried it out with pleasure. Sticking the boot in came naturally; it still does today. He was always available to tear down a member of the Shadow Cabinet or an unhelpful trade-union leader. Ron Todd, the leader of the mighty Transport and General Workers' Union, was one frequent target for Campbell's scorn. The TGWU, the enemy of the modernizers, infuriated Campbell. Noisy left-wing MPs like Ken Livingstone were a favourite Campbell target. Like Kinnock, he frequently found himself at odds with John Prescott, always likely to make a nuisance of himself by speaking up for the left against the modernizers. It is a measure of Campbell's ability to manage personal relationships that he remained on good terms with Prescott. Shortly after the 1992 general election Campbell set about undermining Prescott's campaign to succeed Roy Hattersley as deputy leader. He itemized Prescott's many defects in an article that was almost as vicious as it was patronizing. It accused Prescott of failing to come up with fresh ideas and vented claims that Labour press officers were constantly having to wade in to preserve Prescott from his own mistakes. 'He's what one critic calls "a big girl's blouse,"' concluded Campbell. 'He thinks the *Daily Mirror* is part of the conspiracy against him. The trouble with Prescott is that you're either for him or against him.' The idea of Prescott as John Smith's deputy, asserted Campbell, 'appeals to Tories no end'.

Prescott was furious. He stormed around Westminster like an enraged bull. The following week he was granted the right to reply to the charges against him. 'I can't say I like being comprehensively slagged off. Campbell says I have many talents. I wish he'd devoted more space to saying what they are.' Incredible though it sounds, Prescott's ringing riposte was ghosted for him by none other than Alastair Campbell.[6] Labour politicians were starting to dance to his tune.

Campbell used the political editorship of the *Mirror* to turn himself into a powerful player on the political scene as an instrument of Neil Kinnock. He had instant access at all times to the leader's office. In return he wrote about politics the way Kinnock wanted. Andy McSmith, who worked for Campbell at this time, describes how Campbell gave in to pressure from Neil Kinnock to retract one of his stories. It concerned Peter Mandelson. McSmith reported that Mandelson had to step down from his post as Labour's director of communications as a result of his decision to stand for a parliamentary seat. A day or two later, the *Mirror* published a correction of the story even though there were solid grounds for believing it was true. McSmith now takes up the story: 'The original piece was under my name, the retraction was written by the *Daily Mirror*'s political editor Alastair Campbell. Generally, it is notoriously difficult to induce a tabloid newspaper to retract anything, particularly a story that would obviously stand up in court. Mandelson only achieved it by being able, once again, to call upon his relationship with Neil Kinnock.'[7]

The job established Campbell in the same way that, five years before, Peter Mandelson had been turned into a figure of substance by his appointment as Labour's director of communications. As *Mirror* political editor, he counted for very much more than any mere member of the Shadow Cabinet. Colleagues remember that he could often be seen talking to Tony Blair in the members' lobby. There was no question in their minds about who had the upper hand in these conversations. Blair was merely a rising Shadow minister. Campbell by contrast was a powerful political editor, known to have the ear of Neil Kinnock and well capable of throwing his weight around at the Mirror Group. Blair's attitude was appropriately deferential, almost giving the impression that he was flattered that a man of the stature of Alastair Campbell was ready to give him the time of day.

Two events brought this successful and happy period in Campbell's professional career to a conclusion. The first was the death of Robert Maxwell on 5 November 1991. The second was the general election result of 1992 less than six months later. Campbell was devastated by the election result, but the consequences for him when the tycoon fell over the side of his yacht to his death in circumstances that remain mysterious were equally profound. The collapse of the Maxwell empire had dramatic implications for the ownership and control of the Mirror Group: these in their turn would force Campbell, in very painful circumstances, to leave the newspaper he loved.

He had received a powerful intimation that the Mirror Group proprietor was in trouble six weeks before, at the Labour party conference in Brighton. Maxwell would always travel down for a day's appearance at the conference. Normally he exuded bonhomie. On this occasion he looked troubled. During the course of the day he took a small number of senior *Mirror* journalists and executives individually to one side and poured his heart out to them. It is a sign of the respect and affection in which he was held by the old rogue that Campbell was one of those thus singled out.

His encounter with the desperate Maxwell came shortly before the Mirror Group proprietor entertained Neil and Glenys Kinnock to lunch. Later Campbell informed Roy Greenslade about this slightly macabre experience. He told Greenslade that Maxwell – who was far advanced in his wholesale pillage of the Mirror Group pension fund – was acting 'very oddly'. He went on: 'Just before Neil and Glenys arrived, he took me out on the balcony of the penthouse dining room. He told me, "The whole world's against me. People are out to destroy me."'

The impact of Maxwell's death can hardly be over-stated. It sent Fleet Street into a frenzy of excitement which did not abate for several weeks. Whatever else there is to be said about Maxwell, there is no question that the manner of his departure from this earth was entirely in keeping with the way he conducted his affairs while he was still on it. It was also in character that Alastair Campbell should have strolled onto the stage as a bit-part player in the colossal drama that swept Fleet Street, Westminster and the stockmarkets on the afternoon of 5 November 1991.

Maxwell's champion

There are many interpretations of the now legendary fist fight which broke out on the afternoon of Robert Maxwell's death on 5 November 1991, but no question as to the essential facts. The fight was sparked when Michael White, political editor of the *Guardian*, entered the *Mirror* office in the House of Commons press gallery very shortly after news of the publisher's watery demise had broken over the newswires. He wished to share a joke with the *Mirror* political editor. According to subsequent reports, White said: 'Cap'n Bob, bob, bob, bob ... ' There is an alternative account that White was singing: 'We're bobbing along.' Either way, Campbell did not think it funny. White, taking the view that his joke would be more amusing a second time round, returned a few minutes later. On this occasion he was warned that violent retribution would certainly follow if he did not make himself scarce. When White reappeared a third time, Campbell struck him. White struck back. A fracas ensued.

Both Campbell and White are over six feet tall. But White, whose foreign suits and fastidious but slightly fleshy features cause him closely to resemble the worldly communist mayor of a provincial French town, is the less muscular and well built. Ian Aitken, then a *Guardian* columnist, endeavoured to interpose himself, muttering: 'Come, gentlemen, come.' Neither took the slightest notice of him, and all Aitken got for his efforts was a bloodstained shirtfront. 'I felt rather ridiculous,' he later recalled, 'standing there in the tiny *Mirror* office with these fists flying over my head.' In due course, the two journalists were separated. There was no conclusive winner, though some claim White sustained a cut nose. Sympathy for the two contestants was broadly divided along class lines. Tabloid men stuck with Campbell, while correspondents from the broadsheets instinctively backed White. Later, the pair received an angry letter from the Serjeant-at-Arms, warning of the repercussions if they ever again came to blows within the confines of the Palace of Westminster.

Campbell's motives for striking White have never been established. His detractors, eager to link him as closely as possible to Robert Maxwell, suggest that he was driven to defend the reputation of the dead tycoon, whose criminal activities had not at that stage been revealed. However, in February 1998, Roy Greenslade wrote an article in the *Guardian* aimed at clearing Campbell's reputation from all kinds of slights and innuendoes, in which he suggested that personal venom between Campbell and White was the spark. 'It was a silly spat that had more to do with Alastair's and Michael's own relationship than a display of misguided loyalty to Captain Bob.' Nevertheless, the Greenslade diagnosis of personal vendetta has the hallmarks of special pleading.

All the signs are that White was offering quite enough provocation as it was. Ian Hernon, then political editor for the Central Press, has given a convincing eyewitness account. Hernon is a far more renowned drinker and pugilist even than Campbell himself at the height of his powers and has no reason to do Campbell a favour.[8] Hernon points out that the door to the *Mirror* room was, very unusually, shut when he appeared. Any lobby correspondent as experienced as Michael White would know for sure that this was a sign that the occupant did not want to be disturbed. As speculation about the fate of Robert Maxwell mounted, Campbell would have needed to make dozens of highly sensitive calls to discover for himself what had happened. 'During the course of a very fraught ten minutes Michael White kept coming in making jokes,' Hernon says. 'Alastair snapped but didn't immediately punch him. He warned him first. The idea that Alastair hit Michael because he was outraged that jokes were being made against his great leader is ludicrous.'

Even Campbell's enemies are inclined to believe that Michael White richly deserved to be thumped, and that Campbell was acting within his rights when he hit him. Alastair Campbell is an emotional man. Maxwell had been his boss for seven years. His career had flourished under Maxwell. He knew his family. He had maintained a certain independence from his employer, always sensing that the publisher was not quite sixteen annas to the rupee.

But if Campbell had any reservations about Maxwell's integrity, they were glossed over in his warm and respectful tribute in the following day's *Mirror*. 'He was a big man with a big heart – helping sick employees in need and backing charities,' he wrote.

'Oh, sod off Prime Minister, I'm trying to do my expenses'

The piece of lettuce who passes for Prime Minister.
Alastair Campbell on John Major, Today, 9 May 1994

THE DEATH OF MAXWELL and Neil Kinnock's departure to the fringes of the political stage after the 1992 general election deprived Campbell of two great patrons who had driven his career forward for seven years. He never reached anything like the same intimacy with John Smith as he did with Neil Kinnock. Smith, unlike his predecessor Neil Kinnock or his successor Tony Blair, never saw the point of journalists. He did not share the media's sense of their own importance. He failed to see the need to – as he would have seen it – waste his time with Campbell or, for that matter, any other reporter. There was nothing personal about this. Smith always spoke warmly of Campbell in a way he emphatically did not about, for instance, Peter Mandelson. When it came to the media, he was simply a very old-fashioned politician, a throwback to the days of Attlee and Churchill.

The arrival of David Montgomery, the former editor of the *News of the World*, as chief executive of the Mirror Group in October 1992 sealed Campbell's fate. Montgomery remembers discovering 'a conspiracy of indulgence. While Maxwell ripped off the company, he found it convenient to indulge the journalists.'

Maxwell, with his low peasant cunning, had found it a simple matter to destroy the print-workers' unions. He had found it easier still to outwit the accountants whose job it supposedly was to make sure that the books were straight. But he had taken a profound pleasure in retaining the Mirror Group's reputation for ensuring that its journalists lived like lords. The big cars, the expensive suits and the lavish expense accounts continued as before. Only the best would do for the *Mirror*. In the lobby Campbell was known by envious fellow journalists as 'Club-Class Campbell'. On overseas trips he travelled – like all *Mirror* men – in extreme comfort while fellow reporters on other papers sweated it out economy class.

Joe Haines, Group political editor, was the first to go. Richard Stott resigned as *Mirror* editor soon afterwards. He fled to become editor of *Today* newspaper, and soon his paper became a sanctuary for disenchanted *Mirror* journalists.

Campbell was considered a star in Labour circles. That was not the view of Montgomery who saw him as irretrievably associated with the Maxwell-Stott regime. Even now, he professes himself unimpressed by the *Mirror*'s political coverage during the Kinnock period. 'Politically the *Mirror* had no originality,' says the Ulsterman. 'It had no new tunes. It was flogging a dead horse. Its journalism of the pre-Smith era was going nowhere. It was strident, repetitive and boring.' Montgomery made Campbell's departure inevitable by bringing in an outsider to fill the vacated slot of Group political editor. The figure he alighted upon was David Seymour, a political writer on *Today* newspaper. This was a clear snub to Campbell. He did not take the news well when it was broken to him in early 1993 by David Banks, the latest editor to emerge at the troubled newspaper.

Banks is a generously proportioned man. At a conservative estimate he weighs eighteen stone. It is as well that he does. Shortly after Campbell went into his office, the sounds of screaming, shouting and abuse started to emerge, and then there came a crash – a chair being thrown across the room. It later emerged that the chair had been thrown not by Campbell but by Banks. His subsequent explanation for this act of random violence was that Campbell was ranting, raving and completely out of control; hurling a chair somehow seemed, in the circumstances, the natural thing to do. In due course the tall and usually authoritative figure of Campbell emerged, white-faced. One witness says that he looked 'desolate and totally abject'. He crossed the editorial floor and entered the office of Amanda Platell, the managing editor.

It is ironic that the final rites for Campbell's long occupancy at the *Mirror* were carried out by the exotic Platell. Platell is quite capable, when occasion demands, of behaving like a character from the most lurid novel imaginable about Fleet Street. Campbell came into her office and sat on the comfortable sofa provided only in the offices of the most powerful *Mirror* executives. According to one witness to the scene, who viewed events from the ante-room outside Platell's office, Campbell looked a 'broken and crumpled' figure. The former political editor of the *Mirror* was deeply affected by the course events had taken. In the words of one observer, he was 'tearful but not crying'. He informed Platell: 'This is the worst day of my life.'

Then they got down to business. Platell and Campbell understood one another. They played out their allotted roles to perfection. It became clear very quickly that money was the issue for Campbell. Technically, the *Mirror* believed that there was no case that the appointment of David Seymour amounted to constructive dismissal. Campbell's responsibilities remained the same. His position was not affected one jot. 'Alastair told me,' Platell later told friends, 'that I treated him with such dignity that he felt that under the circumstances it could not have been handled better.' At the end of the conversation Campbell rose to leave. Before doing so, he turned to Platell and told her: 'Having spoken to you I can walk out of here with my head held high.' It was a greatly restored Alastair Campbell who stepped purposefully out of the *Mirror* building for the last time. Though in truth, it was not Amanda Platell alone who had made all the difference. The promise of a severance payment worth approximately £100,000 had also helped. It was a great deal more than some of the Mirror Group pensioners – nearly all Labour supporters – retrieved from the wreckage of Maxwell's empire.

Six years later, in the spring of 1999, Amanda Platell was hired as the Conservative party Head of Media. The first time she attended Prime Minister's Questions Campbell smiled at her across the chamber, and gave her a quiet wave of welcome.

Baiting John Major

Three times Richard Stott has intervened to help Alastair Campbell out of a tight spot. He secured him his first job in Fleet Street. He brought him back to the *Daily Mirror* after his nervous breakdown. And now as editor of *Today*, days after Campbell left the *Mirror*, he offered him the post of assistant editor (politics) vacated by David Sey-mour, whose move to the *Mirror* had just brought about Campbell's departure.

At least Campbell was among friends at *Today*. It was to be his only stint on a Murdoch-owned paper – the Australian tycoon had acquired *Today* when Eddie Shah's vision came to grief – during his fourteen years as a journalist. Richard Stott was giving a dazzling demonstration of how an irreverent left-wing tabloid paper ought to be run. Even so, Campbell's presence at his old stamping ground had a curious feel to it. He resembled a well-heeled traveller living in bed-and-breakfast accommodation while seeking somewhere permanent to stay.

Campbell's column cannot have taken up much of his time. His tone was now more trenchant, assured and savage than in the old days at the *Mirror*. The attacks on John Major were venomous. The Conservative Prime Minister was by this stage a universal target, but no one struck home more regularly or with greater brutality than Alastair Campbell. Even today, Major cannot mention Campbell without a shudder. The relationship between the two is curious. It started on an encouraging note. Campbell was swift to spot Major as a rising force when he joined the Cabinet after the 1987 election, ranking him alongside Tony Blair and Gordon Brown as one of six 'names to conjure with' in his famous article of September 1988. So determined was Campbell to attach him-self to the Major bandwagon that he was the only Tory politician grant-ed his own *Sunday Mirror* profile. When John Major finally secured the Tory leadership upon the downfall of Thatcher in 1990, lobby journal-ists remember an astonishing scene: the *Mirror* political editor thrust his way through the mêlée surrounding Major in the Commons, put his arms round his neck and embraced him as vigorously as he had Maxwell. This typical Campbell gesture could have been taken as an act of either gross impertinence or warm affection. The new Prime Minis-ter – famously tactile himself – responded in kind.

That moment represented the high point in the relationship between the two men. Some psychological insight – or perhaps merely the savage instinct of the playground bully – enabled Campbell to sniff out the Prime Minister's vulnerable points in a lethally effective way: another of Campbell's gifts had been discovered. He refused to give John Major any of the respect that a prime minister is accustomed to expect. The abuse which found its way into print was vicious enough. On one occasion Campbell called Major 'the piece of lettuce who passes for Prime Minister';[1] on another, 'simply a second-rate, shallow, lying little toad of a man.'[2] This kind of language, from a respected political columnist, was unusually strong but capable of being brushed aside as an established part of the game. What was unusual, and shocking, was the abuse that Campbell would dole out to John Major in person. Within a very short time he had made it perfectly plain that he regarded the Prime Minister as a ridiculous figure of no consequence.

At the 1991 Tory conference in Blackpool, when Margaret Thatcher appeared on the platform to shake hands with her successor, Campbell wrote a vicious by-lined attack on them in the *Mirror*. The next morning a tweed-jacketed gentleman marched into the press room at the Winter Gardens, demanding to see the author. He was directed to the *Mirror* desk where he spluttered at Campbell: 'Are you Alastair Campbell?' Without blinking an eyelid, Campbell shook his head 'no' and motioned in the direction of his unwitting deputy David Bradshaw, who was on the phone. Campbell had slunk away by the time Bradshaw came off the phone, to be assailed by the angry Tory who shouted: 'You should be ashamed of yourself, Alastair Campbell! How dare you come to this conference and … ' Bradshaw reeled backwards and tried to explain he was not Campbell. He spotted a grinning Campbell a few yards away watching the confrontation, arms folded, and was about to point him out to his accuser when Campbell raised his finger to his lips, ordering him not to drop him in it.

Lobby correspondents all know the prime minister of the day well. They meet him about the House of Commons, sometimes at formal lobby meetings, and most of all on overseas trips. On long-haul flights and at receptions in foreign embassies the prime minister allows lobby men to gather round and he or she will often talk freely on the issues of the day. It was at these events that Campbell would make his contempt so clear. He would shout derisive remarks in the hearing of John Major.

On one of John Major's earliest trips abroad, on the Downing Street VC10, the Prime Minister wandered back to the press seats. He was full of ebullience, eager to talk. Campbell glared at him: 'Oh, sod off, Prime Minister,' he said. 'I'm trying to do my expenses.'[3]

By far the cleverest jibe of all, because it preyed so precisely on John

Major's own social insecurities, was Campbell's charge that the Prime Minister tucked his shirt inside his underpants. Campbell was among the press pack who accompanied Major in a diplomatic shuttle in the run up to the first Iraq war in 1991. Chatting to a fellow reporter on the plane, Campbell said: 'Have you noticed that Major has got those trousers with a belt stitched in? When he bent over I could see that his shirt was tucked inside his underpants.'4 Some of the journalists thought he was joking, others thought he had made it up, some thought it was true.

During the rest of the trip, the lobby journalists glanced towards Major's waistline, in between filing copy, hoping for a glimpse of the PM's underwear. They didn't get one. And John Major's underpants were never seen in public again.

It was several weeks before the anecdote found its way into print. And when it did, it was not under Campbell's by-line. The underpants scoop went to, of all people, distinguished *Guardian* political writer Ian Aitken, who was not even on the trip. 'Mr Major is now known to be one of those who tuck their shirts into their underpants before they put their trousers on,' he wrote authoritatively. 'How do I know? Because he recently appeared in shirt sleeves aboard his prime ministerial VC10, and a sharp-eyed reporter spotted that his pants were showing above the waistband of his breeks.'5 Aitken was told of the underpants story by his old friend *Glasgow Daily Herald* political editor Geoffrey Parkhouse. Later, when the story became an urban myth, largely as a result of having been adopted as a Major trademark by the *Guardian* cartoonist Steve Bell, an indignant Parkhouse tackled Aitken and told him the caricature was unfair to Major. Aitken told him: 'For Christ's sake Geoffrey, it was you who told me about it.' Parkhouse had completely forgotten. Why Campbell did not write the story himself remains a mystery. Whatever the reason, it is probably just as well that no one told him of one of Major's real fashion hang-ups, which, by chance, one of the PM's officials described to a more discreet reporter on the same trip. Major had refused to wear a short sleeved-shirt in the desert because he was self conscious about his 'flabby arms'.

On overseas journeys with the prime minister, the British press corps have always borne a close resemblance to a collection of clever sixth-formers accompanying a teacher on a school trip. There is a healthy conflict between the teacher's wish for his pupils to do what he thinks is interesting and the pupils' own strong desire to go off and do their own thing. Campbell took this tension one stage further. He ridiculed and humiliated the teacher, destroying his authority by turning him into a figure of fun. After a while, the rest of the lobby caught on and began to treat John Major in the same way. In due course this attitude fanned outwards to embrace fashionable opinion in London, and thence to the rest of the country. There is a strong case to be made that it all started with Alastair Campbell and the underpants. The conversion of the Tory Prime Minister into a ludicrous, comic-cuts figure earned Campbell one of his many Labour campaign medals.

After John Major, the biggest target of Campbell's *Today* column was the royal family. The move from the *Mirror* encouraged him to tackle a broader range of subjects, and in a more rancorous way. There is a very strong argument to be made that Alastair Campbell saved the monarchy from destruction with timely advice in the wake of Princess Diana's death in the late summer of 1997. The Palace remains grateful, and properly so, for the guidance that he offered.

But there is no mistaking, either, the screaming derision and contempt that he displayed towards them in *Today*. The early 1990s represented the nadir of royal fortunes. The Palace was forced to endure the divorce of the Prince and Princess of Wales, the Windsor fire, the absurdity of Sarah Ferguson and much else besides. Kicking the royals was a national pastime as much as kicking John Major. Campbell was even more unpleasant than most. 'There are many reasons for the decline in royal esteem,' he announced in May 1993. 'One is that royals are thick.' He labelled Prince Philip 'insensitive and stupid' and Prince Charles 'an overprivileged twit'. Princess Diana – later to be converted into the People's Princess – was 'vacuous, shallow, silly and egomaniacal' while her brother, Earl Spencer, was a 'hypocritical upper-class little pillock'. As Campbell stated in his *Today* column in February 1994, 'I have never gone for the notion that the royal family represents all that is right in this country. They represent to me much that is wrong in this country, notably its class system, obsession with titles, dressing up and patronage and the arrogance of unelected power.'

Campbell's own core political beliefs are not sophisticated, but they are strongly felt. They still embrace some of the angry rancour of his student days at Cambridge towards the young army officers and Old Etonians who set the social tone for the university. He has never expressed that emotion quite as eloquently as he did when attacking Prince Charles in his *Today* column on 9 May 1994. In an extraordinary outburst he described Britain's future king as 'someone who cannot hold his marriage together, does not see his own kids from day to day, delegates their upbringing to nannies and private school spankers, went to a Spanking Academy himself, needed the power of patronage to get into university, apparently wants to send his own sons to Eton, *the* Spanking Academy, whose advisers all come from similar establishments and are similarly ill-suited to speak about the real world, and who courts his mistress with lavatorial suggestions.'

Here speaks the real Campbell, the angry, disaffected Alastair Campbell who mulled over his many grievances at the Late Night Bar at Gonville and Caius College. That side of Campbell, for worldly and pragmatic reasons, has mainly been kept hidden since. Something about the heady, destructive national mood of the mid 1990s, fuelled by the witty, lucid anarchism of Richard Stott's *Today* newspaper, let it loose in the last months before John Smith's death propelled Campbell towards government.

It is interesting to speculate what would have happened to Campbell if John Smith had not died when he did. In 1994 his career was drifting. He was established as a minor celebrity of sorts. The fisticuffs in the lobby with Michael White had begun the process of building a wider Campbell profile. The flurry of publicity that surrounded his departure from the *Mirror* increased it still further. Alastair Campbell was in any case an extremely accomplished media performer. His rugged good looks worked well on television and he had a pleasant speaking voice. Best of all, from the point of view of television and radio producers, he was always available and would jump through any hoop. He hosted one late-night television show at the height of John Major's back-to-basics crisis from a bed, having failed to persuade any number of Tory MPs to share it with him.

There is a nether world out there where politics and the media meet, and a living of sorts to be made out of a portfolio of chat-shows, occasional columns and paper-reviews. It is inhabited by sepulchral figures like David Mellor and the Labour MP Austin Mitchell. Campbell was heading in that direction in the months before John Smith died. He was out of sympathy with the Labour leadership, his friends were in exile, and he himself was slowly drifting away from mainstream politics. He was spending his life reviewing newspapers very early in the morning and appearing on chat shows very late at night. It must sometimes have seemed to him that there was barely time to get home and shave between the two activities.

But the television makeup girls loved him to bits. They found him madly attractive and voted him 'most popular newspaper reviewer'. They discovered he had replaced his taste for alcohol with a taste for Toblerone bars, and would present them to him at party conferences.

chapter six

John Smith's Death

> I can remember vividly the moment when
> news came of John Smith's death and I felt
> instinctively Tony was going to be the leader.
>
> *Alastair Campbell,*
> *30 January 2004*

Smith's most dangerous critic

AFTER JOHN SMITH succeeded Neil Kinnock, Alastair Campbell emerged as one of the new Labour leader's most articulate, powerful and dangerous critics. This was partly because he found it hard to shake off the legacy of Kinnock. Kinnock's allies resented Smith's obvious belief that he would become the next Labour prime minister on the basis that he was not Kinnock – and nothing else. And, more urgently, they believed that Smith was squandering Neil Kinnock's modernizing legacy.

This mood of despair bordering on prostration is well conjured up by Philip Gould, the media and advertising executive who became a political consultant to Blair. The frustration of the John Smith years seeped out of Gould who, having played a role in President Clinton's 1992 election campaign, felt a messianic urge to teach the lessons of that famous victory to the British Labour party. He saw no signs that John Smith was ready to learn them.

The biggest sufferer of all was Peter Mandelson. He had been elected member of parliament for Hartlepool in the 1992 general election.

But that was no compensation at all for the fact that John Smith promptly thrust him into the outer darkness. He did not appreciate Mandelson and had no place for his skills.

Campbell threw in his lot with these men. He became the strongest public voice of disaffection with what they saw as John Smith's slow-moving and lazy leadership. In the aftermath of election defeat the Labour party was convulsed by one of its great internal debates: this one was about the lessons of 1992. The left said that Kinnock lost because he abandoned Labour's natural working-class base. The modernizers claimed that he failed because he did not abandon it enough. There was no question as to which side of the barricades Alastair Campbell stood on. In article after article he made the case for radical change. Less than a year into the Smith leadership, Campbell was already at it. Taking advantage of a rare invitation by the *Sunday Telegraph* to write a column, Campbell turned on the Smith leadership. 'I see the real divide as between "frantics" and "long-gamers"', he wrote.

> The 'long-gamers' all believe Labour has time on its side. There is no point, they say, in wasting energies and risking the Tory theft of ideas, in a period that will be forgotten by the next election. But what makes the 'frantics' frantic is that the party does not know what it is for, other than to oppose the government in parliament. There is little sense of the party finding itself a wider role.

Campbell had no hesitation in naming John Smith as the leader of the despised 'long-gamers'. He cited as accomplices Smith's deputy leader Margaret Beckett, Robin Cook, John Prescott, Jack Cunningham and Frank Dobson. Campbell had very much more difficulty in identifying his 'frantics', coming up with just Tony Blair, Gordon Brown and Jack Straw as well as 'several lesser known shadow cabinet members'.

Campbell banged away at Smith's leadership right up to Smith's death in May 1994. Less than a fortnight before the Labour leader died, he was at it again in the *Spectator*: 'Labour are so used to enjoying the Tories' troubles that they have stopped thinking about their own,' he thundered. 'If the current line is held to the election, the ducking and diving of Labour will become as big a turn-off as the deceit and dissembling of Conservative ministers.'

There is no question that Tony Blair, Peter Mandelson and Philip Gould were egging Campbell on from the sidelines. According to Tony

Blair's biographer Jon Sopel, the Blair faction steered interested parties towards Campbell's *Spectator* article for an illuminating insight into the melancholy state of affairs that prevailed under their lacklustre leader. The modernizers were going nowhere under John Smith.

All great revolutionary movements need their period of tribulation, suffering and exile. For the handful of men who dreamt up New Labour, John Smith's leadership was that period. It cannot be said that they spent their time of martyrdom in any physical discomfort. They plotted – and there was a great deal of plotting – over well-stocked north London dinner tables and in elegant villas in the south of France.

Well before the spring of 1994, Alastair Campbell and Fiona Millar had concluded that Blair and not Gordon Brown would succeed John Smith. In the summer of 1993, the Campbell-Millars shared a holiday villa in Majorca with Philip Gould and his wife Gail Rebuck. Peter Mandelson joined them. It was a conspiratorial group and the three exiles devoted much time and effort to rubbishing Smith. In between lamenting the inadequacies of the – in their opinion – ponderous leader of the opposition, they speculated about the future. Campbell and Gould expressed their view that Blair was the coming man: they could hardly believe it when Peter Mandelson stood up for Gordon Brown.

Campbell told Mandelson: 'You have got to support Tony. Gordon is insecure and will be just the same if he becomes leader.' Even then, Campbell had decided Brown was flawed. Campbell was supported by Gould who argued that Brown was, by turns, 'brilliant and barmy'. Mandelson defended Brown: 'But Tony is just a little boy and knows nothing about the Labour party. Gordon is a proper grown up politician.'[1] (This was the holiday on which Mandelson made the momentous decision to shave off his moustache, providing a rare scoop for Campbell in his *Today* column upon his return to Britain.)

By the time Smith became leader, Campbell had decided that Blair was a better prospect. Campbell later said he spotted Blair's potential to lead the Labour party the first time they met in the House of Commons members' lobby, shortly after Blair became MP for Sedgefield. Blair was wearing 'an ill-fitting beige suit and a huge smile'. Campbell had been heavily involved in advising the future leader on how to handle the press since 1989 if not before. The connection grew closer still after the 1992 election, when Campbell emerged as the leading Fleet Street voice speaking up for the New Labour modernizers. The relationship was so close that Tony Blair's biographer refers to Campbell in 1993 as Blair's 'proto-press-secretary'.

When Kinnock resigned, and Blair decided against running for deputy leader under Smith, Fiona Millar wrote an article in the *Sunday Express*, stating that many Tories believed Blair 'will one day be the man to take them on'.[2]

The period leading up to Smith's death was – but only to the uncurious eye – a good time in the life of the soon-to-be New Labour leader Tony Blair. He was proving to be a formidable Shadow home secretary and talented performer on the Labour front bench, his star gradually rising at the expense of Gordon Brown, his closest friend and deadliest rival. And yet, when alone with his friends, he fretted. He feared that ponderous, plodding, complacent John Smith could throw it all away and let the Tories back again. He saw himself as condemned to an arid life of perpetual opposition. In his darkest moments, he spoke of chucking it all in and returning to the Bar.

He was advised against doing so by his wife, Cherie, who was deeply ambitious for her husband and was determined that Brown should not deny him the leadership. As far back as 1987, when Brown and Blair emerged as Labour's two boy wonders, she told Blair to be wary of Brown, for whom she developed a deep and lasting mistrust and dislike.

It must be Blair

Today newspaper found it hard to get hold of Alastair Campbell on the morning of John Smith's death on 12 May 1994. The reason was entirely characteristic: he was reviewing the newspapers on BBC television.

During the rest of the day, Campbell spoke to Peter Mandelson on the phone many times, trying to ensure that Mandelson supported Blair not Brown. He told Mandelson that Blair was by far the stronger candidate and the only one who would win substantial backing from the media. 'The impression I got was that there were eight or nine phone calls between Campbell and Mandelson,' says someone who spent much of the day with Campbell. 'He was saying very clearly that it must be Blair, that Blair was the only plausible candidate that the media would buy and Brown would be a problem if he got it. Mandelson seemed to be agreeing. The gist of it was: "You've got to do it, Peter." Campbell seemed to be firming Mandelson up.'[3]

Campbell never suffered the agonizing conflict of loyalties that afflicted his friend Peter Mandelson as the day unfolded. From the start he felt a complete conviction that Tony Blair would and should become Labour leader and threw himself into the Blair campaign. 'I can remember vividly the moment when news came of John Smith's death and I felt instinctively Tony was going to be the leader,' he said later.[4]

Campbell appeared on *Newsnight* on the very evening of John Smith's death to proclaim Tony Blair the inevitable winner of the forthcoming leadership contest. Asked who he thought would be the next leader, he said: 'My own view is that it will be Tony Blair.'[5] He later claimed the remark was 'a complete accident'. That was a ludicrous assertion. His comments on *Newsnight* were made with the same cold calculation applied to all his utterances. Peter Mandelson, who was in the agonizing process of switching from Brown to Blair, was horrified and phoned Campbell to berate him. Campbell was unmoved. He went on to write Blair's glossy campaign leaflet, given the ineffable title of *Principle, Purpose, Power*, and wrote an article in *Today* a few days later in which he nailed his colours to Blair's mast again.[6] He plotted merrily away on behalf of Tony Blair, leaving no stone unturned in an attempt to bury all of Blair's opponents and Gordon Brown in particular. This vigorous activity was noted by the Brown camp with dismay but not surprise. Paul Routledge, Brown's far from dispassionate biographer, records with disapproval that in the days immediately following John Smith's death, Campbell was 'briefing heavily and continuously against Brown'. Routledge contrasts Campbell's unsportsmanlike behaviour with Brown's reverential attitude towards Marquess of Queensberry rules. 'Brown,' Routledge wearily records, 'was reluctant to begin even the softest press campaign against Blair.'

Brown never really held a grudge against Alastair Campbell, in spite of the latter's leading role in extinguishing whatever faint hopes Brown might have had of becoming party leader. Against Peter Mandelson, who did his utmost to keep these hopes alive, he has ever since nurtured a deadly resentment. Brown never reckoned Campbell as an ally, taking him from the very first as a member of the fraternity of north London media folk who – in Brown's considered opinion – conspired to deprive the Labour party of its rightful leader. Alastair Campbell had already formed the view that Brown was too 'psychologically flawed' to become a plausible or satisfactory candidate for Labour prime minister.[7]

At the end of the campaign, the question arose whether to offer Campbell the position of press spokesman. In retrospect the choice looks obvious; not at the time. Nobody questioned Campbell's abilities, his loyalty or his immense personal charisma. But there was his past to consider. It was only eight years since he had emerged from hospital after suffering a breakdown: there was no guarantee that the same thing might not happen again. It was absolutely certain that all the old stories of the pornography and the boozing would come out.

Tony Blair looked to Peter Mandelson for advice about Campbell. There is some evidence that Mandelson did not weigh in as generously on behalf of his old friend as he might have done. Mandelson had his own position as Blair's private media counsellor to protect. He knew Campbell's vast ability, but also the way he did business: direct with the boss. It is possible that Mandelson might have preferred a figure he could control more easily than Campbell. Five years before, he had supported Julie Hall for the position of Neil Kinnock's press spokeswoman, which was never the happiest of appointments. Among her many qualities one stood out: she was never likely to threaten Mandelson in any way.

The evidence suggests that Mandelson did his best to steer Blair quietly away from Campbell. There were a number of powerful candidates. Philip Bassett, then industrial editor of *The Times* but recruited to Downing Street in 1997, fancied his chances. Colin Byrne, the former Labour party press officer, was cited as a contender. Certainly, Mandelson urged the case for others. His close friend Andy Grice, then political correspondent of the *Sunday Times*, was offered the job but turned it down. Derek Draper, Peter Mandelson's former assistant, admits that Mandelson 'made the case for Grice at one stage. And Alastair would know that.'

A further complication was introduced by Neil Kinnock, who was a summer guest of the Campbell-Millars in the south of France that year. Kinnock argued passionately that Campbell would be mad to take the job. He said, with considerable truth, that it would ruin his family life. It was a view which Fiona Millar strongly supported. Kinnock's motives were not entirely selfless. Having rejected Campbell's offer to be his press secretary in 1992 on the grounds that Campbell was more use to Labour in Fleet Street than in Walworth Road, Kinnock offered his friend the job of *chef de cabinet* in his new commissioner's office in Brussels. It seems likely that reports of these discussions filtered through to Tony Blair, because the newly elected Labour leader suddenly also turned up in person at the Campbell-Millar holiday home near Avignon to plead with Campbell to ignore Kinnock's advice. For a few heady days in August, Campbell found himself the object of a tug of love between the past and present leaders of the Labour party.

But Campbell never really had a choice. There is a strong sense in which he had been preparing for his latest attachment all his life. Even his period as press relations man for Robin Fenner, certainly his time at the *Daily Mirror*, above all his years of devotion to Neil Kinnock, had all been useful schooling for this particular post. Campbell had always sought to be the instrument of a very powerful man. Now the ultimate opportunity had come his way. Two years later he said that what eventually decided him was imagining two post-general-election situations. 'Two things came back to me the whole time,' he said. 'The first was that we lost the election and I was there thinking I could have made a difference. And the other was that we had won and I could have been a part of it.'

The New Labour *coup d'état*

Alastair Campbell's appointment as press spokesman for Tony Blair was announced in September 1994, during the TUC conference at Blackpool. The inner core of New Labour was now complete. It comprised just five men. They were Tony Blair himself, Gordon Brown, Philip Gould, Peter Mandelson and Alastair Campbell. This group went on to reconvene in Downing Street under the misleadingly bland nomenclature of 'P5' – 'Political Five' – when Labour won power, and wielded more power than the Cabinet. No one else really mattered. This remained the case for many years despite the partial estrangement of Gordon Brown and Peter Mandelson's resignation from the

Cabinet. It is a sign of the endurance of this tight-knit group that even after his two resignations, Mandelson has remained almost as potent a presence as when he was a Cabinet minister. These five had been the modernizers who fretted and strained under John Smith's leadership. Now they were let loose. They could do what they wanted. Nothing stood in their way. They had secured control of the Labour movement and over the coming two years they would use that dominance to create a new political party and an entirely fresh political force in Britain. The importance of this development cannot be overestimated. Bitter jealousies, enmities and hatreds divided them as individuals – indeed these were so poisonous that Peter Mandelson and Gordon Brown were not to exchange more than three or four consecutive words for the following two years. But more powerful by far were the factors that bound them together: a profound contempt for the traditional structures of the Labour party and existing institutions of British government, a lethal understanding of raw political power and how it can be achieved and then exercised in the modern British state; above all, an awesome will to win.

They included some of the most fascinating men that British politics has thrown up this century. No individual as exotic as Peter Mandelson has blossomed quite so close to the heart of power since George Villiers, Duke of Buckingham, strutted his stuff at the court of James I four hundred years ago. Alastair Campbell was an extraordinary individual: he was soon to turn into an entirely novel constitutional phenomenon. Gordon Brown, brooding and complex, his brilliant political mind quite unable to come to terms with everyday human life, was already a massive figure on the political stage. Philip Gould, the author of the first sacred text of the New Labour movement,[8] was the least known of the five. But for Blair and the others he was a talismanic figure, always at the forefront of the modernizing mission. Tony Blair was the only one of them who seemed normal but that of course was a delusion: he was the most extraordinary of all.

In the summer of 1994 these five men carried out a *coup d'état* of breathtaking brilliance and simplicity: the election of Tony Blair as leader meant that they seized control of the Labour party. It is too easy to take for granted the magnitude of the accomplishment. Labour is a great political party with many hundreds of thousands of members. But with the will, the genius and the luck of the Spaniard Pizarro conquering the Inca empire against massive odds, they won the battle and then consolidated their power.

Looking back with hindsight it is possible to see that the primary architect of this extraordinary feat was Peter Mandelson. This flawed politician of high talent possessed the narrow, desiccated frame of the true revolutionary – a Robespierre or a Trotsky. Mandelson had been there since the beginning. On his route to power he had endured two heart-rending defeats, in 1987 and 1992, as well as those wilderness years under John Smith, until it all came good for him with the leadership election of 1994. He was not to enjoy the fruits of power for long. It was the more solidly built, square-framed, practical politicians – Blair, Campbell and Brown – who survived to reap the rewards of the revolution that Mandelson had worked so hard to bring about, and whose nature perhaps he understood best of all.

Mandelson's and New Labour's genius was to grasp that the key to power in modern Britain was the media. Revolutionaries in the past have focused on the obvious symbols of state – the armed forces, the prisons, government buildings and the royal palaces – and used the mob as their instrument of destruction. Mandelson realized that today the media mattered far more than all these put together. Two hundred years ago the French revolutionaries stormed the Bastille. In 1994 and since, the insurrectionaries of New Labour have taken as their target the BBC, ITV, the newspaper editors, the broadcasters and the parliamentary lobby. They were all there for the picking. The newspapers have never been a negligible, and are sometimes a potent, force in politics. In the 1990s the print media allied with broadcasting combined to turn into a devastating power in the land: they suddenly achieved critical mass.

There have been many attempts to define New Labour. Before the 2001 election Tony Blair made an inept and half-hearted attempt to place a 'stakeholding economy' at the heart of his political philosophy. That swiftly foundered. Since the election the notion of a 'third way' in modern politics has been promoted by New Labour thinkers. This idea has more plausibility, but even less popular force, than its defunct predecessor. 'Third way' discourse has a tendency to oscillate between the banal and the obscure. It is very much more accurate to define New Labour by its relationship with the media: it was the first ever Media Class opposition. In due course it became established as the first ever Media Class government with Tony Blair installed in Number 10 Downing Street as the first ever Media Class Prime Minister.

Campbell's own input into the formulation of these ideas was perfunctory. His role in their projection, however, was characteristic. Tony Blair launched the 'stakeholding' theme with a speech to local businessmen in Singapore in January 1996. It came too late to suit British broadcasters. Campbell therefore arranged for Blair to extract the relevant passages from the body of the text and place them at the very start of the speech so that they could be filmed being delivered by the Prime Minister on film just in time for that night's TV news bulletins back home. In effect, Blair read out a press release and then returned to his speech. 'The guests were utterly bewildered,' recalls one British member of the audience.

The rise of the Media Class

The rise in the status of journalism in all its manifestations has been one of the most striking developments of our time. Very little more than a generation ago, journalism was a dishonourable and poorly esteemed profession. Now talented journalists have become fêted celebrities. They wield immense social, economic and political power which the Media Class has gathered unto itself at the expense of the great institutions of the state, the monarchy and the church.

Nowhere is the elevation of the humble jobbing journalist more apparent than in political reporting. In the immediate post-war epoch, right up to the election of Harold Wilson as prime minister in 1964, the attitude of political reporters to the House of Commons and to politicians was profoundly deferential. It was practically unheard of for parliamentary correspondents – the title political editor and the grandeur that implies did not develop till the late 1960s – to have lunch with a Cabinet minister. Indeed, one of the primary requirements of the lobby man was to arrange, though not to attend, lunches on behalf of his proprietor. Gerald Herlihy, the political correspondent of the *Graphic*, was for a number of years in effect the social secretary to his proprietor's wife, Lady Kemsley.

Political reporters were divided between 'parliamentary' correspondents and 'political' correspondents. It was the function of the former to report, partly in the flamboyant manner of a theatre critic, the events of the previous day in the Commons chamber. These articles were given abundant space. Parliamentary correspondents were considered very much more important than political correspondents, whose membership of the lobby enabled them to share some of the privileges of members of parliament. These lobby men would add a few lines to the account of the previous day's parliamentary drama, modestly drawing attention to items of particular significance. This division of power within the profession indicates how political reporters accepted Parliament on its own terms. Politicians were judged very much in the way they wanted to be judged.

Prime ministers in the post-war period did not deal with political reporters at all, and very rarely even with newspaper editors. They maintained a warm relationship with the great press proprietors, whom they met at society functions and country houses. When Churchill suffered a stroke in June 1953 the illness was never reported. This serious disruption in the life of a serving prime minister was one of the biggest stories the press had had to cope with since the war. Yet it was covered up with ease. Downing Street merely indicated to the great proprietors – Beaverbrook, Bracken and Camrose – that it would be inconvenient if this distressing illness got out, and it never did. Eventually it was Churchill himself, restored and at the despatch box of the Commons, who chose to reveal that he had had a stroke: a tribute to the then inviolate power of parliament.

Churchill, during his second term as prime minister, held reporters in such low esteem that he refused to let them in through the front door of Downing Street when they turned up for their diet of daily official announcements. He banned them from the building and insisted that they use a room in the Cabinet office further up Whitehall instead. When he reluctantly handed over power in April 1955, his successor Anthony Eden attempted to ingratiate himself with the press by rescinding the ban. But the feudal spirit remained. Harold Evans (not the editor of the *Sunday Times*), who served as press secretary to both Harold Macmillan and Sir Alec Douglas-Home, adopted the demeanour and approach of a superior gentleman's gentleman.

Downing Street briefings were conducted in the spirit of the butler at a great country estate addressing the domestic staff. Nobody thought this was odd or offensive. Lord Poole, chairman of the Tory party under Macmillan, once pronounced on the subject of lobby correspondents at a Chatham House discussion. They were very decent fellows, he opined, but not quite the sort of people one would invite into one's own home.

The parliamentary reporter needed two qualities: an outstanding shorthand note and the ability to keep his head down. Very few of them had been to university: they had come up the hard way, starting with local papers in the provinces. Anthony Howard, who later became editor of the *New Statesman*, entered the lobby as a reporter for *Reynolds News* in 1958. He recollects that there were two other graduates in the press gallery: Bernard Levin of the *Spectator* and T. F. Lindsay, the sketchwriter for the *Daily Telegraph*. 'Lindsay practically fell round my neck. He greeted me like a long lost soul,' records Howard. When Harold Wilson entered Number 12 Downing Street (the house which served as the Whips' Hall, the large back room of which was sometimes used for prime ministerial press conferences) to give his first lobby briefing the day he became prime minister in 1964, the room stood to attention as he walked in. That sort of behaviour is inconceivable today. Perhaps the change reflects no more than the impoverishment of modern manners and the collapse of deference. But the collapse of deference is synonymous with and part of the story of the rise of the Media Class.

It was Wilson who first gave parliamentary reporters some kind of self-respect. He regarded them as important people. He called them by their Christian names. He read their work and was able to contrast their individual styles and modes of operation. He was at ease with them socially and they with him. He would invite the more important members of the lobby fraternity down to Chequers. He awarded knighthoods to two working political journalists, Francis Boyd of the *Guardian* and Harry Boyne of the *Telegraph*. He took them with him on overseas trips, and frequently made himself available to brief the lobby in person. On such occasions the sign would go up on the lobby notice-board: 'Sunrise Red at 4 p.m.' This obliged the Tories to respond in kind. Their leader Edward Heath, in the curious Masonic terminology then favoured by lobby men, was known as 'Celestial Blue'.

Wilson was the first prime minister to grasp the rising importance of the press. Alan Watkins, the political columnist of the *Independent on Sunday*, is today an elder statesman of the press gallery. In the early 1960s he wrote the Crossbencher column for the *Sunday Express*. Throughout the two years before the 1964 general election he would see Wilson once a week, on Fridays. The leader of the opposition would take endless trouble to furnish him with political gossip for his column. 'Like Senator Joe McCarthy, he knew the deadlines,' recalls Watkins. On one occasion, Watkins recalls ringing the Labour party to check some minor detail about defence policy. He was surprised to receive a call back from the leader of the opposition himself. 'Even I was surprised,' states Watkins, 'that Harold Wilson was taking an interest in what I might be writing.'

But it all went horribly wrong with Wilson. After a short space of time political reporters started to conclude that they had been taken for a ride. Devaluation of the pound in the autumn of 1967 perhaps sealed things. Thereafter the easy friendliness of the early days was replaced by bitter enmity and mutual contempt. But Wilson's fascination with the press continued. Only this time it was malevolent. He would plot and intrigue against individual reporters. David Wood, political correspondent of *The Times*, was an early case. The Prime Minister went to extreme and demeaning lengths to prevail upon the editor and proprietors of *The Times* to dismiss Wood. William Rees-Mogg, then *Times* editor, responded to these endeavours in the only way possible: by promoting David Wood to the rank of political editor. Another subject of Wilson's obsession was Nora Beloff, the *Observer* journalist who was first to draw attention to the powerful and to this day highly mysterious influence exercised by Marcia Williams on the Prime Minister. Wilson summoned David Astor, the owner and editor of the *Observer*, to see him in his office at the Commons. When Astor arrived, Wilson produced bulky files of Beloff's newspaper cuttings, heavily annotated and underlined. After rambling on like a man obsessed on the subject of the sinister influences at work upon Beloff, the Prime Minister then announced: 'Of course, I know all about the people she sees. In fact our people keep an eye on her to see just what she is up to.' Names, offices and meetings were provided for Astor's inspection. When checked back with Beloff later they proved accurate in all respects. Astor presumed that Labour party trusties rather than MI5 officers were behind the surveillance, though the matter has never been satisfactorily explained.

Late at night Harold Wilson would sit up with his tiny coterie of advisers, among them Gerald Kaufman and Marcia Williams, sifting through the first editions. They would assess likely sources for stories, always alert for signs of conspiracies being hatched against the Prime Minister. Any item that proved particularly difficult would result in a call from George Wigg, the Paymaster-General, to the editor or the correspondent concerned. A generation later, Tony Blair's New Labour would take an even greater interest in the press. For the most part, however, the assessment and analysis were devolved to party officials rather than carried out by the party leader himself.

Harold Wilson was the first prime minister to understand the importance of 'spin-doctoring'. The expression was not current in his day; 'public relations officer' was the expression used then. The word 'spin-doctor', which conveys the greater degree of menace, subterfuge and mystique in the modern PRO's job, came later. It originated in the United States and is said to have derived from baseball. According to Dr Emma Lenz of the *Oxford English Dictionary*, the first recorded use of the term was by Saul Bellow in his 1977 Jefferson Lectures. The *Collins English Dictionary* (1999 edition) defines 'spin-doctor' as 'a person who provides a favourable slant to an item of news, potentially unpopular policy etcetera, especially on behalf of a political personality or party'. The word was not taken up in Britain until the early 1990s, when it was indelibly associated with the rise to public prominence of Peter Mandelson and his school of New Labour media experts.

Wilson's catastrophic error was to try and carry out the task of spin-doctoring himself rather than delegate it to others. His first press secretary, Sir Trevor Lloyd-Hughes, was too scrupulous to fulfil the demands of the job. By the time that Joe Haines, an experienced press gallery hand with a fine political brain, was brought to bear in 1969, the problem had got out of control. Haines was condemned to fight a defensive war. It was often conducted with marvellous tactical astuteness, but the chance to seize and then control the agenda, which was to be grasped with such brutal skill and strategic finesse by his successor

Alastair Campbell twenty-five years later, had been well and truly cast away by the time Haines arrived on the scene.

The Media Class began to sense an intimation of its own future power during the Wilson premiership, but it did not emerge as a fully fledged force on the national stage until the 1980s. Margaret Thatcher was a vital part of the story. The Media Class was her closest ally as she smashed down national institutions and challenged traditional sources of authority. She was often embattled and isolated within parliament and even her own Tory party, and the close alliances she formed with press proprietors, and through them with the political editors, became a key source of her power. The political press was no longer content, as it had been in the 1950s and the first half of the 1960s, to be a passive and neutral player in national debate. In the 1980s it developed with staggering speed into a brilliant, potent and deeply destructive force in its own right. For a long time that force was harnessed to Margaret Thatcher and the Tory party. Some observers lazily considered that the alliance would last for ever.

There was much that was new about the press of the 1980s. Though nobody was yet fully aware of it, the balance of power between reporter and reported had switched. The reporter now met his subject on equal terms. In some areas – financial reporting is an example – the old deference held. But in politics it first collapsed, then went into reverse. The Media Class became an élite at Westminster. It suddenly became the case that journalists, now for the most part graduates, were cleverer, more self-assured, far better paid and very much more influential than most of the people they were writing about. The brightest and the best were going into the media. By contrast it seemed the dunderheads who went into politics. The cold cult of exposure made the problem worse. Brilliant men and women who felt drawn to public life steered clear for fear that some private vice or past misdemeanour would come to light: some of them became journalists and joined the Media Class instead.

Parliamentary correspondents – the old breed of gallery reporters who ruled the roost up to the 1960s – went into rapid, terminal decline. Their shortcoming was that they reported politics straight. Political correspondents – whose training was to put a slant on the news rather than merely report – had become the dominant force. Newsdesks and editors made it plain that they wanted stories with a sharp, polemical edge. Lobby men used their privileges to trawl the corridors of the Commons in search of rifts and scandal. Neither was in short supply.

Television was the decisive force behind the rise of the Media Class. All democratic politicians can have only one overwhelming preoccupation: the voter. There are 45 million of them out there in Britain but no one really knows what these mysterious creatures want or why they behave the way they do. Numerous experts claim special insights of one sort or another. There is no final way of telling whether they are right or whether they are talking gibberish. A previous generation of statesmen at least had the advantage of dealing with the voter direct. Open-air meetings, the verbatim publication of political speeches in newspapers, door-to-door canvassing: all gave that opportunity. Television took most of that away. The last generation of great political orators went out with Aneurin Bevan in the 1950s – Neil Kinnock was born a generation too late. Newspapers abandoned the practice of handing over precious space to unprocessed political discourse not much later. With the rise of television, politicians were handed over, trussed and bound, into the hands of the Media Class.

From then on, politicians could set their own agenda only with the greatest difficulty, and only on the terms set by the Media Class. Media Class values had to apply. The media have no morality in the sense that the word is traditionally understood. But they prefer the short-term to the long-term, sentimentality to compassion, simplicity to complexity, the dramatic to the mundane, confrontation to the sensible compromise. They can destroy with a pitiless and awesome brutality. But they can rarely create anything new, original and good. They yearn for the stark contrast between hero and villain. It is hard to imagine any environment for political decision-making that could be more damaging and unhelpful. By the 1980s, however, the Media Class had established itself as the most powerful force in British national life, comparable in a number of ways to the over-mighty trade unions in the 1970s.

For nearly a decade Margaret Thatcher rode the monster. The Media Class was not her natural ally, though it appeared to be so at the time. Large sections of the Media Class, above all the liberal élites which congregated in the broadsheets and the BBC, were always ranged against her. But they were unable to challenge the dominance she achieved through her alliance with the proprietors of United News-

papers, Associated Newspapers and above all News International. They
gave an agenda to their editors, which was put into brilliant effect by
two newspaper geniuses in particular: Kelvin MacKenzie of the *Sun*
and David English at the *Daily Mail*. Their journalism was so well-
focused and brilliant that its influence was impossible to resist, even by
those who detested it most. And Margaret Thatcher's extraordinary
personality fitted like a glove with the screaming Media Class demand
for heroics, for confrontation and for drama. The eventual downfall of
Thatcher, however, created an entirely new state of affairs and in due
course unleashed the Media Class in a new direction. Under the bland
and weak new Conservative Prime Minister John Major, the Media
Class finally came of age. It threw off the Tory agenda and set about
creating one of its own. It turned on the Conservative party with an
unspeakable ferocity and tore it apart.

Campbell's earliest and most formative political experience was as a
member of the tiny team of Neil Kinnock loyalists. He suffered at first
hand as the Tory political editors ripped the man he loved to shreds and
destroyed his chance of ever becoming prime minister. Nowadays Neil
Kinnock, a warm and decent human being, blames his own personality
defects for his failure to win in 1992. He need not be so hard on himself.
The tabloid campaign to destroy Kinnock was the Media Class at its
most brilliant, effective and repellent. Certainly Kinnock had weaknesses: they were magnified out of all proportion. William Hague, the Conservative party leader between 1997 and 2001, was a victim of the
identical process of slaughter, carried out in many cases by the very same
reporters. Campbell was a senior member of the Kinnock court in both
the 1987 and 1992 general elections. The experience scarred him for life:
former members of Neil Kinnock's court are like dogs which have been
brutalized by a cruel owner as puppies. They are never happy with outsiders, only at ease within a tiny circle of trusted intimates.

Campbell, with his powerful intelligence, made certain that he
learnt all the lessons going from the obliteration of Kinnock, and when
the Tories fell into difficulties in the first half of the 1990s he was ready
to apply them. First of all he did so, to vicious effect, as a journalist. No
one else spotted Major's weaknesses so quickly or exploited them so
clinically. This painfully acquired knowledge is what made him such a
perfect choice to become press spokesman for Tony Blair.

It was immediately apparent to Campbell, just as it was to Tony Blair, that there was an extraordinary opportunity opening up for the Labour party in 1994. The two men discussed it in great depth that summer as they talked about the task ahead at the Campbell villa in the hills above Avignon. The chance was there to claim the Media Class – for more than a decade the insuperable obstacle that lay between the Labour party and government – for themselves. It was a chance that the vilified and despised Neil Kinnock would never have been able to seize. It was a chance that John Smith, with his old-fashioned attitudes and rather admirable imperviousness to the north London media establishment, would never have wanted to grasp. But it was a chance that was tailor-made for Tony Blair, the new media-friendly leader of the Labour opposition.

The best that Neil Kinnock had ever been able to look for was to neutralize the awesome hostility of the British media – and that in itself was a forlorn enough hope. With Alastair Campbell to help him, Blair would pursue a far more audacious objective and seek to turn the domestic media into allies and friends. Campbell's view, which he expressed again and again with considerable force, was that the tabloid press, in the past such an enemy of Labour, held the key. Campbell made it a condition of his job that every possible means should be exerted to bring the *Sun* aboard. Not that the Labour leader, whose own views already lay in that direction, needed any convincing.

Tony Blair raised one other matter with Alastair Campbell in those fleeting days in August. After swearing his new press secretary to secrecy, he informed him of the plan to abolish the Labour commitment to wholesale nationalization in Clause 4 of the party constitution. It was a move that at once appealed to Campbell. Not so much because he was a New Labour modernizer who wanted this venerable and cherished antique moved out of Labour's front parlour: what Campbell liked about it was the strategic genius of the move. It would enable Blair to hit the ground running as Labour leader, make a symbolic statement of who he was and what he was about. 'What appealed to me,' Campbell said later, 'was the sheer boldness of it and the fact that this was someone who wasn't going to mess about.'

For several weeks Campbell harboured the illusion that it would be possible to maintain his broadcasting career while acting as spin-doctor to Tony Blair. It was quite clear to everybody else that the job of press spokesman was to work quietly behind the scenes. Campbell thought that it could be combined with the role of high-profile public spokesman. He felt hurt and slighted when some of the breakfast television programmes that had used his services as a paper-reviewer dropped him for reasons of political impartiality. When the BBC political correspondent Nicholas Jones suggested that there was a contradiction in maintaining both roles, Campbell expressed outrage. He was soon to find out the justice of Jones' remark the hard way. Campbell went on the *Frost Show* to review the papers, a practice he was reluctant to abandon. In a moment of unfathomable ineptitude he allowed himself to be drawn into a discussion of Labour party plans to renationalize the railways. His remarks managed both to contradict the position that had been publicly stated by Tony Blair earlier in the week and to confuse the position that John Prescott was to set out later that day. Shortly afterwards Tony Blair introduced his press spokesman to a newspaper executive with the following words: 'This is Alastair Campbell. He gets more publicity than I do.' This casual remark was delivered as a joke: it was actually a pointed public warning to Campbell to keep his head down. He eventually had the good sense to take it.

Conference debut

Blair's first Labour conference as leader saw the party take its most important decision since World War II. The decision to abolish Clause 4 of Labour's constitution, which, in theory, committed it to nationalizing vast tracts of British industry, was a brilliant success. Yet the media-handling operation was about as efficient as some of the state industries that earned Clause 4 a bad name.

It was not entirely Campbell's fault, for he had not yet severed his link to *Today* newspaper. But he must be held mainly to blame. Journalists working in Blackpool that year quickly discovered that there were no less than three separate spin-doctoring operations going on at the same time. There was the official Labour media team, led by moustachioed David Hill, director of communications since the 1992 election. At this stage, Hill, who went on to succeed Campbell in Downing Street, was regarded by the Blairites with a degree of mistrust. Hill had spent most of his working life as spokesman for Roy Hattersley, a red raw socialist compared to Blair, and had been ruled out as a possible press secretary to Blair. There was Campbell, who was briefing erratically on behalf of Blair, but was not yet fully in control of his own operation. Unseen, but nevertheless omnipresent, there was also Peter Mandelson. This led to numerous clashes as one set of spin-doctors countermanded the other and vice versa. An especially vicious row exploded over briefing for Tony Blair's speech, but there were a number of other examples.

The collision between the Tony Blair operation and the Labour party briefing machine was easy enough to solve. But Peter Mandelson was always going to be a central problem for Alastair Campbell. The two men had been close friends for the best part of a decade by the autumn of 1994; it was with Mandelson that Campbell forged one of his earliest political friendships. As with all relationships which involve Mandelson, this one was difficult, complex, and punctuated by long, frosty periods. Dealing with Peter Mandelson is not at all like doing business with a regular member of the human race. At times the charm can be overwhelming. But the ordinary rules of human discourse do not apply. The smallest dispute or upset can be enough to send him into a sulk for months.

At times the relationship could be very warm indeed. In October 1990, when Mandelson stepped down as director of communications for the Labour party, Campbell fixed him up with a column in the *Sunday People* newspaper, then edited by his old patron Richard Stott. Not content with merely setting up the column, Campbell then actually wrote it. According to Westminster legend, Mandelson would trudge up to Campbell's Gospel Oak home on Wednesday evenings to take dictation. On occasion the support was more personal still. Shortly before the 1987 General Election campaign the *News of the World* ran a story on Mandelson's complex private life. The friend he turned to for support at this time of intense distress was Alastair Campbell, and he spent the Saturday night before the story broke with Campbell and Millar. Nor was it all one way: Peter Mandelson was one of the very first to get in touch when Campbell suffered his breakdown.

At other times, however, distance bordered on hostility. The Campbell/Mandelson relationship was embarking on one of its problematic stages in the autumn of 1994. This was, of course, inevitable from the moment that Campbell accepted the job of press spokesman. There were two distinct problems here. The first was that Mandelson, with very considerable justice, regarded himself as an expert on the media. He felt that he had a lot to offer. Furthermore, he was attached to the press. There was no way that Campbell was ever going to halt the flow of informed briefing from the MP for Hartlepool to selected journalists. All he could do was stem the tide, and try to make sure that he alone was seen as the official voice of the opposition leader.

Campbell's solution was striking enough, and typically robust. First of all he took advice. Finding himself on one of his breakfast television shows with Sir Bernard Ingham, Margaret Thatcher's legendary press secretary, he took the old-timer aside afterwards and asked what course of action he would recommend. Ingham's reply was as laconic as it was brutal: 'Slit his throat.' The opportunity to take offensive action came the day after Tony Blair's conference speech. An over-excited *Times* report credited Mandelson with the authorship of important sections. Campbell chose to take umbrage, professing to believe that the item in question had been placed there by Mandelson himself. He responded in his *Today* column the following day: 'Having been a close friend of his since the days before he started wearing cufflinks, I have none of the traditional hang-ups about Peter, and fully intend on becoming Blair's press secretary to exploit his expertise, which in some areas is second to none. Speech-writing, however, is not one of them, but such is his ubiquitous appeal that *The Times* yesterday suggested he had helped write Blair's speech. I know from the days when Peter was a *People* columnist that writing was never his strong point, and that he had to look to his friends to help him out. Know what I mean?'[9]

To place such an item in a newspaper was a bold strategy. It was a public pronouncement by Campbell that he would be no pushover, and a demonstration that he was in no way afraid of Mandelson. All that was wise, and even commendable. But it also drew attention, in the most public way conceivable, to the tensions and rivalries within the court of Tony Blair. That was unprofessional, the kind of mistake that Campbell would never have tolerated in others.

This minor skirmish was merely a symptom of a much more visceral conflict between Mandelson and Campbell, who, whether they liked it or not, were on the way to becoming direct personal rivals. They now found themselves in the position of two powerful courtiers competing for the attention of the monarch. In 1994 there was no question who was the senior of the two. Peter Mandelson was the more powerful, in terms of age, ability, experience and above all his mesmeric hold over Tony Blair. Campbell seems – with some difficulty – to have been partly ready to accept this secondary role in the autumn of 1994.

But he really had no choice. He had yet to prove himself. He was not yet the dominating figure he was to become. That autumn Campbell accompanied Tony and Cherie Blair to the annual *Tribune* dinner. Halfway through, the Labour leader's consort realized that she had forgotten something in her bag. Campbell was despatched to retrieve the item from the car. It was a very public demonstration of his subordinate status and, as such, inconceivable only two or three years later.

'The Most Brilliant Election Campaign in History'

At least no one can say we peaked too early.

John Major, during the general election campaign, 1997

CAMPBELL THREW HIMSELF INTO the revolutionary changes that Blair immediately began to impose on the Labour party. Campbell can take the credit for the bold decision to change the very name of the Labour party. While Blair, Mandelson and even Philip Gould dithered, Campbell pressed for change. It was he who came up with the 'New Labour, New Britain' slogan for the 1994 party conference. At first it was rejected by the others as too stark, too confrontational. They had suggested the uninspiring 'Labour's New Approach'. Campbell argued them round. It was an example of his rare gift for the simple, telling phrase and the determination to make sure it works. Later Gould, who had himself a strong claim to authorship, generously acknowledged that 'it was Campbell who turned the term "New Labour" into an entirely new identity for the party'. The process was subsequently taken even further, with party membership cards in the name of New Labour. The traditional red was replaced with a variety of colours, depending on the occasion.

Campbell's contribution in pushing through the ditching of Clause 4 was almost as important. Had the operation gone wrong, Tony Blair's leadership of the Labour party might have foundered before it had properly begun. The key problem was securing the whole-hearted assent of John Prescott, Tony Blair's deputy – and put there as the voice of the unions and the Labour left. Dealing with John Prescott at the best of times is much like handling a piece of high explosive. On the question of dropping the cherished commitment to wholesale national-ization he was a potential nuclear bomb. Tony Blair already trusted Campbell enough to hand over this vital negotiation to his press spokesman. Campbell justified his leader's trust completely: the nuclear bomb, despite a few sweaty moments, never went off.

When he signed up to Tony Blair's inner circle in 1994 he was enter-ing a seething world of bitterness, resentment, passion and blind hatred. Brown was consumed with an overwhelming resentment of Blair and not even talking to Mandelson. His relations with another powerful Labour politician, Robin Cook, were worst of all. Mandelson was shortly to fall out with Gould, whose relations with Brown in turn were never easy. Blair's relationship with Mandelson, who once flounced out of a meeting with the party leader and Shadow chancellor, was complex beyond belief. Campbell navigated his way through it all. He maintained satisfactory relations with all parties. By standing aside from the emotional turmoil that surrounded the Labour leader he steadily acquired extra authority for himself.

All things to all men

It was not merely the Blair circle with which Campbell coped in level-headed fashion. He was a popular figure with MPs from all sides of the party. Being Scottish helped. Bernard Shaw once remarked that the moment an Englishman opens his mouth he is either despised by one half of the population or resented by the other. This was not the fate of Campbell. He comes from outside the English class system, and his voice is a curious cocktail of northern vowels and a Scottish lilt. Even more importantly, he has the ability to make anyone who has dealings with him feel that he is a blood-brother. With dour old Labour types, Campbell was able to produce his support for Burnley Football Club and lashings of red-blooded sentiment on the subject of grammar schools and redistribution of wealth. With sharp-suited New Labour adherents, Campbell could provide an acceptable north London address, impeccable modernizing credentials and an awesome set of connections. He was very good with Tories too. Conservative MPs like Alan Clark, Michael Heseltine and Nicholas Soames loved Alastair Campbell. His self-assurance, cynicism, arrogance, instinctive grasp of the nature of power and clear sense that he had been born to rule convinced them against the evidence of their own eyes that he had been educated at Eton. Clark liked Campbell so much that he invited him and his family to his family home, Saltwood Castle. He once, in a moment of impulsive generosity, offered him one of his collection of vintage cars as a gift. Campbell, always immune to temptation in financial matters, had the sense to refuse.[1]

Alastair Campbell's protean personality took in all of these, but most grievously deceived were old-fashioned Labour types. His success in massaging the warm-hearted and instinctive Labour soul – that section of the party which, unlike its brain, remained impervious to Tony Blair – was remarkable. He knows little of, and feels less for, the magnificent history of the Labour party. His father was a member of his local Conservative club. His first political involvement was as the press relations adviser to a Conservative party councillor. Campbell came to Labour late in life and then as a journalist, never as an activist. He has no serious links with the trade-union movement. Every action he has ever taken and every word he has ever written has been on the side of the Labour modernizers, first Kinnock and then Blair. And yet there is no question that the Labour party regards him more or less as one of its own whereas Peter Mandelson and Philip Gould are objects of hatred and suspicion.

This is partly because Mandelson and Gould are more courageous than Campbell. Mandelson had the guts to court unpopularity by fighting for the difficult changes that had to be made by New Labour. The same can be said of Gould, who has often borne the brunt of attack from the left, but never of Campbell, who played a more cunning, calculating and double-edged game. This subtlety has helped the modernizers. It enabled Campbell to act as the bridge between Blair and Prescott over Clause 4. He could play the part of Tony Blair's ambassador to the Labour party in a way that Peter Mandelson could never dream of.

The paradox is that Campbell, for all his red-blooded political opinions, was the biggest modernizer of all. It was the absence of personal Labour roots, the relative ignorance of the party's history and guiding ideas, that helped make him the force he was. Peter Mandelson and Philip Gould were born and bred in the Labour party – it is part of their innermost being, which is why the final irrevocable step towards New Labour felt to them like an act of parricide. When they created New Labour they destroyed some important part of themselves. This was not so with Campbell: he was simply making a neutral, calculated political decision. It was the same for Tony Blair. That neither Blair nor Campbell has ever been fully part of the Labour movement in its traditional sense is one of the things they have in common.

Educating the Blairs

Human nature can harbour many contradictions. Campbell's breast could contain both a clinical indifference to the old Labour party and a passionate commitment to some of old Labour's most bloody-minded notions. Most New Labour compromises or adaptations – for instance the commitment to the market economy and to not raising income tax – he either swallowed or warmly embraced. But neither he nor Fiona Millar would budge on comprehensive education. They took the ultra-montane stanoe. In their book it was not merely sufficient to send one's child to a state school. It must also be non-selective and, for good measure, the nearest. This was what the Campbell-Millars did with their own children, and they expected no less of anybody else.

Early victims of this ferocity were Andrew Marr, the future BBC political editor, and his wife Jackie Ashley, the *Guardian* columnist and broadcaster. The Marrs lived near the Campbell-Millars in Gospel Oak, north London. For a number of years these two high-powered media couples, whose children were close in age, were good friends, in and out of each other's homes, embarking upon joint projects the way families do when they have young children in common. Then the Marrs made the same agonizing decision as many other middle-class families, and removed their children from the state system. From that moment on relations chilled. Fiona Millar would blank Jackie Ashley if she met her in the street. Nor were the Marrs alone. Other friends of the Campbells who had taken their children out of state schools found themselves interrogated at dinner parties hosted by the Campbells. 'Fiona would go on and on about it,' said one parent who dropped out of the Campbell dining set. 'It was embarrassing and easier not to go.'[2]

Next to suffer were Tony and Cherie Blair. Alastair Campbell and Tony Blair did not see eye to eye on education. Right from the first the two men clashed bitterly. This damaging split, which was to dog their relationship right up to the end, was in the open almost from the very first. In the autumn of 1994 young Euan Blair was entering his last year of primary school. The Blairs, like so many Labour-supporting parents, faced the difficult choice of which school to send him to next. The Blairs lived in Islington, where the standard of secondary education was famously poor. Most people sympathized with their predicament when it emerged that they were considering sending their beloved eldest child to the London Oratory. The Oratory was no private school. But it had taken advantage of Conservative legislation to opt out of local authority control and the journey involved crossing local education authority boundaries. Many Labour supporters were bitterly opposed to these 'opt-out' schools, and this group included Alastair Campbell and Fiona Millar. When Campbell heard that the Blairs had decided to send their son to the Oratory he was livid. Like many Labour MPs, he saw the move as an outright act of betrayal. 'You can't fucking do that,' he told Blair privately. So furious was Campbell that at one stage he even threatened to resign.

Campbell was right to warn the Prime Minister that the move would be controversial. The announcement, when it came, caused a storm. Many Labour people accused the Blairs of committing an act of giant hypocrisy by attacking the Conservative system of opt-out – and then favouring an opt-out school themselves. Roy Hattersley, for instance, attacked the way that Labour had come to accept Conservative language on schooling and 'parental choice', which he defined as 'the freedom of the middle classes to talk their way into unfair advantage'.[3]

Campbell's relationship with the Blairs survived the row. But forever afterwards there was a real tenseness when schooling was discussed. Sometimes this came to the surface in the presence of others. In April 1996 *Sunday Times* political editor Andrew Grice asked Tony Blair in an interview if he planned to introduce 'streaming' in schools. The concept was seen as being as far as Labour could ever go in embracing the concept of selection in education. Blair hesitated, and Grice sensed his instinct was to say yes. Blair looked sideways to where Campbell was sitting. 'If you do that, I'll resign,' declared Campbell. He got his way. Blair eventually told Grice he favoured 'setting' – a watered-down version of 'streaming.' The Oratory remained an object of tension between Campbell and Blair. Three weeks before the 1997 election, John MacIntosh, headmaster of the London Oratory, called for grant-maintained schools to be given more power and criticized Labour's education proposals. Campbell was furious. After the general election, the government made the decision to abolish GM schools – effectively cutting the Oratory budget by £250,000. MacIntosh, an accomplished media operator, responded by asking parents, including the Blairs, to make up the shortfall by paying £30 per month for the first child at the school and £15 for the second. Campbell offered to draft a statement on behalf of the school, a move that was rejected out of hand by MacIntosh, who felt there was no need for Downing Street to get involved. Campbell phoned MacIntosh to harangue him: 'Just remember that if it wasn't for the Blair children your school would be nothing'.[4] Shortly afterwards, at a lunch hosted by the Politeia think tank, MacIntosh was overheard calling Campbell a 'pig,' resulting in further headlines.[5]

The Campbell-Millars can be accused of intolerance when it came to education, but not of hypocrisy. There have been better schools than the Gospel Oak primary school in the Labour-run borough of Camden. But the Campbell-Millars did not respond, as many middle-class parents would have done, by taking their children away. Instead, Fiona became a school governor and threw herself into the life of the school. When a government report exposed the institution's many shortcomings, the Campbell-Millars took the lead in a campaign that in due course forced out the headmaster. At a special meeting of more than a hundred parents called to discuss the school's future, one of the most violent denunciations of the hapless head came from Campbell.

Campbell was extraordinarily busy in the early months of 1995: plenty of ambitious men would never have taken the time off work to involve themselves with the problems of their children's school, with all the tedious detail and little tasks that it involves. The Campbell-Millars had strong beliefs and principles which they were prepared to put into practice with regard to the education of their children. They were very unforgiving to others around them who did not display the same unswerving rectitude. This Puritan zeal was soon to claim another victim.

Tarnished golden girl

For the best part of a decade Harriet Harman was one of Campbell's golden girls. He missed no opportunity to build up the career of this clever and well-connected ornament of Neil Kinnock's Labour party. The modernizers wanted her for themselves: on television her fetching good looks, headmistress manner and upper-middle-class accent conveyed precisely the image they wanted. With the arrival of Tony Blair, Harriet Harman's future appeared more assured than ever. That was until Alastair Campbell flattened it.

Ms Harman, the daughter of a Harley Street doctor and niece of the Countess of Longford, threw herself into the turbulent left-wing politics of the 1970s, became a civil rights activist, and in due course married the trade-union leader Jack Dromey, who led the famous Grunwick strike in the 1970s. They had three children: it was the education of these youngsters that sounded the death-knell for Harman's promising front-bench career.

The Dromeys lived in a south London inner-city borough whose high level of burglary, car theft and violent crime was not matched by the standards in its schools. There was no critical mass of local middle-class parents to put pressure on the local teachers as there was in Campbell's more salubrious area of north London. It is hard not to feel sympathy with Harman in her predicament. The eldest child was despatched across borough boundaries to the London Oratory. Even this minor infringement prompted abuse from Alastair Campbell who, when Cherie and Tony Blair followed suit, blamed Harman for setting such as unsavoury precedent. But the real storm only hit when Jack Dromey and Harriet Harman made the decision to send their next son to St Olave's, a grammar school in Orpington. Harman knew it was a provocative act: almost the entire Labour party was opposed to selection at the age of eleven. She told Tony Blair several months before the story broke. One of the major problems was that Blair, knowing the inevitable reaction from his strong-minded assistant, did not dare to inform Campbell. All through the winter of 1995–96 it remained

Harriet Harman and Tony Blair's little secret until, in the third week of January 1996, it was unearthed by Joe Murphy, the political editor of the *Mail on Sunday*. Unluckily for Murphy, the school then alerted Harman: the game was up.

The Harman story was an early test for Tony Blair's already renowned press machine. Campbell decided to squash Murphy. Having learnt about the story on Friday, Campbell promptly denied the *Mail on Sunday* its scoop by handing it over to Labour-friendly journalists. The *Daily Mirror* and the *Independent* were party to this petty larceny. Their half-hearted attempt to portray Harman's actions in a friendly light failed completely. Within hours, the Labour party was ablaze.

Campbell's behaviour at this juncture was self-indulgent. Most of the Labour party, the press and even the Shadow Cabinet were baying for Harman's blood. Only Tony Blair, Peter Mandelson and a very few others wanted to save her. It was one of the biggest tests Tony Blair's leadership has ever faced. Two issues were at stake that week in January 1996. The first was selective education. The second, and by far the more important, was the continued authority of Tony Blair and the entire modernizing project. Campbell's duty was to fling himself into the breach. But he went missing.

It was Peter Mandelson who went in to bat on Harman's behalf. It was enough to save the day, but not before great damage had been done. Harriet Harman had been marked out. The assassins, waved on by Alastair Campbell, would come back to get her. Campbell's disloyalty would have been unforgivable enough from a senior member of the Shadow Cabinet. But Campbell was not an elected politician, he was an appointed apparatchik. And yet he chose to follow a principle of his own rather than spring to the defence of his boss. Yet no one in the Blair inner circle thought that Campbell's behaviour was odd. It goes to show his compelling ability to get others to accept him on his own terms.

Wooing the Media Class

It is a clear indication of the needs and imperatives of New Labour that Tony Blair's two closest advisers, before and after the general election, Peter Mandelson and Alastair Campbell, were trained in the media.

When they were not fighting like ferrets in a sack, their complementary qualities made them a perfect fit. Mandelson was stronger on strategy, Campbell on execution. Mandelson had the more probing, subtle mind while Campbell was more brutal and direct. Mandelson's genius lay above all with television and broadcasters, while – at first at any rate – Campbell really understood only print journalism. Both of them were fully paid-up members of the Media Class.

Mandelson's training was in broadcasting. He was part of that talented generation which passed through London Weekend Television in the early 1980s, then fanned out into national politics and the commanding heights of the British media. It includes, to name a few, Greg Dyke, who went on to become director-general of the BBC; Sir Christopher Bland, former chairman of the BBC governors; Barry Cox, treasurer of the Tony Blair campaign team in 1994; Michael Wills, briefly a junior minister; and – incongruously – Bruce Anderson, future biographer of John Major.

Mandelson has a feel for how broadcasting works, which explains why he was so effective for so long as Labour's director of communications. The widespread view that there was something sinister about the immense influence he exercised for many years is false. Mandelson had a precise grasp of the values, pacing, judgements and deadlines of news stories, and it was this professionalism and insight that gave him such sway with BBC reporters. They would have been mad not to want to listen to what Mandelson had to say. The same applied to their bosses. Campbell offered the same service on the press side. He was able to play the rhythms of the daily news cycle as on a violin. He knew the needs and weaknesses of every lobby journalist and was always as happy to meet the one as he was to prey upon the other. The herd instinct of the lobby, with its mob mentality, was home territory for Campbell.

Between them, these two with others put into effect the new electoral technology New Labour had imported from the United States: the giant media war-room, the twenty-four-hour monitoring of television, radio and press outlets, a rapid rebuttal service, a savage clampdown on MPs and Shadow ministers who spoke out of turn. The move of Labour's headquarters from John Smith House in south London to a new office in Millbank Tower in October 1995 was the symbol of this profound change in methodology. A few souls who wanted to bring the name John Smith across the river as well, in tribute to the recently deceased leader, were swiftly silenced. Smith, who would have hated Millbank and everything it represented, was rapidly becoming a non-person. A team of 150 staff was swiftly assembled, growing to nearly twice that as the general-election itself approached. Before the election campaign Campbell did not even have his own office in the building. On the irregular occasions that he put in an appearance, he made use of a desk outside the office Peter Mandelson used in his capacity as chairman of the Labour general election planning committee. Nothing like Millbank had ever been seen in British politics before. It was American both in inspiration and in its structural preference for process rather than substance. Campbell poured scorn on these foreign influences coming from Washington at first: but he swiftly changed his opinion when he saw their uses.

New Labour introduced a new concept into British electoral history: the permanent campaign. Until the arrival of Tony Blair, election campaigns started the day that the prime minister went to see the Queen to hand over the seals of office and ended approximately three and half weeks later when the British people went to the polls to vote. For the rest of the time the winning party was allowed to get on with government. New Labour, with Media Class connivance, abolished that agreeable mode of life. The general election campaign of spring 1997 had actually begun almost three years before, practically the moment that Tony Blair became Leader of the Opposition.

Labour's ferocious internal discipline was the key to its success. In stark contrast to the Conservative party, then at the height of its self-laceration over Europe, Labour MPs were prevailed upon to limit their public utterances to the bland platitudes imposed upon them by the party machine. Those who found this discipline unbearable were harassed like dissidents in a totalitarian state. One radio producer remembers Clare Short, in the Shadow Cabinet only on sufferance and always regarded by the Labour machine as a liability, showing some spirit and militancy on air. It was shortly after she had made a public attack against 'people who live in the dark', widely regarded as a reference to Campbell and Mandelson. Within seconds of taking off her headphones, she was being bleeped with a request to ring Millbank

Tower urgently and told to shut up. She turned down further interview requests. Austin Mitchell, an unruly Labour backbencher, compared Tony Blair to a North Korean dictator. Instantly he was contacted by Millbank and told not to conduct any more media interviews.

When stories went in a direction Millbank did not like, punitive action was swift. High-profile rows, like the one sparked by the peremptory letter from Alastair Campbell to the BBC director-general John Birt in 1996 demanding that Tony Blair's conference speech should lead the BBC News, were relatively rare. Day-to-day bullying at a lower level, however, was routine. Tim Allan, Campbell's deputy in the Labour press office, was especially awkward to deal with. On one occasion Michael Brunson, then political editor of ITN, had to intervene to separate him and a furious producer. Campbell thoroughly approved of his subordinates' tactics. He cheered them on and gave them useful tips about how to make themselves even more unpleasant.

What gave Labour complaints an edge was that they were inevitably well researched and sensibly focused. The vigilance was extraordinary. Roger Mosey, then the editor of Radio 4's *Today* programme, recalls: 'If you had a line that Labour didn't like on the 6.30 a.m. bulletin you got called instantly. Often Labour complaints had some substance. That was their cleverness. If there was a glimmer of an inaccuracy they were onto you.'

Tory Central Office, once spoken of in hushed tones, now full of anxious and baffled men, was well aware that something was going on. But it could not comprehend exactly what. Eventually, after much deliberation and many meetings, it produced a secret weapon: a junior backbench MP called Alan Duncan. Tory Central Office temporarily suffered from the delusion, fully shared by Mr Duncan, that he was the Conservative party's answer to Peter Mandelson. The two spin-doctors share a fondness for expensive, hand-made suits, but in all other respects Duncan's attempts to emulate Mandelson only highlighted the general Tory hopelessness. 'There was the time when Duncan was appointed spin-doctor to the *Today* programme,' remembers one senior BBC figure. 'For a few days he would ring up at midnight and ask what was going on. The Tories just never understood what it was all about. From time to time Duncan would get angry and threaten to report us. He just didn't have any credibility.'

The legendary Sir Bernard Ingham, whose influence on the young Alastair Campbell can hardly be overstated, had understood the value of denying access. Programmes that irked Margaret Thatcher suddenly found that no senior minister would go on to be interviewed. It was a brave producer who was prepared to live in such a lonely state for ever. The risk of non-cooperation did not exist as far as John Major's Tory party were concerned. Sportingly, they kept coming back for more. Campbell and Mandelson never made that sort of mistake. They controlled who appeared where, and made the fullest possible use of that control. Any programme that questioned the glowing public image of Tony Blair and his Shadow Cabinet found itself ostracized. This was the fate of *World at One*, the influential lunchtime news programme. To the bafflement and blind fury of Labour spin-doctors, it asked hard and probing questions and refused to be put off. The high-profile interviews therefore went to friendlier and more helpful programmes.

Fallen men

Daily political journalists need, above all else, a high-calibre, intelligent and well-informed briefing from someone who has total access to his boss. That Campbell could deliver to the daily lobby. He did not trust journalists, or even like them much, and made no pretence that he did. But he provided a professional service.

He learnt a great deal from Peter Mandelson, in particular about how to handle the broadcast media, but also steered clear of his mistakes. Mandelson's method of doing business with the press was to single out a tiny number of favourites. He had a coterie of trusted souls with whom he would share almost everything: Andy Grice of the *Sunday Times*, Donald Macintyre of the *Independent*, Patrick Wintour of the *Guardian*, the columnist Robert Harris, perhaps Lance Price of the BBC. Before the 1992 election Mandelson, Macintyre and Harris would gather together late in the parliamentary week in one of the many bars deep in the bowels of the House of Commons. Intruders were not made to feel welcome. Throughout the pre-1997 period the members' lobby of the Commons would be treated to an unchanging ritual at 4 p.m. on Thursday afternoons. Andrew Grice would be hanging casually about the lobby. Then Peter Mandelson would stroll in purposefully. Grice would walk up to him in a deferential manner. Mandelson would glare at him, as if he had never seen him before in his life. A few words would be exchanged. The two men would then walk off together, presumably to construct Grice's story in the *Sunday Times* for the weekend.

At first Campbell did not make the Mandelsonian error of cultivating a White Commonwealth.[6] He treated all of the lobby with the same amiable contempt. Even those he conspicuously liked, such as Tony Bevins of the *Independent*, appeared to derive no special benefits from the association, while those for whom he appeared to feel a particular dislike, like George Jones of the *Daily Telegraph*, seemed to suffer no special penalties. Campbell rapidly acquired, as Mandelson already possessed, a reputation for bullying journalists when events failed to go his own way.

Campbell's ruthless determination to win the 1997 election showed at a meeting with BBC political journalist Jeremy Vine, shortly before Blair's election battle bus set off on a tour of Britain. Vine, at that time a BBC political correspondent, informed Campbell cheerily: 'You'll have your daily schedule of course, but my job will be to report the things that aren't necessarily on it.' Vine recalled: 'He went absolutely mad and said, "You will fucking report exactly what I tell you to report, you'll stick to my fucking schedule and nothing else."' When, during the same pre-1997 election period, another broadcaster complained at his constant tirades, telling him: 'Stop bullying us, Alastair – everyone knows you're going to win,' Campbell replied: 'I'm preparing to win the election after next, not this one.'

Some reporters minded about this sort of thing. Others found bruising encounters with Labour party spin-doctors added greatly to their enjoyment of the day. One thing everybody could agree upon. Abuse from Mandelson was somehow vicious and nasty, hissed out as if he meant it, and inevitably followed by a long period of unpleasantness. Campbell's bollockings, though more cogently expressed and often accompanied by the implied threat of physical violence, were less personal and far less long-lasting. They came and went within the hour, like a summer thunderstorm. They were good clean fun, always greatly improved if the victim retaliated in kind. Indeed, Campbell is one of those dominant males who feels fully at ease only with someone with

whom he has entered into bruising public combat. Many theories
sprang up in the parliamentary lobby to account for the difference in
approach between the two men. The commonest was simply that Mandelson was the nastier piece of work. The more generous and perceptive view, from Mandelson's supporters, was that he made the mistake
of thinking of journalists as friends. When they let him down – in other
words did their job – he felt personally betrayed. Campbell, by contrast,
never had any illusions about the profession. He thought of his former
colleagues as fallen men and expected them to let him down. That is
one reason why Campbell was to begin with moderately even-handed
in his dealings with political journalists. He made just one important
exception. He made plain from the very outset that he would do whatever he could to make life easy and comfortable for the *Sun* newspaper,
Rupert Murdoch's mass-market tabloid.

News International

A strong argument can be made that the most potent figure of the latter
half of the twentieth century has been not the great statesman but the
international businessman. Of these the most interesting and important – at any rate in the Western hemisphere – has been Rupert Murdoch who, as a young Oxford graduate in the 1950s, spotted the vast
potential of the media business.

News Corp, with its massive portfolio of international interests – in
Britain it owns *The Times*, the *Sunday Times*, the *Sun*, *News of the World*
and Sky TV – has turned him into one of the most powerful men in the
world. National politicians, even one as successful as Tony Blair, are
permitted only a few years at the top, and just one country to play with.
A man like Murdoch spans the decades and the continents: he possesses far more clout than each transient generation of passing politicians.

For the past two decades all British politicians have faced one central question: how to deal with Rupert Murdoch. For those who have
handled him effectively and well, like Margaret Thatcher, the rewards
have been immense. For those who got it wrong, like Neil Kinnock, the
effect has been catastrophic. Blair and Campbell, with their noses for
power, were wide awake to this. They were equally clear about the
answer. They were willing to prostrate themselves to bring Murdoch

across to New Labour. It was Campbell's conviction – one fully shared by Tony Blair – that the support of Rupert Murdoch's mass-market *Sun* was a necessary, and possibly a sufficient, condition of Labour victory at the general election.

Never has a newspaper group been courted as News International was in the months following Tony Blair's election to the Labour leadership. For the Labour party this was in some ways Blair's most shocking policy-change: it had collectively refused to speak to the Murdoch press since News International, in a union-busting move, shifted its centre of operations to Wapping in east London in the mid-1980s. The relationship had been marked by the bitterest hostility and recrimination, made worse when the *Sun* claimed the credit for the defeat of Kinnock in the 1992 general election.

The courtship operated at a number of levels. First, Rupert Murdoch himself was wooed devotedly. When he came to town, Blair and his lieutenants would drop anything to have dinner with him. After Blair's annual party conference speech, the Labour leader's first priority was to speak to Murdoch. He would allay his concerns on some issues, highlight political movement in others: always courteous, deferential and eager to learn Murdoch's own opinion. One of Tony Blair's most priceless gifts has always been the ability to impress older men and bring them over to his way of thinking. This process of intensive cultivation reached its crowning moment in the summer of 1995 when the Labour leader flew halfway across the world to address a meeting of News International executives on Hayman Island, just off the Queensland coast. Blair's decision to embark on this 25,000-mile round trip, made at the prompting of Campbell, was an extraordinary act of fealty. The Political Class was paying homage to the Media Class.

Campbell defended Blair's trip to meet Murdoch at Hayman Island and his relationship with the media mogul, saying: 'People in the non-Murdoch part of the media are neuralgic about Murdoch and neuralgic about spin doctors. There is a disproportionate interest in the relationship between Blair and Murdoch. Rupert Murdoch and News International don't get treated any differently to any other media organization.'[7] It ranks as one of his most disingenuous statements of his nine years working for Blair. Campbell was obsessed with retaining the support of Murdoch's papers, and succeeded in doing so right until the end, and afterwards. He had the confidence trickster's ability to state the opposite of the truth and defy anyone to prove him wrong.

Only President Clinton counted for more with Blair in those three years of opposition: and even that is debatable. Murdoch's needs and wishes became New Labour's needs and wishes. One of Tony Blair's first acts in office was to inform his MPs to pay 'more attention to the tabloids'. He meant the *Sun*. Relations became warmer still when Les Hinton was appointed executive chairman of News International in the winter of 1994–95. Hinton had been in the United States during the Wapping dispute a decade before, so brought none of the baggage from that time. He invited a succession of Shadow ministers down to Murdoch's hideous east London headquarters, which Blair often visited himself. It was noticed with approval that whenever New Labour politicians arrived, they were conspicuously well briefed on all issues close to Rupert Murdoch's heart.

News International had various practical worries on its own account, all of which Tony Blair acted quickly to address. He promised that Labour in government would not undo the Thatcher union reforms. He produced satisfactory assurances that no privacy laws or statutory controls on the press would be introduced. And he gave every impression that Labour in government would not prove awkward over two issues vital to Murdoch: competition and cross-media ownership. The 1992 Labour manifesto had pledged draconian measures to curb the powerful foreign-owned press: by 1997 these were watered down to become practically meaningless.

Campbell devoted almost as much attention to cultivating News International journalists as News International management. Tony Blair's first article for a Murdoch-supporting paper came as early as August 1994. It was a half-page column in the *News of the World*. Though Campbell had not yet taken over as press secretary, it bore the marks of his handiwork. It was the first of scores of articles by Tony Blair that were to appear in Murdoch papers over the coming years. Few were seen, let alone written, by their ostensible author. This was where Campbell's hard-won tabloid expertise came in handy. When English football fans rioted late at night in Dublin, there was a page-six piece in the *Sun* the following morning. It expressed the Leader of the Opposition's considered opinion that 'a game we love is once more condemned by a group of idiots who shame our country'. This required very fast footwork – a late-night negotiation with the *Sun* newsdesk followed by the swift turnaround of the copy which would appear under the Blair byline. It was Campbell at his most productive and efficient. Other papers woke up to the ease with which Blair articles could be obtained. Soon the Leader of the Opposition became by far the most prolific journalist in Fleet Street. Most weeks would see the publication of half a dozen Blair articles at least, sometimes rising to twenty or more. It was not long before the burden of writing his comment pieces became too great for Campbell alone, and he was forced to farm out the work to junior members of the press office. After the general election the task of writing prime-ministerial articles was delegated to a special Downing Street office, the strategic communications unit. Composed partly of ex-journalists and partly of civil servants, this industrious group has been known to fashion more than a hundred exclusive pieces by Tony Blair in a single week. In due course the market suffered from saturation. Articles by the Prime Minister turned into a shop-soiled commodity and comment editors would greet them with a groan. Downing Street eventually woke up to this and steps were taken to curb production.

Tony Blair articles, even when they were still in fashion, were the least of the many services provided by Alastair Campbell to the *Sun*. It was swiftly noticed by correspondents from other papers that *Sun* journalists were the only ones spared Campbell's routine barbarism and scorn. When they asked questions, he listened politely and with an expression of lively interest, which contrasted with his sneer of contempt for ordinary jobbing hacks. He made a point of praising what he viewed as the *Sun*'s responsible reporting, contrasting it with the alleged recklessness and bad taste of the BBC and the *Guardian*. He developed the warmest of relationships with the paper's editor, Stuart Higgins. On one occasion Higgins and his most senior colleagues were invited to Blair's Islington home. The Leader of the Opposition was effusively hospitable. The same could not be said of his wife Cherie, once alleged to have banned the *Sun* from her home. She was nowhere to be seen, and Blair was obliged to make the coffee.

Wherever possible New Labour would hand the *Sun* exclusives, a habit that soon began to annoy *Mirror* journalists. The *Mirror* had traditionally regarded itself as the only tabloid Labour paper and was understandably proud that it had stuck with the party through the dog days of opposition. Now it found itself left out in the cold. As Campbell accurately surmised, there was nowhere else to go, at least not till after the election. The feelings of resentment and betrayal at Campbell's old paper were never stronger than in the days following the extraordinary *Mirror* budget scoop in November 1996.

On the eve of budget day *Mirror* editor Piers Morgan found himself in uncomfortable possession of one of the greatest newspaper exclusives of all time. He received a dossier of documents containing the contents of the following day's budget, Kenneth Clarke's final effort to win back the voters for the Tory party. It was the first time that budget secrecy had ever been breached on such a scale. To the astonishment of Fleet Street, Morgan played safe and decided not to publish his scoop, preferring to make a great show of virtue instead by handing it back to Downing Street.

However, rather than sit on the budget leak entirely, he gave some hints about its contents to the Labour party in order, so he thought, to help Gordon Brown savage Kenneth Clarke during the budget debate. But the following morning's *Sun*, to Morgan's surprise and dismay, confidently and accurately predicted each and every newsworthy budget item – Clarke's decision to cut income tax, raise car tax, lower corporation tax, the lot. At the time the story went round that a *Mirror* journalist, infuriated by the pusillanimity of Morgan, was responsible for passing over the information. But some senior figures at the *Mirror* refused to be dissuaded from the highly improbable notion that Labour handed over its famous scoop lock, stock and barrel to the *Sun*.

The general election

Well before the general election on 1 May 1997 it had become obvious to most political journalists that Labour was en route to an historic victory, very likely of landslide proportions. They made their dispositions accordingly. Looking back, it is amazing that so many papers felt capable of endorsing John Major and his broken-backed Tories. Among Sunday papers two out of the four broadsheets – the *Sunday Times* and *Sunday Telegraph* – stuck with the Conservatives. Both the middle-market tabloids – the *Express* and the *Mail on Sunday* – stayed firm. But at the bottom end of the market the Murdoch-owned *News of the World* made the switch from Tory to Labour.

The daily market was more fluid. The *Daily Telegraph* gave a despairing endorsement for John Major, but *The Times* felt unable to do so. Instead it sat on the fence. In a move which did nothing for its reputation for sound judgement, it counselled its readers to vote not for the Tory candidate, nor the Labour one, but for the most anti-European candidate. Both the *Express* and the *Mail* urged the virtues of John Major upon their readers. The *Sun*, however, produced its endorsement for Labour the day Major called the general election.

At the 1992 general election approximately seventy per cent of the newspaper market, judged by the number of readers, was Tory. In 1997 that figure was more or less reversed. Alastair Campbell had done his bit in opposition. Now it was time for government.

part two

2 May 1997

Right, let's see what I can tell you about this lot.

Alastair Campbell to Downing Street officials before the first
meeting of Tony Blair's Cabinet, 2 May 1997

EUPHORIA AND WONDERMENT were in the air. People were trying to get to grips with the extraordinary fact the Conservatives were out of government for the first time in eighteen years. On this beautiful late spring morning, Tony Blair and his family posed for photographs on the steps of 10 Downing Street. Again and again the Prime Minister turned to go into inside. Again and again cameramen demanded just one more photocall. Crowds cheered, and waved their flags.

Few noticed Alastair Campbell, architect of the election victory, as he quietly entered the building. Most of the phrases uttered by the Prime Minister on the doorstep – 'I say to the people of this country. We ran for office as New Labour, I say we will govern as New Labour' – had been agreed between them. The idea of New Labour itself had been his personal invention. Tony Blair was the actor showered with laurels, but Campbell was the director.

Though nationally unknown, Alastair Campbell was already a celebrated and much-discussed figure within the closed worlds of Westminster and Whitehall. He was known to be exceptionally close to the Prime Minister. He had been the driving force behind, not merely the election victory, but also Tony Blair's dramatic, well-planned and controversial ascent within the Labour party.

He inspired fear. A major reason the new Prime Minister enjoyed a squeaky-clean public image was because Campbell carried out the dirty jobs for him. He was nominally just the press secretary, but in practice he was very much more than that. He knew secrets, and he was prepared to use the information to threaten and intimidate. 'You go to Tony with a private problem,' a senior member of the Blair Cabinet was later to remark, 'and he tells Alastair. Then later, if he wants to, he will use it.'

As Campbell went into Number 10, officials craned their necks to see him. They saw a tall, commanding man, well built and ruggedly good looking. He was on the verge of his fortieth birthday, and had not entirely lost the open-faced good looks of his youth, but they had been mellowed by the maturity and confidence that comes with the respect of peers and the exercise of power. He was smartly dressed, in the way that high-quality tabloid journalists are taught to be. His suit was not well cut, but it was clean and immaculately creased. His black shoes were shiny and his white shirt spotless. He automatically commanded a room, even when he was not speaking. The Americans have an expression for men like Campbell: Alpha Male.

Jonathan Haslam, the outgoing press secretary, welcomed Campbell into his bay-windowed study overlooking Downing Street. Although they were roughly the same age, there could hardly have been a greater contrast between the two. Haslam has the cautious manner of a man forged in Whitehall, not Fleet Street. Haslam was an official, Campbell a political appointment. Haslam did things by the book. Campbell made his own rules.

Haslam dutifully gave Campbell a twelve-page practical guide to the job of press secretary. He explained how the office worked. He told him the times set aside for briefing political journalists – known collectively within Whitehall as 'the lobby'. He gave him an A–Z map of the Downing Street complex. This was badly needed. Number 10 is much larger than it looks from outside, with many labyrinthine corridors and stairways. When Haslam had finished, he offered to hand over to Campbell formally at the lobby briefing. It was a well-meant offer, but there was perhaps a touch of sadism in Campbell's response: 'Would you like to start by briefing the lobby on Major's last hours?' asked Campbell. He was well aware how fond Haslam had grown of the outgoing Prime

Minister. Haslam, who knew that Campbell had cruelly pilloried his boss both as a journalist and a spin-doctor, smiled, and politely declined.

Moments before he was to address the lobby, Campbell was summoned to Tony Blair's study for the first time. 'Where do I go?' Campbell asked Haslam. Haslam showed him to Blair's 'den', where Campbell and Blair would spend much of the next six years closeted together. Campbell said: 'Look Tony, I'm going to brief the lobby in a few minutes. Where are we on appointments? What spin do we want to put on today?' 'There is only one spin,' Blair replied. 'You spin that today is victory for New Labour.'[1]

Campbell was better prepared for Number 10 than he seemed. Knowing victory was almost certain, several weeks earlier he had sent his deputy Tim Allan to meet officials at Downing Street to discuss the hand over. And Campbell himself [2] went there a few days before polling day. He later admitted it had been a huge risk and that if the press had got wind of it, it would have led to claims of arrogance. Neil Kinnock had paid a heavy price in 1992, when, on the eve of the election, he got carried away with himself at a rally in Sheffield, provoking a backlash from the media and voters. It was a typical piece of chutzpah. There was to be plenty more to come, as Campbell set about imposing his own very personal style on Downing Street.

Once installed in his new office, he toured the building, introducing himself to the elite corps of civil servants who worked in Downing Street. Days after the election Campbell addressed Number 10's three private secretaries in their shared study, the PM's outer private office. These were the staff who worked most closely for the Prime Minister, advising him on home, economic and parliamentary affairs. All had worked for John Major, all had been picked out as Whitehall high flyers. It was the day before the first full meeting of Tony Blair's new Cabinet. The officials were gathered informally to discuss the seating plan proposed by Sir Robin Butler, the Cabinet Secretary, always a contentious issue since great symbolic significance attaches to the places allocated.

Campbell offered a different interpretation of putting ministers in their place. He wandered into the centre of the room and casually picked up a sheet of paper containing the 'place settings' for the ministers due to attend Cabinet the following day. 'Right, let's see what I can tell you about this lot,' he announced. He was taking the civil servants into his confidence, making them want to be part of his team. By being outrageously indiscreet he was inviting them, without quite saying as much, to join him in his conspiracy.

Campbell scanned the list. He paused, looked up, named two Cabinet ministers, both household names, and continued: 'Both of them have trouble keeping their trousers on.' He returned to the list and referred to a senior Cabinet minister who is still in the Cabinet in the spring of 2004, saying of him: 'Mmm, likes the women.' The officials looked at each other, unable to believe what they were hearing. Never in their lives had they come across behaviour like this in Number 10. Campbell glanced down again. 'Yes, Clare Short,' he observed. 'She has a colourful past.' Short had been reunited the previous year with her son, Toby, whom she had given up for adoption when she gave birth to him as an unmarried eighteen-year-old student. Next up were Derry Irvine, the Lord Chancellor, and Scottish Secretary Donald Dewar. Long ago, deep in the mists of time, Dewar's wife had left her husband for Irvine. There were stories that they were so glad to be part of the first Labour government for two decades that they had buried the hatchet. 'Forget the official line,' scoffed Campbell. 'They hate each other's guts.'

He dwelt briefly on Chancellor Gordon Brown, describing him as 'dedicated to his work', which prompted a stifled titter from one of the officials. He then turned to Brown's friend, ally and namesake Nick Brown, then chief whip. 'Nick Brown, ever the bachelor,' said Campbell, smirking. Eighteen months later Brown was to be 'outed' as gay by a former lover. Campbell picked up Foreign Secretary Robin Cook's place setting, holding it up for closer inspection. At that time Cook's adulterous affair with his secretary Gaynor Regan was still a closely guarded secret. 'Robin Cook,' he pondered aloud, before adding, 'he has interesting arrangements with his secretary.' Campbell's remarks did nothing to prevent Cook's secret gaining a wider currency in Whitehall. One of the shocked officials present, a senior civil servant, knew the wife of one of the ministers mocked by Campbell, and was upset. 'I don't believe what he said about ****. I know his wife and he is not the sort to do that kind of thing,' said the official.[3]

Campbell's reckless smearing of Tony Blair's Cabinet was only half the entertainment to be offered that day. He went on to circulate Downing Street staff a spoof version of the Queen's Speech, due to be delivered for real one week later. The first words Campbell put in the mouth of the Queen were as follows: 'Now look, I've been doing this job for a long time now, and frankly it really was time for a change and, boy, have we got it.' Though Campbell had clearly devoted some time to his parody, its level of humour was worthy of a student rag. It does, however, give an insight into the attitudes he was to take with him from Fleet Street into government: a boorish disrespect for the establishment, cynicism even about New Labour's policy objectives, a redeeming readiness to take liberties. The spoof mocked Labour's modest election manifesto: 'Frankly, the people are sick of my governments making grand promises they cannot keep, so my government doesn't intend to make any grand promises at all.'

Tony Blair was often to boast publicly that his programme for Scottish devolution was one of the legislative highlights of his first term of government. Campbell's mock Queen's Speech derided the Scots' 'dead duck' parliament: 'I wouldn't trust the Jocks as far as I could throw them.' Campbell, himself an Anglo-Scot, had always enjoyed an uncomfortable relationship with the Scottish press, which took a traditional Labour line and never concealed its unease with the Blairite agenda. Tony Blair was once overheard referring to Scottish journalists as 'unreconstructed wankers', a view fully shared by Campbell. Most revealing of all was the final line of the speech: 'My government is just hoping that if the style is a bit different, nobody will notice the Substance (Lack of) Bill.'

'We were taken aback by the outrageousness of his behaviour,' said one official who was present during Campbell's briefing on ministers' sexual peccadilloes and who was given a copy of the spoof Queen's Speech. 'But he may have had an ulterior motive. Perhaps he was saying to us, "I know you worked for John Major, but I trust you and you're going to enjoy working with us." It impressed on us from the beginning how powerful he was.'[4]

The day after Campbell issued his spoof Queen's Speech, Tony Blair acted to make sure that his trusted aide's centrality to the New Labour project in government was fully understood. The forum he chose to make this clear could not have been more symbolic: the first Labour

Cabinet meeting for eighteen years. Less than one minute into his opening remarks to the Cabinet on Thursday 8 May 1997, the Prime Minister was already lecturing ministers not on how the government would tackle health, education or crime, but on how it would tackle the press. To drive the point home Campbell himself was sitting silently at the back of the room.

Blair gave a talk on the perils of speaking out of turn to journalists. Well trained by Campbell, he drifted into the argot of news reporting with the unconscious ease of a seasoned editor. 'There's a sense of exuberance, but journalists are not friends,' said the Prime Minister. 'Stories are too easily generated. There's too much chatter. We need to move into a different *modus operandi*. The constitutional commission was leaked to the *Scotsman*. Cabinet committees must stay confidential. I will come down very hard on leaks,' he said accusingly.5 He moved on to the subject of special advisers, the political aides who advise Cabinet ministers and were to play a uniquely potent role for New Labour in government. 'They performed a very good service in opposition, but now we are in a very different position. I don't want to see them talking to the media now we are in government.'

Most important of all he laid the foundation stone for Alastair Campbell's authority over Cabinet ministers themselves. 'All media interviews should be cleared through this office at Number 10, otherwise newspapers will feed off this type of thing,' said the Prime Minister. This announcement was so strong, so emphatic and so surprising that some ministers sought to query it. International development secretary Clare Short, later to resign from the Cabinet on principle and already famous for her independence of mind, asked: 'Does that mean every little interview?' The Prime Minister came back: 'Yes.' Education secretary David Blunkett, one of the most publicity-conscious ministers, was worried about the practical implications of the policy: 'What about when you need to be in the studio within half an hour?' Blair replied: 'Just use common sense. You need to be aware of what's going on. It may not be sensible to do the interview. You need to know what has happened.' The next subject on the agenda was a proposal for ministers' pay rises. Again, Blair's primary concern was how this would play as a story in the media. 'The press are on to this but there's no easy way out,' he said.

This obsession with presentation rather than policy was to become a hallmark of the Tony Blair government. In the second New Labour Cabinet meeting on 15 May, Blair opened by repeating his warning that ministers were not to say or do anything in public without Campbell's permission: 'All press announcements must be cleared through Number 10,' he emphasized. By 29 May, before the government was a month old, the Prime Minister was showing his preoccupation with media criticism. 'I am worried about two kinds of story,' Blair declared. 'One that we can't handle it, and two, that we are arrogant and drunk with power. I have to say that of the two I prefer the latter. We have to tackle this issue and deal with it head on. We must meet these head on and not allow ourselves to be diverted. Bill Clinton said to me that the biggest mistake he made in his first two years was not communicating, that he was too busy governing. Any specific announcement should be linked to a clear message.' Ironically, the charge later made against Blair's first-term record was the opposite: it was that he and Campbell devoted too much attention to communication and not enough to governing.

In this Cabinet meeting Home Secretary Jack Straw gave the first of many Cabinet name checks to Campbell and Peter Mandelson. It is striking that he did not even feel the need to refer to their surnames. 'We must be ruthless about why the Tories lost, that they were incompetent and divided. We need to tell all the stories about it. Peter and Alastair will try all this out on focus groups,' he said. Foreign Secretary Cook entered into the spirit: 'The editor of the *Guardian* told me he was excited to live under a Labour government.'

When the Cabinet met on 12 June, Tony Blair for the first time invoked Campbell by name as a threat to any minister who talked out of turn. 'I am still getting reports of Cabinet committee meetings being leaked. Alastair has been alarmed to get complete read-outs from journalists.' There was an embarrassing moment when Harriet Harman said a report she read about a Cabinet meeting on the Millennium Dome was so comprehensive she assumed it had been authorized. 'It was absolutely not,' snapped Blair. The Downing Street obsession with stories and media handling returned on 17 July when an exasperated Blair told them: 'Junior ministers don't realize how big stories arise from an innocent briefing.' Straw, at this stage eager to ingratiate himself with Number 10, observed that 'lobby journalists deliberately target junior ministers'. Blair complained that the *Today* programme 'didn't help. Hospital waiting lists led the news. In opposition, it would hardly have been covered.' And, in an eerie forewarning of the furore that erupted four years later when Labour spin doctor Jo Moore said 11 September was 'a good day to bury bad news', Straw said: 'The tail must not wag the dog. We are riding high even among those who didn't vote for us. We can still clear the decks with bad news while it lasts.'

'What is the story on Monday?' Harriet Harman enquired obediently. She was beginning to get the hang of things. Blair and Campbell had been in office three months. The triumph of spin over substance – 'story development' over 'policy development' – was nearly complete.

chapter eight

Downing Street

A lot of the changes introduced by Campbell were long overdue.

Sir Christopher Meyer, John Major's press secretary

MANY SYMPATHETIC OBSERVERS thought that Campbell would never last as Tony Blair's Downing Street press secretary. There is all the difference in the world between doing the job in opposition and doing it in government. Opposition calls for opportunism, flair, brilliance, cheek: all qualities that Campbell was known to possess in abundance. Government calls for discretion, meticulous judgement, sobriety of approach, self-effacement. Nobody yet knew whether Campbell was capable of acquiring any of these qualities, but some of the evidence suggested that they were foreign to his nature. The job of a press secretary is to promote the interests of the prime minister, and keep himself well in the background. This too seemed an unlikely feat for him.

The doubters were proved wrong. Before entering Downing Street, Campbell had already earned the respect, though not the universal affection, of the press. Afterwards, he very quickly converted himself into a figure of huge and commanding authority in Whitehall. Officials soon came to value his massive capacity for hard work, the calibre of his decision-making and the fact that he so clearly spoke for the Prime Minister. They rubbed their eyes at the contrast with the dithering and indecision of the final stage of the Major epoch.

Campbell revolutionized the Downing Street media operation inherited by Sir Christopher Meyer when he became John Major's press secretary. 'On my first day I asked where I got the newspapers so I could brief the Prime Minister and was told I would have to make my own arrangements,' said Meyer. 'Luckily, the Indian gentleman who runs my local paper shop in Putney kindly agreed to arrange for his elderly father to deliver the morning papers to my home.' A lot of the changes introduced by Campbell were long overdue.

The punctilious adherence to the civil service's convention of impartiality under Major drove some of his own advisers to distraction. The Number 10 press office refused to draft a speech for him to mark a national newspaper's 'Policeman of the Year' award, arguing it was a political occasion. And the Treasury refused to contribute to a pamphlet promoting the benefits of privatization, arguing it was political, since the Tories had introduced privatization. There were to be no such scruples in Campbell's Downing Street press office.

The post of Downing Street press secretary

The post of press secretary was invented by Ramsay MacDonald upon taking power after the 1929 General Election. The incoming Labour prime minister, bruised by his fleeting experience of power five years earlier, felt that he needed professional advice about how to cope with an overwhelmingly hostile Tory press. He chose a Foreign Office official named George Steward. Over the following eleven years, Steward developed the basics of the job more or less as it existed when Campbell took over in 1997. The press secretary briefed lobby journalists twice a day. The first briefing took place at 11 a.m. in 10 Downing Street and a second at 4 p.m. in the lobby briefing room in the Commons. The press secretary had an office in Downing Street. He travelled with the prime minister on overseas trips and was constantly available to give guidance to accredited political journalists. A good press secretary had always been a source of huge strength to the incumbent at Downing Street. Successive prime ministers discovered that an effective press secretary could play a vital role in imposing their own version of events on Whitehall. That is a function, as successive prime ministers have also discovered, that can easily be abused.

John Major was too scrupulous a man to go along this road. He might have been better off if he had. Three press secretaries served him during his six-year term of office. Being John Major's press secretary was rather like being captain of the England cricket team of the same era: held up to ridicule and derision, batting on a losing wicket, doomed. Given the traumatic circumstances, all three of the men who devoted themselves to serving Major managed well. More surprisingly still, they all flourished afterwards. Gus O'Donnell, always popular with the press, was picked out by Gordon Brown as a high-flyer and went on to become permanent secretary at the Treasury. His successor, Sir Christopher Meyer, skilfully navigated through the horror and carnage of the Major years. He resembled a man in an immaculately cut suit making his way across a muddy and death-strewn battlefield, only to emerge both spotless and unscathed at the other end. Sir Christopher went on to serve as British ambassador in Washington, that most prized of all Foreign Office appointments, later returning to become chairman of the Press Complaints Commission. The third and final occupant of the post, Jonathan Haslam, later found a billet in the City. All three were career officials, whose final loyalty always lay with the civil service rather than with John Major. Strict civil service rules governed what they could and could not do on the prime minster's behalf. Tony Blair decided, long before he entered Downing Street, that this was a handicap that should never be imposed on Alastair Campbell.

Only two press secretaries in living memory bear any comparison with Campbell in 1997. They are, firstly, Joe Haines, who acted as press adviser and hatchet man to Harold Wilson, and secondly, Sir Bernard Ingham, who performed the identical function for Margaret Thatcher for the full eleven years of her famous premiership. Technically, Joe Haines was a Downing Street civil servant. In fact, the niceties of the job did not interest him. Like Campbell, he was a former lobby journalist and Labour partisan who believed that his only function was to serve and protect the prime minister. He did his best to convert the Downing Street press office into a political weapon for Harold Wilson: his first action on returning as press secretary after the Labour victory in the 1974 General Election was to sack half the Downing Street press staff. He used his position to become far more than a press officer. He advised on policy, wrote Wilson's speeches, was heavily drawn into ministerial appointments and even helped compose honours lists. Haines was a forerunner to Alastair Campbell in two ways. He showed how the job could be used explicitly to foster political ends. More striking still, he showed that the title itself could be used as a cover for anything at all if the possessor put his mind to it and that was what the prime minister wanted. Harold Wilson told Haines in his conspiratorial way: 'I'll call you press secretary because it sounds good and it helps conceal what you really do.'

Joe Haines has played a large part in Campbell's life. After the Wilson years, he ended up on the *Mirror*: it was Haines who, somewhat reluctantly, gave Campbell his first job as a lobby man. When Campbell went to work in Downing Street, Haines sent him some advice: 'The press secretary is not there to help the press. He is there to help the Prime Minister.'

But the biggest trailblazer for Campbell was not Haines. It was Sir Bernard Ingham, Margaret Thatcher's press secretary. Periodically, from his well-earned retirement, Sir Bernard takes a fierce relish in issuing thunderous denunciations of his successor for misusing the powers of his office. Since Sir Bernard was not whiter than white himself in this respect, these are typically greeted with wry smiles among those who saw him at work in Whitehall. But Sir Bernard was a towering figure in his day. Novelist and political commentator Robert Harris' biography of Ingham sets out how he used the lobby system to cut the ground from under the feet of ministers who had fallen out of favour. Francis Pym, one of Margaret Thatcher's foreign secretaries and John Biffen, Leader of the House, were two who got the Ingham treatment.

For Campbell's first formative five years in the lobby, until the ejection of Margaret Thatcher in 1990, Sir Bernard was the prime minister's press secretary. The two men had a great deal in common. Both were outsiders.

There is no question that Campbell studied Ingham with fascination, noting how the Yorkshireman used the powers of his office to deadly effect. At one stage Campbell even set about writing a novel with Sir Bernard as the central character. He was 50,000 words into the text when one day Fiona Millar pressed the wrong key and the document was obliterated.

Sir Bernard showed the way for Campbell, just as Margaret Thatcher showed the way for Tony Blair. Campbell shared Sir Bernard's appreciation of the tabloid press. Both men were fond of levelling the charge of triviality, distortion and fabrication at the press in general. Both made a point of exempting the *Sun* – conventionally held to be more guilty of these three practices than any other Fleet Street paper – from these grave criticisms. Both men bullied and blustered their way through lobby briefings. Neither bothered to conceal his dislike of journalists, though the trait is more pronounced in Campbell. Both have been utterly loyal, but it is probably fair to say that Ingham's loyalty was to his mistress alone. Campbell's goes beyond Tony Blair: he is deep at the heart of the New Labour project. Ingham, unlike Campbell, was rarely seriously accused by lobby men of distorting the truth.

There is one other, most important, difference between the two men. Ingham was an accident, Campbell was deliberate. When Margaret Thatcher became Prime Minister in 1979, the last thing on her mind was the appointment of her new press secretary. The appointment ranked so far down her list of priorities that she delegated the task to someone else. Sir Bernard was appointed on the basis of a ten-second interview. Had it lasted any longer, it is possible that he would not have got the job, for she would have discovered that in 1965 he stood as a Labour party candidate for Leeds City Council. More probably she would not have minded. In the opinion of Margaret Thatcher back in 1979, the post of press secretary was as unpolitical as it was unimportant. This was partly because she thought of civil servants as neutral. But it was mainly because, twenty years ago, the rise of the Media Class and the central problem it posed for government was not yet evident to senior politicians.

She very quickly discovered her mistake. By the end of her eleven-year term, Bernard Ingham and Charles Powell, her private secretary, were two of her most trusted and powerful advisers. When Tony Blair entered Downing Street seven years later, he was under no illusions whatever about the importance of his press secretary. He felt that the media now had the power to destroy, and to create, a prime minister or a party leader. For Blair, the identity of his press secretary was a matter of the highest importance. Sir Bernard Ingham came to carry great weight under Margaret Thatcher. But Alastair Campbell was to carry ten times more under Tony Blair. John Biffen, the recipient of the worst of Ingham's bile and poison, once remarked that his tormentor was the sewer but not the sewage. Campbell, to adapt that unpleasant metaphor, was both the sewer and the sewage. With Campbell, indeed, the job entered another dimension.

On arriving in office he was immediately handed a massive new power that no previous Downing Street press secretary had ever possessed. All previous occupants of the job had been civil servants. This meant that they were servants of the state, owing allegiance to the crown, prevented by strict civil service rules from getting involved in party politics. Sir Bernard Ingham, for instance, had to take a three-week holiday during general election campaigns. Tony Blair was determined to find a way around this for Campbell.

The obvious solution was to make Campbell a 'special adviser', one of the shadowy group of figures who are allowed into Whitehall to give ministers political advice. But this solution created a new problem: these special advisers, under civil service rules of impartiality, are never permitted to hold executive powers: they can be observers only.

Following long discussions with senior civil servants before the election, Campbell and Blair boldly cut the Gordian knot: they made Campbell and Chief of Staff Jonathan Powell both civil servants and special advisers. The solution gave Campbell the freedom to throw himself into politics, as well as the power to order civil servants around. It was unconstitutional, and it required a change in the law to allow it to happen. A meeting of the Privy Council was called within forty-eight hours of the election, and special Orders in Council were issued giving Alastair Campbell sweeping new powers and freedoms of a kind that no press secretary had ever enjoyed before.

The decision was taken after a rearguard action by Cabinet Secretary Sir Robin Butler. Butler feared the consequences of giving Campbell and Powell access to two areas of government that should be kept separate from political appointees at all costs: the intelligence services and the honours system. It was a prophetic warning. Campbell saw patrician Old Harrovian Butler as representing everything he disliked about Whitehall. Campbell got his way.

Campbell introduces himself to Whitehall

In opposition, Alastair Campbell and Peter Mandelson had pioneered by far the most sophisticated media machine in British political history. It was all too natural that, once they had won power, they should wish to import the expertise and ruthlessness of the pre-election Millbank office into government. They set about doing this at once. The two men invited the heads of information of every Whitehall department to a reception at Number 10 on Monday 5 May. It was a memorable occasion.

The directors of information of the government information service (GIS), who were Whitehall's interface with political journalists, some of whose traits they shared, poured themselves wine. Teetotal Campbell grasped his mug of tea; Peter Mandelson sipped a glass of hot water with a slice of lemon. Campbell and Mandelson had perfected their trade at Millbank, headquarters of the Labour election-fighting machine. During the three years leading up to the election the two men had revolutionized the information process, introducing rapid-rebuttal units and media-monitoring teams, staffed by fanatical youngsters dedicated to the Labour cause. Campbell and Mandelson breezed into the room. Mandelson sniffed the air, and observed the sober-suited forty- and fifty-year-old men and women, who would be responsible for taking over the task performed by the Millbank zealots, with a critical eye. 'I've clocked you all,' he declaimed loftily. The muffled sound of glasses being replaced on tables and cigarettes being stubbed out could be heard all around.

Campbell got straight to the point. 'We want to work with the system and we need your support to make sure that everything we do raises the game of the GIS. We have had a very successful operation in opposition and we intend to use the same techniques to ensure we get good coverage for government events and the government generally. We are going to take the initiative with the media announcing stories in a cycle determined by us.' One official recalled: 'He said that under Major we had been like, I forget which football team it was, Charlton Athletic or something, but under Blair we were going to be Manchester United.'

'How does parliament fit into all of this?' inquired one member of the audience. Campbell answered: 'We will make announcements when and where and how we think it is appropriate.' It was left to Steve Reardon, the most experienced of all the assembled directors of information present, to mount the case for the defence. Reardon recalled: 'I said we were a very good team and knew how to do our job. Alastair Campbell clearly thought that might be a threat, and that it meant we were mates and regarded ourselves as a unit. I think I signed a dozen death warrants that day. Within hours of the new ministers arriving in departments, we were having to say, "hang on, that is a political message, we can't put it out". They thought we were being bloody minded. Press releases were having huge chunks of the Labour manifesto written into them by special advisers.'[1]

After Reardon fell out with his own secretary of state, Harriet Harman, for opposing Labour 'spin', he was summoned by social security department permanent secretary Anne Bowtell. 'She said she couldn't go on being called every morning by Harriet Harman bellyaching about something the press office had or hadn't done. If I didn't clear out various press officers then it would be my head on the block. I refused to point the finger at anybody to protect my own position. She said, "I'm afraid we've reached the end of the line." There were tears in her eyes.' Reardon was one of the seventeen out of nineteen directors of communication inherited by New Labour who left within two years of the 1997 election.

Campbell set out his rules for the GIS in a confidential letter to all heads of information on 26 September 1997. By now, he had had a chance to see how they operated. He was not impressed. 'There are several areas which need to be addressed,' he wrote. 'Media handling needs to be built into the decision making process at the earliest stage. We need to be in there at the start. I often get the impression that events happen and the mentality surrounding them is one of damage limitation. Big positive announcements are not getting as good a show as they should.'

He laid down his formula for getting maximum publicity out of every announcement. 'There are three parts to any story – the build up, the event and the follow through. There is insufficient attention to advance publicity – the briefing of editors, feature writers and others before and after. Departments must come up with ideas for "the

Sundays".'[2] He rounded off with another rallying cry to civil servants to take a new aggressive pro-active stance. 'We should always be ahead of the game. We should always know how big stories will be playing in the next day's papers. This requires a combination of judgement and telephone legwork, but it is a vital early warning system. Defend your headlines. Sell your story, and if you disagree with what is being written, argue your case.' There was no need to hold a press conference to mark all major parliamentary announcements, as had traditionally been the case in the past, said Campbell. Here was a forewarning of his later battles with Speaker Betty Boothroyd as the Commons was by-passed in favour of other more media-friendly ways of getting New Labour's message across.

One of Campbell's earliest tabloid public-relations coups in Number 10 came at Blair's first EU summit in Amsterdam in June 1997. The Dutch hosts had arranged for the leaders to take part in a 400-metre bicycle race. Campbell asked a Foreign Office aide: 'Do you think Tony should do this bike race?' 'The whole thing sounds very risky,' replied the aide. 'What if he falls off? It'll be a shambles.' The German Chancellor, the overweight and ageing Helmut Kohl, obviously had similar worries. He walked the 400 metres. Campbell told Blair to take part. Blair not only avoided falling off, he came first, prompting the *Sun* headline: 'Tony shows EU fatties a clean pair of wheels.'

Campbell had made it clear how he intended to govern. He would only work with people who would do business with him. He was impatient with the proprieties, decencies and neutrality of the old civil service. He wanted to turn government into an election-fighting machine. They had never seen anything like Campbell before. In those first few weeks in office he displayed many, though by no means all, of the qualities that would come to dominate Downing Street: an overwhelming arrogance, complete impatience with form and protocol, a conspiratorial charm, barbarism, and an utter contempt for what he saw as an old-fashioned British establishment.

Freedom of Information

Campbell's predecessor as Number 10 press secretary, Jonathan Haslam, said: 'There had to be changes in GIS, but Campbell's "divide and rule" style of manipulating the press could only work for so long. You can buy favour after favour after favour but all you are doing is building up resentment among the people who don't get any favours. He turned government information into a saleable commodity.'3 Campbell viewed government information as a commodity to be traded and doled out parsimoniously if at all. It could be used to damage opponents or to support a political case. It could be released as a reward to cooperative journalists and newspapers, above all those from the News International Group. Or it could be withheld as a punishment. He emphatically did not regard it as a neutral, value-free good to which any citizen could enjoy ready access.

It was a ruthless, clear-sighted attitude, which distinguished him sharply from traditional information chiefs. But two problems stood in the way of any rigorous implementation of Campbell's strategy. First, Labour in opposition had accused the Tory government of being obsessive about state secrecy. Labour's 1997 election manifesto pledged to introduce a freedom of information act to force the establishment to let the people know what was being done in their name.

The second problem was human. David Clark, the Cabinet minister given the task of getting any freedom of information bill onto the statute book, was a passionate, committed supporter. Unhappily for Clark, his deputy – in name at any rate – was Peter Mandelson, who shared many of Campbell's qualms about freedom of information. Between them, Mandelson and Campbell set out to wreck the bill – and to destroy the Cabinet minister responsible.

Not long after the election victory, Campbell addressed the 'top management forum', a group of senior civil servants at the Civil Service College in Victoria, London. 'A freedom of information bill is a bad idea and will not work for this government,' he told them. 'It is totally crazy and people who support it are naive. I make no secret of the fact that I do not like it and have no intention of allowing it to be introduced by this administration. How on earth can you conduct effective government if you go round telling people what you are going to do. It is a total nonsense. I know some people in this government want to do it, but I am not one of them.'

At the time he delivered the words, the government's official position was that it was still committed to introducing a far-reaching freedom of information bill. Downing Street could hardly announce baldly that they were doing a U-turn on their manifesto pledge. They found a more effective means. A smear campaign was organized to undermine Clark.

Many ministers in the Blair government believe they have been subject to smear campaigns organized from within Downing Street. The case of David Clark is special. The smears can be traced, and it is easy to prove that they originated within Downing Street.

In October 1997 Paul Linford, political editor of the *Newcastle Journal*, asked a routine question about a cabinet reshuffle. He was astonished by the reply from a Downing Street press officer: 'The one most likely to go is David Clark. He is considered totally to have lost it.'[4]

There is interesting extra evidence that Downing Street smeared Clark in the shape of testimony from the former Labour deputy leader Lord Hattersley. He told the journalist Linda McDougall how, shortly after the 1997 election, 'I was writing a profile of a beleaguered cabinet minister. His friends said he was being given a very hard time by the Downing Street machine and could I do anything to help him. I admired him. I wrote a profile of him for the *Observer*. There was one small fact about his career that I wanted to check so I phoned the Downing Street press office. They confirmed the fact. Ten minutes later they phoned me back and said: "we hear you are writing a profile of this man. Well, it's only fair to tell you that he is a very bad minister, he doesn't get on with his civil servants, his junior ministers are rebelling against him." So there was the press office gratuitously briefing me about the inadequacies of a man who was still in the cabinet and was sacked, I think, three weeks later. I have never known Downing Street to behave in that way before and it seems to me entirely disreputable.'

Two months later Campbell told Hattersley: 'It didn't happen. Pure invention. You are imagining it.'[5] Hattersley added the denial was uttered 'in a dismissive, slightly jokey way'.

The government maintained it was determined to introduce a freedom of information act. But everything it did stalled the bill and watered down its provisions. When Home Secretary Jack Straw finally produced some plans in 1999, they were so tame that many civil liberties campaigners said they were close to worthless. Cabinet records, legal advice to ministers and correspondence between them were omitted, as were the secret services and the National Criminal Intelligence Service. And crucially, the government and public bodies could block the disclosure of anything that might cause 'prejudice'.

Getting the upper hand

It was soon clear that Campbell had an astonishing power to impose his own will on Whitehall, and to override Cabinet ministers. There was only one reason why he was able to exercise this kind of control: he spoke for the Prime Minister. Anyone who observed Campbell together with the Prime Minister instantly got the message. The two men were on terms of complete equality. From their early days together, Campbell did not think twice about talking down to Blair.

Mike Maloney, a *Mirror* photographer, went round to the Blairs' Islington home to take some portrait shots. Campbell was there to mind the event, but was called to the phone. When he returned he discovered that the *Mirror* man had prevailed upon Tony and Cherie Blair to rub their noses together, Eskimo-fashion. Campbell went mad. 'You prat!' he stormed at Blair. 'What are you doing? Maloney is the original baby-faced assassin.'[6]

Campbell would go into a room where Tony Blair is talking to businessmen or party officials and stroll up to him with elaborate casualness. 'Come on, we're off,' Campbell would say and Tony Blair would spring to attention. Campbell did not hesitate to put Blair down in meetings. Once, in front of Stuart Higgins, editor of the *Sun*, he contradicted Tony Blair three times on a sensitive issue of party policy. There was no formality about it, no courtesy, no deference: merely a brusque finality. Officials were surprised by the extent to which Blair relied on Campbell. During a discussion on Princess Diana's campaign to ban land mines, Blair stopped short a meeting to announce: 'Wait, I need to speak to Alastair before going any further.' They had to wait until Campbell could be found.[7]

Once, after a long day of talks at Hillsborough Castle, the Northern Ireland Secretary's official home, Blair wanted to go to a local pub, a couple of hundred yards away in the adjoining village of Hillsborough, for a drink. 'I fancy a beer,' said Blair to one of his officials. 'Let's go over the road to the pub, shall we?' The two were about to leave until a voice intervened. 'You aren't seriously going drinking?' It was Campbell's. Blair looked at him blankly. 'You must be joking,' said Campbell, 'we're all staying here.' Blair looked at the official. The embarrassed official looked back. They put their coats away. But not everyone went to bed. Half an hour after Campbell stopped Blair going to the pub for a quiet drink, some of those who had retired for the night were woken up by a racket coming from the main sitting room downstairs. Campbell was playing the bagpipes.

Political reporters got a privileged view of the intimate Campbell/Blair relationship. Sometimes, at receptions, they could be seen giggling together like a pair of schoolboys. They acquired each other's mannerisms. If you watch the pair together closely, you can sometimes see the identical look of exasperation appear on each of their faces at the same moment. 'They do it independently, without looking at one another. They spend so much time in each other's company that they know exactly what the other is thinking automatically,' said one close friend of both men. Campbell was ubiquitous. His presence in the world of the Blairs clearly made an impact on young Leo Blair, who would crawl around the floor while Alastair advised his father.

A group of officials were once at a meeting with Tony Blair. Leo looked up at one of them, who had Campbell's build, and said 'Alastair'. It was the first time any of the officials had heard the child speak. Blair spent so much time talking to Campbell, much of it while bouncing Leo on his knee in the Prime Minister's study, that 'Alastair' was one of the first words he mastered.

On trips abroad, when Blair and Campbell came back to the press pack to talk, there was never any question that Campbell was the dominant partner. On a prime-ministerial trip to Washington in the spring of 1999, Campbell was briefing journalists in the cavernous jet which had been provided by British Airways. The plane was empty, apart from the small group of officials travelling with Tony Blair and the score or so of journalists. Take-off had been quite frightening: the plane was so underweight that it seemed to project itself vertically upwards after leaving the runway at Heathrow. Not long into the flight, Alastair Campbell addressed the journalists who gathered round to hear what he was saying. Ten minutes later the Prime Minister himself arrived to join them. No one moved to greet him, as all ears were strained to take in what Campbell was saying. Tony Blair stood alone, an isolated figure in the empty plane. Then he quipped: 'Don't mind me: I'm just the press secretary.'[8]

On a flight back to London after talks with George Bush in Washington in the wake of 11 September, Campbell spotted Blair talking to two journalists, and wondered out loud if he 'didn't have anything better to do?' Campbell continued, his feet on the table in front of him: 'Any prime minister who has more than twenty minutes to talk to the media clearly isn't doing his job properly.' 'If it was meant as a joke, Blair did not appear to see the funny side. His face froze and the reporters looked away in embarrassment. Campbell established this semi-public superiority over the Prime Minister from the very first. Not long after Blair became party leader, he went on a trip to Paris. The press came with him, eager to monitor the new Labour leader in action. They travelled on Eurostar and halfway through the three-hour journey Blair and Campbell went to the bar area to meet the travelling lobby journalists. The Leader of the Opposition batted all hard questions in the direction of his press officer, not even making a pretence of answering them himself.

During a regional visit to Worcester shortly after becoming Prime Minister, Blair was accompanied by BBC political reporter Jon Sopel, later his biographer. Campbell had already briefed Sopel that Blair intended to outline new laws whereby young hooligans who kicked in people's front doors would have to repair them. When Sopel joined Blair for breakfast on the train and said: 'I am interested in this idea you have about making young tearaways repair the damage they cause,' Blair looked at him blankly. Campbell chipped in: 'I haven't told him what the speech is about yet.' This master/servant became so pronounced that the Prime Minister and his press secretary took to hamming up the relationship like a couple of mates, which they were.

Broadcasters got an even more astonishing insight into Tony Blair's outright dependency upon his press adviser. The phenomenon was evident to a grotesque extent when Jeremy Paxman interviewed Tony Blair on BBC2's Newsnight in May 2002. Less than a minute into the interview Campbell interrupted Blair during his answer to a question on

Afghanistan. A chronically embarrassing scene followed in which Campbell humiliated the Prime Minister. As Tony Blair boasted to Paxman how one third of Afghanistan's poppy crop had been destroyed since the downfall of the Taliban, an off-screen grunt could be heard coming from Blair's right, where Campbell was sitting in the shadows. Blair looked anxiously towards him: 'Sorry?' Campbell shouted back: 'Fifth.' Blair looked uncomprehending. 'Fifth of the poppy crop,' went on Campbell. Paxman asked Blair if he wants to start the interview again. Blair glanced at Campbell before replying: 'Right … sorry, yeah … sure. OK. If they say it's a fifth, it's a fifth.' Then he said quietly to Paxman: 'It's not what my briefing notes said, but anyway … ' Paxman, clearly irritated, twiddled his glasses before telling Campbell: I don't think we can really stop again, Alastair.' Campbell grunted: 'No.' Blair chipped in: 'No … er, quite.' Blair embarked on the topic of the poppy crop again, this time using Campbell's figures. The BBC cut this extraordinary interjection from the broadcast to spare Blair's blushes.

During another of Blair's interviews with Paxman, the PM brought his son, Euan. While Paxman interrogated Blair, Campbell and Euan sat facing the broadcaster and passed the time by jotting down scores depending on who they thought was winning the debate.

One well-known journalist, who has interviewed the Prime Minister on a number of occasions, said: 'It is quite uncanny. You are interviewing two people. Alastair will sit on the other side of the table, writing notes and handing them across. Blair gets incredibly nervous on these occasions. If the Prime Minister shows signs of getting lost Campbell is quite capable of stepping in and giving him the line.' Joy Johnson, who worked with Campbell in the Labour media team before the election, describes Campbell's awesome influence thus: 'When you heard Bernard Ingham speaking, you heard Margaret Thatcher and when you heard Margaret Thatcher speaking you heard Margaret Thatcher. When you heard Tony Blair, very often you heard Alastair Campbell.'

For television interviews, Campbell made sure that he became an invisible third participant. He was skilled at placing himself within the interviewer's line of vision and making signs such as tapping his watch. As one well-known broadcaster put it, 'It's very hard to tell who's the boss. When they are together it's impossible to say.' Campbell's role was so dominant that some broadcasters cannot resist mocking it.

Once, Campbell and Blair were sitting in the BBC 'green room', the reception area where studio guests wait to go on air. John Humphrys, the *Today* programme and *On the Record* presenter, went into the room to greet the pair. He deliberately walked straight past the Prime Minister and held out his hand with a 'Good of you to come, Alastair'. Then he turned round and, in mock surprise, greeted Tony Blair, who by then was looking somewhat perplexed.[9]

Campbell remained in control from start to finish. After one visit to the television studios, Blair lingered behind, chatting to a couple of journalists. Suddenly the door opened with a flurry. It was Campbell. 'Come on, Tony,' he shouted. 'We're off. Get a fucking move on.'

Campbell would tease Blair in front of Downing Street guests. He ribbed him about having to miss a party hosted by Rupert Murdoch in London owing to an EU summit. As Blair's disappointment registered, Campbell grinned: 'Don't worry, I'm not going to the summit, so I'll be able to go to Rupert's for you.' Blair looked decidedly put out. On another occasion, when Campbell grumbled about Gordon Brown in front of newspaper executives visiting Downing Street, Blair brought him up short: 'That's enough of that.'

Campbell was always happy privately to make his views known when he disagreed with Tony Blair, or thought he had been weak. For instance, he blamed the Prime Minister as much as Gordon Brown for the government's failure to make a decision on the euro. 'Alastair told the PM in no uncertain terms that it was his job to knock heads together, i.e., get Gordon to toe the line,' says one Downing Street insider. 'But he wouldn't do it, Alastair said it was Tony's fault.'

There have been some extraordinary relationships at the heart of Downing Street, but none as extraordinary as this one. It answered the deepest need in each man's character. As Tony Blair's biographers have shown, the Prime Minister has always sought out gurus to guide him through life's intractable complexities. At different times that role has been played by Peter Thomson, the priest he met at Oxford, by Derry Irvine, his head of chambers, by Gordon Brown and by Peter Mandelson. But the person he relied on most, his rock of strength in Downing Street, was Campbell. And Campbell, too, got what he had searched for all through his life. He had always wanted a relationship of privileged intimacy with the most powerful member of whatever organization he has joined. Now he had the **ultimate**: he was on intimate terms with the man who was running the country. And he did a superb job for a long time. He gave first-class advice. He was always by the Prime Minister's side. On overseas trips, long after Tony Blair had fallen asleep, Campbell was still awake beside him, dealing with calls, preparing the following day's business, making sure they were not caught unawares. When asked once how he does it, he replied: 'I don't drink and I don't smoke.' His judgement was never clouded by that half-bottle of wine over lunch. He never woke up bleary, hungover, unable to cope. He woke up ready for action and ready for the problems of the coming day.

Campbell and Blair are often referred to as alpha males. One individual who knows them both very well, offers an alternative view. 'Campbell is alpha male, Blair is beta male. Blair is like a tropical plant. He needs two or three sturdy plants around which to grow. Campbell was the sturdiest.'[10]

A hurried affair

Campbell's role as the formal link between the government and newspaper editors gave him a frightening hold over ministers when their private lives entered the public domain. Labour had been in power for only three months when Campbell had to deal with his first ministerial sex scandal. Campbell had turned Tory 'sleaze' into a double hit by using it to characterize the Conservatives as corrupt and by castigating John Major for trying to hang on to ministers caught with their trousers down or their hands in the till. He once said: 'We decided early on that we are not going to let the media decide who is and who isn't in the cabinet.'[11] Campbell was determined to show that Blair would never be accused of dithering over ministerial scandals. To achieve this aim he was prepared to be utterly ruthless to anyone whose names were plastered across tabloid newspapers. Campbell had had plenty of time to prepare for the exposure of Robin Cook's affair with his secretary, Gaynor Regan. He had known about it since before the general election and had been terrified of the damage it would cause if it had been revealed during the campaign. Once Labour's victory was in the bag, Campbell did not seem overly concerned about Cook's private affairs becoming more widely known. He alluded to it in his briefing to shocked officials days after entering Downing Street.

When Campbell discovered Cook's affair was about to be splashed all across the *News of the World*, he finally had a chance to test his skills at dealing with a sex scandal for real.[12] What followed was extraordinary. Having tracked down Cook at Heathrow airport with his wife Margaret, about to depart for a holiday in the US to save their marriage, Campbell told him: 'You're in the shit,' before adding, 'but I can buy you a few hours.'[13] Campbell did the first of a number of 'deals' with tabloid newspapers, whereby he would negotiate the terms of what they would publish, in return for the minister doing as Campbell instructed to minimize the damage to the government and stop the story running for days or weeks, as had happened under the Tories. The *News of the World* would leave Cook, his wife and mistress alone, in return for a statement. Campbell told Cook that 'clarity in news management' was the only way to stop the story from getting out of hand. Cook rightly took this to mean that he must rapidly choose between his wife and his mistress. He chose his mistress. Campbell's technique was half way between that of a traditional press secretary and that of the celebrated publicist Max Clifford. Even more remarkable, although Cook was humiliated both by the exposé and by Campbell's peremptory treatment of him, he showed no bitterness. Instead he seemed relieved that someone had forced him to make a decision on a matter that he had agonized over for months.

But Campbell was not satisfied. Getting Cook to leave his wife for his mistress was one thing. Now he sought to get it out of the headlines as soon as possible. On the same day that the *News of the World* were exposing Cook, the *Sunday Times* carried a sensational front-page story alleging that the former Governor of Hong Kong, Chris Patten, faced possible prosecution under the Official Secrets Act over material in a book about him by his friend, broadcaster Jonathan Dimbleby. The allegation later turned out to be groundless and the story fizzled out. The reason that it made front-page news was because Downing Street confirmed it. According to a source on the paper: 'Campbell stood it up.'[14] Elsewhere, there were government-inspired reports that Labour might save the royal yacht *Britannia* after all. That was untrue too.

The job of keeping the diversionary tactics going on the following day, Sunday, fell to Peter Mandelson who offered himself for interview of Radio 4's *The World This Weekend*. Reporter Jon Sopel asked him about the Patten story and Mandelson duly confirmed it.

Labour's tactics were exposed. On Monday morning, BBC *World At One* editor Kevin Marsh received an unexpected call from Tim Allan who asked: 'Anything we can help you with?' Marsh told him that *World at One* was 'looking at this string of odd stories kicking around'.

Allan: 'Such as?'

Marsh: 'The royal yacht?'

Allan: 'Not a word of truth in it.'

Marsh: 'The Patten story?'

Allan: 'If you knew where that had come from you'd know there's no truth in that either.'

Marsh persuaded Sopel to confirm on air that he had been approached by a 'senior Labour spin doctor' who had suggested raising the Patten issue with him because they were worried how the Cook story would run. Sopel said it was 'all rather unusual'. New Labour's barrage balloon was shot down. Spinning scandals wasn't quite as easy in government as from the comfort of the opposition benches.

Now Downing Street turned on the BBC. And two days later, during an interview by Martha Kearney on *World at One*, Mandelson launched a vitriolic attack on her for ignoring the government's important achievements. It backfired spectacularly, overshadowing the anniversary of Labour's first hundred days in office and prompting the first major controversy over New Labour spin-doctoring.

Helping out Nick Brown

A much more formidable test of Campbell's crisis-management methods came the following year, during a strange period in 1998, when three gay ministers were 'outed' in the space of two weeks.

The first victim was Welsh Secretary Ron Davies, who was involved in a bizarre incident on Clapham Common. Early in the morning of 27 October, Home Secretary Jack Straw was contacted by police who informed him of Davies' indiscretion. Initially, Campbell defended Davies, but when it was decided he must go, he acted with clinical swiftness. So keen was Campbell to control events that he persuaded

Davies to announce his resignation before the press had got wind of it. It was almost as though he took pride in beating Fleet Street at its own game. A non-plussed TV crew were summoned to Number 10 to interview Davies without even knowing what they were there for. When the TV camera caught a glimpse of Campbell lurking over Davies' shoulder, Campbell dived to one side, eager not to be revealed as the ringmaster. He had even composed Davies' resignation letter for him, an episode rich with insight into Campbell's irregular method of doing business. He read out the letter, allegedly composed by Davies, to a reporter. As he was doing so, the journalist interrupted him: 'That doesn't read very well.' Campbell incorporated the reporter's suggestions in the final version.

Once again, he had over-reached himself. He thought that by rushing Davies into resigning as Welsh Secretary, he could close down the story. He had forgotten Davies had another post, that of leader of the Welsh Labour party. And it was an elected post. Neither Blair nor Campbell could sack him from that. Davies was despatched to a 'safe house' in Wales where a Labour aide spent the next 48 hours trying to persuade him to resign. Campbell kept ringing up to see if Davies had buckled. Eventually he did.

When Davies recovered from the shock, he vented his anger at the way Campbell dealt with him, and especially for writing his resignation letter. 'It wasn't until weeks later that I even read the bloody thing. It was written by Alastair Campbell and officials in my press office. I just thought "sign it and it will go away". It dawned on me after a few weeks. I handled it badly and Number 10 handled it badly.'[15]

The Davies resignation set off a chain of events. Within hours, political writer Matthew Parris blurted out on television what the whole of Westminster had known for years: Peter Mandelson was gay. This non-story did not matter too much in itself. But the outing of two cabinet ministers in two days stimulated the News of the World to rummage around in its files. One gay cabinet minister had been forced to resign: perhaps another one would have to go. If so, the News of the World could claim the credit.

It had an ancient file on Agriculture Minister Nick Brown, a close ally of Chancellor Gordon Brown and therefore treated with deep suspicion by Downing Street. Nick Brown was accused of starting a major row between Blair and Brown earlier in the year when it emerged that he was the main source of a biography of the Chancellor that was deeply critical of Blair. Blair, backed by Campbell, responded by moving him from Chief Whip to Agriculture Minister. It was common knowledge in Labour circles that Nick Brown was gay and, like most other politicians, he regarded his sexuality as a private matter. The *News of the World* had investigated Brown's private life before the election and obtained a tape recording of him talking to a former male lover. But it did not contain the evidence needed to publish a story alleging he had paid rent boys, and the tape had been gathering dust in a cupboard ever since. The paper had no new evidence, but decided to confront Brown with the allegations in any case after the Davies affair. As far as can be judged, the paper was on a fishing expedition.

An alarmed Nick Brown immediately contacted Campbell and talked through the story. At this stage, the *News of the World* had no intention of running a story, because it had no proof Brown was gay, let alone had paid for gay sex. That changed after a conversation between editor Phil Hall and Campbell during which Campbell gave the paper a lengthy statement by Brown about his sex life and his relationship with the former lover who had made the allegations against him.

In it, Brown said: 'This was a relationship based on friendship and not simply sex which ended well before the election. I deny totally that I paid money for sex. I have never done so.'[16]

It was a substantial coup for the *News of the World*. They were able to run a story which was destined for the 'spike' on the front page by printing the minister's confirmation that he had had a gay affair and his denial that he had paid for sex. The paper went on to refer to 'fanciful allegations about gay sex encounters with the 48 year old minister which Mr Brown totally denies and which the *News of the World* has been unable to substantiate in any way'.

Hall made no bones about how the story had been obtained: 'The *News of the World* approached No 10 Downing Street after a young man gave us an unsubstantiated account of a relationship with Nick Brown. Mr Brown then volunteered a statement to the *News of the World* which we have published in full.'[17]

One *News of the World* executive privately put it more bluntly: 'Phil said that Number 10 said it was OK to go ahead.'[18] Hall reacted angrily when he was attacked for publishing the story. He said the *News of the World* would not have run it had it not been for Brown's statement. The *Guardian* suggested there had been a 'trade off between Hall and Campbell ... which led to the public statement in which Brown confessed to being gay'.[19] According to some sources, the 'deal' was that the paper would hold back more damaging allegations about Brown in return for confirmation that he was gay. And yet, by its own admission, the *News of the World* had been unable to substantiate these allegations. The *News of the World* was not the only Sunday paper to run the story that day. Downing Street helpfully made Brown's statement available to the rest of the press during the evening of 7 November, allowing them to print it in later editions. Brown kept his job, but had been humiliated.

According to one of Brown's friends who had a drink with him in Westminster's Marquis of Granby pub a few weeks later, Brown said: 'Those c**ts in Downing Street stitched me up. They told the *News of the World* "Go on, publish it." '

Charlie Whelan, a close friend of Nick Brown, said: 'Nick was tricked. Number 10 wanted to do him in. They made him say far more than he needed to.'[20] But that was not quite the end of Fleet Street's gay feeding frenzy. The following day, the *Sun* printed an astonishing article suggesting Britain was run by a 'gay mafia', at least partly in an attempt to cash in on the series of revelations about gay ministers. (The *Sun*'s owner, Rupert Murdoch, had what one colleague described as 'an old-fashioned red-blooded Aussie' approach to homosexuality. During a dinner with News International executives at J Sheekey's restaurant in London, Murdoch once commented: 'The trouble with Blair is that he spend too much listening to that poof Mandelson.')

The *Sun* article provoked howls of outrage from the mainstream liberal opinion, but once again, Campbell went out on a limb to defend News International. The paper's front page headline the following day proclaimed: 'Blair Backs the Sun Over Gays' and quoted a Downing Street spokesman as saying: 'The papers have treated the Nick Browneissue with sympathy and understanding. It was perfectly fair.'[21] However, it appeared to have gone too far, even for Campbell. Editor David Yelland said Campbell 'went nuts' with him.[23] The backlash forced the *Sun* to promise not to 'out' homosexual politicians in future.

New Labour in power

Few prime ministers have thought so carefully about how they would govern as did Tony Blair before he entered Downing Street. Few prime ministers have had the time. John Major was suddenly propelled into a situation he never anticipated. Harold Wilson was given just months to prepare for the 1964 election after Hugh Gaitskell's death the previous year. Jim Callaghan was too busy clinging to office. Sir Alec Douglas-Home and Harold Macmillan, as true Tories, both regarded thinking about the matter as an unprofitable and faintly disreputable activity.

Only one other post-war prime minister brooded about government as much as Tony Blair and that was Margaret Thatcher. She had four years to do so, between being elected leader of the Tory party in 1975 and becoming prime minister in 1979. In the intervening period, she thought about policy, while Blair, in his three years of opposition, thought about process. She thought about 'what'; Blair thought about 'how'. She thought about content, while Blair contemplated form. It was Blair's special perception that, in a country with few real grievances, a large part of politics is about presentation and the articulation of mood. Thatcher changed Britain profoundly. But she left the British state much as it was. Blair's principal legacy will be the imposition of the most revolutionary set of changes in how Britain is governed since the Glorious Revolution of 1688. He also – and this is a curious thing – wants to change the kind of people we are. Tony Blair and those close to him think that the British people are too grim, pessimistic, drab and sour – in a word, too British. They want to turn Britain into a different country and the British into a different people, with a new set of institutions and a different morality. It is all very ambitious, very complicated, very strange, and, in its way, admirable.

New Labour is hostile to tradition, class, existing institutions, history. This hostility is based on three things: ignorance, hope and, ironically enough, New Labour's own tormented past. New Labour had a gruesome birth, out of the corpse of the Labour party of Keir Hardie, Aneurin Bevan, Clement Attlee and John Smith. The ghosts linger on, and still from time to time their rattling chains must surely disturb the slumbers of Tony Blair. New Labour established itself by turning on its past, on the once-omnipotent National Executive Committee, the trade

unions, the Clause 4 commitment to the nationalization of the means
of production, the singing of the Red Flag at the end of the Labour conference every autumn. Most of all, of course, it has grown to vigorous
life thanks to an act of pure parricide: the murder of the Labour party,
with – as we have seen – Alastair Campbell and Peter Mandelson
playing the parts of first and second assassins. New Labour wishes that
the Labour party had never existed. It thinks, much more strongly than
the Tories, that Labour was all a terrible mistake. Philip Gould, in his
important work *The Unfinished Revolution* (1998), explains this hypoth-
esis at considerable length. 'In establishing itself as a socialist party
immutably linked to trade unionism, Labour broke with Liberalism and
cut itself off from the other great radical movement in British politics,'
mourns Gould. 'The separation of Labourism and Liberalism stopped
dead the possibility of building one united progressive party, similar to
the broader coalitions in the United States and Scandinavia.' Gould and
Blair blame the Labour party for making the twentieth century a Tory
century.

In opposition, Tony Blair turned upon the venerable institutions of
the Labour party. In government, he has turned on the venerable institutions of the British state – the House of Lords, the representation of
the hereditary peerage. Members of the Wilson Cabinet did business
together at Brooks and spent weekends at grand country houses. With
the splendiferous exception of Peter Mandelson – who in his pomp was
sometimes styled Tony Blair's 'ambassador to the upper classes' – the
new government has no time for that sort of thing.

Clubland and the House of Lords were obvious targets. But it soon
became apparent that the peaceful revolution Tony Blair had in mind
went very much further. It became clear that he had no appetite for the
institutions of constitutional democracy which have sustained British
government for the last three hundred years. His contempt for the
House of Commons, for its irritating insistence on discussion and
debate, for the way that it demeaned the authority of the prime minister
by opening him up to criticism and public question, was immediately
obvious. Luckily, thanks to Labour's landslide majority, the new
government has not needed to worry too much about the Commons.
The Prime Minister goes there as rarely as possible. His voting record
is the lowest, by far, of any prime minister since the office took modern

form in the early eighteenth century. Blair attends just five per cent, or one in twenty, of all votes held in the Commons. Even Thatcher, in all her pomp, voted six times as often as Blair.

It is a sign of the degradation of the Commons under New Labour that the office of chief whip, which until 1997 was one of the most feared and powerful in both Labour and Tory governments, has degenerated into a middle-ranking post of no especial importance. It has entirely lost the very substantial mystique that it used to possess. The decline of the chief whip under Blair has been attributed by some to the size of his parliamentary majority, but does not take account of Campbell's usurping the chief whip's mantle. Not one of the tiny clique of advisers huddled around Tony Blair is a parliamentarian. One very senior official close to Downing Street says: 'Basically, in Number 10 Downing Street there is a complete contempt for parliament and that attitude permeates the whole government.'

Most telling of all was the complete eclipse of the Cabinet system. Tony Blair frequently did not attend, and when he did, the show rarely lasted more than forty-five minutes. It remained the case that matters of importance were discussed, but both the quantity and the quality of the discussion about these important matters were negligible. A sign of the tributary status to which Cabinet was condemned was the fact that Alastair Campbell now sat in on its meetings, the first time that a press secretary had been permitted to do so as a matter of course. Decisions were made elsewhere. The impoverishment of the Cabinet was an outward symbol of the way power had been taken out of the hands of elected ministers of the Crown, and pulled towards the Downing Street machine. Once the glory of the British system of government, the Cabinet had been converted into a formal and ornamental part of the British constitution. It had suffered the fate of the Privy Council, which fell into disuse three hundred years ago but maintains a shadowy and inconsequential existence to this day.

The power that had drained from parliament, from ministers, from the Cabinet and other traditional institutions of state has had to go somewhere. It has been amassed instead, in part, by the Media Class which has gained in power and authority at the expense, chiefly, of parliament. But the greater part was seized by Tony Blair at Downing Street. It is fair to say that, before he arrived in power, political power in

Britain had the configuration of a mountain range. Number 10 Downing Street was Everest, the tallest, most potent and most majestic of all the peaks. But there have always been others of size and significance. Tony Blair's Downing Street is like a single enormous mountain, surrounded by foothills.

This structure was the reason Alastair Campbell exercised such enormous power for so long even over the most powerful members of the Blair government. There were numerous glimpses of the unnatural power Tony Blair's press secretary exercised over ministers. Take the early spring of 1999. Alastair Campbell and the Prime Minister made the long trip up to Glasgow. At least, that was how the forty-five minute flight seemed to them. To them, the dour Old Labour stronghold of Scotland's largest city has always seemed further away than Washington or Rome.

Blair, accompanied by Campbell, attended a local function. As they came out, the Scottish Office minister Helen Liddell went up to greet Campbell. She was a former newspaper executive for Robert Maxwell and knew Campbell well. Liddell was one of the rising stars of the government, the local minister, and on her home territory. She was confident and in command. What happened next can best be described by Bill Greig, the political editor of the *Scottish Daily Express*, who was there and witnessed it all. 'Helen bounced in front of Alastair with a cheery greeting. Ali walked straight on. He didn't even slow down his stride for a single second. He just said, "See ya", as he went by, not looking in her direction. It was a cold and calculated snub. You could see her being left clumsy and uncomfortable. She crumpled up. She was obviously hurt. You could see her thinking: that's not just Alastair. That's what the Prime Minister thinks of me too.' A few months later, Liddell was moved out of her job at the Scottish Office.

The removals of both Mo Mowlam and Jack Cunningham as Cabinet Office ministers were anticipated by Campbell. Mowlam, who had had a brain tumour, was subjected to a whispering campaign from anonymous government sources claiming she was no longer mentally capable of doing the job and drank too much. Downing Street was involved in the campaign, though there is no evidence that Campbell was culpable. But he invariably knew which ministers were on their way up and which were on their way down. An official recalls: 'Shortly before Mo left Alastair would say "Oh, don't bother with her, she's not long for this world." And before Cunningham left, he said: "Jack won't be around much longer."' Campbell also had a series of clashes with Derry Irvine, the Lord Chancellor. He tried to stop the Lord Chancellor giving an interview to the Radio 4 *Today* programme[23] in which Irvine said burglars should not be sent to jail. Campbell warned Irvine it would go wrong. He knew the peer's high-handed manner was likely to antagonize listeners. Blair may have been intimidated by his old mentor. Not Campbell. He slapped down the Lord Chancellor publicly the following day in a Downing Street briefing.

At one stage Irvine's press officer, Sheila Thompson, went to see Campbell and asked: 'What is your media strategy for handling Derry?' Campbell replied: 'Two words: shut up.' He went on to elaborate. 'I don't want to see any interviews in the papers or anywhere else. Nothing.' Before Thompson left, he added: 'Everyone round here calls him Melonhead.' But before long Thompson was back asking Campbell for more advice. By now rumours concerning Irvine's love of red wine had circulated round the lobby. Thompson told Campbell: 'The problem is simple: it's Derry and drink. It is only a matter of time before Derry is found face down in the gutter. And if a journalist is there with a camera we are in trouble.' Thompson had been told that Irvine's driver had had to help him into his car on at least one evening. Campbell replied 'Oh God.' He told Thompson that Irvine had promised not to drink during the 1997 election campaign, and said he would have a word with Irvine. Shortly afterwards Irvine called in Thompson and told her he was unhappy with her work. She joined the private sector.

The most noteworthy example of Campbell's contemptuous attitude towards ministers came within a year of the general election. This was the affair of the Harriet Harman and Frank Field memos, despatched in the early months of 1998, when Harman, egged on by Gordon Brown, was trying to block welfare reforms by Field, who had been appointed as her deputy by Blair to implement them. Campbell intervened when their feud became public as a result of leaks.

Campbell acted like a headmaster disciplining two quarrelling pupils. 'I see from today's papers that no matter how much we urge silence, congenital briefing goes on about who is responsible for what,' he wrote. 'It is time facts took over from personalities.' He would take charge of the next announcement on welfare, and he warned: 'I do not want to see interpretation of either in tomorrow's press.'[24] A second letter from Campbell banned them from speaking in public in the run up to the Budget and demanded: 'I should be grateful for an explanation on why the interviews with the *Guardian*, *Woman's Hour* and *World at One* were not cleared through this office.'[25] A furious Harman complained to the Prime Minister. She denied briefing against Field and said Campbell's memos were an affront. To her disgust, Blair shrugged his shoulders and said: 'That's Alastair.' Five months later, Harman and Field were sacked. What was so striking about the affair was that Campbell, an unelected official, should have felt able to write to a Cabinet minister in such terms. Harman never forgave him.

A source close to Harman said: 'Harriet said that she wouldn't treat a dog the way that Campbell treated her. She thought he was an appalling bully who kicked ministers in the face because it made him feel powerful. She told Blair that Campbell told lies but Blair would say: "Alastair assures me he didn't do what you say." Harriet thought that Blair and Campbell had an abusive relationship and that Blair was prepared to tolerate it because he didn't want to lose him. Alastair was like Tony's security blanket. What Tony didn't realize was that Alastair made enemies of people who were his natural supporters.' Field said Campbell's behaviour was 'spineless'. Harman re-joined the government three years later as Solicitor General. Few ministers were as happy as she when Campbell resigned. Her response on hearing he had gone can be summed up in two words: 'good riddance'.

The Harman episode showed, in the most blatant fashion, that power in the Blair administration lay in a tiny coterie around the Prime Minister and not with Cabinet ministers, let alone elected MPs. This was no accident. This is how New Labour in government was always meant to be. Nor did the Prime Minister and Alastair Campbell ever make the slightest secret of their intention. On 10 March 1997, just days before John Major called the general election, Tony Blair addressed the Newspaper Society. He said that people must be clear 'that we will run from the centre and govern from the centre'.

No minister could make an announcement without first clearing it through Campbell's Downing Street office. Every day, around lunchtime, all Whitehall departments were faxed a transcript of the lobby briefing given by Campbell at Number 10 earlier in the day. This, in the words of one senior official at the time, 'is sacrosanct. It is taken with the utmost seriousness by ministers. It gives them their line for the day.' When Campbell spoke at meetings, ministers strained to listen. As one middle-ranking minister said of Alastair Campbell: 'When we meet him, we are in the role of client. He is in the role of boss.'

Tony Blair's court

The new structure of government handed over an overwhelming amount of power in Whitehall and Westminster to a tiny group of men and women around Tony Blair. To an astonishing extent these unelected creatures were to make the decisions and possess the power formerly exercised by cabinet ministers.

In formal terms the most senior member of this group was Jonathan Powell, once a career Foreign Office official. Like Campbell, Powell had worked for Tony Blair when he was leader of the opposition. The two men did not always see eye to eye. In theory Chief of Staff Powell far outranked press spokesman Campbell. Campbell was indeed heavily reliant on Powell in the first days and weeks in Number 10 when he would wander round asking: 'What the fuck do we do now?' Powell, former diplomat and brother of Charles Powell who had performed a similar role in Downing Street for Margaret Thatcher, knew which levers to pull. But as Campbell learned on the job, the relationship changed. The shy and retiring Powell preferred to immerse himself in the complex issues such as the Northern Ireland peace process rather than get involved in Number 10 power struggles.

This concentration on the big issues was valuable to the Prime Minister. But it made Powell vulnerable. More than once, Campbell was heard to say to Powell: 'What exactly do you do round here?' It was Campbell's way of showing who was boss, though he passed off the remark as a joke, not a taunt. A measure of Campbell's authority over Powell was the latter's reaction on finding himself threatened with the sack. Powell found himself under fire when the Bernie Ecclestone scandal erupted in the autumn of 1997. It was Powell who had arranged for Blair to meet the Formula One boss. When Blair's obfuscation rebounded on him, it wasn't only Fleet Street who were looking for someone to blame. Powell was phoned at his home by an irate Lord Levy, Blair's fund-raiser, confidant and tennis partner. At the end of the phone call a shaken Powell was left convinced that he was about to be sacked in the morning. He took the extraordinary step of driving straight round to Campbell's nearby home at nearly midnight to tell him about Levy's call. Fiona Millar reassured him, saying: 'Don't take it seriously, it's just Levy stirring it up.' Campbell rebuked Powell's wife, the journalist Sarah Helm, after she wrote a newspaper article accusing Tony Blair of being 'fundamentally dishonest' about a federal Europe.[26] A few weeks later, Powell and Helm had lunch with the Campbell-Millars and Philip Gould and his wife, Gail Rebuck, at the Campbell-Millars' rented holiday villa in Provence. Campbell turned on Helm and told her she had a duty to be loyal. It was as well he didn't know that the piece was only made newsworthy because its tone had been hardened up by Powell himself.

The member of the Blair inner circle with the longest association with Blair was neither Powell nor Campbell, nor even the Prime Minister's wife Cherie. It was Anji Hunter, the daughter of a plantation manager: a decorative representative of the deracinated, imperial middle classes. Tall, cool and confident, she met Blair when she was a rebellious fifteen-year-old schoolgirl and he was a seventeen-year-old public schoolboy in Scotland. They were reunited at Oxford, where Anji Hunter went out with the bass player of his band, Ugly Rumours. When Blair became an MP, Hunter, by now married to landscape gardener Nick Cornwall (who, coincidence or not, bore more than a passing resemblance to the Prime Minister) came to work for him as his Commons secretary.

As Tony Blair's political career took off, Hunter became his 'gatekeeper', taking charge of his diary while wooing editors, intelligence chiefs, industrialists and anyone else who might be useful to him. She assumed an informal role of linking the Prime Minister to middle England, a role for which her Sussex home and home counties vowels amply qualified her. Anji Hunter's relations with the rest of Tony Blair's inner circle were at best edgy, at worst arctic, as the events on 2 May 1997, the day Blair first stepped foot in Number 10 as Prime Minister, showed. Hunter called Jonathan Powell to find out what job she would be doing, but he didn't return her calls. If she feared Powell and Campbell were trying to freeze her out she was absolutely right: they had got to Number 10 first to stake their claims to desks and offices and grabbed the ones closest to the Prime Minister, leaving none for her. Tony Blair told her to phone the ubiquitous Lord Levy: he helped sort her out with a tiny office near the men's lavatory.

But any coolness between Hunter and Powell and Campbell paled against her broken relationship with Cherie. Cherie's background in the poor quarters of Liverpool, and her socialist convictions, provided little common ground with Hunter's confident gentility. Cherie viewed her husband's ancient connection with Hunter with gloom, and her current role with cold antipathy. When Cherie organized a victory dinner party for Blair's closest friends and allies to celebrate the 1997 election victory, Hunter was pointedly not invited. Cherie's relations were much warmer with another member of the Downing Street inner circle: Sally Morgan, Downing Street political secretary. While Hunter wined and dined city slickers, the job of Morgan, a Labour official recruited to the party by Michael Foot, was to stay in touch with Labour chiefs and union leaders.

This was the little group of courtiers who served Tony Blair in Downing Street: Campbell, Jonathan Powell, Anji Hunter, Sally Morgan, Philip Gould, Cherie Blair, Mandelson. Only a few others were allowed admittance. This inner group, characteristically to be found clustered round the sofa in Tony Blair's little 'den' in Downing Street, spoke what almost amounted to a private language. Decisions were reached communally, sometimes with scarcely a word being uttered. Those who sought to join this inner circle – as Cabinet Secretary Robin Butler tried to do after the 1997 election – found themselves frozen out. Another person who observed it from within Number 10 described Tony Blair's inner circle as being more like a commune than a government. It was riven by little feuds and jealousies. For the most part Tony Blair took for granted those who devoted the best years of their lives to serving him. 'He very rarely thanks you for anything,' said one insider. 'The moment a speech or policy is over he has forgotten who did what and is only interested in the next thing.' Members would find themselves in or out of favour, sometimes without knowing why. But they were united against the outside world.

Campbell's power in Downing Street was not merely a function of his job. It was a function of the strength of his personality, the quality of his advice and his immensely strong personal relationship with the Prime Minister. For all his brutality in dealing with truculent journalists and dysfunctional ministers, he commanded the respect and loyalty of most of those who worked for him. It is hard to think of an unelected politician in modern times who had such sweeping powers at his command as Alastair Campbell enjoyed.

chapter nine

Blairites and Brownites

Two households, both alike in dignity,
In fair Verona, where we lay our scene,
From ancient grudge break to new mutiny,
Where civil blood makes civil hands unclean.

William Shakespeare, Romeo and Juliet, *Prologue*

A little local difficulty at the Treasury

Charlie Whelan is one of the most improbable figures ever to have strutted his stuff on the Westminster stage. Even at the time, it seemed extraordinary that this hard-drinking, foul-mouthed, ex-Communist bruiser was able to play his full part in government. He was certainly the most implausible figure to hold influence and sway at the Treasury since Winston Churchill chose the twenty-six-year-old Bob Boothby to become his principal private secretary in 1926. Churchill later said of Boothby that he possessed 'much capacity but no virtue', a remark which applied to Whelan as well.

For eighteen months, Charlie Whelan, as Gordon Brown's press secretary, had an influential role in governing Britain. The manner of his departure was thoroughly in keeping with what went before. He hated Peter Mandelson with every sinew of his body and when Mandelson went, Whelan went with him. It was almost as if he felt that his job was now complete. The French have a term for it, coined from the battlefield – *le coup des deux veuves*. Mandelson and Whelan died together, locked in mortal combat. It was politics at its most raw, human passion at its most destructive.

Civil servants, eager to ingratiate themselves with the barbaric crea-
ture they found in their midst, since they correctly believed that he carried great sway with his master, presented him with a capacious office
on the first floor of the splendid Treasury building on the corner of Parliament Square and Whitehall. The office accurately conveyed
Whelan's status and importance, but he preferred not to use it. Opposite the Treasury was a public house known as the Red Lion. When the
Red Lion became too hot for him, he would repair to the Two Chairmen
by Queen Anne's Gate. Perhaps he felt most at home at the Victoria
Club, a smoky drinking den frequented by trade unionists; it was just a
few hundred yards in physical distance but several thousand miles in
spirit from Millbank Tower, where Peter Mandelson had masterminded
New Labour's media operation before the 1997 general election.

At these various drinking establishments, Whelan would do his
business. Unlike Campbell – but like Mandelson, another former
member of the Communist party – he preferred to operate with a few
trusted intimates. Kevin Maguire, the political editor of the *Daily
Mirror*, was one. Patrick Hennessy, political correspondent of the
Evening Standard, was another. Much time was devoted to cultivating
Richard Littlejohn, the renowned newspaper columnist and television
presenter. Sometime in the dim and distant past, Littlejohn had been an
industrial correspondent and Whelan a union official: they had done
business with each other then. Littlejohn and his wife were invited to
dinner parties in the flat above Number 10 Downing Street along with
the Chancellor and his girlfriend (now wife), Sarah Macaulay. Paul
Dacre, editor of the *Daily Mail*, was also cultivated. Dacre had
remained impervious to the charms of Tony Blair: Brown made a determined effort to capture him for himself. One night, the two men stayed
up till 2 a.m. drinking whisky. This was fêted as a triumph at the Treasury. It was held that the two men were bound together by a common
gargantuan work ethic, an impossibly strong moral sense and a joint
unease in social situations.

All this was promptly reported back to Alastair Campbell, who
hated it. The existence of Whelan was a direct affront to his own
authority in Whitehall. All other government departments, with their
associated spin-doctors and other specialists, were under his direct
control. But Whelan was allowed to range freely about London and

'media-land' as if he owned it. Campbell ordered his staff to monitor Whelan's activities and report back. Anji Hunter was just one of those who found themselves under the suspicion of spying on Whelan. Invited to the wedding of Ed Balls, Gordon Brown's special adviser, and the Labour MP Yvette Cooper in January 1998, she at one point detached herself from proceedings to talk on her mobile phone. It was immediately assumed that she was talking to Alastair Campbell, then accompanying Tony Blair on a trip to Japan. The wedding was a key Brownite event and Hunter was one of a handful of Blairites invited to it. Relations between the two camps were at an especially rocky stage: the episode did nothing to improve them and was held against Hunter ever after.

Cherie Blair was also blamed, whether fairly or unfairly it is hard to tell, for stirring up difficulties between Gordon Brown and Tony Blair. At the Treasury, she was sometimes called 'Lady Macbeth'. It is likely that news of this fresh insult, too, was swiftly relayed back to Downing Street.

Campbell kept a capacious file of Whelan-related cuttings in his office and would painstakingly sift through it, working out what stories Whelan had given to whom and why. Whelan would very often get blamed for stories that were absolutely nothing to do with him. Once Hennessy – a known Brownite and therefore distrusted in Downing Street – picked up the information that Peter Mandelson was to put his name forward as a candidate for the National Executive Committee. He approached Whelan who, knowing nothing of the plan, denied it. Hennessy ran the story anyway, having ascertained through other sources that it was true. Whelan got the blame for giving it to Hennessy. 'He didn't just get it wrong,' a bemused Hennessy recalled later. 'He got a bollocking for something he didn't do.'

In the Downing Street press office, journalists were not divided up according to whether they were Tory or Labour or good or bad. They were classified as Brownite or Blairite. The destruction of Charlie Whelan became a primary objective of Downing Street policy. For many months, Campbell plotted to weaken Whelan at the 9 a.m. meeting. He wanted him to bring his deputy, a civil servant called Peter Curwen, as chaperone, a move that was intended to undermine Whelan's authority. Curwen was placed in a delicate situation, becoming so concerned that at one stage he went to see the Permanent

Secretary about the dilemma. But there was nothing Campbell could do about the Whelan problem without the active permission of Gordon Brown. Campbell spent hours on the phone to Brown trying to drive home the message that Whelan, his mischievous freelance operator round Whitehall, must go.

Whelan was merely the symbol, though an important one, of a much greater power struggle. He had originally been hired shortly before the death of John Smith by, of all people, Peter Mandelson. Whelan told Mandelson that he would work only for Gordon Brown or Tony Blair. The fact that Mandelson placed Whelan in Brown's office as his press adviser is yet another indication that he was backing Brown rather than Blair as party leader right up to the end. At that point, he would have viewed Whelan, for whom he had secured a job, as one of his own creatures and therefore placed him in the office of the man whom he rated more highly.

Something seems to have gone terminally wrong with the relationship between Mandelson and Whelan even before John Smith died. It may well be that Whelan resented Mandelson's proprietorial attitude. They fell out almost at once, and after the feuding started between Mandelson and Brown, the ill-feeling became yet more bitter, rancorous and destructive.

But it is wrong to see the vendetta between the Blair camp and the Brown camp, which became such a dominant theme of the first eighteen months of the New Labour government, as being mainly about personalities. It wasn't. It is certainly impossible to underestimate the depth of the hatreds which the individuals involved felt for one another. To a normal person, familiar with the proprieties of everyday life, the various ways that ambition and lust for power can alter the human character are shocking. Be all this as it may, the underlying battle was a power struggle between Downing Street and the Treasury.

What made this contest unusually difficult to resolve was the deal struck by Tony Blair and Gordon Brown at the Granita restaurant in Islington at the height of the Labour leadership contest in 1994. Gordon Brown reluctantly agreed to stand down, but he insisted on conditions which Blair, guilt-stricken at the turn events had taken, was weak enough to concede. Brown demanded complete control over the economy and sweeping powers over other areas of policy as well. He demanded the ability to place his own people in key posts. In effect, he demanded, and got, something approaching a dual premiership.

There were many manifestations of this in the government formed by Tony Blair after May 1997. Tony Blair abandoned his right to chair the Economic Affairs Committee of the Cabinet, the first prime minister to leave it to his chancellor since the disastrous early Wilson period of 1964–66. Nick Brown, a close ally of his namesake Gordon Brown, was permitted to become Chief Whip. Most alarmingly of all to Blairite eyes, the Chancellor was allowed to run his own briefing operation independently of the Downing Street machine. All of these decisions amounted to a recipe for grotesque instability at the heart of government, threatening to undermine the kind of presidential operation that Tony Blair was determined to impose from Downing Street. That is why the cheerful, jaunty presence of Charlie Whelan, with his freedom to tell journalists whatever he wanted, a freedom he availed himself of to the full, antagonized Downing Street so much. He became, for eighteen months and whether he liked it or not, a symbol of rebellion against the ever tighter control from the centre. He had to be destroyed if Campbell was to run his own show.

On the day after Labour's election victory in 1997, Gordon Brown and Tony Blair went for a walk in the Downing Street garden. They wandered in and out of the shrubbery for forty-five minutes, relishing the sweet feeling of victory as well as the scents and sounds of the glorious sunlit afternoon. Fifteen minutes of that discussion were taken up with the Chancellor's imminent plan to grant independence to the Bank of England. The remaining thirty minutes of this first conversation between the two most powerful men in Britain, on Labour's first day of power in two decades, were devoted to the vexatious subject of Whelan. The new Prime Minister hinted to his old friend that Whelan's ferocious reputation for briefing against certain members of the new Cabinet would end by harming Brown's own position. The Chancellor was deaf to this suggestion. The proposition was aired at one stage that Whelan could be made welcome as Alastair Campbell's deputy in the Downing Street press office. This, too, was repudiated. In the end, the Prime Minister shrugged his shoulders and gave up. When Campbell bumped into Whelan later, he professed no knowledge of the conversation. 'What was that about?' he muttered.

For the first few months after the general election, both Downing Street and the Treasury did their best to make sure that the relationship between them worked. There was an awkwardness in midsummer when the sheer verve of Gordon Brown led commentators to contrast his hard work and energy with Tony Blair's more relaxed style of doing business. Comparisons were made between Blair, the laid-back company chairman, and Brown, the dynamic chief executive. Brown basked in these comparisons. Blair did not. Campbell sniffed danger. It is hard to say whether these ideas were spread about by the Treasury or not. The important thing is that Downing Street believed they were. After a friendly conversation, both sides agreed to play the notion down and emphasize Blair's forceful, proactive role. This was an example, and not a rare one, of the two sides working helpfully together during the first months of the Blair premiership.

The first crisis to hit the relationship between the Treasury and Downing Street came over European Monetary Union. With the start date for EMU set for 1 January 1999, the single currency was always going to be the biggest issue facing the government in its first year of office. It is a striking commentary on the Blair administration that when the problem hit, precipitated by Robert Peston's story in the *Financial Times* that Britain would shortly be joining EMU, the government was found without a policy. The following three weeks, as Blair and Brown endeavoured to sort themselves out, were a shambles, the dénouement even worse. Whelan and Campbell attempted to bring the messy saga to an end by planting a story clarifying the government position. This story was New Labour spin-doctoring at its worst, cynical, clumsy and deceitful. The techniques used repay close examination.

First, a friendly journalist, who it was hoped could be relied on not to make a nuisance of himself, was chosen in the shape of Philip Webster, political editor of *The Times*. Webster was promised an 'interview' with Gordon Brown. Only what he got wasn't a full interview at all; the most important part of it was a prepackaged quote. Even the quote, suggesting caution about immediate entry into EMU, was anodyne and hardly newsworthy.

All the Chancellor said was that it was 'highly unlikely' that Britain would join the euro by 1999. It did not justify *The Times* headline:

'Brown Rules Out Single Currency For Lifetime Of This Parliament'.[1]
The story was in the spin handed down the phone by Whelan, and
agreed by Campbell, which gave *The Times* licence to go much further
than Gordon Brown's carefully chosen platitudes. Brown's aim was
simple: he wanted to give the impression that he was ruling out joining
the euro until after the next election without actually saying so. There
were two problems. Firstly, *The Times* headline went beyond what
Brown wanted. Secondly, no one had told Tony Blair, who at that stage
still hoped to keep his options open on the euro. Brown was trying to
hoodwink not just the public, but the Prime Minister too. And it is not
inconceivable that Whelan was trying to hoodwink Campbell, though
Whelan maintains Campbell fully approved his actions. The whole
operation was too clever by half, and an object lesson in what can go
wrong when over powerful spin-doctors take over from their political
masters. It should also have been a lesson to *The Times* of the pitfalls
of agreeing to be used as an accomplice to an act of deception by the
government.

Peter Mandelson strongly pressed for Whelan to be sacked in the
wake of this incredible episode. But Campbell – who later said that the
EMU débâcle was the scene of his own biggest mistake – stood by him:
he himself was too strongly implicated in the fiasco to allow Whelan to
become a victim. So the effect of it all, so far as Whelan was concerned,
was limited. He did temporarily move his centre of operations to the
Two Chairmen rather than the Red Lion, a not insignificant change in
his pattern of life. Otherwise, things carried on as before. But, as it
soon emerged, Campbell was merely biding his time.

'Psychological flaws'

The battle royal between Number 10 and Number 11 Downing Street
began three months later, in January 1998. This confrontation began
with the publication of a biography of Gordon Brown by the left-wing
journalist Paul Routledge which was seen by Campbell, accurately, as a
deliberate and premeditated attack on Blair's authority by the Brown
camp. Routledge's book alleged that Blair had broken a promise made
to Brown to allow him to succeed John Smith as party leader, information which Routledge had obtained from Blair's Chief Whip, Nick

Brown. The controversy led to a vicious and calculated counter attack by Campbell which culminated in him describing Brown as having 'psychological flaws' to punish him and his supporters for trying to undermine Blair. Campbell, along with most members of Blair's inner circle had long regarded Brown as being slightly mad. Bonkers, barmy, barking, emotionally stunted were all terms commonly used to describe the Chancellor by Blair's coterie. However, it is only fair to point out that they were content to concede he also possessed a brilliant brain and far greater understanding of most complex issues, in particular the economy, than Blair. Discussing Brown's mental state and changing moods was one of the major pastimes in Number 10 and at Chequers.

This makes it all the more curious that the person who triggered Campbell's famous 'psychological flaws' taunt was not a member of the Blair camp. It was the judicious and well-meaning figure of Sir Richard Wilson, the Cabinet Secretary. Shortly after Wilson succeeded Robin Butler in January 1998, Campbell went to talk to him. It soon became clear that Campbell wanted to talk to Wilson about Gordon Brown. At the time, the Brown–Blair feud had just been ignited by the publication of Routledge's biography. Campbell was brooding on it. 'You've met Gordon Brown,' he asked Wilson. 'What do you think of him?' Wilson gave a thoughtful assessment of Brown, during the course of which he observed: 'Quite a number of politicians who get right to the top have some unusual psychological make up in them that makes them creative.' Campbell was fascinated and pressed him further. 'And how do you handle them?' It was essential to set up a dialogue with the part of the politician that was the 'most sane', said Wilson, who had a lifetime's experience of handling senior politicians. 'Encourage the good,' he summed up, 'and discourage the bad.'

A little later, when Wilson saw the 'psychological flaws' remark emblazoned across the national newspapers, he was shocked and felt guilty. It occurred to him that he might well have planted the idea in Campbell's mind. He was an admirer of Brown and the two had warm relations. Wilson's comment was most certainly not intended as a character assassination. He had assumed he was talking to Campbell in confidence, not being used as a sounding board for potential insults. However, in the hands of Campbell, Wilson's comment could be adapted for precisely that purpose.

Campbell ventilated the phrase in a conversation with John Williams, the political editor of the *Daily Mirror*. Williams wrote a regular column and would sound out Campbell for news, views and comment that he could use discreetly in his column. Williams was taken aback by what Campbell had to tell him on this occasion. When their conversation turned to Brown, Campbell used a phrase about Brown that was the kind of raw meat he needed for a powerful column: 'psychological flaws'. And Williams needed one, as he had fallen out with the *Mirror*'s editor Piers Morgan and his job prospects did not look good. Williams told colleagues he had a great story and promptly filed a commentary detailing Number 10's anger with Brown.

But the column never appeared. In fact, Williams never wrote for the *Mirror* again. It is not clear whether the piece was spiked because the *Mirror* did not want to attack Brown, whether Morgan had tired of Williams, or whether there was another explanation. Williams resigned from the *Mirror* and, aided by some timely support from his old friend and confidant Campbell, embarked on a new career as a Foreign Office spokesman. Asked later about the 'psychological flaws' incident, Williams made no attempt to deny that Campbell said it. 'I know very well what you are up to and why you are doing it,' he said. 'I didn't reveal my sources when I was a journalist and I am not going to reveal them now.'[2]

But in spite of the *Mirror*'s failure to print the smear, it appeared in another newspaper days later. The left-leaning *Observer* columnist Andrew Rawnsley would also regularly talk to Campbell to find out what was going on inside the government. And so it was that Rawnsley gave a wider circulation to the 'psychological flaws' jibe in his column three days after Campbell and Williams had tried to get it into the *Mirror*. This time, the bomb went off just as Campbell had hoped. Under the headline 'What Blair Really Thinks of Brown', Rawnsley wrote: 'The Prime Minister has watched the Chancellor aggrandise power at the expense of other Cabinet Ministers … Mr Brown's acolytes have sought to boost the Chancellor at the expense of Mr Blair … he has heard the talk that Blair is "President" to Brown's "Prime Minister" with the insinuation that Gordon is the substantial figure of the government and Tony merely the shallow showman.' The knife went in. Rawnsley continued: 'According to someone who has an extremely good claim to know the mind of the Prime Minister … it is time for Mr Brown to get a grip on his "psychological flaws".'[3]

Brown was devastated by the wounding remark and rapidly concluded that its originator was Campbell. Blair was angry and embarrassed enough by the messy affair to take Campbell aside and tell him off.

Campbell was not alone in his mistrust of Gordon Brown. If anything, Cherie Blair was even more hostile towards the Chancellor. As the Brown–Blair rift intensified, so did her loathing of Brown. During one anti-Brown tirade, she told a friend: 'Tony has got to sack him. Psychological flaws is the least of it. That was an understatement.' Cherie said Brown was 'fucked up'. 'He needs to be put in his place. He is too big for his boots and is impossible to deal with.'

To complicate matters further, Cherie and Gordon Brown's wife, Sarah Macaulay, did not get on. Brown's friends say that Cherie was very unfriendly towards her and had snubbed her publicly on more than one occasion.

Campbell was probably the only person in the government Brown was frightened of. In some ways, Brown never recovered from Campbell's comment. Campbell would either play the role of peacemaker, referring scornfully to the latest Brown and Blair dispute as 'trouble between the kids', or he would talk about 'putting Brown back in his box'. Brown might rage at Blair in private, but he was more wary of taking on Campbell. Campbell knew how to hurt, and Brown knew that he could and would hit him back hard through his network of allies in the media. Campbell had located his enemy's weak spot with lethal accuracy.

chapter ten

Managing the Media

Explain to me just why I should waste my time with a load of
fucking wankers like you when you're not going to write anything
I tell you anyway.

Alastair Campbell to the Sunday lobby, May 1997

THERE WERE JOURNALISTS WHO adapted themselves to the
new circumstances that prevailed under New Labour – and there were
those who did not. Michael Brunson, political editor of ITN, had
always made it his business to get on with the old John Major regime:
colleagues marvelled at the ease with which he did so. Now he made it
his business to get on with Tony Blair. With dazzling sleight of hand
Brunson converted himself, at any rate in the minds of his colleagues,
from a Tory loyalist to a New Labour loyalist. Much the same could be
said of the BBC political editor Robin Oakley. Oakley had been mildly
embarrassed by disclosures about his friendship with Tory peer Jeffrey Archer; Campbell used this to his advantage. Campbell's view
was that he had 'got Oakley where he wanted him' and that he was
unlikely to cause many problems for Blair precisely because his Tory
connection was known.[1]

There were others who felt a warm and enjoyable sense of coming in
from the cold. The late political editor of the *Independent*, Tony Bevins,
had viewed the Thatcher and Major governments with cold antipathy.
Tory grandees like Alan Clark surmised that he was taking revenge for
slights alleged to have been handed out to his father, Reginald Bevins,
who served with distinction in the governments of Eden and Macmillan. Though a minister of high competence, his middle-class origins

meant that he was never fully accepted by the Tory establishment of the day.

These speculations were wrong, however: there was no vendetta. The Clark analysis failed to take into account the high principles of this self-appointed Savonarola to the political establishment of the 1990s. Tony Bevins hounded the Tory party with unspeakable ferocity, and he played a modest part and took a deep personal pleasure in the downfall of John Major's government. Thereafter, this angular, uncomfortable but curiously warm-hearted man collapsed with a sigh into the embrace of New Labour. He and Philip Webster of *The Times* became the two most prominent cheerleaders for New Labour among the ranks of political editors. They were later joined by, among others, Patrick Wintour of the *Guardian* and Tom Baldwin of *The Times*.

Others travelled the same sort of journey, only in the opposite direction. For more than a decade George Jones, the political editor of the *Daily Telegraph*, had been the favoured recipient of whispered confidences from Cabinet ministers. These dried up on 2 May 1997. Any attempt Jones may have made on his own behalf to ingratiate himself with the new administration was rendered hopeless by the adamantine stand of his editor Charles Moore. Moore could see no good in Blair: correspondingly, Campbell could see no good in Jones. So poor Jones found himself in the wilderness, starved of the oxygen of information which alone can sustain the dedicated political reporter. This state of deprivation turned to torment as he was compelled to watch Philip Webster, his *Times* rival and his closest competitor, drink deeply from the very same sources that had been taken away from him.

Webster was prodigious. An ace reporter with the finest shorthand note in the lobby, his skill and craftsmanship had long been held in high respect by colleagues. *The Times* has always been a paper enjoying a promiscuous relationship to power: its habit of taking marching orders from Downing Street dates back to the 1930s and beyond. Now Webster turned its political news pages into Fleet Street's closest equivalent to a notice board for the government. His efforts were richly appreciated. Stories – such as the change of policy on EMU – started to fall into his lap.

Webster is an extremely talented amateur sportsman, but his knowledge of modern poetry is limited. Nevertheless, he scooped the world with the identity of the new poet laureate, infuriating the Palace, which felt that the decision to leak the news was a discourtesy.

On trips abroad Campbell started to treat Webster as one of the official party rather than as a travelling hack. Before briefing reporters, he would take Webster to one side and try out the official line, rather like a medieval king employing a food-taster at a banquet. If Webster spat it out, Campbell would try a different spin. There were to be occasions when Campbell, unable to be physically present to brief the lobby, to all intents and purposes employed Webster to do the job on his behalf. Philip Webster is the most scrupulous and honourable of reporters, and would never abuse this privileged position. Nevertheless, it caused mumblings of resentment among the travelling pack.

At Westminster the *Times* political team was cleansed of Tories. The process was not replicated, however, at the paper's Wapping headquarters. There Tory thinkers, mainly of the Eurosceptic persuasion, thrived: it was New Labour that struggled to make itself heard. Readers of the top people's paper were presented with a schizophrenic menu. The political news pages endeavoured to place the best possible construction on government policy, while on the comment pages Michael Gove, Anatole Kaletsky, Lord Rees-Mogg, Matthew Parris and others – a brilliant constellation – were all capable of placing the worst. This disjunction reflected the ambiguity of the Murdoch press. On the one hand, it was accepted that Tony Blair was as fine a prime minister as Thatcher. On the other, it was accepted that the Prime Minister's support for Europe – held by *The Times* to be the decisive issue of our day, the vital matter at stake in the 1997 election – was an abomination.

This dilemma also faced *The Times*'s stablemate, the *Sun*. Its readers were starkly presented with two contradictory propositions. On the one hand were informed that federal Europe presented an apocalyptic menace which had to be fought with ceaseless vigilance. On the other they were reminded daily that Tony Blair, the man set on leading Britain towards that feared destination, was not merely a genius of outstanding gifts but also a secular saint. *Sun* readers were asked to stomach one further fact: the one British politician alert enough to share the paper's alarm about the European menace, William Hague, was a contemptible buffoon. At the Conservative party conference of 1998 they portrayed him on their front page as a dead parrot. David Yelland, the paper's new editor, had to be dissuaded by senior staff from hiring an actor to put on a parrot outfit, dash up to the stage as William Hague made his annual conference speech, and then theatrically expire.

Tony Blair, Alastair Campbell and Anji Hunter would regularly meet David Yelland, whose almost star-struck admiration of Blair was regarded as embarrassing by old hands on the *Sun* who remembered the contemptuous attitude of former editor, the brilliant and outrageous Kelvin MacKenzie, towards all politicians. (Mackenzie famously told a simpering John Major on Black Wednesday, when sterling crashed out of the ERM, that he was going to 'pour a bucket of shit' over the PM's head in the paper the next day.) Campbell, too, treated Yelland with a degree of contempt, and showed little reverence for the Blair–Yelland summits. With the two men in deep discussion in the Prime Minister's hotel room during a Labour conference, Campbell walked in and barked: 'Yelland!' The *Sun* editor spun round. 'Your flies are undone,' said a grinning Campbell. While Yelland held forth during another meeting with Blair, Campbell whispered to a News International executive: 'What planet is he on?'

By contrast, Tony and Cherie Blair were unfailingly courteous to Yelland. Cherie invited him to a dinner at the British Embassy in Washington after Yelland ceased to be editor, and therefore of any political use to the Blairs, something that suggested she genuinely liked him. The plain-talking Yelland was an object of fascination to Cherie's American liberal lawyer friends, who surrounded him. Blair went to great lengths to flatter Yelland, interrupting a meeting with the *Sun* editor to take a call from German Chancellor Gerhard Schroeder. He returned to say: 'Gerhard says you must change your mind on the euro.' This was Blair's view too. He lived in hope that if he could not persuade Yelland to back the euro, he might soften the paper's stance enough to give him the confidence to call a referendum. Campbell barged in on one of their discussions and asked: 'Have you two got round to the fucking euro yet?'

Yelland would regularly consult Campbell on the issues of the day. During the Afghan war, he faxed Yelland suggestions for stories including a feature on women's rights under the Taliban. Hunter would also bombard the impressionable Yelland with her charm. Some *Sun* executives thought Yelland was too much in awe of Downing Street. 'He was on the phone to Campbell all the time,' said one. 'He would order everyone out of his room, close the door, and you knew it was Campbell trying to tell him what to do.'[2] One *Sun* journalist adds: 'Yelland thought that Blair was God and Campbell was Jesus. They were happy to use him.' Some of the senior staff on the *Sun* objected to Campbell's constant meddling. He phoned the paper one weekend with a story when Yelland was away and was put through to the deputy editor, who told him abruptly: 'I only take instructions from the editor.'

Campbell was not too bothered about the complexities of the *Sun* editorial line. He was simply happy to have the paper in his pocket. Having got it there he would do whatever was necessary to keep it there. Favours flooded in. Campbell would say to Whitehall press officers at Downing Street meetings: 'Do you know what is going to be on the front page of the *Sun* tomorrow? I want you not just to know, but to help me to write it.' For him, it was the only yardstick that mattered. *Sun* journalists continued to get special treatment. The *Sun* itself suddenly became the favoured vehicle of communication with the British people, not merely for Tony Blair but for foreign leaders as well. This new craze started with the Japanese premier Ryutaro Hashimoko's letter to *Sun* readers ahead of the Emperor's trip to Britain on 14 January 1998. Hashimoko's article was drafted, at least in part, by Alastair Campbell during Tony Blair's trip to Japan following a discussion with *Sun* political editor, Trevor Kavanagh. The *Sun* claimed, in its front-page splash, that the premier was apologizing for the war, a claim that was later challenged by the Japanese. This operation was considered to have gone off so well that it was followed, in October that year, by an identical stunt ahead of the visit by the Argentine president Carlos Menem to the United Kingdom. This was also arranged and drafted by Campbell: the Argentinian, too, vainly protested that he had never apologized for the Falklands either.

Some *Mirror* journalists were convinced that Campbell took a special pleasure in leaving them out in the cold because of the particular circumstances of his own departure from the paper. But this was no long-delayed revenge: it was merely an icy-cold appreciation of the realities of the situation.

Ironically enough, it took the arrival of Kelvin MacKenzie, the editor of the *Sun* during many of those years of Tory dominance, to jerk the paper out of its lethargy. That and the episode of the Clinton letter, which demonstrated the complete cynicism with which Campbell and the Downing Street machine was prepared to treat the *Mirror*.

It was the inspired idea of the *Mirror*'s political editor, Kevin Maguire, that President Clinton should make a personal intervention in the Irish peace process. Maguire spotted that Clinton's presence in Britain for the G-8 economic summit in May of 1998, just days before the Irish people voted on the Good Friday agreement, could be put to good use. He put up the proposition to Campbell that the President should use the pages of the *Mirror* to write an open letter to the Irish calling on them to 'say Yes to peace'. Campbell, after consulting with the US embassy, readily agreed. But he had one stipulation: Maguire must write the piece himself and then submit it for approval. Maguire dutifully rattled off the words he considered President Clinton might have wished to write, and submitted them for inspection.

He swiftly received a reply from Downing Street. His piece was sound, but redrafting was required. The *Mirror* was asked to hold its fire for twenty-four hours. Maguire was happy to agree, but not so happy to see the first editions of the following day's *Sun*. For there, splashed all across the front page, was Clinton's dramatic appeal for peace, much of it Maguire's own handiwork. Campbell would appear to have handed over the *Mirror*'s idea, written up by the *Mirror*'s political editor, to the paper's deadliest rival. It was by any standards – even those of Westminster and Fleet Street – an incredible act of betrayal.

Maguire was incandescent. He rang Campbell, who tried to wriggle his way out. He explained that the British embassy, which had been approached separately by the *Sun*, was responsible. It was all an innocent mistake. Maguire's call was followed up by his editor. 'Piers [Morgan] gave Campbell both barrels,' records a *Mirror* executive. 'It lasted ten minutes. It ended with Campbell grovelling, saying: "Look, Piers, I did this for peace."' 'Sure, peace with Murdoch,' replied Morgan.

But the most astonishing betrayal of all came when the *Daily Mirror* secured the mouth-watering exclusive that forty-five-year-old Cherie

Blair was pregnant. The *Mirror* dutifully went to Downing Street for confirmation before it ran its story. When the first editions appeared it was flabbergasted and horrified to see that the *Sun* had been given the story as well.

A livid Piers Morgan rang Campbell to protest furiously. Things became so desperate that at the other end of the line Campbell recruited Tony Blair to help cope with the furious *Daily Mirror* editor. An extraordinary three-way conversation followed, in which Campbell, hand on heart, explained that the whole thing was just a terrible mistake.

He explained that the *Sun* had got the story thanks to an extraordinary coincidence. Alastair Campbell's explanation went as follows: *Sun* deputy editor Rebekah Wade had happened to have rung Cherie Blair that very day. By a still greater chance, the Downing Street switchboard put Wade straight through to the Downing Street flat. As it happened Cherie Blair was passing as the phone rang, and she picked it up. Finding it was her old friend Rebekah at the other end of the phone, Cherie stopped for a chat, and felt 'that she had no choice' but to tell her the happy news as well. The Prime Minister was silent while Campbell spun an incredulous Morgan this astonishing yarn, though he muttered assent from time to time.

Two months later a seething Morgan expressed his utter outrage about the affair to Fiona Millar, who told him quite a different story. It was nothing like the version that Alastair Campbell had tried to fob him off with, with Tony Blair listening in without protesting. The Campbell-Millars were well aware that the Prime Minister's wife never liked Piers Morgan, or the *Daily Mirror*. So they had waited till as late as possible before telling Cherie the news that the *Mirror* was onto the story. As they had predicted, she was furious, and started shouting at Fiona. Cherie Blair was so angry that she promptly picked up the telephone and rang Rebekah Wade and told her the story as well.

Relations improved as the 2001 general election approached, but became arctic once again after the *Sun* scooped its rival with the date of the general election. (see page 268) Downing Street furiously denied it had anything to do with the leak.

Shortly after the election, when Campbell's former deputy, Lance Price admitted that it was Number 10 gave the election date story to the *Sun,* relations between the *Mirror* and Number 10 disintegrated. It was the last straw for Morgan who said: 'I'm not having this. If they think they can mess about with me, then I'll mess about with them.'

When the US and Britain led the attack on Afghanistan in the winter of 2001, the *Mirror* launched a counter attack – against Downing Street. It maintained this hostile approach to Blair's foreign policy, and his support for Bush whom the *Mirror* had constantly attacked, through the Iraq crisis.

However, *Mirror* political editor James Hardy approached Campbell on a Blair trip to the US before the invasion of Iraq to ask if the Prime Minister would write an article for the paper, setting out why its readers should support the war on Saddam.

'Fuck off,' replied Campbell. 'The only message the Prime Minister has for *Daily Mirror* readers is: don't buy it.' Hardy recalls: 'Alastair's obsessive chase of the *Sun* meant he took the *Mirror* for granted in a way that was contemptuous and arrogant. The Clinton article set the tone. The *Mirror* remained largely benign although more inclined towards Gordon Brown. As political editor of the biggest Labour supporting paper I thought we might get a few titbits from the table, but the few that there were went to the *Sun*.'

Morgan's fall out with Blair became more embittered after the *Mirror* editor discovered that Cherie Blair had criticized him at a dinner with *Mirror* executives, stating Morgan had 'no moral compass'. Morgan threw this back in her face during the 'Cheriegate' affair when a *Mirror* leader asserted that Cherie had no 'moral compass'.

Blair complained to James Hardy: 'What are we going to do about the *Mirror*? I know you are out to get me but there's more to play for than just my future, you know.'[3] Once on the warpath, Morgan wasted no opportunity to taunt the Blair camp. He made Chancellor Gordon Brown blush when he went to Number 11 for lunch with the Chancellor. Spying Fiona Millar down a corridor linking Number 11 to Number 10, Morgan shouted at her: 'We're going to lunch with our real friends.'

When David Yelland held a leaving party in London on 24 February 2003, to mark the end of his four and a half years in the editor's chair at the *Sun*, rubbing shoulders with Page Three girls and TV soap stars were Tony Blair and Cherie, Campbell, Gordon Brown, David Blunkett, Peter Mandelson and Philip Gould. Weeks before British troops went into action in Iraq, Blair found time spend an hour saying 'good-bye' to Yelland and 'hello' to his successor, Rebekah Wade. Campbell didn't care about the *Mirror*. Their readers weren't going to vote Tory at the general election. But *Sun* readers might.

Campbell should have been content with the press New Labour enjoyed for its first six years in government – but he was not. He would not rest until he controlled them all. The mass-market tabloids were Labour, the *Mirror* albeit reluctantly. In the middle market the *Express* had converted itself from Tory to Labour.

The *Mail*, however, the paper of middle England, refused to come across: this was a cause of great distress to New Labour. Intimates revealed that Tony Blair was 'heartbroken' about the *Mail*. The failure to win the paper was not from any lack of effort. Before the general election enormous strides had been made. David English, the newspaper genius who chaired the group, had come close to falling – platonically – in love with the young leader of the Labour opposition.

The handling of David English is another example of the ineptitude of the last Tory government. John Wakeham, the Conservative leader of the Lords, twice urged on John Major the wisdom of converting English's knighthood into a peerage. On each occasion Major rejected the proposal on the grounds that he was not prepared to reward a man whose newspapers had attacked his government so brutally. It fell to Tony Blair to effect the elevation. He felt no Majorish qualms. The fact that English's newspapers had been the bitterest enemy of the Labour party for three decades, and played a large part in keeping it out of power for two of them, did not put him off in the least. Sir David English died just a few days before his elevation was due to be publicly announced.

Tony Blair and Alastair Campbell devoted prodigious efforts to winning over English's successor Paul Dacre, now editor-in-chief at the *Mail*. Blair enthused to Dacre that the *Daily Mail* stood for many of the things that he too believed in – family values, self-reliance, enterprise. The young Prime Minister told Dacre that the *Mail* was 'the only authentic voice in Fleet Street', and would heap opprobrium on the *Guardian*, telling Dacre that 'if the *Guardian* approved of me, something must be wrong'. Campbell revelled in upsetting the *Guardian* by leaking stories on education and health, subjects the *Guardian* considered its own preserve, to the *Mail*. Blair told Dacre: 'I agree with so much that you say about Europe,' and pronounced it 'obscene' that the British people should have to pay forty per cent tax to the state. Downing Street lavished immense energy cultivating right-wing *Mail* columnists like Simon Heffer, Paul Johnson and Lynda Lee-Potter, the embodiment of Middle England woman.

The *Daily Mail* only turned on Blair after his 'forces of Conservatism' speech at the Labour party conference in 1999. Paul Dacre saw this as an attack on everything the *Mail* stood for. Within a few months, Campbell, egged on by Fiona Millar, agreed to the launch of a 'Mail Monitoring Unit', with the intention of exposing what he saw as the *Mail*'s political bias. Blair was nervous about this from the start, believing it would only make things worse. It was closed down within weeks. Relations between the *Mail* and Downing Street were broken off after Blair's disastrous speech to the Women's Institute in the spring of 2000 when he was heckled by members of the audience. Alarmed by how he could have got it so wrong, and by the increasingly hostile tone of the *Mail*'s coverage, Blair invited Heffer to Number 10. Heffer told the Prime Minister that he had deserved to get a rough ride at the WI. He could not expect to make a speech extolling NHS reforms to women – many of whom had direct experience of it, either as patients or as voluntary workers, and who knew its true shabby condition – and expect to be applauded. Heffer was not invited back.

To Campbell's intense annoyance, Dacre maintained close relations with Brown. At the time of the death of Brown's baby daughter, Jennifer Jane, in January 2002 relations between Brown and Blair were so bad that it was only the child's death that prevented Blair from sacking the Chancellor. When Campbell saw Dacre at the funeral he was heard to swear. Later the same year, as the Iraq war loomed, Campbell invited Simon Heffer to see him and discussed the possibility of a rapprochement with the *Mail*. It came to nothing.

Bashing up the lobby

Two years into Blair's first term, Alastair Campbell said: 'Editors told me we would get a six-month honeymoon, but we've been in for two years now and there's no sign of an end to it.'

By the standards of previous political epochs, even including the high noon of Thatcherism fifteen years earlier, New Labour received an extraordinarily good press for most of its first term in office. In many ways, it deserved to. Tony Blair's achievements were generously celebrated, nobody apart from a handful of malcontents dwelt too long on his failures. The contrast with the coverage of John Major's doomed administration was striking. The nation urged on the New Labour government to succeed, just as it had willed the Tories to fail, and the media reflected that novel mood of benevolence.

The peculiar thing is that this was not the mood in Downing Street. At the court of Tony Blair there was a sense of siege. Well-meaning critics were seen as hostile, and balanced assessment was understood as an attempt to damage the reputation of the Prime Minister. It is the central paradox of New Labour that never has there been a political movement that stretched out so far, enjoyed such national popularity for so long, and broke down so many traditional political boundaries. And yet it rapidly came to feel isolated. This wholly irrational sense of isolation found its outward manifestation in the person of Alastair Campbell and in his daily encounters with parliamentary journalists.

Campbell's first briefing to the Sunday lobby set the tone. It was only with a show of great reluctance, which started with a failure to return pager messages and was followed by a claim that he had better things to do, that the Number 10 press secretary agreed to meet them at all. When a time was finally agreed, Campbell turned up late. He strode to the front of the briefing room, followed by a gaggle of his Downing Street civil servants. 'OK, you bastards,' Campbell kicked off genially. 'Explain to me just why I should waste my time with a load of fucking wankers like you when you're not going to write anything I tell you anyway.'

The officials seated behind him looked on stupefied. They, unlike the lobby men at the receiving end of the assault, had never heard anything like it before. Campbell was setting a style which he clearly intended to maintain for the remainder of his term of office. Everyone who knew him at all, either as a reporter or a colleague within Downing Street, agrees that he disliked – some people say hated – most journalists. With the exception of that small number who were prepared to accept his tip-offs and steers unquestioningly, he had a strong dislike for the parliamentary lobby and a visceral loathing of the Sunday lobby. His attitude, interestingly enough, was similar to the one invariably taken by former journalists when they became press secretary at Number 10. Sir Bernard Ingham and Joe Haines both scorned journalists, though neither with anything quite like the passionate disdain which Campbell sometimes communicates. Trained civil servants, by contrast, feel none of this hostility. Gus O'Donnell, Major's first press secretary, liked and respected the lobby and the lobby in return liked and respected him. This did not prevent them, however, turning over his boss whenever they felt like it, which was very often indeed and in an especially nasty way.

If it was necessary to obstruct, bully or mislead reporters in the course of his duties Campbell would do so, for his overriding loyalty lay with Tony Blair. Campbell stopped at nothing to protect the Prime Minister. His defenders argued that his behaviour simply reflected the moral code of Westminster. They argued he was doing no more than Haines and Bernard Ingham had done. Both were prepared to rough up the lobby if it suited their purposes. But Campbell went much further. Neither Haines nor Ingham had a fraction of the power that Campbell had over the whole of Whitehall. Neither had the same status as equal partner to the Prime Minister. Neither had the same politically motivated staff and sophisticated media apparatus at their fingertips. And neither took the art of manipulation and disinformation to such extremes.

Campbell possesses the skills of a playground bully – mimicry and an uncanny insight into his victims' weaknesses – and he puts them to good use. This was one of the things that made his lobby meetings such arresting events, the best spectator sport in town. For a long time he targeted Robert Peston, political editor of the *Financial Times*. Peston is an able journalist, with an aptitude for picking up stories which distress the government. In the lobby, Campbell would mercilessly mock and mimic Peston's mannerisms. Peston had the habit of stroking the hair at the back of his head, which could be taken as a sign of vanity. Campbell got that perfectly. His imitation never failed to raise a laugh.

He also singled out Peston's junior, a bright young reporter called Liam Halligan, for special abuse. Campbell was warmly welcoming when Halligan, now economics correspondent for *Channel Four News*, turned up in the lobby. But he turned nasty after Halligan produced a few awkward stories. He called him 'gel-boy' or the 'Derek Draper of the lobby', a reference to Peter Mandelson's assistant who had gained a reputation for playing fast and loose. When Halligan spoke, Campbell would welcome 'another question from the Peston school of smartarse journalism'. He rubbished his stories.

Halligan hit back, always the best way with Campbell. 'He just thought I was going to be scared of him. I wasn't. I told him: at least I didn't run away from Oxbridge; at least I'm my own person; at least I don't follow other people around; at least I'm not a coat-tails merchant.'[11]

Guto Harri, the BBC correspondent, was another to strike back effectively at Campbell. Shortly before a Blair–Bush Iraq war summit in America, Harri told TV viewers that some critics would call the two leaders 'war mongers', while others would praise them for trying to find peace. When Harri scrambled to board the plane to the summit, he offered Campbell a cheery: 'Hello, Alastair, how are you?' which was met with: 'Fuck off.'

Harri: 'Pardon?' Campbell: 'You are a wanker, fuck off. You called the Prime Minister a war monger. I'm not talking to you.' Campbell turned to talk to other journalists, and when he noticed Harri was lingering, broke off to ask: 'You still here?'

Harri took a deep breath and replied: 'I just wanted you to know, Alastair, that I updated your political obituary last week. Some of my bosses at the BBC aren't sure if you are going to survive the war.' Harri expected another volley of insults from Campbell, but instead he stood there silent.

Campbell enjoyed bullying women journalists. On a trip to the Middle East in the early summer of 1998, he picked out Rachel Sylvester, a young reporter on the *Telegraph*. He mocked her interventions and referred to her throughout the trip as 'Rachel Sylvester of the venal *Daily Telegraph*'. At the end of the trip Charles Moore sent a sharply worded complaint to Campbell. But that did not stop him handing out the same sort of treatment to a woman reporter from the *Scotsman*, Joy Copley, when she accompanied Tony Blair and Campbell on their trip to South Africa in January 1999. Copley's crime was to challenge Campbell too openly in a lobby briefing. Their clash came shortly before Blair made his keynote speech of the trip. The day before, Campbell had briefed that Tony Blair would signal unspecified 'harsh and authoritarian' measures for the welfare state. This line duly appeared in morning papers. When the speech was handed out all mention of these harsh measures had disappeared. Copley accused Campbell of peddling a false line. Campbell's response was typically robust. 'The lobby all write garbage anyway.' Copley was not to be deterred. 'You fed us that garbage,' she said. 'You made us write a story that wasn't true.' Campbell's response was contemptuous. 'I wouldn't wet your knickers about it,' he said. To his credit, he later apologized.

There are very few journalists in the lobby whom Campbell did not attempt to abuse or humiliate at some stage. His only iron rule was to leave the *Sun* well alone. Once he forgot to obey this precept and pinpointed George Pascoe-Watson, the deputy political editor of the *Sun*, who had written an unhelpful story on Labour's attitude towards the single currency. Campbell beat him up verbally for a good five minutes. It was a splendid sight, Campbell in full flow, and a group gathered round to watch Campbell front up Pascoe-Watson and point his finger at his chest. The following day Campbell took Pascoe-Watson gently aside and thrust an envelope into his hand. It contained a fulsome apology. Campbell apologies are rare things, almost never handed out after a routine piece of thuggery such as the one he had dished out to Pascoe-Watson, who in any case was perfectly capable of looking after himself. That Pascoe-Watson got his letter was less evidence of contrition on Campbell's part than testimony to the respect owing to his newspaper, the *Sun*. Pascoe-Watson is said to keep Campbell's note in a drawer by his bed, a unique and valued item.

Insults were deliberately targeted at what Campbell saw as the weak spots of his victim. When the Scottish journalist Ian Hernon – a familiar figure round the bars of Westminster – left a lobby briefing early, Campbell sneered as he left: 'Need a drink, do we?' At one stage Campbell fired a letter off to John Scott, the editor of Hernon's paper the Glasgow *Evening Times*, which accused Hernon of inventing a story. Pending an explanation, said Campbell, 'further action will be taken'. This was taken as a threat to get Hernon's lobby status removed, thus destroying his livelihood. Like many of Campbell's threats, it was never followed up. Even friendship is no bar to a Campbell assault. During the twenty-four-hour period when Downing Street was officially backing Peter Mandelson to survive as Trade Secretary after the revelation of the Geoffrey Robinson loan, *Sky News* political editor Adam Boulton asked Campbell for an interview with the Prime Minister so that he could publicly throw his weight behind the beleaguered minister. 'Oh, fuck off,' came the reply from Campbell. Boulton immediately went on air and conveyed to Sky viewers the flavour of this exchange. Campbell was infuriated, called Boulton on his mobile phone, and informed him that personal relations between Sky and Downing Street had been severed. The following day, when Mandelson did resign, Sky TV was frozen out of interviews with the fallen minister.

New Labour has never hesitated to destabilize journalists by going behind their backs to their bosses. Numerous reporters have had the experience of being run down behind their backs to their editors or proprietors by New Labour spin-doctors. This weapon could be used even against close allies who strayed from the party or government line. Very shortly before the 1997 election, Andrew Marr, then editor of the *Independent*, wrote a critical piece about Labour's European policy. The Marr attack was sparked by some palpably dishonest and disingenuous remarks by Tony Blair in the *Sun* in which he invoked the shade of St George against the European dragon. It was all too much for the fastidious, pro-European Marr, who knew better than anyone that Blair was a fervent pro-European. But it suited him to wrap himself in the flag of St George to win few a more votes. Marr phoned Campbell and told him: 'You idiot, you fucking idiot, what are you thinking of?' Campbell's reply was along the lines of: 'Come on Andy, you know the game.' Marr replied: 'That won't do. I'm really going to put the boot into you tomorrow.'[4]

But Campbell got his retaliation in first. Shortly after Marr came off the phone, the *Independent*'s chief executive David Montgomery came spinning down the stairs, wearing a broad grin, and announced to Marr: 'Guess what? I've been told to get rid of you. You've really upset them.' Marr believed it was a deliberate attempt to get him sacked.

Marr was more determined than ever to make his point and wrote that Blair had backed himself into a corner and that in future he would either be 'betraying the whole emotional tone of his *Sun* piece or betraying our nation's better future'. It was a perceptive piece of journalism. It is highly unlikely that, appearing where it did, it will have cost New Labour a single vote. Marr's article, in the rarefied air of the *Independent* newspaper, had no bearing on the general election campaign. The criticism was made by a man who was one of the closest and most valued allies of the future New Labour government.

Campbell was incapable of distinguishing true friend from foe, or fair criticism from hostile attack. 'If you are ninety-nine per cent for Alastair, then in his view, you are against him,' said one of his friends.

Using the lobby

Campbell would not merely harass journalists: he could sometimes also use them as highly tuned instruments in highwire political negotiations. During the negotiations before the Good Friday Agreement in April 1998, Campbell used live BBC TV to pressurize the unionists to the negotiating table. With the talks on the edge of collapse, the BBC reporter Mark Mardell was broadcasting live on *Newsnight*, preparing to interview David Trimble, the Ulster Unionist leader, when he suddenly received a phone call. Mardell interrupted his TV commentary to answer it.

Campbell had phoned to tell him the Prime Minister was planning to hold a showdown with the unionists. Mardell proceeded to tell viewers. Minutes later Trimble rejoined colleagues, only to be told by colleagues who had been watching television that Tony Blair needed to see him at once.

A second episode related to the appointment of the British cabinet minister George Robertson as secretary-general of NATO. This appointment came up in the wake of the Kosovo War, just as Tony Blair was beginning to develop confidence in his own foreign policy and was eager to extend British influence abroad. When President Clinton said he would back a British candidate, Blair first offered the NATO job to Foreign Secretary Robin Cook, who turned it down. So he made a private approach to Defence Secretary George Robertson, who accepted. At this stage, Robertson's name had not even been mentioned as a possible successor to Solana. It was against this background that Blair and Campbell attended a NATO Balkan 'Stability Pact' summit in Sarajevo

in July 1999. They were determined to use the get-together to win
approval for Robertson's appointment. The new secretary-general was
due to be formally decided the following week. Campbell and Blair
knew they would face opposition from some of the smaller NATO
members who were reluctant to allow the Anglo-American alliance to
gain even greater control.

The conference took place on 30 July in the dramatic setting of a
sports stadium in Sarajevo which was the scene of Jayne Torvill and
Christopher Dean's ice-dancing gold medal in the 1984 Winter
Olympics. The Downing Street team had to be ferried in and out by
helicopter and were accompanied by two reporters, Jon Smith of the
Press Association and John Morrison of Reuters. As the two journalists
waited to be briefed by Campbell on the outcome of the summit, they
were suddenly ordered into the waiting Chinook helicopter to prepare
to leave. As the helicopter prepared to take off, Campbell clambered
aboard. His voice drowned out by the rotors, he motioned to Smith to
pass him a pen and paper and spent the flight jotting down notes.
When they landed in nearby Banjaluka, where the Prime Minister's
plane was waiting to take them all back to London, Campbell ran off,
while the reporters made their way to the plane. They were unable to
file copy to London as their mobile phones would not work. The Prime
Minister's team has rather more effective communications links. An
hour or so later, when the PM's plane took off, Campbell called the two
journalists to the front of the plane. 'I've had to do something a bit
unconventional,' he told them. 'I have filed copy in your joint names
announcing that we have nominated George Robertson to be the new
secretary-general of NATO.' 'You've done what?' asked an incredulous
Smith.

'Don't worry, it's a joint byline,' said Campbell. Smith was shocked
– 'I thought, Christ I'm dead.' He feared that if his editor discovered
that the Prime Minister's press secretary had filed copy in his name, he
would be in serious trouble. Smith leaned towards Campbell and said:
'Alastair, you are going to have to tell me, very slowly, exactly what you
have done. Every detail.'

Campbell replied: 'I wrote a story with the pen and paper you gave
me and used the PM's secure communications to get it to Godric
(Smith) at Number 10 and told him to ring Reuters and PA and file it as

copy by you two.' A seething Smith inquired: 'And are we going to be allowed to see the story you have filed in our name?'

Morrison's account of the incident is less clear. He does not recall being cross and is not sure if Campbell asked his permission or not. Campbell included quotes by Tony Blair, in which the Prime Minister said: 'George has exactly the right mix of defence expertise and political and diplomatic skills. He will do an excellent job.' The story also stated that Robertson had had 'a good war in Kosovo, not least as a media performer', and that his candidacy had the backing of the main NATO powers. Campbell even had the temerity to quote himself as the Prime Minister's spokesman, stating: 'Before the media launches another wave of inaccurate reshuffle hysteria, I tell them they will be making yet another mistake if they do so on the back of this.' Once the nomination was announced by PA and Reuters, both renowned for their authority and crucially, their independence, it was tantamount to an official announcement that Robertson had got the job. Five days later it was duly confirmed by NATO. Robertson's nomination by Campbell effectively sealed his appointment. For NATO to go back on it would cause a major diplomatic row.

The move was a complete surprise to observers in Britain. The *Guardian*'s description of it as 'an unexpected diplomatic manoeuvre to reinforce (NATO's) renewed Anglo-American axis' was typical. It was an even bigger shock to some smaller member states, who believed they had been bounced into accepting Robertson. Four days later, a NATO source was quoted as saying: 'There is a feeling that it was a bit rushed and people wanted a chance to consult their capitals.'[5] The 'Stability Pact' summit gave another example of the British government's obsession with spin. The airport at Sarajevo was so small that the hosts had, in the interests of security and efficiency, asked the visiting politicians to share planes so they could all fly in and out in safety. Some obliged by giving a lift to politicians from neighbouring countries. Blair and Foreign Secretary Robin Cook were so keen to preserve their separate identities that they refused to travel in the same plane. The organizers reacted by banning them from landing at Sarajevo, forcing them to fly to Banjaluka, a detour of more than two hours which meant flying in to Sarajevo by helicopter. Blair and Cook would not even share a helicopter, forcing military commanders to lay on four Chinooks, one each for

Blair and Cook, and one each as a back up.

During the Iraq invasion, Campbell contacted a senior BBC correspondent in Kuwait and told him: 'We are hearing that a quarter of the republican guard are defecting and the numbers are increasing all the time.' The reporter contacted his bosses in London, indicated the source of the information, and suggested it could be 'dodgy', and if it was used, must be accompanied with a 'health warning' to make it clear to viewers it might not be reliable. He was wary of giving the impression the information came from military sources in Kuwait, which would give it greater credence than if it were attributed to Downing Street. The BBC broadcast the claim, but gave it little prominence and ensured it was carefully qualified.

Campbell's cavalier approach to leaking highly confidential information shocked British Airways executives who went to Downing Street to discuss plans to announce a £3 billion BA deal to buy nearly 200 aircraft from the European Airbus Consortium. The contract was an important 'good news' story for the government. BA's decision to switch from Boeing to a European aviation firm was a boost for Blair's standing in the EU, and the deal would safeguard nearly 40,000 British jobs. Blair agreed to interrupt his holiday in France to be in Toulouse when the deal was unveiled. Campbell announced at the Number 10 meeting with BA: 'I think I'll leak this to one of the Sunday papers.' When horrified BA officials explained such a move would be highly irregular because of the market sensitivity of the deal, he remained unimpressed. 'Bollocks,' he told them. One of the BA managers reported back to his superiors: 'Alastair Campbell plans to leak this story. If he does we are in big trouble and could end up in jail.' Campbell got the message. The story was not leaked. The incident was a good example of the dangers that arose when Campbell took his skills from politics to other areas. Spinning a story about a Labour policy or smearing a rival politician might be questionable from an ethical standpoint. But it did not involve any breach of the law. Spinning highly confidential and market-sensitive information was a different matter. Leaking details of a City deal involved big money and there were regulatory bodies to investigate such offences. It was the same cavalier approach to dealing with matters of an even more sensitive matter – intelligence – that led to Campbell's downfall.

During the Afghan war, BBC reporter Jon Sopel, who has friends in the Blair inner circle, was on the front line in northern Afghanistan, in fear of a Taliban counter attack at any moment, when his mobile rang. It was the Downing Street switchboard: Campbell wanted to speak to Sopel. He told Sopel of vital military developments in the Taliban stronghold of Kandahar and suggested he use this information in his report. Sopel told Campbell it was impossible for him to file a report claiming to know what was going on the opposite side of Afghanistan, and declined.

Doing deals with dirty Des

Shortly after his purchase of Express Newspapers for £125 million in November 2000, Richard Desmond told Alastair Campbell: 'I'm not interested in politics.' Campbell replied: 'You soon will be.' The handling of Desmond was another sign of New Labour's dedication, commitment, ruthlessness and constant readiness to subordinate the means to the ends. Desmond, a raucous cigar-smoking businessman who had made his fortune publishing soft pornography, was a natural Tory, though of a primitive type. His own attitudes and prejudices – dislike of regulation, angry alarm at asylum seekers 'flooding' into Britain – were almost exactly in line with those of William Hague. Yet, thanks to great attention to detail and enormous professionalism, Alastair Campbell and Tony Blair won Desmond for New Labour at the 2001 general election.

Downing Street struck at once. Within minutes of news flashing up on the wires in the early afternoon of 22 November 2000 that Desmond has purchased Express Newspapers, the Prime Minister telephoned the newspaper proprietor to congratulate him and ask him into Downing Street for a chat. Desmond warmed to this attention. 'He's great. He's efficient, isn't he?' he raved days later about Tony Blair. 'We are all the same age. He has played the guitar. He has got guys around him that are on the ball like Alastair Campbell and Lord (Waheed) Alli.'[6] An invitation to Chequers swiftly followed[7] while Alastair Campbell at once inaugurated close social relations.

Some suggested that Campbell's own past as a soft pornographer struck an harmonious note with the owner of a stable of raunchy magazines including *Big Ones*, *Asian Babes* and *Horny Housewives*. Indeed Desmond turned out also to be the publisher of *Forum*, the lubricious journal which had launched Campbell's career in journalism.

But Campbell would have got on well with Desmond in any case: he saw it as his job. There were reports that the two men jogged round Hampstead Heath together. Campbell duly attended Desmond's fiftieth birthday party at the Roundhouse. At the party, the Downing Street director of communications played the role of matchmaker between England football coach Sven-Goran Eriksson and Ulrika Jonsson, remarking to the former TV weather girl: 'Here's another Swede for you to talk to.' The two went on to have a well-publicized affair.

Cherie Blair is known for her strong support for feminist causes, and had at one stage banned the *Sun*, with its notorious Page Three girls, from the family home. But she proved to be notably tolerant towards the publisher of *Asian Babes*. At one of the gatherings at which Desmond mixed with the Blairs, Cherie sat on the arm of the chair where Desmond, cigar in hand, was seated. The PM was glad-handing guests over the other side of the room. At length Desmond said impatiently to Cherie: 'Is his Royal Highness going to come and see us?' Cherie replied: 'I'll go and get him.'[8] (She might have taken a different view had she been aware of claims that Desmond had planned to mark Labour's election victory of 1997 with a provocative photograph of a Cherie lookalike on the cover of his salacious publication *Readers' Wives*.)[9]

The comparison between the professional warmth of the New Labour media machine and the desultory Tory handling of Desmond was instructive. Several days after the purchase of the *Express* Desmond received a call from William Hague's office, saying the Tory leader would be on the phone shortly. Desmond stomped around impatiently, but Hague never came on the line. Desmond told *Sunday Express* readers on 26 November 2000 that Hague was 'unprofessional'. He went on: 'If I say to someone "I'll call you," I call them. You do.'[10]

But the Prime Minister wanted more than just the support of Express Newspapers. Soon Desmond and Labour general secretary Margaret McDonagh, who was desperate to raise money for the general-election campaign, had their first discussions about a donation. Desmond's first suggestion was that he should provide Labour with free advertising in his papers during the election campaign. But Labour wanted hard cash. On 7 February, Trade Secretary Stephen Byers announced there was to be no Competition Commission investigation into the *Express* takeover. Eight days later, Desmond secretly wrote a cheque for £100,000 to McDonagh who banked it immediately. If the money had been given just one day later, on 16 February, it would have been affected by new laws on political donations which would have forced the Labour party to disclose the gift. As it was, it stayed secret for another year and half. Only a handful of figures knew about it, including Blair, Campbell and McDonagh. When the donation was finally made public, it provoked an angry public response from ultra-loyal women ministers Harriet Harman and Tessa Jowell. An angry Desmond phoned Campbell and told him: 'I'm not happy about these bitches Jowell and Harman. You told me it wouldn't be a problem.'

Campbell replied: 'Richard, none of these people matter. The only person who counts is Tony and he is in your camp. Tony and Cherie will always back you.'[11]

McDonagh resigned as Labour general secretary after the 2001 election to become general manager of Express Newspapers on an estimated salary of £100,000.

Six of the best for Alan Rusbridger

Shortly before Tony Blair became prime minister, Alan Rusbridger, editor of the *Guardian*, was invited to a private meeting with him in the leader of the opposition's office in the House of Commons. It was suggested that he should bring with him Martin Kettle, the *Guardian*'s chief leader-writer, and his political editor, Michael White. The *Guardian* editor happily accepted. He hardly knew Tony Blair, having met him only once before, at a dinner party given by mutual friends. The *Guardian* team arrived at the Commons under the impression that they had been invited for a friendly chat with the Tony Blair.

They soon realized they had been mistaken. Besides Blair, the Labour team comprised Alastair Campbell and David Hill, director of communications. This was no social event. The leader of the opposition wanted to read the riot act. After perfunctory greetings he brought out a sheaf of cuttings, and went through them all. At one stage the future prime minister demanded to know why the word 'Blair' appeared in a headline. 'I imagine because it was shorter and fitted better than Labour,' came Rusbridger's reply.

'It took me back to public school,' recalled Rusbridger later. 'This sense of being in the senior prefect's study. Campbell said nothing, just looked on. Blair gave this imperious speech about how the *Guardian* was behaving. It was as if he was saying: "It's your attitude I object to."'

The meeting ended frostily. A few days later a version of the events was leaked from the Blair camp to the gossip column of the *Evening Standard*. This conveyed the information that a furious Campbell regarded Rusbridger as a 'public school twat'. Rusbridger wrote a letter demanding an explanation. Peter Mandelson then arrived in the role of mediator, and arranged a private dinner between Rusbridger and Blair at the Labour leader's Islington home. Here warm personal relations were restored, though on a professional level the problems persisted.

It is difficult to know what Campbell and Blair thought they could achieve. The technique used could hardly have been more counter-productive. Campbell and Blair might have had some success in changing *Guardian* policy had they confronted Rusbridger on his own. Doing so in front of two senior colleagues made it impossible for him to climb down, even if he had wanted to, without losing face.

In the months that followed, every technique was used by Campbell in attempts to bring the *Guardian* round. 'He used to ring up to cajole, plead, shout and horse-trade,' says Rusbridger. 'Stories would be offered on condition that they went on the front page. I would be told that if I didn't agree they would go to the *Independent*. They would withdraw favours, grant favours, exclude us from stories going elsewhere.' Gradually, Campbell woke up to the fact the *Guardian* simply wasn't interested in the Downing Street approach to news management. 'Now we have almost no contact,' says Rusbridger.

Even after abandoning the full-frontal approach, Campbell and Blair continued to find other ways of getting at the *Guardian*. The newspaper became a ritual object of attack at meetings of the parliamentary Labour party, the National Executive Committee and even, at times, the Cabinet. 'I don't read the *Guardian*. I prefer to read a Labour paper,' became a standard Blair remark. At one point he is supposed to have urged Labour MPs to read the *Sun* instead. The real preference, however, was for *The Times*. Downing Street found the political reporting in the Murdoch broadsheet gratifyingly reliable. The *Guardian* lobby team, by contrast, produced shudders of distaste.

One main object of Campbell's resentment was the cheerful and bucolic figure of David Hencke, the *Guardian* Whitehall correspondent. To look at, Hencke is nothing much. A beard, a mop of hair, a badly cut suit. He does not have an office and operates out of a tiny desk in a sweaty and overcrowded room just off the Commons press gallery. Yet his stories have been responsible for the downfall of two Cabinet ministers, one for each political party, Jonathan Aitken and Peter Mandelson, and he can also claim the credit for the downfall of Neil and Christine Hamilton. But Campbell smelt danger. He sensed that the same man who had been so invaluable to Labour in opposition could wreak havoc to Labour in government. The existence of Hencke, and his ability to prise out damaging stories, has been one of the major bones of contention between Rusbridger and Alastair Campbell. A correspondence exists on the subject. Once Campbell bumped into Hencke in the lobby corridor of the Commons and barked at him, 'You're just completely insane,' before marching on.

Campbell believed that the best way to get back at the *Guardian* was by hitting the paper commercially. Returning to London from Blackpool after the Labour party conference of 1998, Ewen MacAskill found himself sharing a railway carriage with the Downing Street press secretary, who soon went on the offensive. He listed several recent atrocities carried out by the *Guardian* – an opinion piece by Jonathan Freedland, one of the paper's star columnists, on Labour's maladroit handling of the annual elections to the National Executive Committee appeared especially to have infuriated him – and then made an extraordinary threat. 'If you carry on in this vein,' Campbell calmly told him, 'We are going to tell our people not to buy you.' Campbell indicated to MacAskill – who subsequently sent a memo to his editor about this bizarre train conversation – that 10,000–20,000 readers could be knocked off the circulation of the *Guardian* if the Prime Minister sent out an edict to Labour party members to boycott the paper.

The feud with the *Guardian* shone a most illuminating light on Alastair Campbell's Downing Street machine. Part of it was the sheer unreality of it all – the weird belief that Labour party members could be ordered to give up reading their daily paper, the deluded notion that the *Sun* and even the *Mail* could be true, rather than merely fair-weather, friends of the Labour party. Most revealing of all was Campbell's belief that the *Guardian* was hostile to New Labour. It was not. To think this was to misunderstand the paper's role, indeed to misunderstand journalism itself. There are two ways that a friendly newspaper can behave when its side is in power. It can either act as house journal, repeating the government line in a slavish way. Or it can play the role of candid friend. The *Guardian*'s entire history and character compels it to choose the latter, more complicated route. All previous leaders of the Labour party have complained about the *Guardian*. There were plenty of columnists who were thought to be Blairite – Hugo Young, Polly Toynbee, Jonathan Freedland, Martin Kettle. Roy Greenslade, the paper's media writer, was and remains the most devout follower of the Downing Street line in all Fleet Street, reflecting the alarms and preoccupations of Campbell himself with an uncanny accuracy. Few would dispute that the *Guardian* had been, on the whole, supportive of the New Labour government rather than not. None of this counted with Campbell. And because the *Guardian* produced the occasional story that highlighted the rifts in Labour ranks or an editorial that poured scorn on government incompetence, he thought it was against them. Campbell's suspicions were reinforced when the contents of a private breakfast for Brown, hosted by Rusbridger, were leaked in the autumn of 2003. Brown openly derided Blair's plans for foundation hospitals, saying they were doomed to fail, and criticized university 'top-up fees' as 'ridiculous and elitist'.

Campbell's hostility towards the *Guardian* was an inheritance from the days when he shared Neil Kinnock's bunker. It is strikingly similar to Margaret Thatcher's approach to the media during the 1980s. Thatcher had a series of big and bloody battles to fight. She had powerful enemies who needed to be destroyed. She needed a praetorian guard to stand by her in a hostile world. But Blair, in many ways, is the opposite of Thatcher. Where she brought division, he is a healer. Where she polarized, he unifies. As a political leader it is his mission to reach out and break down the boundaries that divide British society rather than create new ones. And yet Alastair Campbell's Downing Street press office retained and even fostered the narrow, paranoid, sterile mentality

of the 1980s. It could hardly be less appropriate for the new world ush-
ered in by Tony Blair's great election victory of May 1997. This antago-
nistic view was to grow worse and worse as the Campbell years dragged
on, ending up with the tragedy of the David Kelly affair.

Culture of concealment

One important expression of the bunker mentality that Campbell
brought with him to Downing Street was his attitude to revealing the
truth. Though technically he was a civil servant, with a salary paid by
the state, Campbell owed his overriding loyalty to Tony Blair. And it is a
ferocious loyalty. 'Loyalty, that is what I am about,' he once said.[12]

His cynical approach to the release of information was evident long
before he entered Downing Street, indeed before he formally took up
the reins as Tony Blair's press spokesman. The first reporter who
formed the impression that Campbell's account of events could be partial and not wholly reliable was Nicholas Jones, the BBC political correspondent. After Tony Blair dropped his Clause 4 bombshell at the
Labour conference of 1994, Jones suggested on air that 'John Prescott
was only on board a week ago and did advise against it.'

This was, for New Labour, a damaging suggestion. The Clause 4
announcement could not have been more sensitive or more potentially
explosive. Any notion that the deputy leader of the Labour party had
reservations about dropping it was inflammatory. After the broadcast,
according to Jones's account, Campbell asked to see him. He told Jones
that Prescott had been aware of the move for several weeks and had
been 'fully on board every step of the way'. Campbell used the episode
to publicly humiliate the BBC man and demonstrate the muscle and
firepower of his own press machine.

Jones's original broadcast may very possibly have been wanting in
some respects. But Campbell's assertion that Prescott was 'on board all
the way' was completely untrue. Prescott's biographer, Colin Brown,
provides a detailed account of his conversion to the proposal that
Clause 4 should be abolished. Brown records that the 'deputy leader
maintained his opposition right up to seeing the first drafts of Blair's
speech for the conference. Then, like a reluctant craftsman, drawn into
a project to make it work, Prescott relented.'

Another episode before Labour's election showed how obstructive Campbell and New Labour were capable of being. In early 1996 the *Sunday Express* ran a story that a close and intimate political friendship had sprung up between Tony Blair and Roy Jenkins. With Blair facing dissent on the left of the party, the report highlighted the sensitive issue of New Labour collaboration with the old Social Democrats who had broken away from Michael Foot's Labour party in the early 1980s. When the *Express* rang Campbell for confirmation the story was comprehensively rubbished. The denial was specific. It was claimed that the two men had met only once since Tony Blair had become Labour leader, at a dinner with a number of others present. The *Express*, confident of its sources, went ahead and ran its account anyway. The *Sunday Times* tried to follow up the *Express*. Michael Prescott, the paper's political correspondent, rang Peter Mandelson for confirmation, but he too denied it. A month later a television programme made by Michael Cockerell showed that the *Express* story was even truer than its reporters had realized. It proved that Jenkins and Blair had become personally and politically close, and showed that Blair had even been a welcome visitor at Jenkins' country home.

When this programme appeared the *Express* rang Campbell to complain. He said that he 'understood how you might think that you have been misled'. Other papers reported similar episodes with Campbell, but not too much was made of them.

When Tony Blair appointed Campbell his press secretary he already knew that Campbell had a reputation as a man who could not be relied on to tell the whole truth. In May 1996 the then Tory MP Rupert Allason took Campbell and Mirror Group Newspapers to court on a charge of malicious falsehood. The case resulted from a long-running feud between Allason and the *Mirror*, which dated back to the days when Robert Maxwell controlled the paper.

Allason claimed that Campbell had fabricated a *Daily Mirror* story in November 1992 which stated that fifty MPs had signed a Commons early day motion (EDM) urging him to give a £250,000 libel payout from the *Mirror* to *Mirror* pensioners. The *Mirror* admitted the story was wrong. (Only seven MPs signed the motion and the payout was £200,000.) The paper also admitted organizing the EDM. Allason's most damaging allegation was that Campbell had organized it because he had a grudge against the MP. Allason told Campbell in court: 'Your stock in trade is disinformation and half truths.' Left-wing MP George Galloway told the court he saw Campbell in a Commons corridor urging Labour MPs to sign the motion. The *Mirror*'s counsel, Charles Gray QC, told Allason that nobody would be interested in the case 'unless you were calling the press secretary to the leader of the opposition a liar'.

Campbell admitted he couldn't stand Allason, but said he had had nothing to do with the EDM: it was the idea of his deputy David Bradshaw. His story was backed up by Bradshaw.

In his summing up, the judge, Sir Maurice Drake, was scathing about Campbell. He said: 'I did not find Mr Campbell by any means a wholly satisfactory or convincing witness,' adding that 'Mr Campbell was less than completely open and frank, he did not impress me as a witness in whom I could feel 100 per cent confident.'

After the 1997 election, Bradshaw was recruited by Campbell to work in the Number 10 strategic communications unit. One of his jobs was to churn out articles which appeared in national and regional newspapers under the by-line of Tony Blair.

Robert Peston, when political editor of the *Financial Times*, put the difference between Campbell and his predecessors like this: 'With previous press secretaries one always felt that if one asked the right question one would get the right answer. Not necessarily with Alastair. He is more obsessed with controlling the flow of information.'

Many lobby journalists have their own stories of this kind of obstruction from Campbell or his team. And not just lobby journalists. Gordon Brown's spin-doctor Charlie Whelan claimed it was possible to tell when Campbell was not telling the truth by reading his body language, or to be more precise, monitoring his habit of sniffing in a derisive manner. 'Every times he lies, he sniffs,' said Whelan.

A year after the 1997 election, the *Mail on Sunday* learnt that special in-flight beds were being built so that Tony Blair could sleep on long-haul journeys overseas. It was an eminently sensible idea, and the main question it raised was why British prime ministers, who often faced fraught and complex negotiations at the end of their journeys, had not been provided with beds years before. But the government information machine put up a smokescreen. At first it denied that the beds had been ordered at all, then claimed, inaccurately, that the order had been placed by the Tories before New Labour gained power.

This was routine obstruction. The *Financial Times* faced the same kind of difficulty in November 1998 when it ran a story that the government welfare-reform programme had run into difficulties. The paper reported that ministers had dropped plans, announced the previous March, for compulsory saving for pensions, adding that the government pensions review had been delayed. Campbell dismissed the story as 'crap'. Two months later, when the pensions review was finally published and the compulsion element was missing, Campbell was asked in open lobby why he had rubbished the *FT*'s story. He said he could not remember having done so.

In June 1998 a furious row broke out following Ulster Secretary Mo Mowlam's decision to invite both Prince Charles and Sinn Fein leader Gerry Adams to the annual summer garden party at her official residence in Hillsborough Castle. The Prince was deeply irritated and upset, partly because he felt that the Sinn Fein invitation had been deliberately kept from him. A group of the Prince's aides had visited the province three weeks before on a reconnaissance ahead of what was always expected to be a very sensitive trip. They had been told nothing. The Prince found the whole episode particularly disturbing because his great-uncle Lord Mountbatten was blown apart by an IRA bomb, and he himself is colonel-in-chief of the Parachute Regiment. On the Monday after the story broke, the Prince's office was alerted that Downing Street was briefing journalists that the Prince of Wales had been made aware of the meeting some time before and had approved it. The Prince was so angry about this that Mark Bolland, a senior member of his private office, rang up Alastair Campbell personally to complain. In a heated exchange, he informed Campbell that unless he himself set the record straight, the Prince's office was ready to publicly contradict the Downing Street version of events.

These were all everyday incidents in the rough and tumble of lobby combat. What was perhaps more striking was how questions about the integrity of the government machine were often highlighted during moments of acute political crisis. It began to look as if the first reaction of the government when put under pressure was to cover up and to dissemble rather than come clean. This syndrome quickly emerged when the new and squeaky-clean Blair administration was first put to the test with the Bernie Ecclestone affair. The government failed that test, though Campbell himself emerged with flying colours.

The Ecclestone affair started to crackle on Guy Fawkes Day 1997, when it emerged that Tessa Jowell, the Health Minister, was planning to grant Formula One a special exemption from the government ban on tobacco advertising. This news caused a great deal of rumbling on the left, but the problem only really began when the *Sunday Telegraph*, was informed that Bernie Ecclestone, the owner of Formula One, was a giant donor to Labour party funds. The paper rang Downing Street for corroboration of this story on the afternoon of Thursday 6 November.

There followed a great soul-searching within the government machine. Campbell strongly urged that the press should be informed not merely that Ecclestone was a donor, but that he was a very large one indeed, having contributed £1 million to Labour's accounts. It seems to have been Tony Blair, after talking the matter over with Gordon Brown, who ran scared of coming clean. He decided on an alternative course of action. A letter should be written from the Labour party to Lord Neill, chairman of the Committee of Standards in Public Life, enquiring about the propriety of the donation. That way the government would be seen to have acted properly. In the meantime instructions went out that the donation should not be confirmed to any member of the press.

This tactic did not work. The *Sunday Telegraph* published the story anyway. The situation got out of control. In the end Tony Blair made the decision to go on national television for a soul-baring interview to protest his own innocence. *On the Record*, John Humphrys' Sunday lunchtime political show, was deliberately chosen as the vehicle. It was decided that it was important to show that Blair was prepared to face up to Britain's toughest interviewer.

Campbell's advice to come clean was based just as much on his sound strategic sense of how to handle a story as on any belief in open government. But his general aversion to telling the truth in anything like an open and straightforward way was demonstrated by the row that blew up over a lobby briefing given on the morning of 24 March 1998. It followed a front-page story in that day's *Financial Times* by

Campbell's old adversary Robert Peston. Peston wrote that Blair had 'intervened on behalf of Rupert Murdoch ... by speaking to Romano Prodi, the Italian premier, about the media magnate's attempt to acquire an Italian television network.' This was a sensitive story. The government's close relations with Murdoch have always been unpopular with great tranches of the Labour party. Just a month earlier the government had been defeated in the House of Lords over an amendment to the Competition Bill aimed at outlawing predatory pricing. This was directly aimed at the News International policy of reducing the cover price of *The Times* in order to gain readers from less well-endowed rival broadsheets.

There is no absolutely authoritative account of what happened at that lobby briefing. A Downing Street tape was taken of it: it was subsequently, as usual with all such tapes, deleted. Lobby journalists took notes: no one has come forward with a word-for-word account. Perhaps it was simply not possible to make one in the mayhem and confusion.

Campbell was asked why the British Prime Minister was asking Prodi questions on behalf of Rupert Murdoch. He was not eager to answer. Lobby correspondents persisted in their chosen line of attack. There are various techniques that Campbell uses when he is in a tight corner and wants to change the subject. He stonewalls, evades the question, answers a different one from the one that has been asked, puts up a smokescreen of confusion by launching a savage attack on his adversary. On this occasion he settled on bluster and abuse. While not denying that a conversation had taken place, he described the *Financial Times* story as a 'complete joke'. Just to make his meaning even more clear he proclaimed that 'it's balls that the Prime Minister "intervened" over some deal with Murdoch. That's C-R-A-P.'

Two days later the *Financial Times* revealed that Murdoch had told colleagues the previous week 'that he would ask Tony Blair for help in ascertaining whether the Italian government would block his £4 billion acquisition of Mediaset, Italy's leading commercial television network'. When this conversation was confirmed by Ray Snoddy, the media editor of the Murdoch-owned *Times*, Campbell was exposed.

But Campbell did not lie over the Prodi business. For him, much hinges on the definition of the word 'intervention'. He continues to this day to defend, in the pugnacious, no-nonsense manner he has made his own, his stance that morning in Downing Street. Three months later, grilled by MPs on the episode, he was sticking to his guns: 'I described that story as a joke and I happen to think it was a joke. I think it is the oddest form of intervention to sit in your office waiting for a phone call from the Italian prime minister.' He has his defenders in the press. Roy Greenslade, former editor of the *Mirror*, pronounced afterwards that 'Campbell didn't lie to journalists, though he was economical with the truth because he and Blair were punctiliously observing the protocol of protecting the confidentiality of a private conversation between government leaders.'

Most journalists involved in the episode would not accept this gallant defence from Campbell's old friend, at any rate not in its entirety. Robert Shrimsley, then political correspondent of the *Daily Telegraph*, puts this point of view in no uncertain terms:

> Campbell has mastered the trick of conveying a message which conveys the direct opposite of the truth without telling a lie. A good example is the Prodi story. He informed the lobby that the story was C-R-A-P. It later turned out that the only thing that was wrong was that he [Blair] had not actually instigated the telephone call himself. Strictly speaking he can probably defend the position that he did not lie. But any rational person attending that briefing would have drawn only one conclusion from what he was saying and that conclusion would have been wrong. And that was his specific intention, that they should draw the wrong one. One of Campbell's favourite expressions was 'I've told you what I've told you.' This was wide open to misinterpretation. Campbell would fall back on the phrase when he had reached the limit of what he was prepared to say. One reporter, who had a long established relationship with Campbell, assumed Campbell's 'I've told you what I've told you' reply to the same question was a coded 'yes'. He was furious when he did just that only to discover the story he wrote as a result was completely untrue, though it had suited Campbell's purpose for him to write it. The reporter accused Campbell of deliberately misleading him, only to be slapped down sharply. The journalist had done well out of the relationship and had nothing to complain about, said Campbell.

Another victim of what might best be referred to as Alastair Campbell's disinformation strategy was the *Times* columnist Matthew Parris.

Parris has told the story in his autobiography *Chance Witness*. He recalled how in 1994, during the Labour leadership campaign, he and Campbell, then still a journalist on the newspaper *Today*, travelled together in a cab to BBC Millbank to interrogate Tony Blair for *BBC Breakfast News*. Parris wrote that the two reporters had discussed lines of questioning for the interview. He recalled how Campbell successfully urged him not to question Tony Blair on why, as an opponent of opt-out schools, he had sent his son Euan to the elite London Oratory. Parris said that Campbell persuaded him that to pursue that line of enquiry would have been a cheap trick, without adding that he was actually at work on behalf of the Blair campaign, and therefore an interested party.[13]

Campbell's response when Parris published this story was devastating. Writing on Downing Street notepaper to the editor of *The Times*, Campbell insisted that Euan still had a year's primary schooling ahead of him at that date, and could not possibly have been at the Oratory. Simultaneously a letter from Downing Street went to Parris's publishers Penguin: 'In accepting that he [Parris] was factually incorrect, he is accepting that I did not seek to prevent him asking Mr Blair about his choice of the Oratory for his son. At the time I did not know Euan was going to the Oratory. Nor did Mr Parris. Nor did Euan. Nor did Mr Blair.'

Campbell went on to tell Penguin that he had been 'advised' that Parris's remarks were defamatory: 'You say that there can be no question of offering me redress. I ask you to re-examine that statement before I take the matter further. [Otherwise] I will need to consider what steps are open to me to ensure that the book is not published until an appropriate correction is made.'[14]

These letters prompted grave doubt, bordering on panic, in the minds of both Parris and his publishers. If the Blairs had not decided to send their son to the Oratory at this stage, how could Parris have known about it, let alone discussed the issue with Campbell in the back of the car? Parris's first reaction was that perhaps his memory had been playing tricks on him. In fact, subsequent research showed he was mostly right. Though Euan had not yet started at the Oratory, the Blairs had already visited the Oratory to discuss sending him to the school. Furthermore this was public knowledge, so there was no mystery about how Parris knew about it during the leadership campaign.[15]

Parris had, however, made a small mistake. He wrote that Euan Blair was already at the Oratory in 1994. Euan only joined the school a year later. Campbell's art was to seize on this inaccuracy, and seek to use it to prove that the whole Parris version of events was a fiction, that the encounter in the car had never taken place, that he had never sought to dissuade Matthew Parris from asking questions about Euan Blair. On this basis he threatened steps to block the distribution of the Parris book.

The technique here is interesting, because it was used by Downing Street on a number of other occasions. A story might be fundamentally truthful and correct, but Campbell would seize on one minor detail or inaccuracy to create the impression that it was utterly false. Campbell created an atmosphere in Downing Street where the initial recourse was often to suppress the truth, and even on occasion to lie his way out of trouble. An important example of Downing Street mendacity came during the Mittal affair in February 2002. This involved lying and deception on a grand scale, starting with the Prime Minister himself. The scandal started with the discovery of a letter from Tony Blair to the Romanian prime minister, Adrian Nastase, concerning the sale of the Romanian SIDEX steel plant to Lashme Mittal's LNM. The most striking thing about this letter is that it referred to LNM as a 'British company', a blatant falsehood. LNM's parent company is registered in the Dutch Antilles, while no more than 100 employees are employed in the UK out of a 125,000 worldwide workforce. LNM's closest relationship with Britain was perhaps in its capacity as a Labour donor. It had given £125,000 to the Labour party.

At first Tony Blair, and the Downing Street machine stood by the claim the LNM was 'a British company'[16], but rapidly weakened that line, so that by 13 February the Prime Minister was merely expressing his delight that 'a British based company has succeeded'.[17] By 14 February Downing Street was reduced to blustering, 'Look, there isn't any legal definition of what is a British company.'[18]

The claim that Mittal was British is just one of numerous direct falsehoods uttered by the Prime Minister's official spokesman (PMOS).[19] In an attempt to distance Tony Blair from the incriminating letter, the PMOS had asserted that the letter had been drawn up within the Foreign Office and that the 'Prime Minister had signed it and sent it back unchanged.'[20] This assertion was repeated in the afternoon's lobby meeting.[21] This, however, turned out to be false. It emerged that Downing Street staff removed a reference to Lakshmi Mittal, described in an earlier draft as a 'friend'.[22]

Downing Street also seems to have misled reporters by claiming initially that LNM 'had donated to other political parties as well'.[23] When this suggestion was denied, the PMOS blamed 'reports over the weekend' for the error.[24]

Doubt also surrounds the initial Downing Street claim that the letter from the Prime Minister to his Romanian counterpart was simply a formality, and simply 'congratulatory', as Downing Street insisted. But on 13 February the British Embassy in Romania suggested to the BBC that the letter from Tony Blair had been a major factor in helping 'finalize' the takeover.[25] Extra evidence that this might have been the case can be found in *Bucharest Business Week* of 23 July 2001, the date that Tony Blair sent his letter. It reported that even at that late stage the French company Usinor was still confident of winning the contract and that the, 'issue is high on the agenda of visiting French Prime Minister Lionel Jospin who arrives today'.[26] The leading Labour Asian peer Lord Paul, himself a steel tycoon, was quoted as saying, 'The Romanian government were teetering on the edge about whether to give him (Mittal) the contract. They were not satisfied with his credentials. He needed the Blair letter to give his bid a lift.'[27]

The Mittal affair was a bizarre episode, with 10 Downing Street changing its story on a number of occasions in an attempt to make sense of why the Prime Minister should have personally backed a bid by LNM, a company with no significant British links, for the Sidex steel contract. Even today a number of questions remain unanswered. According to the Downing Street account, the idea that Tony Blair should intervene at head of government level to secure the Mittal contract came from the British ambassador in Bucharest. This claim, like many of the official protestations in the affair, is unconvincing. One curious detail is why Tony Blair seems to have displayed no anger or upset at having his integrity called into question after signing a mendacious letter to the Romanian prime minister.

The semi-automatic fib-telling that was the hallmark of Downing Street during the Mittal affair was on display once again after the Prime Minister and his family went on holiday in Egypt in December that year. The luxury holiday came courtesy of the Egyptian government, which paid for the Prime Minister, his wife Cherie and their four children to fly from Cairo to the Red Sea resort of Sharm-el-Sheikh and then to stay at private villas in the grounds of a hotel. The involvement of the Egyptian government became public knowledge when the Prime Minister made an entry in the House of Commons Register of Members' Interests several months later, revealing that he made a charitable donation of an unspecified amount said to be equal to the cost of the stay in the villa and the travel. But at the time Downing Street had told newspapers that the Blairs paid for their holiday and that it was 'entirely private'.[28] Doubtless the Blairs deserve credit for making their charitable donation, but the Downing Street account of events was at best misleading, since the holiday was arranged and paid for by the Egyptian government and the Prime Minister had dinner with the Egyptian President during his stay.[29]

First strike at the BBC

The BBC welcomed the arrival of New Labour. Political reporters and producers were told to report government within its own chosen parameters. Many found this easy to do. Only a minority treated New Labour in the same sceptical way as they had reported the vanquished Conservatives. Few wanted, and fewer dared, to stand up against an accomplished New Labour media regime which mixed bullying, ingratiation and illicit influence to get what it wanted.

From very shortly after the 1997 General Election victory, New Labour set out to control the nature of BBC reporting. Campbell set out what he wanted when, in January 1998, he addressed a private seminar of BBC executives at Nuffield College, Oxford. His main complaint was that the BBC devoted too much time to Labour rows. The corporation's political reporters were unable to 'distinguish what is important from what is exciting', he stated. 'A public service broadcaster,' added Campbell, 'should be providing more coverage of policy and less about rows.'[30] And he had an extraordinary solution to the problem: the BBC should ignore laws forcing them to be impartial, and report Tory splits but not Labour ones.

'The BBC worries too much about balance and the Representation of the People Act,' Campbell proclaimed. 'It could also take a different view of party dissidents. When a government has a majority of only one, then what Teresa Gorman says is significant; but when it has a majority of over 160, Ken Livingstone's and Diane Abbott's remarks are much less newsworthy. Too much attention was paid to the row over lone parent benefits without enough on the substance of what had been decided.'

Newsnight, the *World At One* and *Today* were the worst offenders, he said. 'The treatment of Jack Straw this morning was illustrative. First there were three critics, followed by Straw and some sneering from John Humphrys.'[31]

To a very large extent the BBC establishment fully subscribed to this analysis. Shortly after the general election the *Newsnight* editor Peter Horrocks wrote a memo to his team which might have been written by Alastair Campbell himself. 'The model of five years of Tory coverage must be thrown away,' Horrocks wrote. 'The template of spite, disunity, Europe and chaos may one day apply, but it doesn't yet and we must not behave as if it does.' He continued: 'Labour has a huge mandate … our job should not be to quarrel with the purpose of policy but question its implementation. Ennui is over – for now. Much of our tricksiness and world-weariness was an appropriate way of capturing the repetitiveness of the dying days of Conservatism.'[32]

Very few BBC executives had the will or the motive to hold out against this new culture. Kevin Marsh was one of the few who did. He refused to take at face value the stories pumped out by Millbank and later Downing Street. He insisted that his reporters digged deeper.

The bad blood between Campbell and Marsh first surfaced in March 1997, five weeks before the general election. The *Guardian* published extracts of a Commons Standards and Privileges Committee investigation into 'sleaze' allegations against Tory MP Neil Hamilton. The report led to a major political controversy. Knowing the damage it could do, Major had gone to great lengths to prevent the report being published before the election.

So far this was just a routine Tory sleaze story. But it took another turn when extracts of the committee's report were distributed at a Labour party election press conference, talked up by one of Campbell's deputies as 'the evidence John Major didn't want you to see'. Marsh got his team to check the extracts against those published in the *Guardian*, found that the Labour party appeared to have more information than the newspaper, and decided to tackle the story from a different perspective. Marsh wanted to know if Labour had abused the rules on Commons privilege by leaking the report in an attempt to damage Hamilton and Major.

Campbell's deputy, Tim Allan, got to hear about it and rang Marsh three or four times pleading with him not to run the story. As the clock ticked towards 1 p.m., Marsh refused to drop the item. An agitated Allan rang him again and said: 'If you run this story, I'm finished.' By now there were only minutes to go. Marsh knew the story was risky if not done properly, had the rest of the programme to complete, and decided to play safe and drop it. It was broadcast in the *PM* show later that day, but in a diluted form. Shortly afterwards, Marsh received a handwritten letter from Campbell which accused him of adopting an 'anti-Labour follow-any-old-Tory-guff agenda'.

Marsh annoyed Campbell again by pursuing Labour party confusion over plans to sell off Britain's air-traffic control system. Shadow Transport Minister and opposition spokesman Andrew Smith, the man at the centre of the row, was ordered by Labour officials to go to ground to damp down the story. But on 10 April a *World at One* reporter tracked down Smith and proceeded to question him.

Campbell fired off a complaint to BBC head of news Tony Hall and BBC chief political adviser Anne Sloman. Campbell told them: 'The relationship with the BBC has completely broken down.'[33] Sloman did not want a major falling out with New Labour and replied in measured tones. According to one BBC source, Sloman 'half apologized'. Within days, Allan boasted: 'You can't trust *World at One*, the BBC has had to apologize to us.'

New Labour's technique of using any admission of error as 'proof' that an entire report was wrong was to be one of the main factors in determining its defensive response during the dispute over the Iraq dossier. Once established in Number 10, Campbell tried a different way of influencing *World at One*. He took to phoning *World At One*

host Nick Clarke, offering a briefing on whichever subject the programme was pursuing. Marsh's view was that the BBC political staff
already received the Number 10 daily briefings along with other
Westminster reporters: he saw no reason why Downing Street
should be allowed any special influence. *World at One* could make its
own assessment of a story or interview without Campbell telling
them how to handle it. The next time Campbell rang, Clarke did not
take the call.

Campbell was not alone in his suspicion of Marsh. Marsh threatened to sue Charlie Whelan in October 1997, when Scottish TV made a
fly-on-the-wall documentary about the Treasury in which Whelan said:
'Don't worry Gordon. The editor of the programme is a Tory, Kevin
Marsh. *World at One* have always pissed us about.' The remark was cut
from the programme as a result of a complaint by Marsh, who has
never been a member of the Conservative party. Staff at *World at One*
had T-shirts produced bearing the phrase that Campbell and Whelan
both used to describe them: 'Wankers At One.'

BBC political correspondent Nicholas Jones, who wrote several
books about Labour 'spin', was the butt of many Campbell jibes. After
Jones made an aside on *Breakfast News* about an apparent leak of government information to the *Sun*, Campbell bawled him out at that day's
lobby briefing: 'Hey, I was watching you this morning with one of my
kids and he said to me: "Dad, that bloke is obsessed with you."' The skill
of the comment was that Campbell put the observation in the words of
his son. After a report by Jones about a firemen's dispute during the
1997 election, Campbell raged at him: 'So that's the story, then, a trade
union dispute … I just love the way you guys in the BBC decide what
the issue is … John Major only has to fart to get on the news. If Blair
does something positive, you don't report it.'

The BBC might have been expected to be proud of the fiercely independent and unbiddable Jones. Not so. Under director-general John
Birt, he was treated as an embarrassment. Jones was told privately:
'Your job as a BBC correspondent isn't to antagonize Alastair Campbell.' Campbell even complained about Jones at the BBC Nuffield seminar (with Birt in attendance) stating: 'The BBC's obsession with spin
doctors is way out of proportion. There is one guy on the BBC staff
whose only job is to write about spin doctors.'

Campbell was more outspoken when BBC political heavyweight John Sergeant asked him how Blair would respond to questions about the Bill Clinton's affair with Monica Lewinsky during a trip to Washington. Campbell responded by calling the BBC a 'downmarket, overstaffed, over bureaucratic, ridiculous organization'.

chapter eleven
Campbell Takes Control

Look at that bloody man Campbell sitting on the only chair in the room. He didn't stand up, he didn't even acknowledge me, he just stayed there sprawled out using his mobile phone.

Prince Charles

Deputy Prime Minister

NO ONE WHO WAS THERE will forget the press briefing that Campbell gave on Wednesday 23 December 1998. He dragged himself into the room to meet the waiting journalists, all hungry for news of Trade Secretary Peter Mandelson's next move following the revelation of his undeclared £373,000 loan from Geoffrey Robinson, the Paymaster-General. The story that Campbell told the lobby, both collectively and in individual briefings over the next few days, was a moving one. He told how a contrite Peter Mandelson, upset by the damage he had inadvertently done to the government, had phoned Tony Blair at 10 p.m. the previous night, and told him that he saw no alternative to resignation. The Prime Minister listened sympathetically, told Mandelson to 'sleep on it', but felt in his heart that 'Peter's mind was made up.'[1] The following morning, so Campbell told journalists, Mandelson had duly called Blair at 10 a.m. and told the Prime Minister that he had decided to resign.[2]

It was an attractive story, which put the best possible gloss on events which had hurt New Labour to the core. It presented the Prime Minister as compassionate, and Peter Mandelson as contrite. There was only one problem with this account: it was not true.

On the night of Tuesday 22 December, Mandelson had indeed spoken to Blair at Chequers and admitted he had acted unwisely. He had also made it clear he intended to stay. The next morning, he woke up more convinced than ever that he should not resign, and that he could persuade Blair to agree with him. At 9 a.m. he told a political editor friend, 'I'm confident I can ride out the storm.'[3] He also spoke to Gordon Brown, who told him: 'It is not a resigning matter and as long as you apologize for an apparent conflict of interest that should suffice.'[4] The irony of being supported by the Chancellor, on whose behalf the story of the home loan was leaked by friends who thought they were acting in his interest, was not lost on Mandelson.

But, unknown to him, when he arrived at his office in the Department of Trade and Industry ready to fight for his political life, the decision had been made for him. Campbell had taken the precaution of phoning Blair at Chequers early that Wednesday morning. The two men agreed Mandelson must go, and had even taken the secondary step of deciding who would replace him. While Mandelson was telling friends he was going to stay, Downing Street Chief of Staff Jonathan Powell, acting under Blair's orders, was already at work in Number 10, drawing up the arrangements to hand over Mandelson's job to Stephen Byers, and planning the rest of the reshuffle. Mandelson, oblivious to the fact that his fate was already sealed and a successor in the process of being chosen, was still putting the last touches to his defence strategy with his special adviser Benjamin Wegg-Prosser.

A few days earlier, when it was clear within Downing Street that the story was about to become public knowledge, Blair had spoken to Cabinet Secretary Sir Richard Wilson and told him: 'This is serious.' Wilson agreed, saying that Mandelson should pay the money back as soon as possible, but that he was satisfied there had been 'no impropriety'. The day the story broke, Powell phoned Wilson and asked him to send a formal note to Blair stating his view. Wilson sent a one-line message repeating the view he had expressed to Blair, and then went on holiday. On his return, Wilson was astonished and outraged to learn that Downing Street had attempted to justify Mandelson's departure by claiming Wilson had 'investigated' the matter, thereby implicating him. Wilson felt he had been used by Number 10. It was not the last time.

When Campbell arrived at Downing Street on Wednesday morning, his mind was made up. 'Peter has got to go, Tony agrees,' he said[5] after visiting Jonathan Powell in the Number 10 private office. Campbell and his deputy Lance Price went to the Department of Trade and Industry in Victoria Street to tell Mandelson the game was up. Price, a close friend of Mandelson, was in agony, torn between loyalty to his friend and loyalty to his master. When they reached the DTI fresh-faced Wegg-Prosser attempted to rehearse the version of events Mandelson believed would get him off the hook, but was cut dead by Campbell, who told everyone to leave Mandelson's office, and instructed him to phone Blair. As they waited outside, Wegg-Prosser told Price that the mortgage issue could be dealt with. 'I'm afraid it's much too late for that,' Price told him. He shook his head slowly and drew his forefinger across his throat like a cutlass.

Inside the commodious Secretary of State's office, Campbell listened as Mandelson pleaded with Blair to let him keep his Cabinet job, arguing that he had done nothing improper and that if Blair held his nerve, the fuss would die down. Mandelson told Blair that the story was all part of a plot by supporters of Gordon Brown to bring him down, and Blair would be mad to give them what they wanted. But even the Chancellor had told Mandelson there was no need to resign. So why should Blair sack him? Couldn't he give him a public slap over the wrists instead? Blair was adamant: Mandelson must go. Still he resisted and in the end Blair agreed to give him more time. Mandelson went out to Price, whom he trusted more than Campbell and asked him, 'What do you think I should do?' To his dismay, Price replied, 'You have no choice.' Mandelson's eyes moistened. He went back into his office, phoned Blair again and said tersely, 'You have made it clear that your mind is made up. I'll go.' Blair did make one very large concession, however. He promised Mandelson that in return for agreeing to resign, he would be restored to the Cabinet at the earliest possible opportunity.

Far from nobly falling on his sword, as Campbell had suggested in his official version, Mandelson fought like a tiger to survive until Campbell arrived at his office to tell him he was fired. Campbell wanted people to think Labour ministers in 'sleaze' allegations were different to their Tory predecessors who connived and grovelled to cling on until the last minute. The main difference was that Blair and

Campbell were, from the start, more ruthless in despatching them.

Mandelson was defeated, but Campbell's work was not yet done. His next task was to stop the Tories claiming any credit for Mandelson's downfall. He had been tipped off that Conservative leader William Hague was about to demand Mandelson's resignation. So driven was he by an obsessive desire to put the best possible gloss on the resignation and deny the Tories any kind of publicity coup that, within moments of Mandelson's dismissal, Campbell used the authority of the Downing Street press machine to issue a false account of Mandelson's demise, stating he had decided to resign the previous night.

Campbell had one more trick up his sleeve: he then wrote the resignation letters. Emboldened by his success with Ron Davies' resignation letter and Nick Brown's gay 'confession' to the *News of the World*, he composed both Mandelson's letter of resignation and Blair's reply. The opening line of the letter he wrote for Mandelson displays his bravado. 'Dear Tony,' it started, 'I can scarcely believe I am writing this letter to you … ' The man who had had a large hand in his removal was twisting the knife.

As a further demonstration of his mastery over both men, Campbell composed Blair's reply, in which he praised Mandelson's humility: 'It was typical of you when we spoke last night that your thought was for the reputation of the Labour party and the Government.' Mandelson had said nothing of the sort.

Out of Mandelson's shadow

For Campbell, the consequences of the Mandelson calamity were immense. Inevitably, Charlie Whelan was blamed for leaking the story and this time Blair put his foot down. He forced Brown to fire him. In one single stroke two of Campbell's biggest rivals in Whitehall – Peter Mandelson and Charlie Whelan – were removed from the political stage.

Campbell doubtless hoped he could use Whelan's departure to control Gordon Brown's press machine: a spectacular victory in the running power struggle between Number 10 and the Treasury. In practice, the Chancellor's economic adviser Ed Balls took over Whelan's behind the scenes briefing role, and although he was far more brainy and discreet, in the view of many of Blair's team he was even more deadly than rogueish Whelan owing to his skill in covering his tracks when leaking pro-Brown stories to selected journalists.

The eclipse of Peter Mandelson was just as important for Campbell and a very much more complicated matter – though one would have expected nothing else from this complex and tortured soul. Campbell had gained some of the freedom he really wanted when, in the summer of 1998, Tony Blair gave Mandelson the post of Trade Secretary. Mandelson's Cabinet Office successor, with responsibility for government presentation, was Jack Cunningham, who took a notably more relaxed role than his predecessor. He turned up at two or three of the early morning meetings, then stopped attending on a regular basis. It was assumed that he did not like the early hours. It suited Campbell, with his inexhaustible appetite for hard work, and he promptly seized control of this vital instrument of government and made it his own. Until then Mandelson, as Minister without Portfolio, had been based in the Cabinet Office and right at the heart of government. Campbell had no alternative but to defer to him. Mandelson even sat on the committee which set Campbell's salary and terms of employment. Mandelson would taunt Campbell about this from time to time.

There were claims from within this committee that Mandelson had tried to keep Campbell's salary as low as possible, so as to emphasize his subordinate status. One civil servant who frequently attended meetings with both men remembers: 'There was a definite rivalry but equally no question who was in charge – Peter Mandelson.'

But it was 23 December 1998 when Campbell finally secured the upper hand in the battle for the heart and mind of the Prime Minister. It was Peter Mandelson who, long before Labour won power in May 1997, had understood that Labour would govern by agglomerating power to the centre. A year before the election, he set out some of his ideas in a book he wrote jointly with Roger Liddle.[5] At the end of the day it was Campbell who inherited the machinery of government whose inventor and midwife had been Peter Mandelson. That is just one of the innumerable ironies of their absorbing relationship.

For nearly five years Campbell and Mandelson had been colleagues, friends, comrades – and rivals at the court of King Tony. But until the matter of the Robinson loan reared its head, Mandelson had always been the favoured and senior courtier.

When Alastair Campbell accepted the post of press spokesman to Tony Blair five years before, numerous people had been as close or closer to the party leader: Blair's old mentor Derry Irvine, his friend Charles Falconer, his rival Gordon Brown, his chief of staff Jonathan Powell, his close aide Anji Hunter, Philip Gould and Peter Mandelson. Campbell had had the sense not to take on the existing hierarchies around Blair all at once. He waited. By 1999, partly through his own ability and hard work, and partly through the weakness of others, he had established himself as Blair's principal adviser. After the Prime Minister himself, he was the most powerful man in the country. It was at the beginning of 1999 that well-informed people started calling Campbell 'Deputy Prime Minister'.

The Grid

By now Campbell was well settled into a comfortable routine. When not travelling with the Prime Minister, he would normally leave his home in Gospel Oak, north London, at around 7 a.m. to make the twenty-five-minute drive to Downing Street. More often than not he would use the family Renault Espace or take a cab.[6] In the car or perhaps earlier at home, Campbell would have talked to Tony Blair. Nobody outside the Prime Minister's immediate family talked as often or as intimately to Blair as Campbell. Campbell had become much more than a press secretary. He was by now the Prime Minister's main adviser on politics, his closest and most trusted friend in government.

He would arrive at his Downing Street office around 7.30 a.m. It was a large office on the ground floor of Downing Street, to the left of the policeman guarding the front door. He had made himself at home in this room; numerous drawings by his three children, Rory, Calum and Grace, were displayed. Framed on the wall were an article attacking Campbell and the government in the most lurid and vicious terms by the *Sun* columnist Richard Littlejohn, a *Newsweek* cover story about Tony Blair, and a New Labour election poster in the colours of his favourite football team, Burnley.

From his desk Campbell would take calls from selected journalists. Charles Reiss, political editor of the *Evening Standard*, might well call at this time. London's *Standard* is taken very seriously by Downing Street because it helps set the agenda for the national papers the next day. Campbell also used his first moments in the office to prepare for the Downing Street daily 8.30 a.m. meeting of information officers, known as 'the 8.30'.

He chaired this event, which was attended by key officials from 10 Downing Street as well as representatives from the Treasury, the Foreign Office, the Labour party and other government departments. There was never any doubt that the purpose was not just to present the government in the best light, but to present New Labour in the best light too, a radical concept for a traditionally impartial civil service. At this meeting, held in a first-floor room in Number 10 overlooking Horse Guards' parade, Campbell would sit in the middle of a rectangular table, his back to the window, his deputies, Godric Smith and Tom Kelly, on either side. It was a mirror image of the Cabinet meeting, and the decisions made here were in many cases far more important. In past days the room was indeed the Prime Minister's study, and the PM himself would have sat in the seat occupied by Campbell. He used the '8.30' to tell the assembled press officers and spin-doctors the messages, policies, events or 'lines to take' for the day. Every tiny aspect of the week's announcements would be gone through so the government's programme could be properly co-ordinated. 'Have we got a line on this?' Campbell would ask. 'What are we going to do about that?' and 'I'll need a line on this for the lobby – can you sort it?' and direct one of those present to get him the answers in time for the 11 a.m. lobby briefing. There would be orders to leak certain stories to favoured journalists or papers. And he had a list of preferred ministers who were given priority to go on the lunchtime or evening news. They rarely turned down Campbell's invitations. Press officers were told to chase up stories Campbell regarded as inaccurate, damaging or embarrassing and get them corrected. He would say: 'This is wrong. Make them put it right.'

The '8.30' also reflected the frictions being played out around the Cabinet table. While Brown sulked, occasionally bursting into life to challenge Blair, the same sparring went on at the '8.30' between their respective champions. Charlie Whelan stopped attending after a few months following a series of frosty exchanges with Campbell.

Whelan's successor, the dogged Ian Austin, had none of his predecessor's clout, flair or recklessness and was in awe of Campbell.

In February 2002, Campbell asked Austin about an item on the
'8.30' agenda listed innocuously as 'speech by Ed Balls'. Balls' official
role was as Brown's economic adviser, but he had, in effect, taken over
Whelan's role as Brown's propagandist. He rarely spoke in public, so
mention of a speech by him instantly aroused Campbell's suspicion.
'What's this speech by Ed?' Campbell asked. 'It's just a routine restatement of government policy,' said Austin in his thick Brummie accent.
Campbell frowned and moved on.

The next morning, the front page of the *Sun* screamed: 'Balls to the
Euro!' The paper said Balls had effectively ruled out Britain joining the
euro for years to come. When the '8.30' reconvened, Campbell scowled
at Austin. 'So that was a routine restatement of government policy was
it, Ian?' Austin squirmed in his seat. 'You know what the papers are like,
Alastair,' he replied limply. 'Yeah,' said Campbell derisively, 'I used to
work in them a while ago, and in those days the *Sun* never splashed on a
routine restatement of government policy.' Austin went beetroot red
and stayed quiet for the rest of the meeting.

Martin Sixsmith, the former BBC journalist who worked as head of
communications to Transport Secretary Stephen Byers, painted a vivid
picture of Campbell's virtuoso style at the '8.30'.

> He would sweep in with a breezy 'Morning, you lot!' and a Burnley FC
> mug of tea, before launching into a series of quickfire commands on how
> the Cabinet should tackle the day ahead. His edicts ran along the lines of:
> 'Problem with the unions? Get Steve Byers up on that one, OK? Tell him
> to call them "wreckers". Got that? And tell him to stick to my script,
> OK?' Or perhaps: 'Problem with the intelligence services? Get John Reid
> (the then Leader of the Commons) out and tell him to call them "rogue
> elements", OK?' Or even: 'Get John Prescott on the airwaves. Oh, on
> second thoughts, maybe not.' As the meeting runs through the previous
> day's coverage, few journalists are spared. Campbell ridicules criticism
> of the government with a dismissive: 'Blah, blah, blah, the usual crap.' It
> is Campbell who decides what the ministers will say, including the Prime
> Minister. 'We'll get TB to do this and say that,' is the way he puts it.[7]

The agenda for the '8.30' came in the form of a document known as the
'Grid'. This elaborate construction expressed Campbell's vision of

government communications as encompassing not just events in Whitehall but everything that was going on in Britain and the rest of the world on any one day, from parliamentary announcements to pop concerts. Campbell's aim was to take advantage of them all to paint the government in the best possible light, using them to highlight some aspects of the government's record, and to conceal others.

The Grid was marked 'Restricted' and consisted of six vertical columns, one for each weekday and one for the weekend. Each one listed events under a series of headings: main news, statistics, other government news, Europe, general and other themes expected during the week. It gave a privileged insight into the news values of the Number 10 press machine, reading as it does like a newspaper news schedule, with separate sections for politics, world news, show business and sport.

The grid for the third week of August 2003 [see page 362], prepared right at the end in the final weeks of Campbell's long spell in Downing Street, included the Hutton inquiry into the death of the government scientist Dr David Kelly alongside the Notting Hill carnival. The following week features a meeting between Jack Straw and Italian Foreign minister Franco Frattini directly above the UEFA Cup draw. The same week's Grid finds room for the Bob Hope memorial service, Hollywood, cancer statistics, Belgian Grand Prix, new figures on poverty and the sixth anniversary of Princess Diana's death. All these events were to be 'factored in' to the government's publicity campaign for that week. September's Grid included a report on disabled children and the Emmy Awards, Los Angeles.

The top section, listed under 'main news' is dominated by Hutton, not surprisingly since this was the week that many of the key figures in Downing Street, including Campbell himself, gave evidence. But the same Grid finds room for England v Croatia (football) friendly, a UN debate on the Middle East, Lee Ryan of Blue in court re drink-driving and Notting Hill carnival.

Campbell always loved to mock the media for its obsession with 'trivia and froth', comparing it with his alleged priority: the big picture and the big issues. But as the Grid illustrates, trivia was at the heart of his communications plan. As this grid of August 2003 demonstrates, Whitehall was run much more in the style of a tabloid editor than a traditional civil servant.

The '8.30' meetings were like the newspaper conferences Campbell
had sat in on in his days as a political editor – only now he was in the
editor's chair. He would congratulate executives who had provided
good 'stories' and reprimand those who had failed to stop 'bad' stories
getting into the press. As with any newspaper, his senior staff instinctively knew the editorial line to be pursued. Critics of the Grid maintain
that it was the blind faith in this all-seeing attempt to make government
announcements tie in with and take advantage of other news events that
led to DTI spin-doctor Jo Moore's disastrous suggestion that 11 September 2001 was 'a good day to bury bad news'.

The Grid for the third week of August 2003 illuminates yet again the
depth of Campbell's relationship with the *Sun* newspaper. The eighteenth of August marked the start of a week in which the *Sun* alarmed
its readers with a succession of hair-raising stories about the terrifying
threat posed by asylum-seekers.[8] Downing Street knew all about the
Sun campaign in advance, as the Grid entry under 'main news: during
the week' indicates. It is listed there: 'Sun asylum week'.

Not merely that, Downing Street had planned its response before
the conflict even began. There in bold ink in Thursday's Grid is:
'Blunkett asylum interview in *Sun*'. On Monday, a *Sun* leader thundered: 'the flood of shirkers, scroungers and criminals has to be
stopped'. Three days later, bang on cue, the Home Secretary came to
the rescue. 'I am not in dispute with the *Sun* on this week's coverage,'
he told the paper, promising 'draconian' measures to deal with the
problem.

The Grid provided lighter moments too. Once Campbell spotted a
mention of the Oxford and Cambridge boat race. It represented everything he hated about Cambridge. 'What next, Ascot races?' he
exclaimed. He didn't stop officials including all major champions
league matches involving British soccer teams, particularly Manchester United, and the occasional Burnley game. Campbell was as master-
ful and as mordant at these early morning meetings as he was at the
lobby.

He would display his disdain for what he regarded as the irrelevant
parts of Labour's manifesto, such as Europe, Lords reform, voting
reform and social issues with the sarcastic: 'Now we come to the
People's Priorities.'

When Campbell stepped back from the daily lobby meetings, he would give official spokesmen Godric Smith and Tom Kelly their marching orders and told them which 'lines to take'. 'Tom and Godric were the public face of Number 10 but Alastair was pulling the strings the whole time,' said one official.

Campbell rarely relaxed his grip, and never at weekends, in politics often the most dangerous time. Sunday papers were more unpredictable than the dailies. At around 9.30 p.m. each Saturday night, Campbell would collect the first editions of the following day's papers. At 10 p.m. he would stage a conference call of all the ministers he had lined up to appear on the Sunday political programmes, mainly *Breakfast with Frost*, John Humphrys' *On The Record*, Jonathan Dimbleby on ITV, GMTV and BBC Radio 4's *World This Weekend*. The Downing Street 'switch' – the switchboard renowned for being able to track down any minister or official anywhere in the world – would be used to call ministers out of restaurants or dinner parties to be told by Campbell how to rebut any unhelpful Sunday paper stories and how to keep the interviews 'on message' with whatever theme had been agreed for the weekend.

A strategic view

Campbell did not merely bring a new efficiency and drive to the ramshackle structure he had inherited. He changed the Whitehall architecture entirely, so that the technology of Millbank could be brought into the heart of government. Within weeks of Labour's general election, the Permanent Secretary at the Office of Public Service, Sir Robin Mountfield, was commissioned to make a report into the government information service.

Sir Robin, hitherto an expert in financial regulation, was walking a tightrope. Campbell was pressing to emasculate the civil service, end its political independence, and make it subject to New Labour. Mountfield was well aware of this. In the end the report amounted to a compromise between the two men. Mountfield stopped the politicization of key civil service appointments. But in return he opened the door to the modernization of the government information service. A new body was set up to co-ordinate departmental announcements and government initiatives. This became the strategic communications unit.

Mountfield also announced the creation of a central media-monitoring unit 'to provide 24-hour monitoring of emergency stories, and immediate warning to departmental press offices and the centre'. Mountfield referred to plans for a new computer to replace the Cab-E-Net electronic information system which had served the Tories. Cab-E-Net had been constantly dogged with technical difficulties; not so its replacement. Given the name Agenda, it listed forthcoming events, lines to take and ministerial speeches. It became a vital tool of government. The media-monitoring unit was almost identical to the one Campbell and Mandelson had run at Millbank. It monitored every major newspaper, radio and TV station, including Sky and CNN. By 7.30 a.m. each morning its summary of overnight events and the morning papers was on Campbell's desk to prepare him for the early-morning meeting. The range was prodigious. BBC political correspondent Guto Harri learned the scope of Campbell's campaign to monitor every word published and broadcast about Number 10 when he was challenged over a column he had written for the Welsh-language newspaper, *Cymro* – which translates as 'The Welshman'. Welsh speaking Harri wrote a light-hearted article for the paper which described how, when he phoned Downing Street out of hours, he was put through to a duty press officer and could hear the sound of splashing in the background. The press officer was at home, having a bath.

Three days later at a lobby briefing, Campbell approached Harri, winked and said: 'Hey you bastard, what are you doing writing about my staff in a Welsh-language paper?' Harri's column had been monitored, translated, and, along with hundreds of others, sent to Number 10 for Campbell's inspection. In April 2003, Labour MP George Galloway gave an interview to Abu Dhabi TV, broadcast in Arabic, in which he called Tony Blair and George Bush 'wolves'. The interview went unnoticed by Fleet Street, but not the all-seeing Campbell. Downing Street obtained a translation.[9] The interview formed the basis of Galloway's expulsion from the Labour party.

As far as Campbell was concerned, the media-monitoring unit and the strategic communications unit were there to achieve his stated aim of seizing the initiative from the media. A common refrain of Campbell's in conversation with Downing Street officials inherited from John Major was: 'How did the last lot fuck this up and how do we make sure we don't?' The strategic communications unit, made up of a cadre of Labour appointees and civil servants, was part of the answer to the second question. Given an office in 10 Downing Street formerly used for the appointment of bishops, its task was to look forward. Government announcements were to be co-ordinated to make maximum impact.

Lèse-majesté

Long before entering Downing Street, Campbell had stated in his *Today* column, 'I have never gone for the notion that the royal family represents all that is right in this country. They represent to me much that is wrong in this country, notably its class system, obsession with titles, dressing up and patronage and the arrogance of unelected power.' Office did nothing to modify Campbell's contempt for the royal family: if anything familiarity increased it. Campbell's views on Princess Diana nearly landed him in trouble during a visit to a council estate by Blair. Cambell waited outside a council house with a TV journalist while Blair was filmed having tea in one tenant's cramped front room, accompanied by a lone cameraman. Campbell and the journalist discussed their mutual interest in Diana's sex appeal. 'Mind you, she's completely bonkers,' added Campbell. When Blair emerged the cameraman took the journalist to one side and said: 'When you feed the film down to London, I suggest you use channel one, not channel two.' The reporter had unwittingly left his microphone switched on, allowing the cameraman to listen in on Campbell and the journalist's bawdy conversation blaring through his headphones while sitting a foot away from the PM and his hostess. If the film had been sent to London via the wrong line, viewers would have heard Campbell's rude musings about Princess Diana drowning out the Prime Minister's cosy chat over a cuppa.

His rival Peter Mandelson made little secret that he richly enjoyed his links with royalty, going out of his way to build connections between Prince Charles and the New Labour establishment, and at one stage gratefully accepting an invitation to stay at Sandringham.

Campbell remained aloof. He told one courtier: 'The royals are irrel-evant to us. They have no power and symbolize something that belongs to yesterday.'

However, Campbell knew that there was no point pursuing an openly Republican agenda, and did not seek to do so. Indeed during the early years in Downing Street, when New Labour intuitively caught the mood of the nation, he put this great expertise and professionalism at the disposal of the royal family on more than one occasion. He gave bracing and badly needed advice in the aftermath of the death of Princess Diana to a royal family in complete disarray.

Diana had been one of the Blairs' first guests at Chequers in the immediate aftermath of the 1997 election victory and he promptly offered her a semi-ambassadorial role to promote both her charities and British interests. Diana had wasted no time in flaunting her friend-ship to her ex-husband. 'She would phone up and say: "I've been talking to Cherie and she is so nice and we get on so well",' recalls a royal offi-cial. '"Did William tell you what a great time we had at Chequers? Do you know the Blairs?" Diana told Charles how the children played foot-ball together, how they all swam in the Chequers pool, how they had swimming races. Diana knew that the way the Blairs had embraced her got under Charles' skin. He was furious because he saw it as her using the kids to engineer a relationship with the Blairs.'[10]

More than infuriating though this undoubtedly was, Charles never-theless had good reason to thank New Labour's spin doctors for bailing out both himself and the Queen in the aftermath of Diana's death on 30 August 1997.

Campbell and Tony Blair put a stop to the royal family's blinkered insistence on abiding by protocol and denying Diana a state funeral. They insisted that she was given the full pomp and circumstance befit-ting her status as the 'People's Princess'. Campbell's good sense came to the rescue as public anger mounted at the Queen's and Prince Philip's decision to remain at Balmoral, where they were on holiday. Campbell attended a hastily arranged meeting at Buckingham Palace where royal officials had arranged a conference call link up with the Queen and the Duke of Edinburgh in Scotland via a 'squawk box'. 'It was a very awkward discussion,' said one official who was present. 'There we were, with various officials politely trying to tell the Queen she had better come to London soon or there would be a serious problem. You could hear Philip grunting in the background. Campbell's view was that Buck House and St James' should stop squabbling, get their act together and have a corporate view.' Campbell's tabloid skills were called on again to help the Queen's televised address to the nation. When a copy of her address was faxed to Number 10, he decided it was too harsh and made several amendments to give it more warmth. It was he who inserted the saccharin phrase 'speaking as a grandmother' which was used by the grateful monarch.[11]

Despite the coolness engendered by the close relations with Diana, Campbell retained links with some staff at St James' Palace. In November 2003, when the Prince found himself in the middle of a row over claims that he had been involved in a compromising incident with former royal aide Michael Fawcett, St James' Palace rang Campbell to seek his advice on how to handle the matter. He approved their strategy for trying to quell the media furore.[12] Downing Street also offered advice to Charles on whether he should marry Camilla. During the Queen's Golden Jubilee celebrations in 2002, Number 10 suggested that the Prince of Wales could take advantage of the wave of support for the royals to marry Parker-Bowles. Charles ignored the advice.[13]

As Campbell became more assured and confident in his job, he made less effort to hide his contempt for the royal family. He treated them casually, taking liberties as if they were old friends who could be trampled upon at will. An example of Campbell's high-handed approach came during an official visit by the Prime Minister to Charles' Highgrove estate in September 1998. This event took place just over a year after Diana's death, and its purpose was mainly to discuss progress with the Diana Memorial Fund. The Prime Minister had gone on ahead by helicopter, while Campbell and a group of Number 10 officials arrived later by car. The Prince and the Prime Minister were about to start their discussion when Charles' butler Tony Rabey interrupted them. 'I have just had a call from some of the Prime Minister's entourage who are on their way, sir,' said Rabey to the Prince. 'Yes?' asked a puzzled Charles. 'They would like to know would it be possible for them to use the swimming pool, sir?', said Rabey. 'Who?', asked Charles. 'Mr Campbell,' replied Rabey. 'Who the hell does he think he is?' demanded Charles. When Campbell arrived, he stripped off into his trunks and dived into the ornate heated outdoor pool.

This was a minor case of Campbell's insolence. A much more grievous case occurred five months later, in February 1999, when Tony Blair and Prince Charles flew to Amman, Jordan to attend the funeral of King Hussein. Campbell, as ever, went with the Prime Minister. More than forty heads of state attended the funeral of the great Middle-Eastern potentate and survivor: space was at a premium. The Prime Minister and the Prince of Wales were obliged to share a small meeting room in a hotel while they waited to attend the ceremony. It had just one chair in it. At one stage Prince Charles entered the room to discover Tony Blair and Alastair Campbell already established. The Prime Minister, who was standing up, greeted the Prince warmly. Campbell, who was slumped, legs wide apart and tie undone, on the chair in the corner, did not greet him at all. In this kind of situation the Prince is accustomed to find people leaping to their feet, offering the chair, generally bowing and scraping in the way that a British subject is traditionally expected to do when he meets his future monarch. Campbell simply ignored the Prince of Wales, acted as if he were not in the room, and carried on making phone calls on his mobile. Charles was affronted. He muttered to a Palace aide: 'Look at that bloody man Campbell sitting on the only chair in the room. He didn't stand up, he didn't even acknowledge me, he just stayed there sprawled out using his mobile phone.' It was indeed an extraordinary piece of effrontery from the press secretary to the heir to the throne. It is impossible to imagine Tony Blair, on the whole a well-mannered man, behaving in anything like the same disrespectful way.

Charles was still bristling with indignation a few minutes later when an official entered the room and addressed Blair: 'President Clinton would like to see you now.' The Prince said with a smug grin: 'You had better run along, hadn't you?' A Palace source later said: 'It was Charles' way of getting revenge on Blair for what Campbell had done to him. Campbell had treated him with contempt and he wanted to take it out on someone. He always felt that Alastair was sneering at him behind his back.'[19]

Relations were always edgy between the royal family and Downing Street. Tony Blair was less assiduous than any other Prime Minister in attending audiences with the Queen: he attended just nine between December and June 1999: not much more than one a month. The Palace was annoyed when the appointment of Andrew Motion as Poet Laureate was leaked to *The Times* on 19 May 1999. Number 10 seemed the only possible culprit.

It could hardly fail to notice, either, the way that honours lists found their way into Labour-supporting newspapers with unfailing regularity. It has traditionally been the case that honours are kept strictly private until they are gazetted by Buckingham Palace. Only those in receipt of honours know in advance, and they receive a ferocious warning not to share their happiness with the world until the day itself.

Victory for New Labour brought a brutal change in this position. Often it was George Pascoe-Watson of the *Sun* who would bring the happy news of the latest award for a celebrity or sportsman: he was first with the honours for the 1966 England squad, the knighthood for Tesco boss Terry Leahy and tycoon Richard Branson. Pascoe-Watson always did his best to make clear where credit was due, and that the Prime Minister and not the Palace was behind the award.[15]

The Blair government's habit of playing politics with honours, and leaking details of awards to the media, led to serious problems. William Hague was so angry at the way that details of his recommendation of a peerage for Tory treasurer Michael Ashcroft had been leaked that he told Conservative officials not to have any dealings either with Campbell or Jonathan Powell. 'Eventually we would only deal with Sir Richard Wilson because we didn't trust anyone else in Downing Street over honours,' said one of Hague's officials.

Relations between Charles and Downing Street reached a low point after the Prince and Blair dined together at St James' Palace and disagreed over an issue over which both men had passionate views. The Prime Minister was a strong supporter of GM foods; Charles, who refused to eat or serve them to his guests, believed they posed a threat to mankind. On 27 May, four weeks after their private clash, Blair went on the offensive, attacking 'media hysteria' over GM foods. Four days later, on 1 June, Charles hit back hard in a by-lined article in the *Daily Mail*, the newspaper most hated by Downing Street. St James' Palace had been in negotiation with the paper about the article ever since Charles' face-to-face showdown with Blair. It was an act of provocation that, in Number 10's eyes, heightened the very 'hysteria' Blair had complained about. Charles openly derided as 'emotional blackmail' the Prime Minister's claim that GM food was needed to fight Third World hunger. The initiative won him his best headlines for years. Campbell for once refused to rise to the bait. At the Downing Street lobby briefing on 1 June, journalists were told: 'There is a desire among you for a "Blair at war with Charles over GM food" story, but I'm afraid I will frustrate you in your endeavour.'

The attack on the World Trade Centre on 11 September 2001 brought a reconciliation between Prince Charles and Downing Street. The Prince met Tony Blair on 25 October, six weeks after the attack, to offer his help at healing the deep wounds that divided the Arab world from the West. Charles seemed the ideal man for the job. He was known for his pro-Palestinian sympathies, had close links with the ruling royal households in Saudi Arabia and Jordan and a long-standing interest in relations with Muslim groups in Britain.

Charles floated the idea of a diplomatic initiative. He proposed to visit America and then fly straight to a Muslim country, probably Saudi Arabia, in a journey that would symbolize sympathy and understanding for both sides. Charles was keen to improve his standing in America, where Diana had been a stunning success on the celebrity circuit during her visits and was generally seen as the innocent party in her divorce from the Prince. Campbell supported the idea, but warned Charles's team: 'If the Prince is going to do this, then he has got to do it and he has got to do it properly. If you all wimp out about this we will be very pissed off. It's a good thing that the Prince wants to do this. It would be very helpful to the Prime Minister and would improve understanding between the communities. But we know the moment the Foreign Office gets its hands on it, they won't be happy and will say it shouldn't happen.'

The Prince's press secretary Colleen Harris observed to a colleague: 'This had better happen or our credibility with Number 10 will be kaput.'[16] Campbell's doubts turned out to be fully justified. Charles's own private secretary, Sir Stephen Lamport, the Queen's private secretary, Sir Robin Janvrin, and the head of the diplomatic service, Sir John Kerr, were all nervous of the proposal. Charles was warned, says a Palace source, 'that he would be aligning himself far too closely with the government and that it would look as though we were being used by Number 10'.

One royal courtier says, 'The Foreign Office thought Charles was treading on their feet. And they were worried he would say something that would upset the Americans such as by suggesting they had to be more understanding of Islam. It is true that some Americans see Charles as a bit anti-American, but Alastair could see that all that was irrelevant after 9-11.'

One Palace official observed: 'Charles hoped he could show Downing Street that he could make a valuable contribution on a serious issue. In the event, their scepticism was justified, though it was not for the want of trying.'[17]

The Prince's trip was abandoned. He held a series of private meetings with senior British Muslims, but his intervention did not have the impact he had hoped to make. Campbell was contemptuous. He later told royal officials: 'I told you it would never happen. You just wasted my time.'[18]

Operation Gobble

With his exceptionally acute nose for the language and etiquette of power, Campbell had always played the Tory party like a violin. During the late 1980s he had exploited the convergence of interest between Neil Kinnock and Michael Heseltine against Margaret Thatcher.

Now Campbell rekindled the relationship with Heseltine: only this time the target was not Thatcher but William Hague, the Tory leader. In the autumn of 1998 Campbell, with a grin, announced the appointment of Michael Heseltine as chairman of a new Anglo-Chinese trading body. The news came while Tony Blair was on a trip to the Far East, but few accepted it was sheer coincidence that the announcement was made during the Conservative party conference. A few months later Michael Heseltine made an apparently spontaneous speech welcoming the positive, mood-changing announcement from Tony Blair on the single currency in February 1999. It emerged later that Heseltine's speech had been choreographed in advance with Downing Street.[19]

This cultivation of Heseltine was part of a larger and more sophisticated operation, referred to privately by Peter Mandelson as 'Operation

Hoover'. Campbell, by temperament earthier than Mandelson, referred to it as 'Operation Gobble', a phrase he would occasionally accompany with loud and disgusting gulping noises.

Heseltine was an early and willing victim of Operation Gobble, but by no means the only one. A large raft of the Tory left were also targeted, among them Blair's Commons 'pair', the former chief whip Sir Alastair Goodlad, the former chancellor Kenneth Clarke and Chris Patten, the former Conservative party chairman.[20] The plan was to take them out of the arena by offering them jobs. Goodlad and Patten succumbed. Campbell had a conscious and deliberate strategy. He wanted to edge the Conservatives away from the middle ground of politics and turn it into a hard-edged party of the far right capable of being labelled extremist. It was probably no coincidence that Michael Portillo, whose long journey to the Blairite centre of British political life was only just beginning, was offered nothing. There were some indications that the former defence secretary might be available for hire in the aftermath of the 1997 election,[21] but Downing Street took no notice. New Labour preferred the prospect of a return by Portillo to active Tory politics, and the mayhem that was expected to bring about.

Campbell tried to lure Alan Clark over to New Labour, on at least one occasion offering him a peerage. 'I love the company of intelligent and powerful people,' Clark would claim, justifying the Campbell connection, 'It's one of the most seductive drugs in politics.'[22] Clark took Campbell, while he was still a journalist, as his guest to the Beefsteak, the Tory luncheon club near Leicester Square. Campbell disgraced himself when his mobile phone rang in the middle of the meal. A ringing mobile phone is the ultimate solecism at the Beefsteak, and Clark looked on in amusement as Campbell rushed to the exit with his phone.

Clark would provide Campbell with useful inside information and links into certain Tory factions. Clark's unlikely friendship was very interesting, for instance, to Clark's friend and dining companion the Tory MP Nicholas Soames. Clark claimed that Soames sought to use him as an envoy to intimate to the Downing Street press secretary that he would like to be ambassador to France. Clark passed on the Soames interest. In the 1998 Euro-summit at Vienna Campbell created mischief for the Tory party by hinting that Soames was angling for a government job. Soames admired Campbell's passionate commitment and considered him to have done the establishment a favour by destroying the Old Labour party.

Downing Street's greatest Tory coup of all was to engineer the Tory split leading up to the sacking of Robert Cranborne, Conservative leader of the Lords. Campbell induced Cranborne to enter into negotiations with the government about Lords reform without informing William Hague, the Tory leader. The two men met secretly in 10 Downing Street ahead of the announcement that the hereditary peers were to be reduced to ninety-two in number. When Cranborne's conniving with Downing Street came to light Hague dismissed him.

Campbell also played a major role in arranging the defection of Shaun Woodward, the Conservative MP for Witney, to New Labour. Campbell's role in securing Woodward's defection gave rise to complaints from Conservative that Campbell was abusing his role for party political advantage. This brought a po-faced response from Cabinet Secretary Sir Richard Wilson who implied Campbell could take part in political activity, so long as it was during the lunch hour. Campbell's first meeting with Woodward took place in Downing Street, noted Wilson, but 'subsequent meetings took place with the approval of the Prime Minister, away from Number 10 either at lunchtime or outside office hours'.

Operation Gobble was not only aimed at Tory wets like Goodlad, Patten and Heseltine, or grandees like Cranborne. It was a sign of Campbell's breadth and subtlety that he was equally at ease operating at a subterranean level among the Thatcherite right. Indeed cultivation of this section of the Conservative party dated back to before the general election of 1997. Part of the strategic brilliance of the run-up to that campaign was the way Tony Blair and Alastair Campbell helped open up a second front against John Major, forcing the beleaguered Conservative prime minister not merely to face New Labour head on but also to deal with a secondary flanking operation led by a highly effective group of Eurosceptic 'death squadders', who despised John Major so much that they saw a Labour victory as preferable to the continuation of what they believed to be a bankrupt regime.

Campbell and Blair actively fostered this coterie both before and after the 1997 general election. Great attention was focused on the recruitment of two powerful right-wing columnists, Simon Heffer and

Paul Johnson. Their attraction for New Labour was all the greater because both opened the way to the *Daily Mail*, whose editor Paul Dacre proved hard to convert. The central intellectual problem facing both Heffer and Johnson was how to reconcile their avowed enmity towards the EU with support for a pro-EU Prime Minister. Blair and Campbell did their best to solve it for them by invoking the *Fuhrerprinzip*. Blair's famous comment to John Major at Prime Minister's Questions in 1995 – 'I lead my party. He follows his' – was aimed just as much at the Thatcherite right as at the Labour party.

chapter twelve

Campbell Goes Worldwide

Rein your man Campbell in, he's been briefing against me.

President Bill Clinton to Tony Blair

Best friends with Sir Alex

DURING THIS PERIOD OF HIS LIFE, a fulfilled Alastair Campbell was absorbed with his job. When not with the Prime Minister, he was at home with his family. He remained, within the limits of his demanding schedule, a conscientious father.

His social sphere, such as it was, was mainly an extension of his work. He spent his time with politicians, or occasionally the handful of political reporters he felt were on his side. He did, however, build a strong new friendship with one man from far away from the daily pressures of Westminster: Sir Alex Ferguson, the manager of Manchester United. On the face of things this association between Britain's most successful football manager and Tony Blair's spin-doctor was incongruous. In fact it made perfect sense, and the friendship was revealing about both men.

Ferguson and Campbell were similar in outlook and approach. They were ruthless, hard working and very successful. They both lived lives that were distorted beyond belief by the glaze of public attention. This produced an important paradox. Everything they did or said was pored over and analyzed beyond the point of exhaustion in the newspapers and on television. This transparency created the impression that everything was known about them that could be known. This was false. The actual lives they led and the world they lived in were governed by a set of rules that was invisible to the public at large.

To understand these rules it is essential to grasp that both men were wholly clannish. They were driven by profound, unbreakable personal loyalties. This characteristic accounted for most of their success. It meant that both of them were charismatic leaders of a team, loyal to the point of savagery to those on their own side, and very bad enemies indeed. But this clannishness was also a weakness. There were times when their unbreakable ethic of private loyalty came into conflict with public expectations or morality. In these cases both men unhesitatingly plumped for their private ethic. Thus when the England defender Rio Ferdinand failed to take a drugs test, Ferguson backed him to the hilt. When the passionate Manchester United skipper Roy Keane fell out with the Irish football management during the Tokyo World Cup, Ferguson sent the Manchester United private plane to collect him.

This clannishness had some malevolent effects. Campbell and Ferguson put the interests of New Labour and Manchester United respectively above anything else in the world. Ferguson is famous for threatening and abusing any newspaper or TV channel which shows Manchester United in an unfavourable light. He has been prepared to mislead reporters from time to time when he felt that Manchester United's interests are threatened. By and large he gets away with it, because people understand the boundless depths of his passion and commitment. It is part of the reason why Manchester United is so successful.

Campbell is just the same. He too has manipulated the truth, bullied and threatened, created a world divided between us and them. To do him credit, he seems rarely to have brutalized or abused the truth for personal or selfish motives. He has been driven on by a deeper and over-riding purpose – the interests of New Labour. In the end Campbell, unlike Ferguson so far, was to pay a price.

But, to begin with Campbell's intensity and focus was a great strength. It drove New Labour on, gave it cohesion and boosted morale. It played a large part in the winning of the 1997 general election, and perhaps that of 2001 as well. But running a country is not like being in charge of a football club. Higher demands are made, and a much broader and more generous vision required. In the end Campbell's passionate clannishness came into dramatic conflict with the public purpose of the government he served. He sought to adapt the machinery of state to private New Labour ends. To Campbell there was never a conflict. For him, the interests of Britain and New Labour were identical. Indeed the 1997 manifesto had explicitly stated as much when it defined the New Labour as the 'political arm of the British people'.

But to others the distinction was much less clear, and New Labour's lack of clarity led to allegations of corruption. In due course Campbell's readiness to distort the truth in the interests of his party led on to a crisis of trust and identity. Worst of all, without really understanding what he was doing, he was turning New Labour into a faction rather than a national party. The longer he lasted in office, the worse it got. In the end there was no contradiction between Sir Alex Ferguson's clannishness and Manchester United's overwhelming success. But there was a fundamental and glaring contradiction between Campbell's loyalty to the New Labour cause, and New Labour's integrity in government.

Ferguson and Campbell had been introduced by the late Jim Rodger, a friend of Ferguson's who had been a colleague of Campbell on the *Daily Mirror*.[1] Ferguson, a keen Labour supporter, often rang Campbell during the 1997 election campaign. They spoke so often that sometimes, Campbell's mobile phone would ring only for him to hear shouting in the background. Ferguson had accidentally pressed the automatic redial button containing Campbell's number while berating one of his players.[2] Campbell was later to credit Ferguson with coming to his rescue when he was in danger of succumbing to the kind of pressure that led to his breakdown on the *Today* newspaper. With Campbell nearly at the end of his tether, Ferguson rang him on Blair's election battle bus at the height of the 1997 campaign. 'I was getting to the point where I just couldn't cope,' Campbell later recalled. 'Alex said, "Imagine you are in a tunnel. At the end of the tunnel is the Premiership and anyone who isn't part of that, you have got to get them out of the way." I took his advice and have adopted that approach ever since.[3] Campbell's conversation with the football manager formed the basis of his approach to his work inside government: ' I started saying, "This is your problem. I don't have to deal with it." I came across as being a bit hard and even brutal when I was with the government because of it – but it worked.'[4] Ferguson was happy to donate money to party funds, and helped the 1997 campaign with supportive messages. He allowed himself to be filmed kicking a ball around with Tony Blair.[5] Campbell even sought Ferguson's advice about how Labour's front-benchers should keep mentally and physically fit in the face of the demands of an election campaign.

The two men continued to work together closely when Labour won power. Ferguson came to the rescue of New Labour's faltering European election campaign with a last-minute broadcast in 1999. 'If you want Britain to continue to get results in Europe,' said Ferguson, in a reference to Manchester United's famous European Championship triumph in Barcelona just two weeks earlier, 'then there's only one leader: Tony Blair.' Campbell had been to the game, enjoying one of the best seats, as Ferguson's guest.

Four days after the match, Ferguson was awarded a knighthood, something that came as no surprise to readers of the *Sun*, whose reporter George Pascoe-Watson had learned from a 'Whitehall source' of Ferguson's impending honour some weeks earlier.[6]

Soon after Ferguson's knighthood came an affair that cast a sharp light on the parallel agendas of Manchester United and New Labour. It centred on Manchester United's withdrawal from the following season's FA Cup in order to play in the World Club championship in Brazil. The move was supported by Tony Blair and Alastair Campbell. Both men, intensely conscious of the symbolism that linked sport to politics, believed it would help gain support for England's bid to host the 2006 World Cup. But the Brazil tour was controversial. It meant that Manchester United was turning its back on English football, and devaluing the FA Cup, the premier domestic cup competition with a famous history, by its absence.

The *Sun* backed the United decision, but the *Daily Mirror* was leading the campaign to make the club do a U-turn. On 29 July 1999, Kate Hoey replaced Tony Banks as Sports Minister. She received clear instructions from Campbell, on the very day of her appointment: 'Don't say anything to the press about Manchester United pulling out of the FA Cup to play in Brazil. Alex Ferguson is angry about the *Mirror* campaign and we don't want to rock the boat.'[7] But in one of her first interviews in her new job, Hoey was put on the spot. BBC Radio 5 Live had done their research thoroughly and discovered she had criticized the United decision while a backbench MP. She was asked whether she held the same view now she was Sports Minister.

Outspoken Hoey decided to ignore Campbell's advice and tell the truth. 'Manchester United should be playing in the Cup. I am just amazed that they have treated their supporters in what I would say was a quite shabby way.'

Hoey soon learned the perils of defying Campbell and Ferguson. She received a terse message from Number 10 the next morning. 'I was told I had been instructed not to criticize United's decision,' she said.[8]

She was so cross about Campbell's role in Ferguson's knighthood and the decision – against her advice – to give an MBE to Arsenal footballer Ian Wright, despite her plea that his record of bad behaviour in the game made him a poor role model, that she complained to Sir Andrew Turnbull, the civil servant in charge of the honours system. Shortly after her run-in with Downing Street, she was sacked. 'Maybe that's why I am no longer Sports Minister,' she told MPs investigating the honours system in March 2004.

Top gun in Kosovo

Late on the evening of Tuesday, 18 May 1999, Bill Clinton phoned Tony Blair. The two men were probably closer, politically, culturally and personally than any British prime minister and American president had ever been. But on this occasion Clinton was furious. And the target of his ire was Alastair Campbell.

Clinton was enraged by an article in that day's *New York Times* from their London correspondent, reporting that Clinton was under pressure from Britain to drop his opposition to sending ground troops into Kosovo. It was the latest and most strident in a series of newspaper stories on both sides of the Atlantic, inspired by Number 10, portraying timid Clinton as reluctant to match heroic Blair's determination to use any force necessary to get rid of evil Slobodan Milosevic. The President detected the hand of Campbell.

Clinton told Blair: 'Rein your man Campbell in, he's been briefing against me.' He proceeded to vent his frustration on the White House hotline with both Campbell and Blair for the next ninety minutes. So great was Clinton's annoyance that his relationship with Blair nearly foundered there and then. Blair spent most of the ninety minutes trying to reassure the President that he could trust his British allies.

The Kosovo war saw Campbell's unique skills brought fully into play. A series of disputes over bungled air strikes came to a head on 14 April, when American F-16s, flying at a height of three miles, mistook a group of Kosovar refugees for a Serbian military convoy and slaughtered more than seventy innocent people.

The media machine at NATO HQ in Brussels was not coping well. Campbell decided to get a grip and, within days of the massacre, flew to Brussels and took personal control of the media machine.

He used the methods perfected in Labour's 'war room' at Millbank in a real war. Hand-picked spin doctors from London and Washington were flown over to take charge. The manner in which he transformed the way the NATO briefings worked was masterly. The office of NATO press spokesman Jamie Shea was in a parlous state. Shea was under-resourced, overworked and had no media strategy. He had only three support staff and was obliged to write up his own notes before each press conference. There was no system for monitoring each day's press; Shea was vulnerable to being caught off-guard and unprepared for running news stories.

Shea, though liked by defence correspondents, lacked the level of access to NATO bosses that Campbell was able to take for granted in Downing Street. The first day that Campbell attended the briefing at the NATO summit in Washington to celebrate its fiftieth birthday, there was a rambling twenty-five-minute statement from Shea about the war, followed by fifteen minutes from a NATO general. Watching the performance, Campbell turned to a colleague and said: 'He stands there and says too many different things.'

Afterwards, Campbell took Shea outside. He asked: What was the top line? What did you want the story to be? The following day's press conference was transformed. Shea delivered a short five-minute statement, with a clear message. Afterwards – as Campbell had previously arranged – both Tony Blair and President Clinton congratulated Shea in person. 'It was a masterly performance,' says one well-informed observer. 'Alastair could have humiliated Shea and stepped forward and taken the credit for himself. But he didn't.'9 It was a re-run of Campbell's Whitehall shake-out after the general election two years earlier. It had worked for the Labour party, it had worked for the Government: now it was set to work for the Western Alliance.

War brought to the fore Campbell's short-tempered intolerance of hostile or inconvenient press comment. On 16 April *The Times* political editor Philip Webster wrote a front-page story recording government anger at John Simpson, the BBC correspondent in the Serb capital Belgrade. Downing Street was angered by Simpson's account of the carnage after the mistaken US air strike on 14 April.[10] *The Times* said: 'John Simpson, the BBC's veteran foreign correspondent, has run into fierce criticism from the Government over his coverage from Belgrade. Mr Simpson ... has been accused by government sources of falling short of the standards expected of a leading journalist. In an astonishing attack, senior officials accused him of ... swallowing Serb propaganda.'

Two days before the *Times* story about Simpson, British journalists were with Campbell at NATO's Brussels headquarters. After the official briefing he wandered over to a group of reporters and candidly told them that he would like 'to send a cruise missile through Simpson's hotel room'.[11]

Three months later, when the Kosovo war was over, Campbell made a rare public appearance to denounce British war reporters. In a lecture to military experts at the Royal United Services Institute in London on 9 July, he accused them of giving too much weight to the 'Milosevic lie machine' and of playing to Serb propaganda by emphasizing NATO's bombing errors. He claimed that UK press and broadcasting coverage of the conflict had given other dictators a 'template' to exploit the Western media in future wars. He said they had made British politicians look like war criminals. Simpson countered by defending the way NATO's mistakes were reported, stating it was 'a matter of public importance and interest'. Campbell took a swipe at war reporters, saying it was 'striking' how few journalists entered Kosovo to find out about atrocities before the NATO troops went in and how few even tried. 'The day of the daredevil reporter who refuses to see obstacles to getting the truth, and seeing it with his or her own eyes, seems to have died.'

And yet the very BBC reporters who angered him most were those same people: the Omaars and the Simpsons, all intrepid newsmen prepared to risk their lives behind the lines for a story, 'daredevils' in Campbell's words. Campbell's journalistic allies who lived in the cosy environs of Westminster were rarely criticized. Perhaps it was not surprising that when, four years later, the BBC was attacked by Campbell over the Iraq dossier, Simpson was among those who defended the BBC vigorously. 'If the BBC apologised to Alastair Campbell because it had upset the British Government at a time when the British Government was out on a limb, it could say goodbye to its reputation for independence,' he wrote. 'The BBC would be right where governments would always prefer it to be: comfortably on their side, broadcasting soothing information. Or, in this case, trying to persuade the doubters that war is best.'[12]

By the end of the Kosovo campaign, Campbell was one of a handful of people intimately involved in running the war. He was on the way to becoming a significant and even celebrated figure on not just the national but the world stage. By the time Clinton left office he was so impressed by the man he once ordered Blair to rein in that he is said to have jokingly offered him a job. Joke or not, it was a measure of Clinton's regard for Campbell's effectiveness.

The Kosovo war showed how effective the New Labour media machine had become. The lessons from the Clinton White House had all been learnt and absorbed. Now Downing Street was going out and teaching some of its own. It resembled in some ways an international media consultancy. After the NATO mission there were reports that Campbell was being drafted in to sort out the disaster-prone European Commission. Most telling of all was the moment when New Labour aid was sought to help Hillary Clinton's campaign for the Senate.[13] His cool-headed and professional handling of the Kosovo war had made Campbell's reputation on the international stage.

Campbell preens himself

By the time of the new millennium, even Alastair Campbell couldn't believe how well Labour had done in its first three years in office. He was pleased with his own success too. He should have been at ease with himself. And yet there were signs of frustration. At Westminster, the behind-the-scenes adviser always has to pay a price. The politician utters his phrases, adopts his strategies, does what he says. Always Blair got the credit, not Campbell.

That was the deal. But Campbell was not cut out for the role of an anonymous adviser. As the 2001 election approached, he started to push himself forward, and seek out his share of the glory. There was a problem here. Campbell could only stress the importance of his own role by diminishing Tony Blair.

When Charlie Whelan invited the cameras into Number 11 Downing Street, two years earlier, Campbell warned him it was a fatal error. Whelan's enhanced profile contributed to his downfall. Yet Campbell repeated Whelan's error, and the consequences were far more damaging, and not just for Campbell. Perhaps he felt so powerful that he thought the rules that had applied to Whelan did not apply to him.

Campbell said his reason for allowing Michael Cockerell to film a 'fly-on-the-wall' documentary *News from Number Ten* was to 'lance the boil' of media fascination with him and his job and expose 'cynically corrupt' journalists at work. But the programme achieved neither of his aims. All it did was to expose his own cynicism in action, and create an even greater fascination in him.

The comedian and impersonator Rory Bremner had already spotted that Campbell was Blair's Achilles' heel. A one-off comedy show by Bremner, *Blair Did It All Go Wrong*, to mark Blair's third anniversary in office in May 2000, showed a bullying Campbell bossing around an indecisive Blair.

Bremner had no idea how realistic the sketch was until it was played out for real by Blair and Campbell in Cockerell's documentary a few weeks later. The scene was set up and directed by Campbell himself. Campbell may have wanted to be in the limelight, but clearly Blair did not want to be seen to be part of a double act and wisely avoided being filmed with his press secretary. Campbell the puppet-master had other ideas.

'We had been filming in Number 10 for several weeks and I said to Alastair that we didn't have enough interaction between him and Blair,' said Cockerell. 'Alastair said: "The trouble is he gets stiff if he knows in advance that you are going to be there. He will only relax if he doesn't know you are there." He was trying to help.'

Cockerell's team was stationed behind the door of Campbell's office, cameras rolling, when a jacketless Blair marched into the room, walked towards Campbell and started talking to him, oblivious to the fact that he was being filmed. When he cottoned on, he stopped in his tracks, as a laughing Campbell casually gestured to him to proceed, while deftly turning down the TV news in the background so the soundman could pick up their conversation.

As Blair went to leave the room, Cockerell coralled him, and pressed him about his relationship with Campbell. 'He's the best in the business,' said an uncomfortable Blair.

'Was it true that they spent their whole time working out how to 'spin' their way to victory in the next election? "Rubbish," said Blair. "I'm supposed to have spent my holidays with him last year ... " His answer trailed off.' (In fact, they had been on holiday together, though not the previous year.)

Cockerell: 'Was the press cynical?'

Blair: 'What is important for me is that it doesn't disturb me from doing the things that are really important. Y'know, for the country. Otherwise there's no point in doing this. You can believe it or not, but that's what I spend my time doing.'

It was at this point that Campbell, arms folded nonchalantly, interjected witheringly: 'That's why you've just spent seven minutes talking to Michael Cockerell.' Blair momentarily froze, before walking away to hide his discomfort.

Cockerell recalled: 'To some, it looked like the schoolboy coming into the headmaster's study, and Dirk Bogarde in *The Servant*.'[4] That, undoubtedly, is what it looked like to millions of TV viewers.

By coincidence, the day after the film was shown, Bremner and Cockerell bumped into each other at a charity cricket match in Sussex. 'I watched your film last night and I'm studying it frame by frame,' said a gleeful Bremner. It became the highlight of his weekly *Bremner, Bird and Fortune* show. Was the Cockerell film Campbell's psychological revenge upon his boss Tony Blair? In some ways, the Bremner show's comic-strip portrayal of Campbell was flattering. He may be shown as a thug, but he was an attractive one. His main complaint was that Andrew Dunn, the actor who played him, was too fat. Campbell was in the early days of a keep-fit regime and was taking much greater care of his appearance than before, to such an extent that he would cringe with embarrassment whenever he saw press photographs of himself in his overweight days. By contrast, Bremner's 'Blair' was shown to be timorous and vacillating, ordered around by Campbell, his blunt Northern enforcer. In its way, the caricature was every bit as damaging as the *Spitting Image* show in the 1980s which had portrayed Liberal leader David Steel sitting on the shoulder of his SDP ally, David Owen. Steel's reputation never fully recovered.

No sooner had the film been broadcast than Campbell had a lobby revolt on his hands. George Jones, political editor of the *Daily Telegraph*, told Campbell that, since he had invited the cameras in to Number 10 to observe the lobby without asking its permission, from now on, the *Telegraph* would refer to him by name instead of referring to him as the Prime Minister's official spokesman. Campbell complained, writing to Jones: 'I do not accept that I "agreed" to change the formulation of "Prime Minister's official spokesman". There is nothing I can do to stop the *Telegraph* naming me, but I am writing none the less to ask you not to do so.'[15] Jones wrote back, saying it was too late. 'In the immortal words of Cecil Parkinson, the toothpaste is out of the tube and cannot be put back,' he said. Judging by the mild, at least by Campbell's standards, tenor of his letter, it is possible that Campbell did not want it put back.

A forgotten telephone call

Alastair Campbell's growing authority in domestic affairs caused him to be listened to with a new respect in Downing Street. But he was still not strong enough to prevent Peter Mandelson's return to the government. Within six months of the home-loan affair, Blair was pressing for the recall of Peter Mandelson to the Cabinet. Campbell said it was too soon, but Blair honoured his promise to recall Mandelson as soon as possible. By the autumn of 1999 he was back as Northern Ireland Secretary. His comeback lasted fifteen months. This time, Alastair Campbell would play an even more central role in the events surrounding his removal.

At the heart of the new problem was Peter Mandelson's acquaintance with S. P. (Srichand) and G. P. (Gopichand) Hinduja, a pair of multi-millionaire businessmen. They had been involved in problems in India, and were inclined to look towards Britain as a way of making a fresh start. Their applications for British passports were turned down in the early 1990s.

Following the change of government in 1997, they set about wooing
New Labour and G. P. Hinduja's second passport application succeeded in autumn 1997. The Hindujas met Blair at Number 10 in June 1998,
and four months later they offered to give £3 million to the Millennium
Dome, Blair and Mandelson's pet project.[16] In March 1999, S. P. Hinduja was given a British passport.

The possible connection between his donation and the granting of
his passport hit the headlines in the New Year of 2001. Campbell
learned that there was a Mandelson story afoot only when he saw the
first editions of the Sunday papers on the evening of Saturday 20 January. Initially, it looked a routine affair. Claims that improper influence had been exercised made little impact and Mandelson shrugged
it off, insisting that any representations about the Hindujas' passport
applications had been handled by his civil servants, and not by him
personally.

In a phone call between Mandelson and Blair that Sunday morning,
the *Observer* report about the Hinduja affair was not even mentioned;
Mandelson was far more concerned about a *Sunday Times* report concerning a dispute between him and Gordon Brown over election plans.
Campbell phoned Mandelson, who told him he had not made any representations to the Home Office, but that his office merely sought
information about the government's policy on naturalization. At the
following morning's lobby briefing, Campbell told journalists: 'Mr
Mandelson had not got involved in the matter – beyond being asked to
be involved, which he refused to do.' There matters rested for a few
hours, until a confidential Home Office briefing for the department's
own press officers contradicted Campbell's statement. It said Mandelson had indeed made 'verbal inquiries' of Home Office Immigration
Minister Mike O'Brien. Campbell spoke to Home Secretary Jack
Straw, who confirmed that Mandelson had spoken to O'Brien. Moreover, Straw told Campbell that he had phoned Mandelson the previous
Wednesday to remind him of this.

An alarmed Campbell convened a three-way conference call
between himself, Mandelson, who was at Hillsborough Castle, and
Mike O'Brien. O'Brien continued to insist that Mandelson had raised
the Hinduja application with him in a phone call. Mandelson said he
had no recollection of it, but O'Brien was insistent and said it had been

recorded in a Home Office note. Campbell said: 'We have got to say you two had a conversation and that what I said to the lobby on Monday was wrong. And we have to do it as soon as possible.'[17] Campbell told Mandelson privately: 'This is looking bad for you. I have had a record of the phone call read out to me.' Mandelson replied: 'That is amazing.' Mandelson later claimed that Campbell had been confused and that the 'record' was not of a phone call between him and O'Brien, but merely a Home Office e-mail referring to the approach for information with regard to the government's policy on naturalization.

Mandelson told Campbell that when he spoke to the lobby, he must make it clear that at no stage did he seek to help the Hindujas get passports. At that stage there still seemed no undue cause for alarm. It was the Downing Street briefing to the lobby on Tuesday morning that catapulted what was becoming known as a 'passports for favours' story into a full-scale crisis. Campbell's deputy, Godric Smith, said there had been a mistake at the previous day's briefing – in fact, Mandelson had 'forgotten' the phone call. 'Although Mr Mandelson had no recollection of the call, it clearly took place,' he said. This prompted newspaper headlines stating Mandelson had lied. Mandelson then made things worse by giving an interview to Channel 4 television in which he gainsaid Smith. Asked how he could now remember a conversation Number 10 had said he had 'forgotten', Mandelson replied: 'You will have to ask them that. Nobody asked me these questions.' In Mandelson's mind, he had not 'forgotten' the phone call; he still didn't believe it had taken place, but had agreed to go along with the Home Office's version of events. At best it was a sloppy, casual performance, at worst it was downright disingenuous. The result was that Mandelson was now publicly at war with Campbell. There could only be one winner.

Once again Jonathan Powell was despatched to consult Cabinet Secretary Sir Richard Wilson. Wilson, who still felt sore at the way he had been used to justify Mandelson's first resignation, agreed to find out the facts, but stressed he would not carry out an investigation. It was not the job of a civil servant to investigate a minister, he said firmly. It was up to the Prime Minister to decide for himself if a Cabinet minister deserved the sack; the Cabinet Secretary was not there to act as his 'hangman'. Wilson set about his task with despatch and reported to Blair on Tuesday morning that there was 'not a shred of evidence' that

Mandelson had done anything wrong.

Just before midnight on Tuesday, after the conflicting accounts given by Campbell and Mandelson had led to banner headlines in the Fleet Street first editions, Downing Street was panicking. Campbell told Blair that the government was in major trouble. Blair phoned Wilson, who was in his car accompanied by his wife, returning from a dinner in his honour at the Japanese Embassy. 'I am extremely worried about Peter,' said Blair. 'There is a firestorm developing. We are going to have to have an inquiry.' Wilson replied: 'I don't think that is a good idea.' He advised that the whole thing would blow over if Blair only kept his nerve. 'It's just a storm in a teacup,' he told him.[18]

But Blair and Campbell ignored Wilson and ordered their own investigation. Campbell was certain Mandelson had not told him the truth. Some Labour insiders say he had another motive to dispose of Mandelson. 'The two of them always vie for control in election campaigns,' claims one. 'The election was only months away: Peter was behaving irresponsibly and it was an ideal chance for Alastair to say to Tony: "We can't have him doing this in the election campaign."'

Blair and Campbell met in the Prime Minister's Downing Street flat at 8 a.m. on Wednesday morning. There was a palpable air of panic. Blair, Campbell, Hunter, Powell and Wilson were surrounded by scores of documents relating to the case strewn across the floor. Campbell sat on the window sill while the others plucked at pieces of paper trying to make sense of the paper trail. At one point, Blair knocked over his cup of tea, reducing a pile of papers to a brown mush. Cherie breezed in and out of the room.

'What do you think?' Blair said to Wilson.

Wilson replied, 'You have two choices: ride it out or hold an inquiry.'

Blair said, 'Or Peter goes.'

Wilson was taken aback. 'But why?' he asked.

'Because he has lied to Jack (Straw),' Blair answered.

Powell supported him enthusiastically: 'He's lied to Alastair, he's lied to the press and he's lied to parliament.'

'So it's a question of character, is it?' asked a baffled Wilson.

The Prime Minister's allies have subsequently contended that Mandelson was obliged to resign because of media pressure. But this account of events is not consistent with that morning's headlines.

Though there was heavy coverage of the story, there were few calls for Mandelson to go. That was not the picture in the Prime Minister's flat. When Mandelson arrived at Number 10 shortly after 10 a.m., it was like a replay of the final hours before his first resignation: he thought he was there to persuade the PM he had done nothing wrong and that if they all kept their nerve, he could prove his innocence and survive. Blair, supported by Campbell, had already decided to fire him. The meeting went on for more than an hour.

Campbell was worried about his rapidly approaching 11 a.m. daily appointment with the lobby. He wanted to announce that Mandelson had resigned – a clean kill. But when 11 a.m. arrived, Mandelson was still battling away in the PM's study. Campbell interrupted the meeting twice to ask if they had reached a decision – i.e. had Blair sacked him yet? On the second occasion, he told Blair: 'What am I supposed to tell the fucking lobby?'[19] Even while Blair was talking to Mandelson, Powell, sitting a few doors away in his own office, was phoning other senior civil servants to inquire if there were any grounds for concluding that Mandelson had broken the ministerial code, to provide firmer grounds for sacking him. To his dismay he was told there were none. In the end, Powell gave up.

Mandelson begged for more time, but neither Blair nor Campbell was disposed to grant it. Campbell arrived late at the lobby and told journalists that Mandelson was meeting the Prime Minister at that moment, and it might be best if they hung around; he would be 'more useful upstairs' in the PM's study. His meaning was plain. Had Blair at this stage changed his mind and allowed Mandelson to stay, Campbell's own position would have become untenable. In the event, Blair stuck to his guns. Mandelson crumbled and agreed to go. Outside the Prime Minister's study, Anji Hunter was sobbing. 'It's terrible,' she moaned. 'It's the end of New Labour. It was all due to Peter, Gordon and me and now Peter is going, it's all over.' Mandelson announced his resignation on the steps of Number 10 at lunchtime.

Hunter later told Mandelson: 'It was Alastair who pushed it because he thought he had misled the lobby as a result of you misleading him.' Mandelson told a friend: 'To protect Alastair's integrity, I had to take a fall. It had to be a Peter Mandelson lie and not a Downing Street cock-up, which is what it was.'

The ink was barely dry on Mandelson's resignation statement when he decided he had been bounced out for no good reason – and that Sir Richard Wilson was to blame. Mandelson phoned Wilson and told him, 'I have been the victim of a terrible injustice and I want to know what you are going to do about it.' 'Richard was very unhappy,' a Whitehall official recalled. 'Mandelson's tone was very hostile, threatening almost, but Richard had had nothing to do with the decision to make him step down. He had been the only one to defend him.'

Wilson's concern turned to horror when a series of reports, all blaming him for Mandelson's fate, appeared in the press. Wilson made a formal protest to Blair, pointing out that the media coverage was grossly unfair and asking Blair to defend him by putting the record straight. Blair nodded sympathetically and told him: 'Of course, it may take me a couple of days. I'll speak to Alastair about it. If I get the chance to mention it in Prime Minister's Questions I will do so.' Nothing happened, leaving Wilson feeling aggrieved – so much so that he decided he had no choice but to share his simmering discontent with his fellow permanent secretaries. At their regular Wednesday meeting in conference room 'A' in the Cabinet Office Wilson told them of his outrage and how he had advised against dismissing Mandelson only to find himself blamed for it in anonymous briefings. 'People are telling lies about me,' he told them, adding later, 'I have been stitched up and I think it is Alastair's doing.' At one stage, Wilson threatened to resign in protest. 'He felt utterly devastated, isolated and betrayed,' said one official. As a direct result of the row over the handling of Mandelson's resignations, Wilson, fed up with being made the fall guy, suggested that a special system be established ready to deal with any future allegations against ministers. Blair immediately ruled it out, believing, with some justification, that once the press got wind of it, it would be a red rag to a bull.

As Mandelson belatedly tried to salvage his reputation and career, Campbell suggested he was finished not just as a minister but as an MP too. He told journalists, 'I think Peter's making clear from his statement that he is looking to wind down his political activity.' He went even further after a phone call from Mandelson on the morning of Friday 26 January. Mandelson had been contacted by one of his former civil servants, who told him that it was she, and not Mandelson, who had made the crucial phone call to O'Brien. Mandelson phoned Campbell and told him he had proof that he had been wronged. 'Don't give me that,' Campbell replied. 'I'm fucking sick of hearing this.' Campbell warned Blair that Mandelson was determined to clear his name at all costs. In one last effort to save his reputation, Mandelson set about writing an article to appear in that weekend's *Sunday Times*, setting out how, in his view, he had been 'assassinated'.

But, ever alert, only an hour after the Mandelson phone call, Campbell suppressed his habitual distaste for the Sunday lobby and invited them to a meeting in the Number 10 briefing room. He walked to his chair in the briefing room and said: 'Right, what do you lot want?', knowing full well they wanted a Mandelson story. He had come prepared with one. Mandelson was 'mad' – or at least that is how his comments were interpreted by the journalists, left and right, tabloid and broadsheet alike.

Campbell said Mandelson had been 'curiously detached'. The last time he had used such language was after Ron Davies's 'moment of madness', said one of the reporters. Was Mandelson's behaviour in the same category?

'I think it was,' said Campbell. He was entering into shark-infested waters, and the lobby smelled blood. Was it anything to do with Mandelson's personal life? they asked.

'I got the sense that he's fed up with it, he's kind of had enough,' said Campbell. 'He sees media and political alarm bells ringing all over the place – you know, "What are they on about now? What's this I'm supposed to have done now?" and therefore, mentally speaking, he thinks, "Get me out of here, I don't want to be here."'

Scarcely able to believe what they were hearing, the lobby asked Campbell if he feared for Mandelson's mental health. 'It is an absolute tragedy that his entire career is in tatters,' he replied ambiguously.

Would he be given a role in the election? 'He is not going to be in Millbank. He is not going to be advising on the general election.'

When Campbell's comments suggesting he had questioned Mandelson's sanity made front-page news, he angrily claimed they had been taken out of context. But Kamal Ahmed, political editor of the left-leaning *Observer*, who is close to Campbell and who attended the briefing, wrote: 'Mr Campbell is not someone who just breezes into meetings and says the first thing that comes into his head. There was no pushing him towards saying something he did not really want to say. He returned to the subject several times. The tone of the briefing was clear. If he (Campbell) wanted to kill the Downing Street end of the story he could have given us a few bland statements. Mr Campbell never says anything by mistake.'[20]

The events surrounding the second Mandelson resignation showed the fragility and emptiness, verging on semi-hysteria, that lay at the heart of the New Labour project. They demonstrated that, though Campbell was often accused of telling falsehoods himself, he was utterly unforgiving to anyone he thought had lied to him, and that he was prepared to dispatch them to the political wilderness with utter ruthlessness.

Mandelson's account of his actions with regard to the Hinduja passport affair was at times deeply confused, but Campbell was far from blameless. In an article headlined 'It Was Alastair Campbell Who Led An Iniquitous Panic', *Guardian* columnist Hugo Young wrote that 'it was only when Campbell told journalists on Monday that Mandelson had had no personal involvement whatever – a statement the minister had never made, either publicly or privately – that the world was substantively misled.'[21] Not for the last time, Campbell's main consideration appeared to have less to do with the reputation of the minister involved in the controversy, but rather his own reputation.

Mandelson held Campbell responsible for his resignation. Yet the Saturday after he left the Cabinet in disgrace for the second time, the Campbell-Millars threw a party at their home in Gospel Oak and Mandelson rolled up as a guest and led a singsong. But the show of unity did not conceal the private reality. The two men barely spoke for a year.

Mandelson remains bitter at the way he was treated by Campbell. 'I wouldn't mind, but he has never said sorry to me,' he told a friend.

Setting the election date

Two months after Mandelson's second Cabinet departure, on a cloudy day at the end of March 2001, Campbell walked into the daily meeting of information officers after a blazing row with Blair. Blair had to decide whether to stick to their decision to hold the election on 7 May, or delay it, to avoid appearing insensitive to the plight of farmers during the foot and mouth epidemic. The strain of life in Number 10 was beginning to catch up with Campbell. The constant phone calls seven days a week; keeping Gordon Brown at bay; constant disruptions to family life and preparing for another election campaign. His growing notoriety added to the pressure.

For once, the normal dividing lines in Downing Street were cast aside. Campbell's determination to stick with May was vociferously supported by Gordon Brown and his adviser Ed Balls. Hunter and Mandelson, already back as an unofficial adviser to Blair, wanted it put back.

While Campbell was trying to manoeuvre Blair into going ahead with the May poll, Hunter was doing the opposite. As the end of the March deadline for deciding whether or not to call off the May election approached, Hunter asked a senior civil servant: 'Do you think the election should go ahead?' The official replied: 'If it's not sorted out soon there are going to be major problems.' Hunter gave a wry smile. 'That could be very useful,' she commented as she walked off.

As the debate raged on inside Downing Street, someone told the *Sun* it had been settled. On March 20 March, it proclaimed: 'May 3rd: Election Day: Official.' For an official announcement, it didn't last long. Within days, Blair told Campbell he was considering delaying polling day. Campbell was furious. His allies on the *Sun* launched a campaign to make Blair stick with 3 May. On 26 March, the paper ran a front-page article showing Britain as a jail under the headline: 'Sorry We're Closed: Foot And Mouth,' warning Blair that a delay would send the wrong message to the world.

But Blair ignored everything that Campbell and his friends at Wapping threw at him. On 30 March he told Campbell the election was to be delayed until 7 June. Campbell marched into the meeting of information officers, who were blissfully unaware that the election date had been put off, or that Campbell was seething with rage.

'The moment the foot and mouth discussion started he exploded, banging his fist on the table, effing and blinding,' said one official. Campbell erupted: 'You're a complete fucking joke, the lot of you. When are you going to get your act together over this? I have never in my life known people make such fucking stupid decisions.

'I'm sick to the death of all the balls ups. When are you lot going something right for a change? What a ludicrous day,' he rambled. It was only afterwards, when the officials heard on the grapevine that the election was to be put off, that the penny dropped and they realized the real cause of his anger. It had nothing to do with the handling of the foot and mouth crisis. He was angry with Blair for ignoring his advice.

But how was Campbell going to pacify the *Sun* who had got it so wrong? To help him out, Blair agreed to delay the announcement so that the *Sun* could be first with the new election date. On Saturday 31 March, eleven days after announcing exclusively that the election was to be held on 3 May, the paper declared: 'Now it's June 7th as Blair puts country before party.' Five days earlier the paper had claimed that Blair would be closing down Great Britain plc if he put off the election; now it hailed his statesmanship for doing just that.

chapter thirteen

Second Term

> There has been talk of a bill to protect civil servants from ministers. What we need is a bill to protect ministers from civil servants.
>
> *David Blunkett, 7 March 2002*

Dealing with Gordon

TONY BLAIR'S VICTORY IN JUNE 2001 gave him the chance to relaunch his government. Robin Cook was thrust aside as Foreign Secretary to make way for Jack Straw. Asked why the pro-euro Blair had replaced the pro-euro but prickly Cook with the anti-euro Straw, Campbell gloated to a journalist: 'Because Jack will do what we tell him to do.' Tony Blair could change the rest of the Cabinet at will, with the massive exception of the Chancellor of the Exchequer. Blair and Brown had spent the entire election campaign arguing over tactics. And no sooner had Blair chosen his new Cabinet than he had the first of a series of confrontations with Brown that brought Blair to the brink of firing him four times over the next two and half years.

The Chancellor stormed into Number 10 following the June 2001 victory to demand of Blair: 'When are you going? I want to know now.' Shortly afterwards, he told Blair to 'fuck off' and let him take over. Blair complained: 'All he does is shout and swear at me. I can't handle it when he's like this.' Campbell and Lord Levy were among those who urged Blair to sack Brown there and then. Blair refused.

Six months later Blair decided he was wrong to keep Brown, but the death of the Chancellor's baby, Jennifer Jane, made him relent. He considered it again in the spring when, to his fury, Brown ruled out joining the euro yet again. Campbell blamed Blair as much as Brown for failing to resolve the impasse. 'Alastair told Tony to knock heads together, i.e. get Gordon to toe the line. But he wouldn't do it.'[1] The fourth threat came in the autumn when Brown opposed Blair's education and NHS reforms and used his Labour party conference speech to challenge Blair's leadership. Campbell was delighted when the speech backfired. He told a colleague: 'Brown got high inhaling his own self importance.'[2]

Campbell complained: 'I am sick and tired of having to go round putting out bush fires started by Gordon Brown. What is the matter with the man? When someone makes a joke in Cabinet, I look round the table and there's always one person who isn't laughing: Brown.'[3]

Campbell tries to quit

The growing friction between Blair and Brown – and the increasing amount of time spent by Campbell on keeping up appearances – was just one of the reasons he was tiring of his job. Tony Blair had to work hard to get him to stay. By the eve of the general election, Campbell had had enough. He told Tony Blair he was underpaid, overworked and wanted out. The decision was partly because of Fiona. She had been most reluctant that he should take the job in the first place, and now she was eager for Alastair to go. He in turn was suffering from a deeper physical and mental exhaustion than can perhaps be readily imagined. Campbell may also have sensed that his time was running out, that he was turning into a liability, and that the era of his special type of spin-doctoring was drawing to a close. In retrospect it would have been better, both for him, and for New Labour, if he had stuck by these instincts and elegantly left the stage to general applause at the 2001 general election.

But Tony Blair refused to countenance the prospect of a Campbell-free Downing Street. He was determined that his friend should stay, although he was equally certain that he must retreat from regular contact with the lobby owing to his growing anger with them. As so often when confronted with delicate personnel issues, Blair recruited the Cabinet Secretary Sir Richard Wilson, urging him to do anything he could to get Campbell to change his mind. Blair told Wilson he was worried that he was going to lose both Campbell and Hunter, and asked

Wilson to talk to both about their roles and look at the possibility of increasing their salaries.[4]

In April 2001 Campbell and Wilson had a series of meetings in which they discussed ways of relieving the burden on the press secretary. Campbell told Wilson how he was fed up with the pressures of the job, and that Fiona Millar wanted him to give it up. If he was going to stay on, he wanted to 'pull back' further from the front line. Wilson recruited a personnel expert to assess Campbell's job. Exactly how Campbell described on paper some of his more irregular tasks, some of which had little to do with those of a conventional Whitehall mandarin, is not known, nor what the expert made of it all. At the end of this process the Cabinet Secretary was able to come up with an offer generous and thoughtfully enough structured to persuade Campbell to stay. In reality, Campbell had been afforded the unique privilege of being able to write his own job description – because the Prime Minister was terrified of losing him. Campbell was given the option of a four-day week and staying at home on Fridays if he wanted to, relieved of the chore of briefing the lobby and granted a new title – director of strategy and communication – and a substantial pay rise, to over £125,000 a year.

Campbell himself was content to take a back seat. For four years his lobby briefings had been famous events within the closed world of Westminster, a guinea a minute, well worth paying entrance money to go and see, the best variety act in town. Now they were abruptly closed down. The problem was partly that they were too good. Campbell himself was in danger of becoming the story.

The Downing Street information machine was rearranged. Campbell's old job of daily briefing to lobby journalists was split between two career civil servants, Godric Smith and Tom Kelly. As his parting shot Campbell requested that 'the media should attribute their comments as coming from the Prime Minister's official spokesman (PMOS) and not named individuals. Who they were was not important. What they had to say was, as they were speaking on behalf of the Prime Minister.'[5]

Campbell himself retreated to the shadows. Nobody, perhaps not even Campbell himself, knew exactly what his grand new title meant. This element of mystery was of no consequence; if anything it helped a bit. The point was to give Campbell an alibi. He remained in Downing Street, more powerful than ever, but much less visible.

These were sensible changes. Not so Campbell's second decision. He moved himself out of his cramped, scruffy, office on the ground floor of 10 Downing Street to the much grander Whip's Hall twenty-five yards down the road at Number 12. The status of Chief Whip Hilary Armstrong was so low that at Prime Minister's Questions she was for a time forced out of the chief whip's traditional position of power to the right of the prime minister immediately adjacent to the gangway and sometimes obliged to crouch on the gangway itself, a humiliating position for a chief whip whose ability to do the job rests partly on the ability to inspire fear. Armstrong was booted out of Number 12 in undignified fashion and left to hunt for offices elsewhere.

A deep symbolism underlay this move. The whips had occupied their splendid Georgian home for more than a century. They had been responsible for party discipline and patronage. They had exercised, at times, an awe-inspiring power, and always been the enforcing arm of the prime minister of the day. But they were important only in terms of a parliamentary democracy, and had no place in the presidential style of government which Tony Blair and Alastair Campbell were eager to impose. The decision to evict the chief whip from her historic office was an unambiguous sign that the real government enforcer was not the hapless Armstrong but Campbell and his information machine.

There was a price to pay for this, both for Campbell and the government. By downgrading the chief whip, Tony Blair was downgrading parliament. In the years that followed the 2001 general election, Tony Blair was to be knocked off course by an escalating series of formidable backbench rebellions. He had deprived itself of the command structure to keep them in check.

For Campbell there was a different danger. It was surprising that a man so acute to the nuances of power should have forgotten the merits of quiet authority. By making his move, he was boasting of his strength throughout Whitehall.

Sorting Cherie and Anji

Tony Blair's biggest personnel difficulties in the aftermath of the 2001 election were nothing to do with his Cabinet, still mainly in a state of subdued acquiescence. They lay elsewhere, among the inner group of courtiers and advisers in Downing Street. Here the difficulties had been stress-inducing from the start, and the general election brought the issue into the open.

Ensuring that Alastair Campbell was found a new role was the smallest part of the problem. By 2001 the hostility between Cherie Blair and Anji Hunter was becoming an embarrassment. On one occasion a dressing-gowned Cherie had screamed at Hunter to get out of Blair's hotel room when she was helping him on a speech. On another there was said to be an incident between them in a Number 10 corridor involving pushing.

But the personal nature of Hunter's role made it inevitable that she had to spend much of the time at Blair's side. Cherie's jealousy grew into a visceral loathing of Hunter, whom she called 'that bloody woman'. Cherie would secretly check Blair's e-mails and fly into a rage at what she considered to be the over-familiar tone of messages from Hunter, though they were generally about mundane matters. Hunter would send Cherie e-mails too, instructing her on photo calls with Blair, when to be where and what she should wear. These would infuriate her too: she would complain at what she felt to be their impertinent tone.

Anji Hunter and Tony Blair had the kind of bond that is unique to people who have been friends since school days: shared jokes, memories and adventures. Cherie felt excluded. Usually, such relationships are between members of the same sex. All this played on Cherie's sense of insecurity. At the back of the minds of wives whose husbands are still in touch with girls they knew at school is the nagging thought: had their friendship been anything deeper? Hunter and Blair laughed off any suggestion of a romantic link. 'Anji said they may have been at the same all-night parties, but they never slept together,' said one of her friends.[6]

It is hard to overstate Cherie's suspicion of Hunter. 'Cherie thought Anji was a terrible flirt and was petrified of the power she had over Blair,' said one New Labour source. Once a mutual friend made the mistake of passing on a chance remark Hunter had made about Cherie. Cherie hissed: 'Don't ever ask that woman what I think. Do you understand? Don't ever talk to her about me. She knows nothing about me.'[7]

Cherie's feelings about Hunter were so intense that she took the extraordinary step of raising Hunter's behaviour with Cabinet Secretary Sir Richard Wilson. She alleged Hunter had far too much power over Blair, and made a series of allegations about her general conduct. .

Either way, Blair realized he had to act and agreed to change his working routine to meet his wife's concerns. 'A compromise was reached and the problem was dealt with, for a while at least,' said one person with close knowledge of the Blair inner circle. Initially, Alastair Campbell could be prevailed upon to act as peacemaker between Hunter and Cherie. But that became harder when Cherie recruited Fiona Millar into an alliance against Hunter. Hunter's friends believe Cherie 'turned Millar against Anji' by playing on precisely the same fears that possessed her. She suggested Anji was too close to Campbell as well as Blair.

The Cherie Blair/Fiona Millar alliance was bolstered by Sally Morgan, the Downing Street political secretary. Morgan and Hunter were trying to pull Blair in opposite directions. Morgan, a lifetime Labour official, sought to strengthen Downing Street's links with the unions, while Anji Hunter worked on right-wing newspaper editors and business leaders. By 1999, relations between Morgan and Hunter had become so bad that Hunter urged Blair to move Morgan from Number 10. Cherie immediately leapt to Morgan's defence and told Blair that if anyone should go, it should be Hunter. On this occasion Campbell acted as intermediary and calmed things down.

The Prime Minister's dependency on Campbell and Hunter is reflected by the fact that the two of them had long since agreed a 'six-month pact'. They agreed that since Blair depended on them so heavily, if one of them left Number 10, the other would wait six months before departing to help cushion the blow. But the six-month pact broke down before the 2001 election. Anji Hunter told the Prime Minister she wanted to leave at roughly the same time as Campbell. An alarmed Tony Blair recruited Sir Richard Wilson, the Cabinet Secretary, in an attempt to make her stay, just as he did in the case of Campbell. Hunter had always been jealous of Campbell's and Powell's special powers to issue orders to civil servants. She wanted the same privilege. Blair supported her request, but Wilson said 'no'. Instead Hunter was offered a generous pay rise, taking her annual wage to £120,000, the cost of which was to be shared between the taxpayer and the Labour party. In addition, she was given the grand but wholly meaningless title of director of government relations. Even so, Tony Blair's attempt to persuade Hunter to carry on hit a problem. Sally Morgan had made the same threat as Anji Hunter: she would resign unless Hunter was moved. And, crucially, Cherie supported her. Hunter concluded that enough was enough. She had been offered a £250,000-a-year job at BP and decided she would accept. She told Blair she was leaving. Cherie was delighted, and so was Morgan. At last, 'that bloody woman' was going.

But as Hunter and Blair travelled the country on the election trail, the Prime Minister made one last attempt to persuade her to stay on. One close Number 10 aide notes Tony Blair's habit of retaining old shoes for as long as he possibly can. He buys them from Church's of Regents Street, established 1873, and popular with American businessmen and James Bond. He has even taken one of his ministers to a shoe shop to try and convert them to Church's. Once worn out, the Prime Minister's shoes are constantly sent off to the cobblers for repair rather than simply thrown away. He is like that with people too. He likes to hang on to old favourites for as long as possible, shrinks from putting on anything new. Perhaps it was this characteristic that led the Prime Minister to go to these extraordinary lengths to retain both Alastair Campbell and Hunter after the 2001 election. It would only be for a few months, he told Hunter, long enough to help him carry out a major Cabinet reshuffle and reorganize key government departments. Hunter agreed. But Blair did not tell Cherie. The day after winning his second term in office, Blair returned to Downing Street from Buckingham Palace. He was in his office, shattered after weeks on the road. He had a series of major ministerial and administrative changes to make. Cabinet ministers, Downing Street officials and mandarins throughout Whitehall were waiting on tenterhooks. Downing Street staff were receiving calls from some permanent secretaries anxious to know what was the cause of the hold-up. Before Blair could break the bad news about the reshuffle to any ministers, he had to break the news about Hunter to Cherie. The Prime Minister and his wife were alone in his office for nearly half an hour. He finally told her that Hunter was not leaving. Not only that, she would have a new title and status. Cherie was furious. A bitter row ensued. She swept out of the room, with a face like thunder and stomped off to the flat. So in the end it was Morgan who left Downing Street. She was given a peerage and a job – Minister for Women – to make up for it.

Hunter's victory soon turned sour as she found that her new title did not by any means give her the enhanced role she had hoped for. She had fallen in love with Sky TV political editor Adam Boulton, an additional complication, and was about to leave her husband. She was also anxious that the communications director post she had been offered by BP might not be held open for ever. She told Blair she was leaving Number 10, but delayed her decision after the 11 September attack on the World Trade Centre. She felt duty bound to help the Prime Minister in his worldwide diplomatic shuttle to gain support for the attack on Afghanistan. Weeks later, her work done, she resigned and made a clean break, starting a new life with BP and with Boulton. Morgan returned to take Hunter's job, salary and office. She and Cherie celebrated. Alastair Campbell, Fiona Millar, Baroness Sally Morgan and Cherie Blair were conspicuous by their absence from Hunter's leaving party at a wine bar in St Martin's Lane, a stone's throw from Downing Street. Blair called in, but only briefly. Campbell did not attend. He said he didn't know how he would have explained it to Fiona.

Buddies with Bush

Alastair Campbell was to forge the same matey friendship with Republican George Bush as he had with the priapic, saxophone-playing third-way exponent Bill Clinton. When Clinton visited the Labour party conference after stepping down as president, Campbell took him for a stroll along Blackpool's Golden Mile and treated him to a Big Mac in McDonalds. Campbell forged his bond with Bush through jogging. Both conquered serious drinking problems to become teetotal and are fanatical runners. They had long discussions about jogging times, how often they ran, how far they ran and what was the best diet. Bush sponsored Campbell in the 2003 London marathon, though Campbell did not cash the cheque, saying he might auction it for charity in a few years. The President loved to challenge friends and bodyguards to join him in a two-mile run in 100 degrees Fahrenheit at his ranch in Crawford, Texas. Few completed the course. Those who did were given honorary membership of the President's '100 Club'.[8]

And yet when Bush first met Blair, he tried to freeze out Campbell from their private discussions. The President was no stranger to spin doctors, and Bush's political and personal image owed as much to his most trusted adviser, Karl Rove, as Blair's did to Campbell. But the extent of Blair's reliance on Campbell was a shock to the Bush team and led to awkward exchanges between the two leaders when Blair went to the US after the World Trade Centre attack.

Tony Blair and his entourage arrived in Washington on the afternoon of 20 September, just nine days after the World Trade Centre outrage. They were to have their first face-to-face talks on the plan to invade Afghanistan. It was not the practice for Campbell's opposite number, White House spokesman Ari Fleischer, to sit in on the President's meetings with other leaders. Fleischer would be briefed afterwards and would convey the briefing to the White House press corps. It was the same relationship that most press advisers had with prime ministers or presidents, but it was not the relationship between Alastair Campbell and Tony Blair. Campbell was not just a messenger; he shaped the message. And he shaped the policy that shaped the message.

When it was clear that Blair expected Campbell to attend the talks, the Americans resisted. They insisted that it would be restricted to leaders and policy advisers, and that spin-doctors were emphatically not included. When Blair turned up with Campbell at his side for one of their first meetings with the Bush team, and Campbell chipped in from the outset, Bush said: 'Who is this guy?' The same problem occurred at the White House supper: Campbell had been left off the seating plan. Blair asked for his media adviser to be allowed to accompany him. The Americans were puzzled. It was only after a British official took one of Bush's officials to one side and explained Campbell's role that the penny dropped with Bush. Blair not only wanted him there, he needed him there. 'They had no idea how powerful Alastair really was and when they did, they let him in,' said a diplomat.

Other American observers were struck by Campbell's influence on Blair's trips to the US. 'The plane would land at Andrews Air Force base and Blair and Campbell would retire to a private room,' said one diplomat who witnessed Blair and Campbell's unique working relationship. 'Campbell would lay down the law and tell him what the press was likely to ask and what the best lines to take were. Blair listened and repeated what Campbell told him.'

Campbell's success in winning Bush's trust is all the more interesting bearing in mind Fiona Millar's strong views about the President. She made no secret of her opposition to the Iraq war and her low opinion of Bush. She said: 'Look at his eyes, they're too close together.'[9] Millar was totally opposed to the war with Iraq and disagreed with Blair's support for it. 'She said the war was outrageous, Bush was a war monger and that Blair was his poodle,' said one friend.[10] Millar was not alone in her scepticism about Bush. When the Blairs flew to America for their first meeting with the Bushes, Cherie asked her husband why they had to be so nice to 'these people'. Over dinner, she challenged Bush over his support for the death penalty.[11] In fact Blair commented wryly on the opposition to the war of all the partners of his inner circle. Cherie, Millar, Powell's wife, journalist Sarah Helm, and Morgan's husband, left-wing lawyer John Lyons, were all strongly against it.

Campbell himself can hardly be described as a natural Bush supporter. His most revealing comments about the President were made after he left Number 10. 'George Bush. I speak as I find. And I am not going to pretend that we share the same political bed at all. We do not. But nor am I going to sit here and say that everything about George Bush is terrible, because it is not.' Campbell got into a tangle when he tried to elaborate. 'I suppose what I'm saying is that he is a lot cleverer than he looks. Sorry, I didn't mean that. He is a lot cleverer than some of you people think that he looks like he is, OK?'[12]

Whatever Campbell's true feelings for Bush, he was clearly able to use the kind of iron will that Alex Ferguson had taught him and shut out from his mind everything that might distract him from his target: the defeat of Saddam, including his partner's abhorrence of the President, and his own reservations. By the time the Iraq war began, Campbell was writing Bush's script as well as Blair's. He toned down a speech made by Bush which coincided with the Commons vote on the war, when the government faced the serious possibility of defeat. The message of the speech was clear: war was inevitable. But it could further antagonize Labour rebels by reinforcing their claim that Bush was a warmonger. Bush was so desperate to retain Britain's support that he allowed Campbell to change the speech, inserting the phrase 'if war comes'. Bush's version was honest. Campbell's version was pragmatic. The government won the vote.

Tackling the Taliban

Campbell had been well prepared for the Afghan crisis talks in Washington in the aftermath of the World Trade Centre attack. Aware that war was a certainty, he took with him a ready-made plan for handling the media. The Americans were sceptical: they were still trying to work out their military strategy. Campbell told them the media war would be crucial. Ironically, it took the Taliban to help him win them over.

In the first stages of the bombings, the Taliban ambassador to Islamabad, Abdul Zaeef, gave the Americans a lesson in how to manipulate the press. Taking advantage of the fact that the media in Pakistan started work several hours before Europe and America got up, Zaeef had a platform to set the agenda, and made the most of it. Showing a remarkable degree of affability and humour for a group known for its extremism and intolerance, the Taliban daily press briefings became hugely popular. A cleric in a black turban, Zaeef's deadpan response to allegations that the Taliban had nuclear weapons – 'We can't even produce glass' – was both politically compelling and a novelty act. Blair and Bush, with missiles and gunships aplenty, were left chasing Zaeef's tail. Campbell felt he was banging his head against a brick wall and fumed in his Downing Street office: 'The bloody Americans don't think the sun has risen until it appears over the Potomac River.'

In mid October Campbell flew to Washington where he and Bush's media adviser, Karen Hughes, finally agreed on plans to set up a Coalition Information Centre, based in Islamabad, London and Washington. Two weeks later, it was up and running. The CIC was almost identical to the media-monitoring unit and rapid-rebuttal unit used by Labour in Britain to defeat John Major's Tories and in Europe to defeat Milosevic. Now he was using it to try and defeat Osama Bin Laden and the Taliban. Campbell had gone worldwide.

He was well prepared. In their four years in Number 10, Blair and Campbell had developed close links with the intelligence services. In the past, even under Conservative administrations, the latter had been kept at arms' length. 'They would operate from a dingy office in the back end of nowhere, dump their reports at Downing Street and wouldn't be seen for months,' said one former Defence Minister. 'Labour gave them more resources and made them feel loved. The intelligence agencies were hugely flattered and were anxious to please in return.'[13] Downing Street's intimacy with the intelligence agencies was a vital weapon in Campbell's armoury.

In his first public comments on the CIC on 2 November 2001, four days after it was launched, Campbell said its aim was to 'rebut the drivel and lies that come from the Taliban ambassador'. He continued: 'The dictatorship and terrorists have no compunction about lying, no compunction about killing innocent people, no compunction about using the media when it suits them. Democracies have got a duty to communicate. It is important that the media does not allow this sense of moral equivalence . . . as though there were a moral equivalence between an elected leader of a democracy and the leader of a murdering terrorist group.' His US counterpart Hughes said on launching the CIC: 'He (Campbell) felt he was getting hit with things the Taliban were saying while we were still asleep in Washington.'

The CIC in Islamabad was run by US diplomat Kenton Keith and staffed by three press officials from Whitehall, including Alan Percival, who had worked for Campbell at Number 10, three Americans and one Dutch aide. One of its most noteworthy triumphs was persuading al-Jazeera TV, Bin Laden's preferred broadcasting station, to interview Blair. Campbell's task was made easier when the British and Americans succeeded in persuading the Pakistani government to close the Taliban embassy in Islamabad, effectively reducing Zaeef to the status of tourist.

A typical CIC day would kick off with a briefing in Islamabad at 10 a.m. designed to highlight efforts to minimize civilian casualties, or to rebut a Taliban 'lie'. Where possible it would try to coincide announcements with major TV bulletins in London. Several hours later, as London was waking, Campbell would arrange a conference call with colleagues from other nations in the alliance to discuss progress and the media strategy for the day. Five hours later, the CIC 'war room' in Washington would take command. And a few hours after that, it was back to the Pakistan CIC base.

An adviser to Canadian Premier Jean Chretien who took part in the conference calls, said: 'Alastair would hand out orders to everyone. He could be very rude but things got done.' Campbell's handling of the propaganda effort in the Afghanistan war was a great success. But it was marred by a wild outburst against the BBC. In the Kosovo campaign, he targeted the BBC's John Simpson. This time it was the turn of Simpson's BBC colleague, Rageh Omaar.

At war with war correspondents

Two months after the attack on the World Trade Centre, the coalition forces were close to taking the Afghan capital, Kabul. But Downing Street and the White House had been shaken by a series of reports from inside Afghanistan of mistakes by Allied bombers, with claims by the Taliban of hundreds of innocent men, women and children killed. Only a handful of Western journalists had managed to get behind enemy lines into Kabul. Inevitably, their ability to report what was happening depended largely on what the Taliban authorities in the city were prepared to show them. Two BBC reporters, Rageh Omaar, who went on to report on Saddam's fall in Baghdad, and Willie Reeve were among those in Kabul. Campbell's temper finally boiled over when he heard a report by Omaar of an alleged blunder by Allied bombers which, according to the Taliban, had caused civilian casualties.

Richard Sambrook, the BBC's head of news, was at home on the evening of Saturday 10 November 2001, when the phone rang. It was Campbell bellowing down the line: 'What the fuck's going on with this Rageh Omaar report? You're being duped by the Taliban.' Sambrook replied, 'Rageh's report was very careful and measured. He made it clear that he could only show what the Taliban was showing him. Our own people on the ground know what they are doing, Alastair.'

Campbell: 'I'm telling you: get your fucking people out of there!'

Sambrook: 'We can't do that.'

Campbell: 'Get them out of that fucking place!'

Sambrook: 'I've told you Alastair, we just can't do that.'

Campbell: 'I'm warning you. If you don't stop doing this we will throw everything at you.'

The conversation ended before Sambrook discovered precisely what

Campbell meant by 'throwing everything' at the BBC. Three days later, Omaar's BBC colleague John Simpson walked into Kabul to announce its liberation from the Taliban.

Burying bad news

When Alastair Campbell announced the resignation of Martin Six-smith, head of information to Transport Secretary Stephen Byers, on 15 February 2002, he thought it would be the end of what was, at that time, the biggest controversy involving spin-doctors since Labour was elected.

Sixsmith's resignation was announced simultaneously with that of Jo Moore, Byers' special adviser. Sixsmith and Moore had been at odds ever since Moore's infamous e-mail three months earlier, stating that 11 September was 'a good day to bury bad news'.

There was only one problem: Sixsmith had not resigned. Campbell had done it on his behalf – and without telling him – out of his desperation to punish Sixsmith for his part in exposing Moore's behaviour. Campbell had spent five months fighting a rearguard action to defend Moore. Even by the driven standards of New Labour's special advisers, Moore's methods stood out as ruthless and earned her the fear and hatred of officials. Her e-mail on the day New York's twin towers were attacked was not her first offence. Sixsmith's predecessor, Alun Evans, had been moved from his post after complaining about Moore's order to civil servants to smear Bob Kiley, the London Transport commissioner appointed by Ken Livingstone.

When Blair first arrived at Number 10, Sir Richard Wilson had arranged for the mild-mannered but diligent Evans to take on the job of running the SCU precisely because he was regarded as 'straight'. Wilson hoped he would act as a check on Campbell and co. But Evans was soon moved out of Downing Street. He was taken on by John Prescott at the Transport Department because, unlike most other ministers, Prescott saw Evans' aversion to 'spin' as a virtue. It was Evans' ill fate that Prescott was succeeded by the most spin-obsessed minister of all, Byers.

Incredibly, Moore did not stop her cynical manipulation of government information. When Sixsmith feared she was planning a similar stunt to take advantage of Princess Margaret's funeral, he warned her off in an e-mail. 'There is no way I will allow any substantive announcements next Friday. Princess Margaret is being buried on that day. I will absolutely not allow anything else to be.'

When the e-mail was leaked to the press, Godric Smith told the lobby that it 'doesn't exist. It's a fabrication.' Within twenty-four hours, Smith had been forced to put the record straight. The e-mail did exist. The wording was not precisely as had been reported, but the meaning was the same.

Furious at suggestions that he had been made to look a liar, Smith told the lobby: 'Clearly, there's a game going on here. I'm not prepared to have my integrity and my credibility put on the line because they are commodities which are precious, which I value.'

In fact, the moment the e-mail was first reported, one of Campbell's deputies asked Sixsmith if the e-mail existed. Sixsmith confirmed it did, but pointed out the wording was slightly different. The official said: 'So we can say the e-mail in the papers is false?' Sixsmith: 'In lawyers' terms, yes.' Official: 'Will you go along with that line?' Sixsmith: 'No, but I will keep quiet.' Within an hour of Downing Street stating that the e-mail did not exist, civil servants who knew otherwise phoned contacts in the lobby to tell them it did. Later that day, as the Number 10 version of events unravelled, Sixsmith was outside Harrods department store in London, when two senior Downing Street press officers contacted him in a joint phone call. 'We've got a bit of trouble over this morning's line,' said one. 'Will you ring the Press Association and say that you approved it?' Sixsmith refused, saying: 'I didn't approve it, I said I'd keep quiet.'

Even Campbell knew Moore could not survive this time. Campbell tried to broker a deal between Sixsmith and Byers. 'The wounds are very fresh,' Campbell told Sixsmith. 'Byers promised Jo that if she went you would go too.' Sixsmith refused, claiming he had done nothing wrong.[14] Campbell responded by announcing Sixsmith's resignation, even though he had done no such thing. It was later reversed and the government was forced to pay Sixsmith £100,000 in compensation.

But Sixsmith's ordeal was not over. He found himself the victim of a crude smear campaign. Press reports appeared about properties he owned in Knightsbridge and Paris. Sixsmith says he has no doubt who was behind the reports. 'Downing Street told journalists to investigate my property portfolio. The implication was clear: how can he have bought all this on a journalist's salary?'[15] In fact the properties were legitimately acquired as a result of a highly successful and well-paid career as a foreign correspondent.

'It was he (Campbell) who told the media – falsely – that I had resigned,' said Sixsmith. 'He who got the Downing Street spokesmen to deny the existence of an e-mail they had in front of them on their desks. He who fed smear stories to the papers.'[16]

Weeks after Moore's exit, Byers himself had to resign after he admitted he had lied over his role in Sixsmith's departure. It is impossible not to contrast Campbell's 'die in the ditch' defence of Moore, surrendering only after five months of bloody siege warfare with the press, with his treatment of government ministers who had committed lesser crimes. Robin Cook was given hours to choose between his wife and mistress; Nick Brown's homosexuality was handed to the *News of the World* on a plate, and Ron Davies was hauled before the cameras and ordered to resign in a matter of hours. None of them had caused the public outrage provoked by Moore's conduct. New Labour could survive without the Browns, Davies and Cooks, but not without the Jo Moores. She can be seen as a proxy for Campbell. They were both tribal Labour supporters who had been hardened by the bleak years of Tory dominance.

Like Campbell, Moore was prepared to go to extremes to get her way and twist the truth to the nth degree to serve her party. Her boss, Stephen Byers, was the most Blairite minister of them all, and more dependant on her even than Blair was on Campbell. The civil service had endured years of being cowed and sidelined by Campbell and his New Labour apparatchiks. Now it had fought back and claimed its first victim. A couple of slingshots hurled by a junior official or two who had enough of being bullied and cajoled had brought the New Labour Goliath to its knees. Alarm bells were ringing in Campbell's head. Moore's scalp had been claimed. Campbell knew his would be next.

The betrayal of a Cabinet Secretary

The Jo Moore affair highlighted the way in which Tony Blair's method of ruling through a tiny New Labour clique was coming into conflict with the traditional civil service.

These tensions simmered under the surface for the first five years. But they came to a head at an astonishing Cabinet meeting three weeks after Moore was forced to resign. It was the moment New Labour declared open war on the mandarins. Ministers queued up to accuse officials of treacherously seeking to undermine the government of the day.

Sir Richard Wilson, Cabinet Secretary and head of the home civil service, sat silent as Cabinet minister after Cabinet minister came forward to insult him. They did not single out Sir Richard personally, but the ferocious attacks on the civil service as a whole were intended to be, and taken as, a direct and brutal assault on his honesty and competence and that of the entire civil service.

Moore was New Labour 'family', an emissary to Whitehall from the Downing Street inner faction. Whitehall saw her dismissal as purgation. But Campbell, Blair and New Labour Cabinet ministers felt it as a humiliating defeat. They believed, correctly, that Moore had been leaked against by the civil service. If civil servants in other departments mounted the same kind of resistance, the entire edifice of political control on which the New Labour's command structure was built could collapse.

The Cabinet Secretary always takes notes of Cabinet meetings. So Sir Richard was obliged to sit silently writing on a note pad, headbowed, as if it were a normal Cabinet meeting and he was not under vicious personal attack. Witnesses say he was pale and shaking, but his normally expressionless features showed 'serious shock'. Convention demands that civil servants never speak at Cabinet meetings. So Sir Richard was unable to answer back as insult after insult was rained down at the organization which he headed. To begin with the Cabinet meeting ran through the usual subjects – the economy, foreign affairs, and the publication that day of a Downing Street pamphlet on public-service reform.

John Reid, the combative Northern Ireland Secretary and Alastair Campbell's closest Cabinet friend and ally, led the attack. Reid declared that 'ministers are always entitled to expect loyalty, professionalism and competence from press officers'. He added that when he had worked at the Department of Transport he 'had never been able to trust his officials'.

Next to weigh in was Helen Liddell, the feisty Scottish Secretary. She reiterated Reid's criticisms before passing the baton on to Home Secretary David Blunkett. 'Blunkett launched into a savage diatribe against the civil service,' remembers a participant. 'It went on for several minutes. Much of it was incoherent and rambling.'

Blunkett fumed about the way that the civil service 'looked after itself', how difficult it was to sack incompetent civil servants, and the incompetence of many officials. 'There has been talk of a bill to protect civil servants from ministers,' he thundered. 'What we need is a bill to protect ministers from civil servants.'

At this point all eyes flashed across the table to the forlorn figure of Sir Richard Wilson. Everybody knew that he had been pressing for months for a civil service bill, whose central purpose was to curb the excesses of the Jo Moores of Whitehall. Blair was on record as supporting the bill, but had avoided any firm commitment. Now Blunkett tore apart Wilson's flagship. At the end of the room the small group of civil servants who always attend Cabinet sat watching Sir Richard, their boss, being savaged. One participant wondered at this stage what Wilson would do. Would he break all the rules and speak out at the Cabinet table? Would he stop taking notes and walk out of the room? But the Cabinet Secretary stuck to his task, kept on scribbling his notes, head down.

After some minutes Blunkett stopped speaking. There was heavy silence across the Cabinet table. All eyes turned slowly from the broken Sir Richard Wilson to Tony Blair. One witness remembers wondering how the Prime Minister would react. Would he join in the savaging of the civil service? Would he rush to the defence of the beleaguered Cabinet Secretary?

Tony Blair did neither. He cracked a joke. 'At least you know, Sir Richard' declared the Prime Minister, 'that you have the full support of the Home Office.' Some saw this as an attempt to lighten the atmosphere and reduce the tension. But others saw it as a sly aside at Sir Richard Wilson's expense. And it was noteworthy that, while he made no attempt to endorse David Blunkett's remarks, the Prime Minister made no attempt to distance himself either.

It was John Prescott who finally did lighten the mood. He made a few generous remarks about the civil service, paid tribute to the loyalty and calibre of many civil servants, and did something to alleviate the icy chill in the room.

At the end of the meeting Cabinet ministers scuttled away, failing to meet Sir Richard's eye. Only one went up to speak to him – Chief Whip Hilary Armstrong. 'Are you all right, Sir Richard?' she asked. 'Not really,' he replied faintly.

Though the immediate cause of the pent-up anger in that Cabinet room on 7 March was the Jo Moore affair, its true nature and depth can only be understood by reference to the first five years of New Labour in government, and the long battle fought by Sir Richard Wilson, supported by other permanent secretaries, to prevent Tony Blair's inner clique turning the British civil service into an arm of New Labour.

Well before the 2001 General Election Tony Blair and Alastair Campbell had decided that the changes to the civil service structure pushed through four years before had not gone far enough. Blair and Campbell wanted instant change. There was a great deal of naivety in this attitude. Tony Blair had travelled light in opposition, like a guerilla fighter. His ammunition had been newspaper headlines, and in Alastair Campbell he had had the best special operations man in the business. His speeches and photo-opportunities went out over the airwaves with instant effect.

Government was different. Blair suddenly found himself general not of a tiny militia but of a conventional army, and he found it hard to adapt. What was in retrospect culpable was that he did not even try to do so. He retained the casual, informal structure and battle plan which had worked beautifully in opposition. This meant that he brought with him into government the same gang who had been round him from the first. He sought to operate through them, and beyond this inner council through to a wider elite of seventy or eighty special advisers, effectively New Labour commissars imposing order and direction upon the wider civil service from above.

Tony Blair did not merely import his own people, he imported his own habits from opposition. Before the election victory, decisions had been made on the hoof by the tiny inner core. The clumsy decision-making structure of the Labour party was simply ignored. This was the way Tony Blair addressed himself to government as well. He disdained large, formal meetings. Decisions tended to be made inside his tiny

Downing Street 'den' on the sofa with a few intimates. Minutes were rarely taken.

It was not just the status of the Cabinet that was downgraded under Blair. Cabinet committees, once the scene of the most fiercely contested debates inside any administration, were similarly neutered. What was the point in arguing? The ministers knew the real decisions were taken at a new complex strata of semi-formalized gatherings of the Blair inner circle. Campbell was at the centre of the hub of this new ad-hoc system of government. At 9 a.m. each day, directly after his meeting with heads of information and special advisers, Campbell and Hunter met Blair in his Number 10 'den' to brief him on the day's events. A 9.45 a.m., Campbell attended the 'message' meeting with Mandelson and Gould. On Tuesday, at 5 p.m., Blair, Campbell, Brown, Mandelson and Gould met at the 'P5' – the 'Political Five'. On Thursday at 11.30 a.m. after Cabinet, Blair, Campbell and Mandelson met to discuss strategy. Others, including Sally Morgan and Jonathan Powell, would sometimes join in. One official who watched them at work said: 'They would go into a huddle and the conversation would often seem to end hanging in the air. Then someone, usually Campbell, would go and do something. Only they knew what had been decided.'[17] One mandarin challenged Blair over his insistence on conducting most of his serious business via one-to-one meetings and unminuted cabals. 'I said he must hold more ministerial meetings, and told him he could not proceed like this. He (the Prime Minister) would say: "Why not?" I said because it would lead to trouble eventually. He would smile and say: "No it won't."'

This became clear to a wider public when the Hutton inquiry painstakingly sought to reconstruct the decision-making process which had led to the naming of Dr David Kelly. It was discovered that the Prime Minister had chaired no fewer than four meetings in the forty-eight hours leading up to the release of Kelly's name. Permanent secretaries and Cabinet ministers had been present. Not one of these meetings had been minuted, a shocking and serious breach of traditional Whitehall procedure. In the event a retrospective minute, drawing upon the memories of those present, was laboriously prepared for the benefit of Lord Hutton.

This was one way Tony Blair challenged the existing machinery of government: by pretending that it wasn't there. But New Labour also tackled Whitehall head-on. It proudly disclosed that it meant to govern with what Downing Street aides audaciously liked to call a 'Napoleonic' method rather than the traditional British Cabinet system. Many of the early decisions – to double the number of special advisers, the creation of special powers for Campbell himself and Jonathan Powell, the transformation of the government information service – were a direct assault on the British system. To begin with the civil service, awestruck by the sheer scale of the landslide election victory, did its level best to co-operate. But Tony Blair was really straining for an entirely new structure, and this the mandarins could not or would not deliver.

This overwhelming contradiction between the controlling zeal of the Blairites and the system they inherited was explicit from the very start. But it began to unravel from the start of 1999, as ministers felt embarrassed that they had failed to improve public services in their first two years in office. Hospital waiting lists and school class sizes continued to grow. At some stage during late 1998 the Prime Minister pronounced that 1999 was to be the 'year of delivery', a claim that turned out to be as arbitrary and ill-informed as the targets he subsequently set. He shouted orders, willed the change, pressed the button. Nothing happened.

During this period he embarked upon a long, agonized dialogue with Sir Richard Wilson who tried to explain to the Prime Minister that results could never be instantaneous, that turning round giant organizations like the National Health Service or the education system took several years, if not decades, could not be undertaken in a few months.

Wilson tried to explain that it was easier to achieve change acting with rather than against the grain. In the words of one senior civil servant, he told Tony Blair that 'the Prime Minister has very few executive powers. The people with the power, the money and the ones who are actually legally responsible are the Cabinet ministers.' He urged the Prime Minister to see himself as the chairman, and look to the secretaries of state to take charge of implementation.

At one stage Wilson wrote a series of notes to the Prime Minister setting out the role of Cabinet ministers, and how they could effect change. But these were ignored, possibly not even read. Tony Blair was not interested. He wanted to know from Wilson if the Prime Minister was the chairman, who was the chief executive? Gordon Brown? Wilson said that neither he nor Brown were chief executives: Cabinet ministers were the only ones with the power to make things happen. Harold Macmillan said that when he entered Downing Street, he felt as though he had taken delivery of a new Rolls Royce. All he had to do was to sit inside, turn on the engine and let the car take him effortlessly and silently to his destination. Blair said that he too felt as though he was sitting in a Rolls Royce, but that he didn't know how to make it move. Wilson told him that in trying to run the government by by-passing the Cabinet in favour of ad hoc cabals, and ignoring the civil service in favour of a tiny group of special advisers, he was trying to move the car without turning the key.

It didn't help. Eventually Wilson and Blair fell out. The first major argument came at a private meeting with just a few members of the Blair inner circle present. The Prime Minister was pressing Wilson over public service reform.

He had made clear that he wanted rapid, instant change. But Wilson kept on laboriously making the point that real reform was not something that would take place over weeks or months. Close to despair, Wilson rounded on Blair: 'The problem with you is that you have never managed anything in your life. Do you have any one around you who has ever managed anything?' A shocked Blair struggled to find something to say. Then he replied indignantly: 'What do you mean? I managed the Labour party.' But Wilson brutally replied: 'You didn't manage the Labour party, you led it. There's a difference.' Word soon escaped to a wider Whitehall audience of this dramatic clash between Cabinet Secretary and Prime Minister, the forerunner of the later Cabinet attack on the civil service.

After a while Wilson gave up trying to get through and resigned himself to the humiliating ritual of having to reach Blair via Campbell. No Cabinet Secretary had ever been reduced to such a lowly status.

Wilson nevertheless worked hard to find a structure which would enable the Prime Minister to take dynamic charge of the system. He suggested Cabinet committees, which had been the mechanism adopted by previous governments. Tony Blair rejected these as too bureaucratic. Blair preferred to chase progress on a more direct, one to one

basis, with Cabinet ministers and their permanent secretaries reporting directly to him.

The Prime Minister became accustomed to set five- or ten-year
plans, full of ancient resonance from the Soviet Union, with impossible
targets, fabricated outcomes and distorting effects. These rarely if ever
lasted the course. Later still, another problem loomed. Frustrated by
the lack of progress on the domestic front, he became bored. After the
2001 general election he set up the 'delivery unit' inside the Cabinet
Office run by the civil servant Michael Barber to chase progress. This
took the day-to-day burden of stimulating public-service reform off the
shoulders of the Prime Minister. The truth of the matter was, as everybody who worked in Downing Street came to recognize, that only foreign affairs, Northern Ireland and headline-grabbing initiatives could
be guaranteed to raise Tony Blair's interest.

Impartiality and integrity

This great issue of public-service reform was not the only matter that
divided the Blairite centre from Whitehall. There was a second grievance, less fundamental than public-service delivery itself but in its way
even more vexatious. Tony Blair, perhaps influenced by Alastair Campbell, had little appreciation of the independence and fundamental
integrity of the traditional civil service. Civil servants owe their allegiance to the Crown: Campbell and Blair wanted officials to give their
basic loyalty to New Labour, and could not understand why they did
not. This in some respects understandable attitude brought them up
against the tried-and-tested civil-service structures that were in place to
protect the civil service against favouritism. Labour wanted its own
men in key jobs.

One fundamental principle of the civil service, sacred since the
Northcote Trevelyan reforms of the mid nineteenth century, was the
principle of promotion by merit and open competition. Again and
again New Labour sought to place its own people in top jobs A good
example of this was the case of Jeremy Heywood, Tony Blair's principal
private secretary. When Heywood started working for the Prime Minister in the late 1990s, he found it hard to get accepted. As time passed,
however, Tony Blair came to rely more and more on this youngish,

clever and hard-working civil servant. He became reluctant to let him go. In order to keep Heywood in Downing Street, Tony Blair wanted to by-pass the traditional structures and promote Heywood directly to permanent secretary, the highest rank in the service. But this was blocked, greatly to the disgust of the Prime Minister and his political aides.

The Heywood case was an interesting example of how Tony Blair and his coterie wanted to change the civil-service structures by rewarding successful civil servants with supercharged promotion. They also sought to have civil servants sacked. The emblematic example here was Sir Richard Mottram, the permanent secretary of the Department of Transport who became heavily embroiled in the row which led to the resignation of Jo Moore. In the wake of this episode, many Cabinet ministers and political aides within Downing Street wanted Mottram out – this was said to be one of the bones of contention behind the Cabinet attack on Sir Richard Wilson. In the event, once more to their disgust, Mottram moved on to a new job of identical seniority.

Blairite aides and most of all Campbell himself found Whitehall procedures forbidding civil servants to take part in political activity incomprehensible. Campbell treated these rules with contempt. The classic example of this clash of cultures came when it emerged that Alastair Campbell had played a role in wooing Shaun Woodward, then a Conservative MP, over to New Labour.

Concern about the propriety of Campbell's behaviour was raised by Whitehall officials at a meeting with Jonathan Powell in Downing Street. Powell came to Campbell's aid, asserting that his conduct was entirely legitimate. 'Alastair Campbell may be a civil servant, but he works for the government and the government's job is to increase its majority in the House of Commons,' declared Powell, prompting horrified expressions on the faces of officials. The implication of Powell's simplistic analysis, that it was part of a civil servant's job to increase the government's majority in the Commons, took their breath away. Such was the power of the Blair inner circle that not one of them challenged him, though they later regretted their silence.

In their desperation to produce figures that showed the government in a flattering light, senior government figures applied pressure to the Office of National Statistics. Like the Government Information

Service, it was told to 'raise its game'. For some civil servants, this was interpreted as meaning 'give us the figures we need to win votes'.

During the four or five years after Labour gained power, a state of armed neutrality was maintained between the Blair faction and the civil service. Much of the time the two sides were cautiously friendly. But there were frequent border incursions and diplomatic rows. Sir Richard Wilson was criticized within parts of the service for giving too much ground to the government. Equally, the more he sought to defend the integrity of the civil service, the more Downing Street thrust him into the outer darkness.

After the 2001 general election Tony Blair conjured up a plan to enhance Wilson's role by making him permanent secretary on top of both the Cabinet Office and 10 Downing Street. But the fastidious Sir Richard, conscious of the need to keep the two roles distinct, refused.[18] He did however swallow an almost equally potent organizational change, permitting the merger of the Number 10 Private Office and the Number 10 Policy Unit, thus formally ending the separation between the career civil service and politically appointed special advisers.[19] In due course Wilson became so concerned about the relationship between politicians and civil servants that he pressed for, and believed he had secured, the Prime Minister's support for a civil service bill setting out protections for officials and defining the boundaries between political party and state.

In retrospect it can be seen Blair was doing little more than stringing him along. Blair was happy to pay lip service to the idea in the same way that he had paid lip service to the idea of a Freedom of Information Act. In reality, he had little sympathy for either. Just as the FOI Act posed a direct threat to Campbell's vice-like grip on the control of information, the Civil Service Act posed a direct threat to New Labour's vice-like grip on the control of Whitehall.

The moment Jo Moore was forced out, relations between Blair and Wilson were polarized dramatically. Blair, still fuming at Moore's dismissal, abruptly withdrew his pretence of supporting the Civil Service Act. Some Cabinet Ministers were reported as describing it as 'a Richard Wilson stunt to entrench the incompetence of the civil service'.

For his part, Wilson no longer felt the need to hide his passionate support for it. The latent hostility between New Labour and the civil service burst out into the open.

Determined to avenge the Cabinet for the mauling they gave him two weeks earlier, a demob-happy Wilson, his retirement only weeks away, cast caution to the wind. On 26 March 2002, he publicly called for new curbs on special advisers. The speech was as close as a Whitehall mandarin ever gets to an act of open defiance.

Wilson's speech, at the Cabinet Office's Centre for Management and Policy Studies, remains an extraordinary document. 'It is fundamental to the working of our constitution,' he declared, 'that governments should use the resources entrusted to them, including the Civil Service, for the benefit of the country as a whole and not for the benefit of their political party. The non-political character of our Civil Service underpins that convention.' Entitling his lecture 'Portrait of a Profession Revisited', Sir Richard insisted that 'Special Advisers should not ask civil servants to do anything immoral or illegal' nor 'do anything to undermine the political impartiality of civil servants to give their own best advice to ministers'. He did not name Jo Moore or Alastair Campbell, but he didn't need to.

'Very often the issues are about boundaries: the boundaries between what is and what is not acceptable,' he said. 'The boundaries between government and party; grey areas where judgements are difficult and different people acting in good faith may properly come to different conclusions. There is a danger that if we continue to leave these issues unattended they will fester. They will increasingly become rubbing matters, matters of political controversy used to embarrass governments, damaging the civil service and perversely making it more difficult to bring about the changes which are needed.'

It was a fitting epitaph for the first five years of Blair government. The reaction from Downing Street was vicious. When Sir Andrew Turnbull was appointed as Wilson's successor, Downing Street arranged for the new Cabinet Secretary to give an interview in *The Times*. In a blatant snub to his predecessor, Turnbull blithely dismissed any need for a civil service act, and indicated that he was relaxed about the need for more special advisers. Turnbull's words could not have been more supportive if they had been composed by Campbell himself. But the interview provided the compliant Turnbull with his introduction to Downing Street's calculating style. Number 10 arranged for the interview to take place on the day that a string of former Cabinet secretaries and mandarins were due to support Wilson's crusade for a civil service act in a House of Lords debate. The aim was to spike the guns of Wilson's supporters. Sources close to Turnbull claimed he had been 'set up'. Former Cabinet secretaries, angered by Turnbull's remarks, mounted a counter attack in the Lords debate, stating that the Jo Moore affair had shown the impartiality of the civil service was under threat.

The same battle was played out again two years later when there was another head-on clash between those who wanted to rein in Blair's special advisers and Blair's own Whitehall priority: to protect special advisers and force the civil service to deliver better results for New Labour. On 23 February 2004, the outgoing Commissioner for Standards in Public Life, Sir Nigel Wicks, delivered a stinging rebuke to the Prime Minister for failing to restrict the powers of special advisers. He criticized the Prime Minister's 'puzzling reluctance' to curb the number and power of special advisers. He made it clear he thought it was wrong that Campbell had chaired meetings of the JIC in the run-up to the Iraq war. The choice for Blair was simple, said Sir Nigel. He could either 'establish the necessary clarity about the proper boundaries within the executive' or put it off until he was forced to do so by 'unfortunate events', i.e. another spin-doctor scandal. Yet again, Blair had his riposte ready. Twenty-four hours later, the country's senior civil servants were summoned to hear a speech by Blair at the Orwellian-sounding 'delivery and values event' in London. He praised the civil service's impartiality and integrity. And then he came to the point: the lowest-performing twenty per cent of civil servants would be 'moved out' – fired – unless they improved. Wicks' call to curb special advisers was ignored. Seven years after he had come to power, Tony Blair was as determined as ever to protect the Jo Moores and Alastair Campbells of Whitehall who had impugned Whitehall's reputation for integrity and impartiality and as determined as ever to attack the 'Sir Humphreys' who had defended it.

Few would argue that Whitehall could not benefit from opening its musty corridors to fresh talent. But civil servants argued that it was Blair's insistence on handing their traditional powers to special advisers, who often had little experience, training or knowledge of management, and who were often selected more for their political or personal loyalty than for their talent, that prevented them delivering the results he craved.

In an incisive commentary, *Times* columnist Peter Riddell said the government had 'a blind spot over standards in public life – whenever proposals have been made for new ethical safeguards, 10 Downing Street has often dragged its feet'.[21] And he was dismissive of Blair's attempt to reform Whitehall. 'Tony Blair has never understood how government works. He has a brilliant intuitive sense of the public mood and of power. And he knows what he wants. But he has little understanding of how to get there.'[22] One former mandarin with forty years' Whitehall experience observed: 'Margaret Thatcher had the most radical programme of any government for fifty years and Whitehall managed to deliver that. You can't deliver candy floss.' The problem lay not just with Blair's lack of management skills. Ever since he had become Labour leader, the emphasis had been on communication and presentation. Blair's closest advisers, Campbell, Mandelson, Gould and Hunter, were experts in presentation, not policy. Blair's policy advisers, David Milliband, Andrew Adonis and Geoff Mulgan, were secondary figures, as was Chief of Staff Jonathan Powell, who lacked the authority to establish a proper balance. Campbell's personality and style dominated not just Downing Street, but the whole of Whitehall. He had become Press Secretary, Chief of Staff and Cabinet Secretary rolled into one.

chapter fourteen

Guerrilla Warfare with the Media: from Black Rod to Cheriegate

We'll get him one day.
Alastair Campbell on Black Rod

A new settlement with the press

THE JO MOORE AFFAIR was a turning point, not just for New Labour, but for Campbell. It was his first significant public defeat. Until then, his power had increased steadily from the day he entered Number 10. His power over the Prime Minister was demonstrated by the lengths Blair went to in order to make him stay on. He had cowed the Chancellor; seen off his main rivals, Charlie Whelan and Peter Mandelson. He had large tracts of Fleet Street in his pocket; he had reproduced the 'spinning ' skills learned in Millbank's media 'War Room' set up to wage war with the Tories, to win real wars. He had gained the confidence of two US presidents. He had his own Downing Street department. And many of those who worked for him would walk through fire for him. But Alastair Campbell was not content. Over the course of the next year, he was to make a series of mistakes that had calamitous consequences for himself, the Prime Minister, the government and others.

The enforced resignation of Stephen Byers' press aide Jo Moore was followed in due course by that of the minister himself. The episode broke Alastair Campbell's rules. He had determined from the moment they entered Downing Street not to repeat the experience of John Major's government between 1992 and 1997, with embattled ministers constantly being forced out of office by press campaigns.

The general election victory seemed to have made no difference. For the last quarter of 2001 and early months of 2002 it seemed as if the government was constantly at the mercy of the press, over Jo Moore, the Enron collapse and the Mittal affair.

This was not the way New Labour had planned it to be. In the New Year 2002 Campbell and a small group of ministers discussed their objectives for the months ahead. 'We've got to change the culture', he ruminated. When one of the ministers pressed him to explain, he added starkly: 'The media culture.'

In some ways it is hard to understand what he was talking about. Campbell's campaign to control the media had been surprisingly successful. The Blair government suffered from nothing like the daily torment that had been the fate of the Major government from 1992 to 1997.

But New Labour was intent on achieving something hugely ambitious. It was determined to change the nature of the media itself. It wanted to change what Peter Mandelson and Alastair Campbell both called, in an elegant phrase, the 'grammar of reporting'. Downing Street believed that British political writing was focused to the point of obsession on the manufacture and elaboration of rifts, rows and controversy and was guilty of failing to cover the real issues that affect the ordinary people of Britain.

Campbell's model was mainly the Clinton White House. In the United States, with its strong culture of regional newspapers, there is no élite political corps with the strength to impose its interpretation on the nation at large. New Labour was deeply impressed by the way the president communicates direct with the American people either through personal appearances on television or through a relatively unsophisticated regional press. It watched, fascinated and absorbed, as President Clinton sustained his popularity with the American people throughout the Starr investigation.

Campbell set out these ideas early on in a Fabian Society seminar on government and the BBC. He accused the writing press of creating 'cynicism about politics, about politicians, about people who work in public life'. The speech is worth quoting from at some length:

> As a public sector broadcaster, the BBC does have a special duty to give most coverage to the stories and issues that most affect people's lives.

This will often mean having a different agenda from newspapers and often going against the flow. It means accepting that conflict is not the only source of news. It means that just because businesses are not, as predicted, attacking the National Minimum Wage, people are still interested in and have a right to be informed about it. It means that policy success stories – such as the New Deal and the part it has played in cutting youth unemployment – should be covered just as much as policy rows which may emerge from a leaked memo. This is not a political point. Such an approach should not mean that the government secured more coverage or that opposition criticism was muted. Indeed, oppositions are more vulnerable than governments to the tendency of only being covered when there is a row. This is a plea to the broadcasters not always to wait for the leak, the row, the scandal, before deciding to examine a particular government or Opposition proposal. Because if they do, like as not they'll be travelling in the press's wake. That journey is a one-way road to cynicism, and while cynicism is an essential part of politics and journalism, when it dominates most judgements, the media's dominant role becomes the erosion of politics.[1]

Even at Westminster, there have been few more shameless examples of hypocrisy than Campbell's speech to the Fabian Society. He was effectively asking listeners to ignore his previous career as a journalist and polemicist which had been devoted to coverage precisely of the 'leak, the row, the scandal'.

They were also being asked to ignore New Labour's behaviour in opposition. Between 1994 and 1997 Tony Blair's Labour opposition was the most brilliant in history. Its campaign against sleaze, which was masterminded by Campbell and a handful of others, cleverly seized on a few individual cases to give the impression that the majority of British public figures were in it for the quick buck. No opposition has ever done more to foster cynicism about public life than Tony Blair's.

Now, having won power through the co-operation of the broadcasters and the press, Campbell was turning his back on his old allies: no wonder the denunciations rang out so fiercely and strongly. Tony Blair had seized power by using the media in the most flagrant way imaginable to undermine confidence in the government of the day. Having done so, Campbell was doing his best to make it impossible that the same should not be done to him.

So the attack on the press had been a long time in preparation. In the

spring and summer of 2002 Campbell was masterminding a conscious
and deliberate attempt to change the terms of trade between government and the media. The aim was to create a political press corps which
was ready to report government in the way it wished to be reported and
within parameters set by Downing Street itself.

There were numerous prongs to the campaign: the undermining and
partial replacement of the lobby system; an assault on the long-estab-
lished practice of unattributable briefing (except when it came from
authorized Downing Street sources); the maintenance of a friendly
power block of friendly newspapers and political editors; an even
greater ruthlessness in the old trick in the exchange of information and
access for friendly copy; a new willingness to attempt to isolate and
smear journalists who wrote 'unhelpful stories'.

Campbell had launched a preliminary attack on the lobby system
four years before. Through the early summer of 2002 he pushed
through much more thoroughgoing changes. Number 10 briefings were
moved out of Downing Street for the first time since Winston
Churchill's eccentric experiment half a century before. Instead 11 Carlton House Terrace, headquarters of the Foreign Press Association and
the former London home of the great Victorian statesman William
Ewart Gladstone, was rudely commandeered. Campbell and government ministers claimed that the move was about bringing a new openness and transparency to political reporting.

Cameras were allowed in, government ministers encouraged to
attend, specialist reporters and foreign correspondents admitted. The
government's numerous apologists in the press, most of them columnists with no experience of hard reporting, praised the new arrangement. At first glance the government case that these moves were driven
by a desire to be more open appeared plausible, but in fact the reverse
was the truth. Though it had its weaknesses, there was a kind of rough
democracy about the old lobby system. True, the briefings were not
held in public. But all political reporters, from the political editor of the
BBC to the political editor of a minor regional paper, enjoyed the same
status. The quick, intimate atmosphere made it possible for reporters
to get at the truth – and it continued to survive in the afternoon briefings in the House of Commons and on the less formal Carlton House
occasions. If fobbed off with an evasive or incomplete reply by a

government spokesman, journalists can and do press the point. The new system which operates at 11 Carlton House Terrace when ministers are present is designed to prevent that. Reporters get one question if they are lucky. It is hard to press on with inadequate replies. Proceedings now have the air of general-election campaign press conferences, which are dominated by the big broadcasters with awkward questions brushed aside. At the first lobby briefing under the new arrangement, in mid October, with David Blunkett present, the BBC were granted four separate questions while there was only one from the regional lobby, and he represented Blunkett's local paper.

Traffic between Downing Street and its favoured political editors became more intense and fruitful than ever. Only it has become completely secret, behind doors and out of view. The new lobby system became more conspiratorial than ever. In the name of openness and transparency the changes tended to make reporting more secret. Reporting of the fireman's strike, just weeks after the new system was introduced, provided a good example of this syndrome. At the Carlton House briefings the Prime Minister's spokesman said nothing of significance. But away from the main press pack a Downing Street source told *The Times* that the Prime Minister believed the firemen were behaving in a 'Scargillite' fashion. This made big news. *The Times* was one of Number 10's most trusted outlets, and would never reveal its source. The story could be denied if need be, and no fingerprints were left behind. The old lobby system had been replaced by a new elite more shadowy, shameless and underhand than anything that went on under Harold Wilson: the antithesis of transparency, which was exactly how Campbell preferred it.

The attack on the lobby, though a longstanding New Labour ambition, was only a small part of the job. More important was the battle of ideas. Campbell, government ministers, and their apologists and partisans in the press[2] went on the offensive. Steven Barnet, Professor of Communications at the University of Westminster, came forward with a striking proposition. 'Evidence is growing', he claimed, that 'the increasingly hostile tenor of political journalism in the twenty-first century may be helping to undermine faith in the democratic system itself.' John Lloyd went to war in *Prospect* magazine, blaming 'the media' for the cabinet resignations both of Stephen Byers and Peter Mandelson, and taking newspapers to task for putting Derry Irvine and Robin Cook through 'media hell'. Lloyd's contention was that 'they were pursued not for large derelictions of duty, or crimes, or corruption – but essentially for being human. They were pursued by men and women who would deeply resent the same kind of "standards" being applied in this way to them'. Charles Clarke, then Labour party chairman, embarked upon a series of lively private seminars, arranged by the political hostess Carole Stone, in which he endeavoured to convince journalists of the error of their ways. He claimed that much criticism of the government 'is pious and hypocritical, sometimes entirely manufactured, coming from parts of the media which themselves have done their best to bring democratic politics into disrepute'. Clarke's message has been supported by other government ministers. Around the same time Home Secretary David Blunkett claimed that the media was 'almost on the verge of insanity'. Similar attacks were launched by Jack Straw, John Reid and Peter Mandelson.

Ministers and their supporters were now close to claiming that it was illegitimate for the press to criticize politicians. A good example was the riposte after Estelle Morris's resignation as Education Secretary. Robin Cook, leader of the House of Commons, complained that she had been 'hounded out of office'. Deputy Prime Minister John Prescott, escorting her out of her department for the final time, turned to waiting reporters and asked: 'Haven't you lot done enough?' Home Secretary David Blunkett claimed that she had fallen victim to a 'feeding frenzy'.

The assumption behind all these remarks was that 'the media' had driven Estelle Morris out of her job. But for the most part Morris was treated generously in the press. Newspapers would have been neglecting their proper democratic function had they not reported her role in the shambles surrounding 'A' level marking, her often tense relations with the 10 Downing Street Policy Unit, the delay at the start of term because of inadequate checking procedures for teachers, or the way she misled the House of Commons over a promise to resign if standards were not met. Estelle Morris was soon rather charmingly to undermine all these protestations by admitting that she considered herself incompetent to run a large government department.

Structural changes to the methodology of political reporting counted for something. So did the attempt to take away the legitimacy of the press to expose government scandals and criticize ministers. But above all a man of Campbell's aggressive temperament was eager for a raw test of strength. He was eager to take on not merely Fleet Street in general but named publications and political editors, and return with the scalps to Downing Street. Campbell's belief that he could single-handedly change the grammar of political reporting was doomed to end in failure.

Black Rod

The Queen Mother's funeral had aroused deep emotions in the British people. Allegations that the Prime Minister tried to muscle in on the event led to a major confrontation between Downing Street and the very parts of Fleet Street Campbell wanted to tame.

Campbell believed that the coverage of events by three newspapers – the *Spectator*, the *Evening Standard* and the *Mail on Sunday*[4] – provided the opening he needed to enable him to 'change the culture' once and for all. These targets were the more alluring because the titles were owned by the two newspaper groups – the Telegraph Group and Associated Newspapers – which had most retained their independence from Downing Street.

The dispute over the Prime Minister's role in the Queen Mother's funeral first surfaced in the *Daily Telegraph*. On 10 April, the day after the Queen Mother's funeral, the *Daily Telegraph* Peterborough diary published a two-paragraph item suggesting the Prime Minister's office had 'wanted him to appear, on foot, just a couple of minutes before the royal procession . . . their idea was to get Tony and Cherie walking along glad-handing the crowd and "looking sombre"'. The following day, the *Spectator* magazine published a fuller report alleging that Downing Street had intervened, demanding changes in the arrangements for greeting the coffin to give Mr Blair a more prominent role.

Alastair Campbell phoned the Press Complaints Commission. 'The stories in the *Telegraph* and *Spectator* are untrue,' he said. 'I am going to tell the *Spectator* to publish a correction and we are writing to the *Telegraph*.' The Prime Minister's private secretary Jeremy Heywood duly wrote to the *Telegraph* stating its report was 'without foundation'. Campbell told the Number 10 press office to denounce the *Spectator* version as a 'complete fabrication' and a 'lie'.[5] On 12 April, the London *Evening Standard* published an article repeating the allegation of meddling.

Blair's private secretary Clare Sumner, a civil servant and one of the most trusted if least well-known members of Blair's inner circle, phoned the parliamentary official who had taken charge of the lying-in-state, Lieutenant-General Sir Michael Willcocks, otherwise known as 'Black Rod'. She asked him to issue a statement denying the story. Sumner knew exactly what had really gone on: she had liaised with Black Rod and the Palace over the Prime Minister's part in the funeral arrangements. Sumner asked Sir Michael: 'Would you be prepared to make a statement?' Willcocks replied: 'Yes, I agree the PM did not specifically demand any changes.' But he warned: 'However, you and I know exactly what really happened and if you go any further I cannot support you because I am not prepared to lie. All it needs is for someone to look round the edges and they will discover what went on. If you are not careful, this will end in tears.'

Black Rod issued a carefully worded, hand-written statement. He was determined to keep control. It seemed to work. Most of the media took the denials at face value and the story seemed to go away. But it resurfaced on 14 April in the *Mail on Sunday*. This account, published over two pages, described how Sumner phoned Black Rod's office to ask if the Prime Minister would be able to meet the coffin and the royal family when they arrived at Westminster Hall. Number 10 wanted Mr Blair to be at the head of the official party that greeted the Queen Mother's coffin after it arrived from Clarence House. It stated that Downing Street was 'disappointed' when Black Rod insisted that he would stick to the protocol which limited the Prime Minister to a walk-on role.

Campbell phoned the PCC again. 'We want to make a complaint, where do we stand?' he asked. He was told by PCC secretary Guy Black: 'You can complain under the accuracy provisions of the PCC Code of Practice and we will follow the normal practice of handing it to the publications to ask their views.' But he sounded two warnings. 'There is an issue here regarding confidential sources. Normally, if there is a clash of evidence between a newspaper and a complainant, we would expect the complainant to be able to prove their complaint with an on the record source. We will need a statement from those involved, including Black Rod. Secondly, if you make a complaint of that sort you should only do so if you are 100 per cent sure what all the parties involved are going to say.' In other words, if the stories were true, Campbell should back down before it was too late. The PCC had good reason to urge caution: Black Rod had told them it was true.

But Campbell replied confidently: 'We are 100 per cent certain and you will get on the record statements from Black Rod and from Robin Janvrin [the Queen's private secretary] at Buckingham Palace.' Campbell's confidence was surprising given the terse exchange that had already taken place between Sumner and Willcocks when she sought his support a second time. 'You know perfectly well that this story is true,' he told her. 'I told you I would not lie and I am not going to do so. If you go any further you are crazy and you will lose.' Equally, officials at the Palace also knew it was true. A royal equerry had been present when the Queen Mother's coffin arrived at Westminster as Downing Street made a frantic last-minute attempt to get a bigger share of the limelight for Mr Blair. On 21 April, the *Mail on Sunday* went even further, publishing new details of how Number 10 tried to get a bigger role for Blair.

It was time for Campbell to call upon Roy Greenslade, media columnist for the *Guardian* and always a faithful stalwart. Greenslade wrote that the stories were 'untrue and malicious', claiming they were part of a right-wing media plot to blacken Blair's reputation.[6] But they contained the first sign of Campbell's irritation that Black Rod was refusing to sing from the Downing Street hymn-sheet. Clearly echoing Campbell, Greenslade said: 'A single source doesn't make a story correct. Blair's reputation has been unfairly blackened and I would expect some harsh questions to be asked today of Black Rod's office. Growing public cynicism about politics stems directly from the papers' inability to tell proper stories truthfully.'

Greenslade was wrong. The story did not originate from Black Rod. Number 10's meddling was so clumsy that it was common gossip among royal, parliamentary and military officials involved in the lying-in-state. Far from revealing all, Black Rod initially collaborated in the attempt to cover it up, but in the end, decided he could not lie. Willcocks, whose military career had culminated in a spell confronting Serbian warlords in Bosnia, rang the PCC and warned: 'Tell the *Guardian* that if there is any more of that I will post my evidence up on every lamp post in Fleet Street.'

Campbell's complaint to the PCC, which he leaked to the *Guardian*, rang with outrage. 'The Prime Minister has many things written about him that are untrue and which he lets pass,' he said. 'But he finds the suggestion that he would wish to change the long planned arrangements for these events, in order to gain himself a higher profile within them, deeply offensive, and he also knows these allegations to be untrue.'[7] It was the first time any Prime Minister had complained to the press watchdog over a political issue, rather than private family matters.

The next day, 25 April, in one of those dramatic coincidences which a novelist might be chary of inventing, all of those involved – the PCC directors, the journalists and editors, and a group from Downing Street led by Campbell – assembled at St George's Hall, Windsor Castle for a media reception specially thrown by the Queen in her jubilee year. Guy Black took the opportunity for a quiet word with Sir Robin Janvrin. He wanted to ask how the Palace statement on the Black Rod affair, promised by Campbell two weeks earlier, was coming along. 'I'm looking forward to receiving your submission on the Black Rod business,' said Black. Sir Robin's blunt reply came as a surprise. 'You won't be getting anything from us,' he said, 'we're staying a million miles away from it.' Campbell managed to avoid Guy Black at the party. However, he did bump into a reporter from the *Mail on Sunday*.[8] 'I've got one thing to say to you,' he snarled. '*Mail on Sunday*; PCC complaint upheld.'

On 26 April, the day after the Windsor Castle party, Guy Black phoned Campbell and told him: 'Janvrin says he won't be writing to us about the lying-in-state.' Campbell maintained a bold front: 'Don't worry, you'll be hearing from Black Rod very soon.' Incredibly, he still believed he could make Willcocks back down. Downing Street had one remaining hope: that Willcocks would perjure himself and get Campbell and Tony Blair off the hook.

But Black Rod stood firm. He had discovered within twenty-four hours of the Queen Mother's death on 30 March just how determined Downing Street was to enhance Blair's role at the ceremony. The day after the Queen Mother's death, Clare Sumner called him on his mobile phone while he was driving from his home in Oxfordshire to

Westminster for a hastily arranged meeting at his Lords office to put the lying-in-state plans into action. As Willcocks described in a letter to the PCC that became known as his 'killer memo': 'The substance of this call was to query the role of the Prime Minister in the coming ceremonials. Phrases such as 'doesn't the PM greet the Queen', 'doesn't he meet the coffin' and finally 'well, what is his role?' were used. I answered all such questions by pointing out firmly, there being no latitude in the planning, that the PM had no such roles but would merely lead the tributes of the House of Commons and if possible be present with the House in Westminster Hall for the arrival of the coffin on Friday 5 April. I explained how, on Parliamentary, as opposed to Government, occasions, such roles are undertaken by the triumvirate of the Lord Great Chamberlain, the Lord Chancellor and the Speaker.'[9]

Willcocks added that there was no mention at that stage, as was later claimed by Campbell, that Downing Street was working from 'internal guidance' written in 1994 suggesting a different role for the PM. 'None of our many iterations of the plan for the Queen Mother's lying-in-state ever included a central role for the PM.' His memo continued: 'However, after this initial contact, and throughout the next five days, my staff and myself were telephoned, at times it seemed constantly, by staff at Number 10 repeating these questions on the role of the PM, but also exerting rather more pressure along the lines of: "don't you think the PM ought to be at the north door? (of Westminster Hall)" . . . "he must have more of a role surely" . . . "don't you think that he ought to be given a role?" etc. The records show at least a dozen or so of such calls and a personal visit by a member of Number 10's staff, all of which followed the pattern above. The feeling we had was of sustained pressure from that quarter . . . My outer office . . . was set up as an operations room for this period and a constant flow of people passed through it at all hours. It is therefore possible that many of these gained the sense of our frustration at the constant querying of Number 10 and some would have heard the exchanges and subsequent staff discussions. At one stage on the telephone I had to take a Number 10 official through the entire ceremonial for the arrival of the coffin, minute by minute, and person by person.'

As a result of the pressure, Black Rod changed the plan to allow Blair to file past the coffin and exit via the north door, where he would be

seen by the TV cameras. But any hope of keeping Number 10's meddling quiet was wrecked when it made a final audacious bid to muscle
in. As the coffin was being transported along the Mall on its way to the
lying-in-state, Black Rod received a message from Number 10 telling
him the PM planned to walk to Westminster Hall from Number 10 and
enter via the north door, where the royal family were to greet the coffin.
This was a sharp departure from the previous plan to enter via the
south door at the far end, out of camera shot. His PCC memo stated:
'Shortly before the arrival of HM the Queen at the north door. . . I
received an urgent message from Number 10, via the Co-Ordinating
Officer for the Police Protection Officers, saying that the PM intended
to walk to the Palace from Downing Street and wished to know if he
could enter via the north door. I had a fairly public discussion on the
merits of such a walk, with among others the Lord Chancellor, and sent
back a message to say that I didn't advise it.'

The policeman relayed Black Rod's blunt advice back to Number 10.
But they came back again, this time more forcefully. The PM would
abandon his plan to walk across from Number 10, but still wanted to
enter via the north door. By now the Queen Mother's coffin was only
twenty minutes away and if the PM turned up out of the blue he could
collide with the Queen's party. His memo continued: 'By return I
received a more insistent request that in any case the PM be allowed to
enter through the north door. I said I didn't think it was a good idea so
close to the Queen's arrival but also that "he is the PM so of course he
can if he really wants to". In the event he arrived by car and not via the
north door.'

In fact, Black Rod's language was more outspoken. He told the
policeman: 'It would be crazy. He is a prime minister not a president.
Tell Number 10 that he is the Prime Minister and can do whatever he
likes, but I strongly advise against. It will look as though he is trying to
get in on the act. Even if he does enter by the north door, the cameras
will only catch the back of his head, they are pointing inside the hall.'
He added caustically: 'There are better photo opportunities at the other
end.' An embarrassed Lord Irvine observed limply: 'It's not Tony, it's
his aides.'

Compare Black Rod's account of the last-minute haggling with
Campbell's version in his 2000-word complaint to the PCC. 'Before

leaving Number 10 it was suggested that the PM might walk.' It does not say who suggested it: in fact it was Downing Street. 'It was decided within Number 10 with no feedback from Black Rod, to drive.' The statement added that when Number 10 asked if the PM could enter via the north door, 'Black Rod said this was not a problem.'

Eager to avoid the embarrassment of having to reject a personal complaint by the Prime Minister, the PCC tried to broker a deal between Number 10 and the newspapers. There were several witnesses to various aspects of what had happened at the lying-in-state, but for the most part their knowledge was partial. And most were in no position to testify. Only one man knew the whole story: Black Rod. Campbell gambled that he would not dare give evidence against the Prime Minister. He sent Sumner to visit Black Rod at his office in the House of Lords. She produced a copy of Downing Street's version of events, approved by Campbell, told Sir Michael she hoped it reflected his feelings, and asked him to sign on the dotted line there and then. If he agreed, Campbell would with one stroke, achieve a crushing victory over the press.

Willcocks looked Sumner in the eye and told her: 'But this not what I feel at all.'

Sumner: 'What do you feel?'

Willcocks: 'Do you really want to know?'

Sumner: 'Yes.'

Willcocks: 'I feel totally hacked off with the way you have behaved over this from start to finish. I told you at the outset that you were making a big mistake by trying to deny it. I told you then I would do what I could to help but I would not lie. And I am not going to do so.'

Sumner claimed she had been working from a Downing Street plan drawn up in 1994. Willcocks brushed aside her protest and said no such document existed. In any case, why had she made no mention of it before the lying-in-state? In theory, the PCC could throw out the PM's complaint. In practice, it was quite hard to do so. The PCC was a self-regulating body run by the press itself. But there were many members of the government who had long wanted to abolish it and replace it with a new, tougher, statutory group. Willcocks refused to be drawn into commenting on Downing Street's version of events, suspecting a trap. He insisted he was not in dispute with Number 10; the row was between Number 10 and the press. He insisted on preparing his own account of what had happened, agreeing to submit it in draft form, to give the PCC and Number 10 more time to find a way out: the moment it was formally presented, copies would have to be sent to the publications involved as well as Blair.

When Black Rod's draft report, or 'killer memo' as it came to be known, arrived at the PCC at the beginning of May, acting PCC chairman Robert Pinker and Guy Black read it with disbelief. Black said: 'It made the hairs on the back of my neck stand up.' They had no idea of the extent of Downing Street's intervention. Professor Pinker went to see Black Rod on 27 May and told him the PCC would prefer 'an elegant compromise'. Black Rod insisted he was not prepared to 'remove' certain sections of his evidence. It was agreed to delay a decision until the following week to avoid spoiling the Queen's Golden Jubilee celebrations planned for the weekend.

The Queen's private secretary Sir Robin Janvrin had good relations with Downing Street, but he was alive to the dangers of Blair treading on the toes of the royal family through his presidential style. The Queen had not been not amused when the Prime Minister and his wife upstaged her by conducting a royal-style walkabout in Westminster on the day of Blair's first Queen's Speech in 1997. 'There was always a worry that the government would try and hijack the Jubilee,' said a senior royal adviser. 'We didn't know how but we thought they might want to do so. We always had the sense that they wanted to maximize the Prime Minister's profile in these things. Robin used to talk about it.'[10]

In the meantime, Guy Black visited Campbell at Number 10 to relay the contents of the 'killer memo' to him. 'I'm afraid the story is clearly true,' he told him, 'and if you go ahead with your complaint you will lose.' Campbell's face bore a resigned look. Black inquired: 'Why on earth did you go into this when I told you to be absolutely certain if you were going to do so?' Campbell responded by blaming others. 'There were two people behind this: Cherie Blair and Derry Irvine,' he told Black. It was a curious remark. It is hard to imagine Mrs Blair insisting her husband be in the limelight at the funeral. And the Lord Chancellor had witnessed first-hand what happened on the day and had appeared to apologize for Blair, blaming 'Tony's aides'. Black Rod had deliberately referred to his conversation with Irvine in his statement, as a warning signal to Downing Street.

By now Willcocks was tired of all the obfuscation. If the matter was not resolved soon, he told the PCC, he would go ahead and publish his report. Guy Black told Campbell: 'You must make up your minds. If you want to push ahead then so be it, but you must decide soon.' Campbell replied: 'I'll talk to TB.' Blair had independently asked Sir Richard Wilson to examine the case. It took Wilson less than twenty minutes to conclude that the Prime Minister must withdraw immediately. He conveyed his advice to Blair. The following day Campbell phoned Black to formally concede defeat. 'We are withdrawing the complaint,' he said, then paused before adding: 'but we'll get him one day.' The 'him' was Willcocks.[11] Blair's statement on 14 June, confirming he was withdrawing the complaint, sought to put a favourable gloss on his decision, stating he had settled the matter 'on the basis that the newspapers had made clear that they accepted I did nothing wrong or improper'.

It was not true. None of the publications involved gave any assurances. They were not even informed officially of Number 10's withdrawal, but learned of it when they read it in the *Guardian* on 11 June in a report by Roy Greenslade. Greenslade said the 'mystery at the heart of the affair' was 'what part was played in the story reaching the press by Black Rod'. For Greenslade, as for Campbell, the central question was not whether the story was true, but how the truth had got into the public domain. Black Rod had initially tried to suppress the story, but when it did come out, he refused to lie. In the eyes of Campbell, and apparently Greenslade, that was the real crime.

An attempt to 'get' Black Rod arrived in the shape of the Labour-supporting *Sunday Mirror*, where Campbell was once political editor. Willcocks discovered the paper was investigating false claims about his private life. They never appeared in print. And three days after the Prime Minister's withdrawal, on 17 June, another apparent attempt to 'get' him surfaced. This one caused Willcocks genuine alarm. Not just because of its contents, or because it was the lead story in *The Times*, but because of its timing. The story was headlined: 'Palace fears funeral row may taint Jubilee.' One of the by-lines was Tom Baldwin, a political journalist with close links to Campbell. It said: 'There is real concern that a member of the Royal Household is behaving in a partisan political fashion. The Queen is unhappy that the memory of her mother's funeral is being tarnished by this squabble.' It quoted an anonymous source as saying: 'If he (Black Rod) is co-operating with the press you have to ask what the hell is going on.' It echoed the *Guardian*'s warning, but with added venom. Hours after reading the *Times* report, Black Rod arrived at Windsor Castle for a lunch hosted by the Queen. Her private secretary Janvrin had also read the report. He saw Willcocks and realized what was troubling him. 'Don't worry, it's not true,' the Queen's man reassured him.

Trashing Cherie Blair

The so-called Cheriegate affair brought a bitter, ugly and final close to the happy, harmonious relationship that for so many years had bound the Campbell-Millars to the Labour leader of the day. The underlying cause of the disaster was Carole Caplin, a former topless model who has played a formidable role as Cherie Blair's 'lifestyle' guru for the last ten years. It is not hard to understand why Cherie Blair should have warmed to sexy, scatty Caplin. Downing Street is hard to bear. Cherie found herself trapped in a dour, male, power-driven world. Lacking the gratification of office or satiated ambition, she was entitled to some escape. One of her predecessors, Sir Denis Thatcher, had found it on the golf-course. Cherie Blair found it in Carole Caplin's dotty world of bath crystals and designer clothes.

Alastair Campbell, with characteristic good sense, smelt trouble right from the moment when the presence of Caplin was publicly revealed at the Labour party conference of 1994. Campbell and Blair had a stand-up row in a Blackpool hotel over Caplin's presence. But then, and for the next decade, Blair refused to act. It was not simply that Campbell saw Caplin as a threat to the wholesome family image he worked so hard at maintaining for the Blairs. As Caplin and Cherie became closer and closer, she supplanted Fiona, Cherie's official personal assistant at Number 10. Caplin was paid approximately £3000 a month by the Blairs, chiefly to organize Cherie's wardrobe.

Millar, with her strong political and moral convictions, was astounded and affronted that Cherie seemed to pay more attention to the views of the outlandish Caplin. This animosity was returned in full. Caplin referred to Fiona as 'the bitch from hell'[12] and was convinced Campbell was responsible for many of the damaging stories about her and Cherie in the press. 'He has always been trying to damage me, he's the one who's behind all this stuff that appears in the papers about me. He is the person who puts it there,' she would say. 'Alastair doesn't care about Cherie, all he cares about is men's games. All he is interested in is keeping Tony and Alastair in power.'[13]

Carole Caplin had her own explanation for why she got on better with Cherie than Millar did. 'Cherie's just a hippy chick, we're a couple of hippy chicks together,' she said. 'Fiona tries to control Cherie and stop her having fun. When I'm with her we have lots of fun and lots of laughs.' One of Caplin's confidants said: 'Cherie was very bad at choosing clothes that made her look good; Fiona wasn't very interested in that, but Carole is a natural. You have to remember how much flak Cherie was getting for her dress sense. She and Carole would go to a fashion house and Cherie would sit there while Carole talked to the designer as though Cherie didn't exist. She'd say things like "No, she can't wear that, her hips are too big," and Cherie wouldn't blink an eyelid. She would refer to Cherie in the third person in Cherie's presence.'[14]

The first direct warning that Campbell and the Blairs had that Cheriegate was about to break was on Wednesday 27 November 2002, when Special Branch police told them that the *News of the World* planned an undercover 'sting' to record Cherie in conversation with Caplin and her boyfriend Peter Foster about the purchase of two flats in Bristol. The police told the Blairs of Foster's background as a conman.

It was the second attempt by tabloid journalists to penetrate the private world of Cherie and Caplin. The first involved a covert bid to lure Caplin into getting involved in a health and fitness centre project in the Middle East. Its real purpose was to get close to Caplin and discover details of her relationship with Cherie, but the plan was uncovered and Cherie was informed. The day after Special Branch informed Number 10 of the second 'sting', Caplin, accompanied by Foster, went to MacLaurin Media, a wised-up public-relations firm, for some badly needed advice. She told director Ian Monk: 'I need someone to protect the reputation of my business because I will get slagged off over my relationship with Peter. And I want to keep Cherie out of it. The press will use my relationship with Peter to damage Cherie.'

Monk, a highly experienced former tabloid newspaper executive who had worked alongside Campbell some twenty years earlier, immediately phoned his former colleague. Campbell was in Cardiff with the Prime Minister. Within two minutes of Monk's call to Number 10, Campbell phoned back. And in a lengthy conversation, Monk gave Campbell the details, referred to Foster and told him the story was likely to be published at the weekend, adding: 'You don't seem very surprised.' Campbell replied: 'Nah, I know most of it.'[15]

Just after midday on Saturday 30 November, the *Mail on Sunday*, which had obtained the story from a different source to the *News of the World*, phoned Downing Street with a list of questions to the Blairs about the flats deal, including whether Foster had negotiated the price for Mrs Blair. Campbell spoke to Cherie who told him the story was 'ridiculous' and denied Foster was her financial adviser.[16] Accordingly, Campbell authorized a Downing Street statement which said it was 'not true' to say Foster 'was or is a financial adviser to the family'. He was confident the story would not take off, commenting, 'It'll be a one-day wonder.'[17]

On Sunday, he managed to persuade most daily papers of his view, claiming there was no truth in the story and dismissing it as a 'smear'. (Note for example the superior tone in the coverage of the story in the *Guardian*, 2 December: 'The Number 10 statement to the Sunday tabloid also said: "It is not true that Mr Foster was or is a financial adviser to the family", a claim inherently unlikely for two such well-connected lawyers.')

Godric Smith, the Downing Street spokesman, stuck rigidly to Campbell's line in the lobby briefing on Monday morning, telling reporters: 'Should it be the case that they [the Blairs] have purchased any property, the negotiations for that would have been conducted by Mrs Blair and her legal advisers.' But the denials fell apart on Wednesday night when the first edition of the following day's *Daily Mail* arrived at Number 10. The paper had obtained e-mails from Mrs Blair to Foster confirming that he did buy the flats for her. One said: 'I cannot thank you enough for taking these negotiations over for me.' The revelation sent Downing Street into a crisis. It was forced to admit publicly that it had been wrong to deny that Foster had acted as Cherie Blair's financial adviser. The admission caused a spiral of recrimination inside Number 10. Smith felt that he had been deceived and came close to resignation.

Campbell was furious that Cherie had not given him the full facts, leading Smith inadvertently to mislead the lobby and fuelling further claims of deception by Number 10. At the height of the Cheriegate row Campbell walked into a meeting in a rage. 'He sat down in a terrible sulk cursing under his breath and ignored the rest of us,' recalls one official. 'He didn't listen to a word we were saying and was muttering: "they won't listen to a bloody word I tell them."'

Campbell was not the only who had been misinformed. Nor did Tony Blair know the full details of the Bristol flats deal. He was under the impression that Cherie had bought one flat, not two.[18] Blair may have been prepared to forgive Cherie, understanding the pressure she was under. Indeed friends said that, if anything, the row over the flats brought them closer. But the Campbell-Millars were not. Guests to Downing Street during the Cheriegate row were taken aback by the painfully clear breakdown in relations between the Campbell-Millars and Cherie. During a dinner party at the height of the controversy, Campbell arrived late to be asked by Cherie: 'Where have you been?' Campbell replied: 'Getting you out of more trouble.' Cherie said: 'I'm sorry, it's all my fault again.' The conversation around the table came to a halt as embarrassed guests looked away. By the end of the affair relations between the Campbell-Millars and Cherie had collapsed. At one charged moment at the height of the row, Cherie asked Fiona: 'Why aren't you giving me more help?' Millar replied: 'Because you never listen to me and you don't tell me the truth.'

Alastair Campbell resented the fact that, as a result of the affair, his reputation, as well as that of the Blairs, had been tarnished. He at once set out making sure that Cherie Blair took the blame for the denials. A typical report in the following day's papers read: '*The Times* has learned Mrs Blair told neither Alastair Campbell nor Godric Smith about Foster's involvement in the negotiations when they discussed the matter by telephone on Saturday.'[20] *The Times* report said Campbell was ill in bed on Saturday afternoon when he was told the story was about to be published, giving the impression he had little chance to react. It failed to point out that he discussed the matter in a detailed phone call with Monk the previous Thursday.

However, people in Westminster and Whitehall saw what was happening and realized that, in Campbell's eyes, scapegoating Cherie was a necessary operation, however sad, clinical and ruthless. Campbell's reputation needed to be protected at all costs, and if the cost was sacrificing the good name of Prime Minister's wife, then it was a price he was prepared to pay. What followed that weekend, however, went far beyond professionalism and smacked of spite and a desire to punish Cherie Blair. The *Sunday Telegraph's* headline on Sunday 8 December 2002 read 'Blairs Ignored Warnings by Campbell Over Cherie's "Guru".' The story revealed how Campbell had warned about Caplin before he had been aware of the Foster relationship, only to be told that it was none his business. An 'aide at No 10' was quoted that 'Alastair and Fiona were told it had nothing to do with them. It was Cherie's private life.' A 'senior figure at No 10' was quoted saying, 'Alastair has made clear in the past that he has had deep doubts about Caplin. Fiona has made no secret of the fact that she does not like Caplin.' Campbell himself was quoted as telling 'a colleague' that Cherie Blair 'treats us as though we are in the same category as the *Daily Mail*'.

Amazing though it may seem, *Sunday Telegraph* Political Editor Colin Brown was briefed by Campbell in his office in 12 Downing Street, directly beneath the Blair's Downing Street flat. Campbell had not simply been content to make Cherie Blair the scapegoat. He had wanted to punish her and rub her face in it as well. Blair reacted furiously. He felt he could no longer trust Campbell to advise him on the issue and turned to Mandelson for help. Mandelson was in the USA to deliver a speech at a dinner hosted by Bill Clinton's Secretary of State Madeleine Albright, when Blair called him, pleading for help and complaining that Campbell had turned against Cherie. When Mandelson landed at Heathrow late on Sunday, he spoke to Blair again and went straight to Number 10. The Blairs arrived from Chequers and spent the evening in the flat explaining the whole story to Mandelson. An emotional Cherie explained how Foster had used Caplin to inveigle himself into her confidence.

Blair was initially annoyed at Cherie for not telling him what had been going on, but when Campbell turned against her he was quick to defend his wife. Mandelson barely left Number 10 for the next four days while he effectively took charge of the Number 10 briefing operation from Campbell. Fiona Millar told Cherie that Campbell was responsible for the *Sunday Telegraph* story and said he had been wrong to do it. There was no apology from Campbell. Cherie was deeply hurt. A vigorous debate ensued over how to rescue the situation. Mandelson told Cherie she had done nothing fundamentally wrong. A minor mishap had got out of all proportion as a result of confusion and a communications breakdown in Number 10. The only solution was for Cherie to make a public statement explaining what had happened. The Campbell-Millars opposed the idea strongly, causing Cherie further hurt. 'They argued that she should withdraw completely from public life, no longer have a public role as the Prime Minister's wife because she had become unbelievable and had lost all credibility,' said a source. 'Basically, they wanted her to disappear.'[22] Mandelson argued against them, insisting it was a totally unacceptable way to treat the Prime Minister's wife. He said the problems were as much the result of mistakes by the Number 10 press office as by Cherie. 'We are not giving in to the media frenzy,' he said. The Blairs spent Monday evening in the Downing Street flat with Mandelson and agreed to his suggestion that Cherie should make a public statement. Blair told his old friend and confidant that the situation reminded him of the events leading to Mandelson's resignation over the Hinduja affair when Campbell's insistence on a quick decision to and determination to protect his own position was the main driving force. 'This is déjà vu I can't believe what is happening here,' he said. 'It's just like what happened to you last year.'[23] Once the decision was made, Campbell and Millar rallied round. Mandelson, Millar, Sally Morgan and Charles Falconer gathered round Campbell's computer in his office and composed the statement.

The *Sunday Telegraph* was not the only weekend paper which took the Campbell-Millar line against Cherie. So did the *News of the World*, in some ways an even more fascinating case. *News of the World* editor Rebekah Wade had known Cherie Blair well. But the two had fallen out badly. Relations started to cool when Cherie opposed Wade's *News of the World's* populist 'Sarah's law' campaign calling for tougher laws against paedophiles after the murder of schoolgirl Sarah Payne. In the aftermath of this dispute, Wade made an equivocal peace offering, sending Cherie a crib for baby Leo, wrapped in 'For Sarah' posters.

But their friendship fractured when Cherie was told about the two separate undercover 'stings', at least one of which was set up by the *News of the World* to shed light on her connection with Caplin's boyfriend, Foster. When the story appeared in the *Mail on Sunday*, Wade invited Cherie to take part in a sympathetic interview by the paper, telling her side of the story. When Cherie turned this offer down, the *News of the World* unleashed its fury on her. It published a story headlined: 'Sex, Crystals and Witchcraft' claiming Caplin 'washed off naked Cherie's toxins in the shower' and got her to do 'bizarre sexual exercises'.[24] The *News of the World* quoted an unnamed Downing Street source saying that Cherie always knew Foster 'had a dodgy past'. While David Yelland at the *News of the World*'s sister paper, the *Sun*, was backing Cherie solidly over Cheriegate, a *News of the World* editorial made it clear where Wade's Downing Street loyalties lay. Describing Cherie as 'foolish, arrogant and dumb', it continued: 'It was only a matter of time before Cherie Blair's misguided loyalty to her friend Carole Caplin would lead to trouble. Skilled aides Alastair Campbell and Fiona Millar urged the Prime Minister's wife to keep Carole at arm's length. Instead, she ignored their advice.'[25] Two weeks later, the Campbell-Millars visited the London home of Wade and her partner, actor Ross Kemp, over Christmas.

There was something curious about Campbell's ambiguous loyalty to the Blairs during this troubled period. The Downing Street media operation was all about sustaining the purity of the Prime Minister, salvaging the reputation of the Campbell-Millars, and trashing Cherie Blair. Some figures close to the Prime Minister still feel that this was the wrong way around and that the Campbell-Millars owe their very great importance and influence only to the patronage of the Prime Minister. They argue that it would have been proper if, in return, the Campbell-Millers had protected the Blairs when they were in trouble. As it was, there was a stream of vindictiveness in the briefing against Cherie Blair. Campbell himself put it differently. 'My job is to protect the Prime Minister and I don't care what it takes to do it,' he said.

Cherie was not the only one in his sights. He had a series of brutal exchanges with Monk after accusing him of fuelling the row. These exchanges, while robust, illustrate the lengths to which Campbell would go, and the enemies that Campbell was prepared to make, as he sought to defend Tony Blair. In one call, Monk accused Campbell of blaming him for leaking details of the Cheriegate saga.

Campbell told him: 'You are acting for a con man. It doesn't matter what it takes, we have got to find out where these stories are coming from.'

Monk: 'Call your dogs off me. I know as many journalists as you do and I've probably got more friends than you.'

Campbell: 'Just fucking shut it sunshine, shut it.'

Monk: 'Don't talk to me like one of your Westminster lapdogs.'

Campbell calmed down. 'You're acting for a conman.'

Monk: 'It depends how you define a conman. What about the guy you are working for?'

Days later, Campbell called Monk in a rage after it was disclosed that Campbell had been tipped off about 'Cheriegate' several days before the story was first published, by Monk himself. Campbell told him: 'You are a complete c**t and have stitched me up. You have been briefing people about our conversation.' Monk denied it.

Downing Street was now split into two camps: the Campbell-Millars and Cherie Blair. Somehow Tony Blair himself remained detached, though quite how he was able to do so while his wife was trashed in the press by Campbell is hard to fathom. It was a miserable little story. For two decades Campbell-Millars had given service to Labour leaders, but their period in charge was reaching its end. After Cheriegate, Campbell somehow remained on cordial terms with Tony Blair, but the relationship had changed for ever. Blair felt partly responsible for what had happened to Cherie. He had long felt guilty at the strains imposed on his wife and children as a result of his being Prime Minister. And when his initial anger subsided, he was prepared to forgive her. Campbell, however, held her responsible for inflicting yet further damage on his own reputation, and that of the Downing Street press office. Blair was deeply resentful of the way Campbell had treated Cherie: Campbell felt Cherie had betrayed Millar.

There was an echo here of the estrangement between the Campbell-Millars and the Kinnocks after Fiona Millar and Glenys Kinnock co-authored a book (see page 68). Now the same had happened with the Blairs, only with much more grave consequences. Fiona, for so long a friend and adviser to the Prime Minister's wife, resolved to leave Downing Street. As with Mandelson's resignation over the Hindujas, Cherie's biggest crime appeared to be not that she had bought two flats using a crook, but that Campbell and the press office had lost face. Cheriegate scarred everything. Even today the wounds have not healed. After it, Campbell's own hatred of the media started to border on the pathological.

chapter fifteen

Nemesis

I am trying to calm him down.
Tony Blair to Gavyn Davies,
chairman of the BBC, 7 July 2003

LONG BEFORE THE END OF his time in 10 Downing Street Alastair Campbell had assumed an air of biblical self-righteousness. He felt to a fanatical extent that only he, Tony Blair, and perhaps a few like-minded journalists working mainly for News International titles, saw the truth and the light. His job was to defend the Prime Minister against a fetid and corrupt press and broadcasting media.

It was a heroic self-image, and not without its grain of truth. The press did get things wrong, sometimes wilfully. On the other hand, it sometimes brought to public attention facts that Downing Street would rather have kept hidden. Either way it was a nuisance. This is a predicament that has confronted all modern governments. Most have shrugged their shoulders, and got on with it. Thanks in large part to Campbell, New Labour had the problem under control better than most. Nevertheless, for Campbell, the problem of the press reached devilish proportions. It consumed him – and therefore the machinery of government – with anger and fury. It was his obsession.

A boundless energy drove him on. The Conservative politician Enoch Powell famously remarked that politicians who complained about the press were like sailors who complained about the sea. Campbell was determined to hold back the tide. Newspaper and broadcasting editors arriving at work would find waiting for them on their desks long typed, or sometimes scrawled, letters from Downing Street complaining about a story that had in some way affronted him.

Instead of filling out, as most men do as they enter middle age, Campbell had become more lean and muscular. So had Tony Blair. Diplomats in Washington would be amused as the two men would get off the plane, go straight to the Washington embassy, put on their shorts and T-shirts and have a forty-minute work out in the embassy gym before going on to meet George Bush. Photographs of Blair and Campbell in the 1997 election campaign show Blair with an almost puppy-like glow, and Campbell burly but not overweight. After seven years they were gaunt. In the spring of 2003 Campbell entered the London Marathon. Never a man of moderation, he threw himself headlong into the sport of jogging. For months beforehand, and indeed afterwards, he could regularly be seen pounding the streets of North London or around Hampstead Heath, battling on and on. His hard work was rewarded and he recorded a creditable time of under four hours. He dedicated his run to his old friend John Merritt and raised large sums for a leukaemia charity. Campbell gave several media interviews about the run and was gradually emerging as a public figure as he prepared to bow out of Number 10. He quite frequently discussed resignation, on one occasion remarking wearily to a colleague: 'Tony couldn't cope without me.' Nevertheless there were cracks in his relationship with Blair, and by the beginning of 2003 those cracks were becoming faultlines.

The road to the 'dodgy dossier'

When war against Iraq started to loom on the horizon in early 2002, Campbell put his mind to resurrecting the Coalition Information Centre (CIC). This time, though its techniques remained the same, its purpose had fundamentally changed. In Kosovo and Afghanistan, Campbell was trying to control the media after the fighting had started. Before Iraq he was trying to persuade the public that British forces should go to war in the first place.

The CIC was Campbell's baby. He loved and cherished it. Though it was technically attached to the Foreign Office, officials within the CIC owed their allegiance to him alone. The unit was almost entirely made up of men, for the most part under the age of thirty-five. Known as 'Alastair's boys', they bore the same sort of relationship to the rest of the government information service as the Secret Intelligence Service to the conventional diplomatic service or the SAS to the regular army. People queued up to join the CIC because it was exciting to work for. Many were inexperienced. To begin with this was an advantage: they were prepared to give Campbell what he wanted regardless of official protocol. In an address to the young turks on the eve of the Iraq war, Campbell rallied them with the kind of fighting talk normally used by military commanders in the field. 'We are going to win this bloody war and the first thing we need to do is to win the information war – and you are the people who are going to do it.' One official said: 'Nothing like that had ever been heard in the Foreign Office. It made some people feel they were part of something really special. Some of the older ones looked embarrassed.'[1]

As 2002 progressed, Campbell came under enormous pressure from Tony Blair to address public hostility to war with Iraq. The CIC, which effectively answered to Campbell himself, was the ideal means to address this massive task. As one British diplomat observed: 'He became disillusioned with the limits on what the Foreign Office, Ministry of Defence and intelligence services could and would do. To him, they were dominated by pen-pushing bureaucrats who followed the rule book. When he pulled their levers, sometimes nothing happened. When he pulled the CIC levers, he knew things would happen because he was directly in control. At last he was getting the service he wanted. Not only that, he could circumvent the MoD, the FO and the security services if he wanted to.'

Campbell also knew that, as with any guerrilla force, it would only retain maximum effectiveness if it remained small and highly motivated. At one stage, when its numbers threatened to exceed thirty, he ordered a cull. Initially, the Foreign Office was happy with the CIC, mainly because it operated from within the FO. Only later, when they realized that the CIC was controlled by Campbell, did some diplomats become suspicious. By then it was too late. 'They kept their work away from everyone else and knew they couldn't be touched because they had been empowered by Campbell,' said one official. 'It was all very secretive and they were left to get on with it. No one in the FO, including Jack

Straw, could question Alastair's authority. Alastair thought it was great, they were giving him what the rest of the system had denied him.' Campbell was provided with an early warning that the CIC was capable of going over the top. Its first major contribution in the build-up to the Iraq war was a pamphlet designed to commemorate the first anniversary of 11 September. This contained photographs of the aftermath of the twin towers attack and allied successes in Afghanistan, and was designed to whip up anti-Iraqi sentiment. But it was cancelled at the last moment after Philip Bassett told Campbell it was inappropriate. It is hardly surprising Campbell had not devoted his full attention to the pamphlet: he was in the middle of producing the September dossier on Iraq's weapons that was to cause him so much grief nine months later.

As the Hutton inquiry later revealed, this was a tortuous process. Campbell had to squeeze every paragraph out of an institutionally cautious security service that was disinclined to gear its work to the needs of a tabloid propaganda machine. After considerable pressure from Downing Street, the dossier famously proclaimed that the Iraqis 'are able' to deploy chemical weapons in forty-five minutes, inspiring the bloodcurdling headline 'BRITS 45 MINUTES FROM DOOM' in the *Sun*. But Campbell was disappointed with the dossier's overall impact. In the final stages of the drive to rally public opinion behind the war with Iraq, he asked the CIC to produce another document detailing the horrors of Saddam's regime.

As a result of the devastating personal and political consequences of the row over the 'sexed-up' dossier of September 2002, it is sometimes forgotten that the flaws in that dossier would, in all probability, have never been uncovered had it not been for the 'dodgy dossier' of February 2003. The means of distributing the latter was sufficient in itself to arouse suspicion. It was slipped beneath the hotel room doors of a handful of sleeping Sunday newspaper journalists in the early hours of the morning of Friday 31 January during Blair's visit to Bush in Washington. Entitled 'Iraq: Its Infrastructure of Concealment, Deception and Intimidation', it was intended as one last, dramatic account of every single bad thing Saddam had ever done. This time, there was no searching exchange of e-mails as there had been between Campbell and others in Number 10 and the intelligence services over the wording of each claim. The CIC had a blank sheet of paper and was ready and able to fill each one as it saw fit. Two Labour-supporting Sunday newspapers duly took the bait and published sensationalized accounts, claiming the dossier provided new evidence of Saddam's deceit and the full extent of his reign of terror.[2] They were just the headlines Campbell wanted, though he must have been disappointed that once again, another dossier had only been a limited success. Several of the newspapers who had correspondents on the Washington trip with Blair and Campbell saw it as rehashed material and didn't report a word.

Never mind; the Sunday lobby journalists whom Campbell despised so much proved to be rather more discerning than one of the other individuals who had been presented with a copy of the 'dodgy dossier'. In his keynote address, the US Secretary of State Colin Powell cited the 'fine paper' produced by Number 10 which 'described in exquisite detail Iraqi deception activities'. Powell's intervention had given Campbell the kind of publicity he craved for his work and his comments were flashed round the world. Powell had helped to give it legitimacy too. The document was placed in the library of the House of Commons and Tony Blair hailed it during a parliamentary statement on 3 February: 'We issued further information over the weekend about the infrastructure of concealment,' he informed MPs. 'It is obviously difficult when we publish intelligence reports, but I hope people have some sense of the integrity of our security services. They are not publishing this, or giving us this information and making it up. It is the intelligence that they are receiving, and we are passing on to people.'[3] The Prime Minister was misleading parliament.[4] Any reasonable person listening to Tony Blair that day would have concluded that Tony Blair was inviting MPs to regard the CIC report as an intelligence document, but it was nothing of the sort. It is a study in how to give a document a spurious legitimacy without at any stage telling an outright lie. It was produced by Campbell's propaganda volunteers in the CIC, who were not subject to any control either by the intelligence services or by Whitehall, but only by Campbell himself.

The dossier was speedily exposed as a fraud. In his determination to give Campbell what he wanted, one of the CIC's most eager recruits, Paul Hamill, copied large sections of an article written by a Californian postgraduate student and posted on the Internet. The plagiarizing was so clumsy that the Number 10 document even reprinted grammatical mistakes by the author, Ibrahim al-Marashi, a student at Monterey Institute of International Relations. The thesis was twelve years old and yet was presented in the dossier as being up-to-date intelligence information. The names of officials associated with the dossier were inadvertently printed on the Number 10 e-mails. The names listed, and their Orwellian job titles, provide a telling insight into the way Downing Street was turned into a 'story factory' under Campbell. Young Hamill's official nomenclature in the FO was as 'head of story development'. One of his colleagues was Murtza Khan, 'news editor of the Downing Street website'. They were joined by John Pratt from the SCU, by now run by Peter Hyman, one of Blair's main speechwriters, and Alison Blackshaw, Campbell's personal assistant.

On the day the 'dodgy dossier' story broke, a devastated Hamill was consoled by Labour friends over a drink in a Commons bar. He phoned Campbell, admitted it was his fault for forgetting to annotate the Internet material, and said: 'I'll resign if you want.' Campbell replied: 'Sleep on it: tomorrow's another day.' Campbell arranged for Hamill to be whisked away to work for the CIC in Baghdad to stop the media pack tracking him down.

Looking back ruefully on the episode, one civil servant says: 'Alastair judged the September dossier to be a failure. He had pushed the security services as hard as he could, but they wouldn't go far enough. The February dossier was produced by very junior people which is why it all went pear shaped.' Neither the security services nor Jack Straw even knew it was being produced.

Campbell was forced to admit that the dossier had been a 'mistake' and apologized to intelligence chiefs. The second dossier was a nonsense on an enormous scale. It had caused the Prime Minister to mislead parliament. It had embarrassed Britain with her American allies. It had discredited the British government's attempt to sell the case for war. For most ministers or officials, responsibility for that kind of shambles would have led to resignation or the sack. Not so to Campbell.

A week after the origins of the 'dodgy dossier' were unmasked, Campbell had bounced back, playing a pivotal role in the government's anti-terror strategy. He asserted himself when the intelligence services were said to have told Blair they feared Al Qaeda might be planning a missile attack on a passenger jet over Heathrow. It followed a number of similar Downing Street-inspired reports of possible terrorist attacks since November, including a 'dirty bomb' on the London Underground, a 'killer bug', a 'smallpox alert' and a 'ricin poison factory'. With the nation's nerves frayed, on Monday 10 February Blair called a meeting of Cobra, the committee that meets in the Cabinet Office briefing room 'bunker' beneath Downing Street. Senior ministers, together with intelligence, military and police chiefs discussed what to do. Campbell was there too. According to one witness: 'Blunkett was his usual agitated self, Gordon Brown glowered and Alastair Darling was in a blind panic. We had just been told that terrorists might shoot down a Jumbo over Heathrow and the entire Cabinet was paralysed. Alastair bided his time and then said: "The way I see it, there are a number of possible options." Tony took his lead from Alastair and then a decision was reached.' At 6 a.m. the following morning, 450 soldiers from the 1st Battalion Grenadier Guards and the Household Cavalry, with armoured fighting vehicles, surrounded Heathrow. Months later, it was reported that the Heathrow terror alert was the result of a false tip off from an Al Qaeda prisoner.

Enter Andrew Gilligan

During the Kosovo War the object of Campbell's blind fury had been the BBC war correspondent John Simpson. The invasion of Afghanistan saw him vent his rage against Rageh Omaar. The Iraq conflict and its aftermath saw Campbell turn his animosity against the BBC correspondent Andrew Gilligan. This time Campbell's hatred would turn into an obsession. This obsession grew from quite small beginnings to claim every last ounce of Campbell's own immense stores of energy and consume Downing Street itself. In the end it claimed a life, that of the distinguished government scientist Dr David Kelly CMG.

The story of the feud with Gilligan, the war with the BBC and the wretched death of Kelly, forced Alastair Campbell to end his dithering about whether or not he wanted to stay in Downing Street. But it meant more than the end of Campbell. The war with Gilligan and its tragic conclusion marked the end of the long experiment in government which had started so hopefully in May 1997. The Hutton inquiry which followed lit up Downing Street and its methods like an outsider turning on the lights during a game of 'murder in the dark'. It showed how Britain had been run for six years by a tiny group of men, neglectful of parliament, contemptuous of the Cabinet, scornful of the facts except when they suited their purposes. At the heart of this system was less the vanishing figure of Tony Blair than his large, confident hatchet-man Campbell.

The story started with Gilligan. Gilligan was a loner. Although he was to make his name by causing trouble for the government, he was no radical agitator. If anything, he was a supporter of the Iraq war. He worked on his own and kept away from the pack: this in itself was enough to make Downing Street suspicious of him. Campbell was excellent at handling the press when it worked collectively. He calculated its moods, lured it on, made it turn on outsiders. Those who worked separately were inherently a threat.

At the *Today* programme Gilligan brought in a series of scoops about faulty bombs, guns and radios, a lack of desert boots, combat suits, night goggles, medical equipment and even soldiers' camp beds. This meant that there was a long history of antagonism between Gilligan, the MoD and Downing Street even before the summer of 2003. The MoD was enraged as his scoops were eagerly followed up by the rest of Fleet Street. Geoff Hoon's director of news, Martin Howard, had been tormented by Gilligan from the moment he took charge of the MoD press machine in January 2000, when he heard a Gilligan scoop about faulty equipment while driving into the MoD on his first day. Gilligan's *Today* boss, Rod Liddle, said: 'A bunch of MoD guys including Martin Howard came to see me under the pretext of improving relations with the *Today* programme. But their primary aim was to denigrate Andrew Gilligan who caused them problems with his stories. Their message was "restrain Gilligan". I told them to go away. Andrew was doing what I had recruited him to do: getting stories, and good ones at that.' By a quirk of fate, Martin Howard was to play a crucial role in the Kelly affair. By then he was the deputy head of defence intelligence, and was Kelly's boss. Howard's role in the process, which led to Kelly's name being leaked, prompted the Kelly family's QC,

Jeremy Gompertz, to accuse him of 'playing Russian roulette' with the scientist's life. But when Gilligan turned from defence to political stories, Campbell intervened directly. On the eve of the EU summit in Nice in December 2000, with the Eurosceptic press in Britain claiming the proposed Nice Treaty posed a new threat to UK sovereignty, *Today* broadcast a Gilligan report on an issue which at the time virtually no one in Britain had heard of. He claimed that EU plans for a 'Code of Law' amounted to a putative EU constitution which, in theory, could form the basis of an EU federal superstate. Downing Street, fearing the right-wing press might latch on to the issue in the run-up to the Nice summit, derided him as 'gullible Gilligan' – a classic piece of Campbell character assassination.

The BBC conducted a full inquiry into Gilligan's story and declared it was fair and accurate. However, Campbell's attack succeeded: the story died within days. It was two years before it became clear how right Gilligan had been. Reports about the proposed EU constitution finally became a major political issue, to such an extent that in April 2004 Blair said he would hold a referendum on the matter.

Having failed to persuade Liddle to 'restrain' Gilligan, Hoon tried again when Liddle was succeeded in December 2002 by Kevin Marsh, Campbell's old enemy from the *World at One*. Hoon invited Marsh to the MoD for tea and said: 'One of the things about Andrew is that he is in with the wrong crowd. We are much more used to dealing with BBC correspondents who are well connected. He is not of the mainstream.' Marsh and Liddle both regarded some of the BBC's previous defence correspondents as having been much too well connected to the MoD establishment. Hoon complained about Gilligan's reports about poor equipment and uniforms: 'I know these stories are embarrassing but they aren't the full picture.' Marsh left the meeting convinced that Hoon would like to see Gilligan replaced: Marsh was equally determined to keep him. On the eve of the Iraq war Gilligan caused anger when he reported that Hoon had slipped away for a skiing break in the Alps.

The first stage of the fatal confrontation between Campbell and Gilligan over Iraq came two days after the fall of Baghdad. Gilligan, one of three correspondents in the Iraqi capital, filed a grim account of the lawlessness and looting that broke out in the aftermath of the coalition victory. 'Baghdad may in theory be free,' reported Gilligan, 'but its people are passing their first days of liberty in a greater fear than they have ever before known.' Within hours he was being denounced by Number 10. 'Try telling that to people whose relatives had been dropped head first into shredders or people who had been tied to a post and had their tongues cut out or been beaten to death in the main square,' fumed a spokesman.

On the morning of 29 May 2003, the *Today* programme reported claims that Downing Street had in some way amplified the first dossier regarding weapons of mass destruction prepared the previous September, six months before the invasion of Iraq. Gilligan's report came at a difficult time. The British and, to a lesser extent, the American government had claimed to have gone to war over Iraq's weapons of mass destruction. None had turned up, and people were beginning to notice. That was why Gilligan's story, first broadcast at 6.07 a.m., struck a chord. He claimed to have been told that the government inserted the claim that Iraq was capable of deploying WMD within forty-five minutes of an order to do so, even though it knew it was 'probably' false. This claim, which later became the focal point of the Government's complaint, was dropped from Gilligan's subsequent reports on *Today* that morning, and indeed, received little attention at the time. Not was it ever substantiated. Furthermore, as Gilligan was subsequently to confess to the Hutton inquiry, his source, Dr David Kelly, never said that the Government probably knew the forty-five-minute claim was false.[5]

Whatever its flaws, there was a great deal of value in Gilligan's report. He revealed that the forty-five-minute claim had come, in breach of usual intelligence service procedure, from a single uncorroborated source, an allegation that was to be swiftly confirmed by a defence minister. Gilligan claimed that Downing Street had 'sexed up' the September dossier. Abundant evidence was to emerge, in the course of the Hutton inquiry, to support this contention. His assertion that people in the intelligence community were unhappy with the forty-five-minute claim was likewise confirmed during the course of the Hutton inquiry when it emerged that senior officials within the defence intelligence staff had been so disturbed by the way it was presented that they mounted a formal protest.

On the day of Gilligan's fateful report, a jacketless, white-shirted Blair was in Basra, posing for photographs with triumphant British soldiers, savouring the greatest single achievement of his premiership. Ninety minutes after the 6.07 *Today* broadcast, Downing Street issued a statement: 'Not one word of the dossier was not entirely the work of the intelligence agencies.' Its defiant brevity had all Campbell's hallmarks. Even now, his line of defence was clear: the dossier had been approved by the Joint Intelligence Committee (JIC).

That weekend, writing in the *Mail on Sunday*, Gilligan went a step further and identified Alastair Campbell as the person responsible for 'sexing up' the dossier. Tony Blair was to tell the Hutton inquiry, in a remark that put Campbell's personal significance in a new perspective, said this article gave 'booster rockets' to the story.[6] There was no evidence to start with that it did. Downing Street's initial response to the *Today* report was comparatively muted. The story was denied but it generated just two private letters from Alastair Campbell to the BBC.[7]

By Campbell's own heroic standards of irate rebuttal, this was pretty mild stuff. BBC bosses were accustomed to receiving a stream of furious letters from him, and there seemed no more reason to pay attention to these than they had to any of the others. This was especially the case since Campbell made no fuss at all about the claim that Downing Street had deliberately inserted false information into the dossier, later to become such a controversial point. He preferred to concentrate on other matters, partly to do with claims made by Gilligan about the structure of the JIC, Gilligan's use of a single anonymous source, and whether or not Campbell had apologized to the heads of the intelligence services about the second 'dodgy dossier'.

The letters did not seek an apology, or a retraction, nor did they single out the 6.07 a.m. broadcast, later to become such a binding issue of principle for Downing Street, for special attention. There was no attempt to pursue the complaint either through the Broadcasting Standards Commission or the BBC's programme complaints unit.

Two weeks after Gilligan's initial report, BBC executives including Richard Sambrook went to lunch with Tony Blair and Alastair Campbell in 10 Downing Street. Campbell made no attempt to raise the issue face to face. If Campbell's later utterances are to be believed, he and Blair regarding the reputation of the entire Government to have been challenged by Gilligan's report on the BBC news. And yet neither of them saw fit to raise it with the man directly responsible for BBC radio news, Sambrook. Campbell left it until the end of June, nearly a month after Gilligan's report, to launch his own public fightback. The venue for this inordinately delayed counter strike was his appearance in front of the Foreign Affairs Committee on 25 June. The FAC was investigating the background to the Iraq war. Tony Blair had told Campbell not to appear in front of the committee. But at the last minute, Campbell – alarmed by a press report that as a result of his refusal to appear before them, the committee was likely to deliver a harsh verdict against him – agreed to give evidence. This was a decisive moment. From now on, Campbell made his own decisions. In the words of one of the Prime Minister's most senior advisers, 'Tony was swept along in Alastair's wake.'[8]

The real question facing the FAC was whether the government had misled the British people about the reason for war. It was not the first time Campbell had effectively been put in trial in public, and he knew he had to stay calm. When he gave evidence in his libel case against Tory MP Rupert Allason in 1996, his lawyer suggested he held something in his hand to release tension if he felt he was losing his temper. On that occasion, he used a toy duck belonging to his daughter Grace. This time he was offered an earring by Downing Street aide Catherine Rimmer. But Campbell decided it wasn't sharp enough and used a pin instead. When he returned to his office and put his papers on his desk, they were speckled with spots of blood.

Appearing alone before the committee, Campbell freely admitted the February dossier had been a mistake. He had little choice, since the previous day, Jack Straw had told the committee it was 'a complete Horlicks'. Typically robust, Campbell launched a ferocious attack upon the BBC over the September dossier, accusing it of telling an outright lie. Once again, he resorted to this tactic without telling Tony Blair, who had no idea that Campbell intended to use the occasion to launch an all-out assault on the corporation. 'The PM agreed with Alastair that the BBC had behaved appallingly,' says one Downing Street adviser today, 'but Alastair went awry because his emotional state weakened his better judgement.'

The pin must have been in Campbell's left hand, since he used his right to make slashing gestures in the direction of the committee as he told them: 'Let's get to the heart of what the allegation is: that the Prime Minister, the Cabinet, the intelligence agencies, people like myself, connived to persuade parliament to send British forces into action on a lie.' Repeatedly jabbing his finger into the table, he pressed home his case more forcefully than any witness had ever done at a select committee. 'That's the allegation. And I tell you. Until the BBC acknowledges that that is a lie, I will keep banging on . . . they had better issue an apology pretty quick.' These tactics had all the hallmarks of a classic Campbell diversionary tactic to take attention away from the far more serious issue of weapons of mass destruction. Indeed later that day, Campbell seemed to admit as much when he noted in his diary: 'Opened up a flank on the BBC.'

At the time of the committee's investigation, the Government still maintained WMD would be found, even though Downing Street had already been told privately that this was highly unlikely. If, as seems likely, Campbell was trying to distract attention from WMD, it would be perfectly consistent with his known methods of news management. Martin Sixsmith, who had resigned as Stephen Byers' head of information over the Jo Moore affair, described Campbell's methods: 'When a story was true, and couldn't be denied, your advice was always to create a diversion.'9

In the words of BBC counsel Andrew Caldecott in his summing up to the Hutton inquiry, 'Mr Campbell used more than battlefield munitions. He went strategic. He said that large parts of the BBC had an anti-war agenda and that the BBC allegations against the government were lies.' It was as grave a charge as it was possible for Downing Street to make. Only at this point, nearly a month after the original Gilligan broadcast, Campbell demanded an apology. The following day, he raised the stakes yet further. He sent off a furious private letter to the BBC director-general Greg Dyke asserting that the Andrew Gilligan story was '100 per cent wrong'. A still angrier one went to Richard Sambrook, demanding an apology, asking a series of questions and demanding an answer by the end of the day. Sambrook was astonished when the letter was leaked before he had even received it. Dyke later said he regretted the BBC was hurried into a reply by this demanding deadline. 'I do not accept the validity of your attacks on our journalism and on Andrew Gilligan in particular,' wrote Sambrook. 'We have to believe that you are conducting a personal vendetta against a particular journalist whose reports on a number of occasions have caused you discomfort.' By now the two men were responding to each other's correspondence on an almost daily basis. Sambrook's riposte was at once rejected by Campbell. 'BBC standards are now debased beyond belief. It means the BBC can broadcast anything and take responsibility for nothing.'[10]

Campbell was at Wimbledon on the afternoon of Friday 27 June, watching victories by Andy Roddick and Venus Williams. He was accompanied by two of his closest friends in the lobby, Philip Webster and George Pascoe-Watson. Two days had gone by since his appearance at the FAC and the controversy was intensifying. Campbell took another gamble. By now he was no longer acting mainly to defend the Government's reputation, he was defending his own. It had become a private war between himself and the BBC. Without consulting the Prime Minister, who only learned about it shortly before it was broadcast, he decided to give an interview to Channel 4 news. Campbell was out of Blair's control. Campbell left the centre court around 6 p.m., and within an hour had arrived unannounced at the Channel 4 studios in Grays Inn Road, London. His face still bore a healthy outdoor glow. 'The first thing I knew about it was when I was told by someone in the gallery through my earpiece, "Alastair Campbell is in the building",' Channel 4 News presenter Jon Snow said later. What followed was an extraordinary, live, unprepared confrontational tirade. Until this point in his extraordinary career Alastair Campbell had barely been a public figure. He had lived his life in the lobbies of Westminster and the corridors of power. Though exceptionally well known at Whitehall, he was barely recognized by the wider public.

Campbell had changed dramatically since his days as a young political reporter when he was regularly interviewed on television. Looking at the pictures, he could be seen to have changed in an unusual way. The softness, charm and vulnerability had left his face. Instead he looked tough and hard, like a soldier just back from a long, unpleasant mission. Emerging from nine years in the shadows, Campbell had become a frightening and tormented figure. He shouted, wagged his finger vigorously, looked intense and on the edge. At one stage he picked up a pencil and jabbed it towards Jon Snow. There was none of the humour that had made Campbell such compelling company in the bar when he was a drinker or such great value when he had to take charge of daily lobby briefings before 2001. It was all serious, passionate, fanatical. Jon Snow, who had only been given two minutes' notice before confronting this loud, angry figure, handled the situation with equanimity. 'Well now,' he breathed, as Campbell sat down opposite, 'we are joined by Alastair Campbell, a rare moment, thank you for coming in.' Snow appeared as unperturbed as if he was meeting an old friend for a drink in his club. 'The row between you and the BBC, I mean, many will see it as a diversionary tactic … '

This was the cue Campbell needed. 'Well, if people wish to see it as a diversionary tactic they may. The media are constantly telling people never to take things at face value. This isn't a row between me and the BBC, this is an attempt by the government to get the BBC to admit that a fundamental attack upon the integrity of the government, the Prime Minister, the intelligence agencies, let alone people, the sort of, evil spin doctors in the dark who do their dirty work in the minds of a lot of journalists, let them just accept for once that they got it wrong.'

Campbell's state of mind was given away by his bizarre response when Snow raised one of the BBC letters. 'That letter is about as robust as Blackburn Rovers' defence when they played Trelleborgs,' he said. Scarcely a single Channel 4 viewer would have recognized the reference to a shock defeat suffered by Blackburn Rovers FC, the hated local rivals of Campbell's Burnley, to Swedish part-timers Trelleborgs in the UEFA Cup, a match that had occurred a full decade earlier.[11] The interview soon became a shouting match as the two men contradicted one another.[12] BBC director-general Greg Dyke watched Campbell's performance and said: 'He's gone bloody barmy. When they come at you like that, you don't just stand there, you poke them in both eyes.'[13]

Campbell later admitted in his evidence to Hutton that his performance on Channel 4 'left something to be desired – I was extremely angry'. Alastair Campbell was under overwhelming pressure at this time. By now he was very close indeed to the edge. His demeanour showed it. Hunched up, intense, utterly convinced that he was right, he had ceased to behave rationally. There were numerous signs of this. One lobby correspondent said: 'He kept phoning me and would say

"I've forgotten why I've called you" or the line would just be silent. He was in a bad way.'[14] At this time, as Campbell launched his super-charged attack on the BBC, *Daily Mirror* editor Piers Morgan rang him up. 'Have you gone mad? Have you taken leave of your senses?' asked Morgan.[15]

A further insight into Campbell's desperation is provided by the circumstances surrounding the unexpected and timely intervention on his behalf of his occasional Tory sparring partner, Nicholas Soames. Very late on the evening of 2 July, hours before the FAC was to meet to decide whether Campbell was guilty of 'sexing up' the dossier, Press Association political editor Jon Smith was at home in bed when his mobile phone rang. 'It's Nicholas Soames here. Is that Jon Smith?' Smith: 'Yes.' Soames: 'Take this down. I have just met the head of the security and intelligence services and he has given me a categorical assurance that the government made no attempt to interfere with intelligence information. It's all nonsense. D'you hear? Nonsense, nonsense, nonsense.'

With that, Soames ended the conversation as abruptly as he had begun it. Fearing he may have been the victim of a hoax, Smith called Soames back and asked: 'Mr Soames, I just wanted to check that you want me to put out a story saying you have spoken to Richard Dearlove ... ' Soames: 'Not the name, don't say the name. Just say that the head of intelligence has told me it is completely unthinkable that the government would put any pressure on the intelligence services.' Smith phoned his office to tell them he was about to file a story about Soames only to be told not to bother: his PA colleague Chris Moncrieff had beaten him to it. Campbell had left a message with Moncrieff telling him: 'Phone Nicholas Soames at home, he has got a very interesting story for you.' Moncrieff recalled: 'Mr Soames was very animated and said the head of intelligence had told him Alastair Campbell was as straight as a die and it was nonsense to say the report had been sexed up.'

A frantic Campbell anxiously awaited confirmation that the story was running on the PA wires that went to every major newspaper and broadcasting organization. By now it was the early hours of the morning. He phoned Smith. 'Jon, it's Alastair.' Smith replied wearily: 'Yes, he has rung me.' He knew full well that Campbell had put Soames on to the PA. Campbell: 'Did you get it out? Is it running?' Smith reassured him: 'If it hasn't, it will be soon.' If Campbell's intervention was aimed at getting Soames, who was known to have contacts with intelligence, to say what Dearlove could not say himself and sway the FAC, it worked. When the committee met on 3 July it narrowly voted to clear Campbell of the 'sexing up' charge. The *Guardian* stated: 'The committee's vote to clear Mr Campbell of the main charge is understood to have been influenced by a last-minute intervention by Nicholas Soames.'[16]

But Campbell was by no means finished that night. With Smith eager to get back to bed, Campbell pressed the PA man to send out another story involving the Defence Secretary, Geoff Hoon. Hoon was due to go on the *Today* programme the following morning. As often happens when ministers appear on *Today*, there were advance negotiations about what questions could be asked, and what areas covered. This time, it emerged, these negotiations were not going to the government's satisfaction. A desperate Campbell urgently wanted Smith to report that *Today* had refused to allow Hoon to make a series of points about whether Andrew Gilligan had given the Ministry of Defence adequate advance notice ahead of the contentious 6.07 a.m. broadcast back in May. Jon Smith, by now eager to go to bed, told him: 'Alastair, it's nearly midnight,' he eventually yawned. 'If you want to have a row with the BBC then go ahead but don't get me involved.'

At this point Campbell started to shout at Smith down the end of the phone: 'But it's vital, it's vital.' Smith tried to calm Campbell down: 'Alastair, stop it, stop it.' Campbell replied: 'I can't, I can't. They're all after me, everyone's after me.' Smith has never been afraid of candour. 'If you don't stop this,' he told Campbell, ' you are going to go round the twist again.' Eventually Campbell rang off. Early next morning, an agitated Campbell rang Smith again. 'Are you going to run the Geoff Hoon story?' he demanded once more. Jon Smith replied: 'Look, I've told you: I'm not interested. My advice to you is calm down and go to bed.'

Smith was so bemused by Campbell's behaviour that he considered ringing Downing Street to report that he thought Campbell needed help. But he decided it was not his business. Shortly afterwards, Jon Smith took Campbell's deputy Godric Smith to one side and gave him a warning. 'I had Alastair on the phone the other night and he was in a hell of a state. I have known him for a long time and if I were you I would watch out for yourself. You don't want to get caught up in all this.' Two weeks later, after Kelly killed himself, and a visibly uncomfortable Godric Smith was left trying to put out the firestorm started by Campbell, he confided in the PA man: 'I have often thought back to the conversation we had and I am very glad we had it.'

In the days running up to Campbell's appearance on Channel 4 News there had been some quiet contact between the government and the BBC. Attempts were made to explore ways of bringing the conflict to an end through a negotiated settlement, with Downing Street withdrawing some of its most extreme demands while the BBC admitted some mistakes. Campbell himself was not involved. The approach was made by Peter Mandelson, through Caroline Thomson, a senior BBC executive and wife of Mandelson's best friend, Downing Street adviser Roger Liddle. The deal was that the BBC would say sorry and, in return, the Government would acknowledge that the corporation had a right to publish the story. But the BBC's Greg Dyke and Gavyn Davies rejected it on the grounds that there was 'no reason to withdraw the story' and their 'view at the time was the source was valid'.[17] Mandelson's response had a menacing air. 'In that case we will go for the BBC with the full force of the state and the Government,' he said.[18]

The BBC and the government had turned into two armed camps. Only one side could win. It was at this highly charged moment, with battle lines drawn, that Dr David Kelly, the source for the Gilligan story, made himself known to his seniors at the Ministry of Defence. The stage was set for tragedy.

The death of Dr David Kelly

The quiet, thoughtful and unobtrusive government scientist Dr David Kelly had nothing in common with the world that Alastair Campbell inhabited. Kelly had served his country bravely as a weapons inspector in Iraq for many years. His skill was at facing down dictators, not assassins from Whitehall and the media. Dr Kelly had many contacts in the press. The government used him to brief journalists on a regular basis. He had met Andrew Gilligan at London's Charing Cross Hotel on

22 May.[19] Kelly confided to Gilligan his doubts about the September dossier, the reservations felt more widely in the intelligence services and his belief that Downing Street had intervened to 'sex up' the dossier. According to Gilligan, Kelly told him the dossier had been 'transformed in the week before publication'. When Gilligan asked: 'To make it sexier?' Kelly is said to have replied: 'Yes, to make it sexier.' The forty-five-minute claim was 'the classic', said Kelly. Gilligan: 'How did it happen?' Kelly: 'Campbell.' Gilligan: 'What? Campbell made it up?' Kelly: 'No. It was real information but it was included against our wishes.'

Kelly was the primary source for Gilligan's broadcast a week later. On 30 June, as the great public row blew up between Downing Street and the BBC, Kelly dutifully wrote to his MoD line manager confessing about his meeting with Gilligan. The Hutton inquiry was to hear details of a flurry of e-mails sent to and from Downing Street figures in the run up to the publication of the September dossier. They did not prove that Campbell had personally 'sexed up' the dossier or that he or anyone else had forced the Joint Intelligence Committee chairman John Scarlett to change it. But they did reveal graphically the pressure in Downing Street to produce a document that would result in the headlines that Campbell – and Blair – needed to make their case for war.

In one, Downing Street adviser Philip Bassett commented: 'We have a long way to go. It's intelligence lite. We have got to find a way over this.' In another, Jonathan Powell wrote: 'What will be the headline in the *Evening Standard* on the day of publication?' Campbell e-mailed Scarlett: 'Another dossier memo! I do worry that the nuclear section will become the main focus and as currently drafted is not in great shape.' In a letter to Scarlett, Campbell complained that the word 'may' in the dossier's statement that Iraq 'may be able to deploy' chemical weapons in forty-five minutes was 'weak'. Scarlett replied: 'The language you queried . . . has been tightened.' The final version said the Iraqis 'are able' to deploy such weapons in forty-five minutes instead of the weaker 'may.' After a discussion with Campbell, Scarlett issued a plea to secret agents to produce more information for the dossier. 'Number 10 wants the document to be as strong as possible within the bounds of available intelligence. This is a last (!) call for any items of intelligence agents think could and should be included.' Number 10 got the headlines it wanted. '45 MINUTES FROM ATTACK,' screamed the *Evening Standard* on 24 September, the day the dossier was published. The *Sun* proclaimed the next day: 'BRITS 45 MINUTES FROM DOOM' and 'HE'S GOT 'EM, LET'S GET HIM.'

Campbell learnt on 4 July that Gilligan's source had come forward, though he seems not to have learnt the actual name till a few days later. Instantly, he saw the potential to use the source – whoever he or she was – to destroy the BBC and achieve a spectacular victory. There were two reasons why he felt so confident. First, in one of his interviews, Gilligan claimed the source came from the intelligence services, while Kelly was in truth a Ministry of Defence scientist. He did have close connections to the intelligence services and had been asked for his views on some drafts of the September dossier. But Campbell pounced on the mistake in line with his tried and trusted technique for attacking any story that embarrassed the government. This was to pick on any element that was wrong, and use it to destroy the credibility of the entire report.[20]

The second reason for Campbell's confidence was that Kelly denied that he had said many of the assertions attributed to the source by Gilligan in his radio interviews. On 4 July an exultant Campbell recorded in his diary:

> Spoke to Hoon who said that a man had come forward who felt he was possibly Gilligan's source, had come forward and was being interviewed today. GH [Geoff Hoon] and I agreed it would fuck Gilligan if that was his source. He said he was an expert rather than a spy or full-time MOD official. GH and I agreed to talk tomorrow. [21]

This diary, which he was obliged to present to the Hutton inquiry, gives a gripping insight into the way the row with the BBC came to occupy not merely Campbell himself, but Downing Street, the Prime Minister and all of the top machinery of government. The next entry in Campbell's diary, on 6 July, records,

> Spent much of the weekend talking to TB [Tony Blair] and GH re the source. I wanted, and GH did, to get it to the BBC Governors that we may know who the source was, that he was not a spy, not involved in the WMD dossier and was a WMD expert who advised departments. GH said he was almost as steamed up as I was. TB said he didn't want to push the system too far. But my worry was that I wanted a clear win not a

messy draw and if they presented it as a draw that was not good enough for us.[22]

On 7 July, the FAC published its report, clearing Campbell of 'sexing up' the dossier. By now, he was prepared to settle for nothing less than a complete victory. As Number 10 plotted its next move, Dr Kelly was summoned for interrogation by his MoD bosses. Campbell and Tony Blair produced another ruse to get the name out into the open. They hoped that Kelly's name could be released by writing a letter to the Intelligence and Security Committee offering the chance to interview him. But committee chairman Ann Taylor would not be drawn into the affair and rejected the suggestion. 'TB came back and continued to try and sort out the source issue,' recorded Campbell in his diary for 8 July. 'He met Scarlett[23] and agreed to try and resolve through letter from Ann Taylor. Word then came back she didn't want a letter on it. That meant do it as a press release.'

The problem obsessed Downing Street for days on end. Tony Blair chaired no fewer then four meetings in two days at which the issue of Kelly was discussed. The fourth of these was the most crucial. Campbell, Jonathan Powell and, strange though it sounds, the Joint Intelligence Committee chairman John Scarlett were sent off to draft a press release providing information about the identity of the source. They clustered round the word processor of Godric Smith, the Downing Street press spokesman, and drew up a form of words. The previous day, in the MoD, Kelly had been shown the draft of a proposed press statement. It contained no information which could conceivably enable a journalist to identify him. Indeed Kelly was explicitly told that his name would not be revealed. This new, supercharged press release was a different matter entirely. It was bursting with information. Journalists were later to tell the Hutton inquiry how – along with a new Question and Answer brief to guide MoD press officers – it enabled them to track down Kelly's name within hours.[24]

MoD personnel director Richard Hatfield called Dr Kelly to clear the final version of the press release with him. That evening, as Dr Kelly and Mrs Kelly watched the Channel 4 News report about the unnamed source, the scientist turned to his wife and said: 'That's me.' Campbell was well on the way to achieving his objective of releasing David Kelly's name to the press. On 9 July, a question and answer strategy, whereby the MoD agreed to name Kelly if a journalist put the name to them first, was agreed by Number 10 and the MoD. No civil servant had ever been treated in this way before. Campbell wrote in his diary that day that 'the biggest thing needed was the source out'.

Once again, Campbell's relationship with News International was a major factor in events. *Times* associate editor Tom Baldwin was among those leading the Fleet Street chase to obtain Kelly's name. On 5 July, a *Times* report by Baldwin, quoting 'BBC insiders', stated that the BBC had indicated that the source was a 'military expert ... based in Iraq'. The report appeared after the BBC's Richard Sambrook had met *Times* executives, including Baldwin. Asked during the private meeting in the office of *Times* editor Robert Thomson if the reason the BBC had not contacted the source was because he or she was out of the country, Sambrook said: 'Something like that.' Sambrook was furious at the way *The Times* had misreported his comment and forced the paper to publish a correction. One *Times* executive who attended the meeting called the report a 'travesty' and complained to Thomson. The meeting took place on 3 July, two days before Baldwin's report. It was on 4 July that Campbell was first told that an MoD official had admitted speaking to Gilligan.

Jonathan Powell told the Hutton inquiry that Baldwin told Number 10 what had happened at the Sambrook lunch. When Powell was asked who told him that *The Times* had got its information from Sambrook, Powell replied: 'I believe I was told by Alastair Campbell.'

'Do you know who told him?'

Powell: 'I believe it was Mr Baldwin of *The Times*.'

MoD director of news Pam Teare said the *Times* report was one of the reasons they believed the scientist's name was bound to be discovered. It is curious how the Government was using the disclosures of the lobby journalist closest to Campbell to explain why it was inevitable that Kelly would be named. It is even more curious bearing in mind that *The Times*'s first attempt at identifying Kelly, describing him as a 'military expert based in Iraq', was hardly likely to expose him. If Fleet Street flew to Baghdad to find him, they would be going on a wild goose chase, and Kelly could have lived happily, and anonymously, ever after in Oxfordshire. The BBC was convinced that the government was trying to get Kelly's name into the public domain by making it appear that it had leaked from the BBC. And *The Times* appeared to be collud-ing in this strategy. Shortly after Kelly was named, a senior executive at News International boasted that Downing Street had helped *The Times* identify Kelly.

The Times's next clue in the Kelly name game landed much closer to the target. Godric Smith told Hutton that at 6 p.m. on 7 July, he went to Campbell's office and heard him talking to Hoon on the phone, and that during the conversation Campbell 'floated the idea' that the news that a source had come forward could be leaked 'that evening to one paper'. An alarmed Smith advised him not to do it.

Campbell's diary entry for that day read: 'It was agreed … we should get it out that the source was not in the intelligence community, not involved in drawing up the dossier.' The next day's *Times* carried a report that used almost exactly the same words. Number 10 was con-vinced that the a source was 'not a member of the intelligence services and … not involved in drafting the report,' it said.[25]

Godric Smith was not the only one alarmed by Campbell's behav-iour. The Prime Minister was horrified by Campbell's antics and was trying to restrain him, with no success. Blair revealed his worries over the phone to Gavyn Davies on 7 July, the day Campbell was noting in his diary his determination to get more details concerning the source into the public domain. It was the first time they had spoken directly since the dispute began. Blair thanked Davies for the BBC's statement that it did not question the PM's integrity, but merely asserting its right to report a valid story.

Blair: 'That is not enough. The story is totally wrong. You need to withdraw it.'

Davies: 'Alastair has put us in an impossible situation.'

Blair: 'I realize that, but I am trying to calm him down. He has a jus-tified grievance but his behaviour has been too loud.'[26]

Davies recalled: 'Blair told me that he had been trying to calm Campbell down and that he was troubled by the way he had behaved.'[27]

By now the net was closing in on Kelly. On 9 July, the MoD press office, normally one of the most secretive in Whitehall, confirmed his name after journalists were invited to use the clues already provided to try and work out his name. When they mentioned the right one, the MoD confirmed it. *The Times* was ahead of the game again. It stated:

'No. 10 is "99 per cent convinced" that Mr Gilligan's source was David Kelly.'[28] 'We were trying to get Kelly's name from the MoD but we got it from Number 10 first,' said a News International source. This contradicts Campbell's repeated assertions that Downing Street did not leak Kelly's name.

No one had prepared Kelly for what happened next. In a forty-six second phone call, an MoD official told him he was about to be named in the morning papers. Kelly told his wife he felt betrayed by the MoD. They packed their bags in minutes, left home and went into hiding in the West Country to escape the press pack. Campbell had got what he wanted. The source was out, and what was needed now was to move onto stage two of his strategy. This was to use Kelly to – in Campbell's words – 'fuck Gilligan'.

The government set about doing this in two ways. The first was by denigrating Kelly. The government machine set out to downgrade his credibility as the BBC source by claiming that he was simply a 'middle-ranking official' of no special consequence. When it was embarrassingly revealed that Kelly accompanied Foreign Secretary Jack Straw as an expert when he gave evidence in parliament, Straw, apparently concerned to play down Kelly's authority, said he was upset that he had been fobbed off with someone so junior.[29] These were slurs. Kelly was a very senior figure, probably the leading expert in his field. He had been awarded the CMG in recognition of his work, a very high-ranking honour indeed, known within the diplomatic service as 'Call Me God'. In due course it emerged that he was up for consideration for a further honour, which would most likely have been a knighthood. This government campaign against Kelly was to continue after his death. Forty-eight hours before Dr Kelly's funeral, Tom Kelly, one of the Prime Minister's official spokesmen, in a private briefing to *Independent* political journalist Paul Waugh, labelled the late scientist a 'Walter Mitty' character.[30] Campbell berated Tom Kelly for being a 'fucking idiot'.

Tom Kelly appeared to be notably more enthusiastic than Godric Smith in embracing Campbell's aggressive style. As Downing Street tried to force the BBC to back down, Tom Kelly sent an e-mail stating: 'This is now a game of chicken with the Beeb – the only way they will shift if they see the screw tightening.'

Campbell's manic mood marred a Downing Street reception hosted by the Blairs in July for Number 10 foreign affairs adviser Sir David Manning, who was leaving to become Britain's ambassador in Washington. In the presence of George Bush's National Security Adviser Condoleezza Rice, JIC chairman John Scarlett and other diplomats and their wives, Campbell, to the embarrassment of some of those present, vowed to wreak vengeance on 'that fucking little shit Gilligan'.

The second part of the attempt to use Kelly to 'fuck Gilligan' went well beyond a simple smear. To achieve the victory over the BBC they desperately sought, it was essential for Downing Street to show that Gilligan had misrepresented much of what Kelly had told him. Several horrible days of negotiation, and interrogation of Dr Kelly, followed. Defence Minister Adam Ingram dropped a menacing public hint over the airwaves that Kelly might lose his job. Challenging the BBC to state that Kelly was not the source, Ingram told the *Today* programme: 'Hopefully this would allow Dr Kelly to carry on with his career in the MoD.'[32] On 11 July, while visiting the Lost Gardens of Heligan in Cornwall, Kelly was told that he would have to give televised evidence in front of the Foreign Affairs Select Committee. His wife said she had never known him to be so unhappy.

At this point Kelly found himself in a terrible situation. He could tell the truth about his conversation with Gilligan, or he could please the MoD and Downing Street. He could not do both. When Kelly was grilled by Richard Hatfield, Personnel Director at the MoD, he denied having given Gilligan the basis for his sensational story. 'Kelly said,' reported the MoD minute, 'that he had not described the dossier as having been transformed the week before publication, and could not recall using the term sexier.' Later in the interview Kelly denied telling Gilligan that the forty-five-minute claim was included in the dossier against the wishes of the intelligence services. 'Kelly replied that he could not believe he would have said this; he did not say that it was not in the original draft; and he didn't know the wishes of the intelligence services.'[33]

Dr Kelly's tragedy was that he had told Andrew Gilligan a great deal more than he let on to the MoD. And not just Andrew Gilligan. He had also expressed reservations to BBC reporter Gavin Hewitt and Susan Watts of *Newsnight*. The day after Gilligan's *Today* broadcast, Watts taped Kelly telling her: 'The forty-five minutes was a statement that was made and it got out of all proportion. They were desperate for information. They were pushing hard for information that could be released. That was one that popped up and it was seized on and it is unfortunate that it was. That is why there is an argument between the intelligence services and Number 10.'

The gap between what Kelly had told the MoD and had told BBC journalists was mercilessly exposed at the FAC meeting. Gilligan, desperate to protect his own reputation, inadvertently piled yet more pressure on the scientist. Without telling the BBC, Gilligan got in touch with two of the MPs on the committee, Liberal Democrat David Chidgey and Conservative Richard Ottoway, suggesting Kelly had spoken to Watts. Chidgey read out Watts' tape of Kelly's conversation. This visibly shocked the scientist who told the FAC: 'I do not recognize those comments,' he said. In fact they were made by him. The Watts tape was critical in proving Kelly did have doubts about the dossier, thereby bolstering Gilligan's claims. But by denying he had spoken to Watts, presumably through fear that it would show he was indeed Gilligan's main source, Kelly had lied. This may have been the final trigger that led him to take his life. As Lord Hutton was to comment in his report, 'It is probable that one of the concerns which must have been weighing heavily on Dr Kelly's mind during the last few days of his life was the knowledge that there appeared to be in existence, known to members of the FAC, a full note of his conversation with Ms Susan Watts on 30th May.'[34] What made the knowledge quite especially painful was the fact that Kelly had specifically said the words on the tape. Graver still, he had told his MoD bosses that he had not spoken to Watts about the September dossier.[35]

On the afternoon of 17 July, two days after appearing before the FAC, Dr Kelly informed his wife Janice that he was going to take a walk. He left his home, an eighteenth-century farmhouse in the Oxfordshire village of Southmoor, at around 3 p.m. During the course of the evening his family felt increasing alarm that he had not returned. Late in the evening two of his daughters went out searching for their father. When they could not find him, they called the police. It was 12.20 a.m. The search began at once. By the following morning, forty police officers were looking for him. In the end, however, it was two local people, Louise Holmes and Paul Chapman, who, with the aid of a trained search dog, found Dr Kelly. His body was at the base of a tree, his legs stretched out in front of him, and his head and shoulders slumped back. He had cut his left wrist and bled to death.

Catharsis

PM's lost his brain.
Sun, 30 August 2003, the day after Campbell resigned

The aftermath

AS DAVID KELLY LAY DYING in an Oxfordshire wood, Tony Blair and Alastair Campbell were together in Washington. The Prime Minister was responding to an invitation to address Congress. He was only the fourth British premier to be asked to do so. This was meant to be one of the crowning moments of Tony Blair's premiership: he and George Bush basking in the glory of their triumph in the Iraq war. There was no question of Blair's popularity in the United States: standing ovations interrupted his half-hour-long speech on no fewer than nineteen occasions.

Nevertheless, unease marked the occasion. President Bush and Prime Minister Blair, more particularly the latter, were becoming ever more embarrassed by the failure to discover Saddam Hussein's WMD in post-war Iraq. This was the issue that underlay the vicious row with the BBC. Tony Blair devoted part of his speech to a public contemplation of the non-emergence of WMD. 'Let us say one thing,' he declared. 'If we are wrong we will have destroyed a threat that, at the least, is responsible for inhuman carnage and suffering. That is something I am confident history will forgive.'

That night Alastair Campbell and Tony Blair parted company. Blair was to fly on to the Far East on a trade mission. Campbell didn't consider it worth his while to accompany the Prime Minister. As the lobby journalists stood in the White House, Campbell approached them and sneered: 'I'm going home, enjoy your week-long trade trip.' He could see few headlines in the week ahead and nor could they. Campbell's deputy Godric Smith, with Jon Smith's words of warning not to get too entangled with Campbell still ringing in his ears, took over Campbell's role.

The night before Kelly died, Campbell was at Michael Foot's ninetieth birthday party in Soho. Fiona Millar was chatting to a guest at the party, *Mail on Sunday* deputy editor Rod Gilchrist, when Campbell homed in on them. When Gilchrist introduced himself, Campbell proceeded to bark 'scum!' in his face repeatedly. Campbell moved off, but returned later and repeated the manic performance, his forehead a couple of inches from Gilchrist's. 'Lighten up, you're out of control,' Gilchrist told him. Campbell burst into a smile, brushed his hand across Gilchrist's face and walked off.

News of David Kelly's disappearance broke very early the following morning. Alastair Campbell was a ruthless man. For years it had been his customary practice to treat individual human beings as political commodities. That was his trade, and he did it for a cause, and he did it supremely well. But now someone had died. Kelly was a civilian who had crossed the barrier into the killing zone of modern politics. Politicians, spin-doctors and the press corps had the thick skins, the cynicism, the cunning, the body armour to survive. Kelly had strayed in unarmed, and never came out.

Perhaps something of this struck Alastair Campbell as he lingered in his Gospel Oak home on the morning of 18 July. He was as close to being a broken man as at any time since his emotional breakdown seventeen years before. A friend who spoke to him that day said: 'He was completely distraught. He could barely speak and he knew then that he would have to resign. He had tried to hang on to clear his name, but he couldn't go on and he knew it.'

It was time to quit. After Kelly's death it was just a matter of time before Campbell went. But first there was one last battle to fight. Campbell had to clear his name and Tony Blair's: it is a measure of his immense resilience that he was to have the strength to do so. But he was in exactly the wrong place. As Campbell loitered in Gospel Oak,

Blair was on the other side of the world, fighting for his political life aboard a plane from Washington to Japan.

The news that David Kelly's body had been found reached Blair's Boeing 777 plane some two hours before it was due to land in Tokyo, Japan. Blair used the plane's satellite communications phone to speak to Charles Falconer. The two old flatmates agreed that a public inquiry into Kelly's death was the only possible response. Within hours Falconer chose the Northern Irish law lord Brian Hutton to chair it. Godric Smith left it so late to brief the lobby that he didn't start until the undercarriage was being lowered, and finished ten seconds before the plane hit the tarmac. It was just enough time to inform political reporters travelling with the Prime Minister about the public inquiry. This tactic minimized the chance of questions, and the likelihood of the increasingly uneasy Smith being dragged personally into the crisis.

Long-planned photocalls were hurriedly scrapped or toned down. Instead a white-faced Prime Minister made a statement to TV cameras in the corridor in his hotel, with only one agency reporter allowed to be present. Blair did not want reporters shouting hostile questions at him. He praised Kelly as a 'fine public servant' and mourned his death as a 'terrible tragedy'. It was not until later in the day that he confronted the media in public. At a press conference he was asked about the Kelly affair by reporters from ITV and the BBC. Blair ignored hands that shot up from other British newspaper correspondents. But before he could leave, he was ambushed by Jonathan Oliver of the *Mail on Sunday* who shouted: 'Have you got blood on your hands, Prime Minister? Are you going to resign?' Blair's eyes blazed with outrage. He had never been treated like this and stood glaring at Oliver for several seconds, before turning and leaving the stage.

For forty-eight hours after Kelly's death Tony Blair looked ill. He only returned to anything like his normal self when the BBC, after consulting the Kelly family, confirmed that David Kelly had indeed been Andrew Gilligan's source. Any other name and the Prime Minister would surely have been finished. Those travelling with the Prime Minister say that the colour returned to his face there and then. The news perhaps emboldened him to make what came very close to a fatal mistake. Four days after Kelly's death, as he flew to Hong Kong, he strolled back from his private compartments to the reporters on the plane. He at once ran into a barrage of hostile fire from the lobby reporters who had agreed on their own strategy to try and force some meaningful answers from Blair, a master at deflecting single questions.

'Why did you authorize the naming of David Kelly?' *Daily Mail* political correspondent Paul Eastham asked him. 'That is completely untrue,' snapped Blair, who leaned forward jabbing his forefinger at the seated journalist, clearly angry. Minutes later, when Eastham asked: 'Did you authorize anyone in Downing Street or in the Ministry of Defence to release David Kelly's name?' Blair answered: 'Emphatically not.'[1]

Normally Campbell would have provided the sound bites, anticipated the hostile lines of questioning, and then hovered at the fringes, ever alert for potential troublemakers. On this one occasion, Campbell was at home and Blair was defenceless. There is little question that the Prime Minister misled reporters that day, and it could easily have cost him his job. The Hutton inquiry was later to reveal that he did indeed play a luminous part in the process that led to the outing of David Kelly. Indeed even the report itself, extremely forgiving of Downing Street lapses, went close to saying as much.[2]

In all probability Campbell would have stopped Tony Blair going back to talk to reporters, realizing that there was little to gain and much to lose. Godric Smith did not have the weight, the experience or the strong personal relationship with the Prime Minister to give that kind of advice. In any case, as the Far East trip dragged on, Smith seemed increasingly detached. By the end of the trip the journalists joked among themselves: 'Shall we ask the Prime Minister if Godric will give us a briefing?' Smith had been badly scarred by the Carole Caplin affair, when he had misled the lobby as a result of being misled by the Blairs, and he wasn't going to go out on a limb to clean the Prime Minister's dirty washing again if he could help it.[3]

Resignation

It was a long, hot, horrible summer for Alastair Campbell and the government. August, normally a month when politicians relax, was spent giving evidence to the Hutton inquiry. Every day brought new, damaging headlines. Campbell himself was called twice before the inquiry.

In his first appearance on 19 August, he admitted he had wanted to use Dr Kelly in his battle with the BBC while acknowledging that with 'hindsight' the Government should have made a better job of the way Kelly was named. In five hours of evidence, during which, in the view of most observers, he acquitted himself well and made no obvious errors, Campbell said no one involved in the case imagined that it would end with Kelly's suicide. 'I don't think it crossed anybody's mind that it would take the turn it did,' he said. He denied point blank any responsibility for the inclusion of the forty-five minutes claim, stating: 'I had no input, output or influence on them in any stage of the process.'

By the second time he was called on 22 September to be cross examined, however, he was no longer in Downing Street.

Campbell had been trying to resign for some time. Always, Tony Blair persuaded him to stay. First he urged Campbell to help establish New Labour's second term, then to deal with the crisis after 11 September, finally to win support for war with Iraq. By the spring of 2003, Alastair Campbell very badly wanted out. In April he told the Prime Minister that he and Fiona Millar had decided they would both leave by the summer holidays. This time Blair agreed.

Gilligan's grave allegation that he had 'sexed up' the September dossier caused Campbell to reconsider: he concluded that he would not walk out of Downing Street until he had won his argument with the BBC. Thereafter Blair and the Cabinet had no choice but to watch in something approaching horror as Campbell went to ever greater extremes.

Campbell's defence was that he was protecting not just his own good name, but that of the Prime Minister, the government and its justification for taking the country to war. Blair agreed that the BBC was in the wrong, but was aghast at Campbell's hysterical reaction and the damage it had inflicted on the government. He had gone too far. Much too far. Worse, Blair had told him to get a grip and Campbell had ignored him.

For his part, Campbell was frustrated that Blair was not prepared to take a more aggressive stance. Some officials and ministers thought that the war against the BBC had the valuable side effect of distracting attention from the failure to find weapons of mass destruction in Iraq. Others backed him out of simple loyalty.

The only real issue was timing. Blair also knew Campbell had to go. 'Tony realized he should have parted with Alastair at the general election,' said one Downing Street source. 'Alastair was taking everything personally. He couldn't stop talking about the *Daily Mail* and the BBC. He had lost all perspective.'[4] Tony Blair reluctantly concluded Campbell was threatening the reputation of the government he purported to defend.

There followed intense negotiations between Blair and Campbell over his exit. Initially, Campbell wanted to stay until the Hutton report was published. 'He was determined at all costs that it should not look as though he was cutting and running,' said a source.[5] Blair felt that was much too long. Campbell offered to bring it forward to the end of the Labour conference, and then to the end of the Hutton hearings in September. Still Blair was not content. He insisted Campbell should announce his resignation by the beginning of September. The damage caused to the government's reputation for honesty was too great for him to remain any longer. Eventually, Campbell agreed to resign the day after Blair gave evidence to the Hutton inquiry.

An angry departure was in the interests of neither man. Campbell managed his resignation on 29 August with the same consummate skill with which he had sent off so many ministers.

One advantage to Campbell was that he would be gone before Dr Kelly's widow, Janice, had given evidence the following Monday, 1 September. Both Blair and Campbell were concerned that she might say something so damning about Downing Street's conduct that Campbell would be forced to go there and then in disgrace. Much better to go at a time of his own choosing.

On the morning of Friday, 29 August, Campbell sent round an e-mail summoning his staff to his office. 'It won't come as any great surprise to you,' he told them, 'but I am announcing today that I am leaving Downing Street. Most of you know that I've been thinking about it for some time.' There were emotional scenes. As ever, Campbell took the precaution of alerting his lobby friends. Philip Webster and George Pascoe-Watson were driving through the highlands of Scotland on a golfing holiday. With them were two New Labour friends. One by one their mobiles went off as Campbell rang them with the news.

Meanwhile, back in London, Blair paid tribute to the retiring spin-doctor. 'The Alastair Campbell I know is an immensely able, fearless, loyal servant of the cause he believes in, who was dedicated not only to that cause but to his country. He is a strong character who can make enemies but those who know him best like him best.' The Prime Minister chose his words carefully. His description of Campbell carried a trace of ambiguity. What was 'the cause he believes in'? New Labour? Tony Blair? His own? There were no qualifications of any kind from the *Sun*. It gave him a send-off fit for a military hero with a giant double-page headline, flattering to Campbell though much less so to Blair: 'PM's lost his brain.'

Campbell knew his resignation would cause celebration in 11 Downing Street. Tension between Brown and Blair was at boiling point and about to erupt into the open at the forthcoming Labour conference. Campbell briefed friendly journalists to say that he, Mandelson and Philip Gould would remain at the heart of Blair's team, regardless of whether they had formal titles. 'Say that the Brownites shouldn't be laughing up their sleeves, because we'll still be in there,' he said.[6]

Campbell the supreme spin-doctor had performed his final act in office: by 'spinning' his own departure. As was so very often the case with Alastair Campbell, nothing was quite as it seemed. Campbell had spent two years trying to get out of Downing Street, only to be talked out of it by Blair who had felt unable to cope without him. In the end, he didn't walk, he was pushed.

Retirement

After leaving Downing Street, Campbell made no attempt to get a major new job. He made well-paid speeches at private corporate events at which he raged against the press to audiences of baffled executives.[7] He undertook a series of one-man shows in provincial theatres, where he sought to dazzle his audiences with stories of life inside Number 10. Having spent a decade in the shadows, he appeared intent on becoming a celebrity. For the first time in a decade, the public could see him in the flesh and hear what he had to say. His performances met with mixed success and Labour supporters were drummed up to fill empty seats. Campbell paid generous tribute to Blair, though it rarely got beyond 'a great bloke doing a good job'. There were inconsistencies: his disapproval of George Bush's views was evident – 'they're not my politics'. But he staunchly defended his crucial role in supporting the only Bush policy known to most of the audience: the war with Iraq. He went on and on and on about the power of the *Daily Mail*. He railed against the superficiality of the modern mass media, yet recruited stars like *EastEnders* actor Ross Kemp and Simply Red singer Mick Hucknall to host his one-man shows to whip up media and public interest.

And there were one or two revealing moments. The first question of Campbell's first show was put by *Daily Telegraph* theatre critic Charles Spencer, who suggested: 'Speaking as a recovering alcoholic I get the feeling you're a dry drunk, which is why you're so obsessive.' Campbell was speechless, and later told a friend: 'I was completely floored by the question. I just didn't know how to answer it.'

Spencer wrote afterwards: 'In my view, Campbell simply swapped the bottle for the Labour Party. It's what's known in Alcoholics Anonymous as being a "dry drunk" and the symptoms are usually obsessiveness, bullying, and sudden switches in mood. Sound familiar? Even when he's trying to be charming there is something faintly chilling about Alastair Campbell, a worrying sense of hollowness.'[8]

Campbell was seen lunching with his friend Rebekah Wade, editor of the *Sun*. This paper had printed barely a word of criticism of him throughout that torrid summer, and had at times seemed more concerned about defending Campbell's reputation than that of Blair himself. This was the newspaper where he had made a showy Fleet Street debut as a Riviera gigolo nearly a quarter of a century earlier, the newspaper he came to hate as it destroyed Neil Kinnock, the newspaper he had wooed away from the Tories to New Labour.

The *Sun*'s owner, Rupert Murdoch's News International, was said to have signed up Alastair Campbell's diaries for an estimated £2 million as part of a wider deal to work for the group. Campbell insisted, however, that he would not publish the diaries till Blair left Downing Street. Whether they were worth that sum of money remained an open question. The Hutton inquiry brought to the surface as evidence an early example of this fabled creation. His diary entries turned out to be hastily scribbled notes, little more than an aide memoire, from a strictly literary point of view a disappointment. It was obvious that Campbell was never going to rival his friend Alan Clark or Chips Channon.

His new patron, Rupert Murdoch, following in the footsteps of Neil Kinnock, Robert Maxwell and Tony Blair, appeared to be rather more successful than they had in saying 'no' to Campbell. Campbell wanted a regular media column on *The Times*. It was rejected because they feared he would use it as an outlet for his anti-*Daily Mail* obsession. He had to make to do with a sports column instead. He wrote occasional articles for the *Sunday Times*. But the *Sun* also turned down his request for a column, mainly because it did not think readers would be interested in his views.

Campbell got his comeuppance from two old rivals when he addressed a gathering of News International executives in Cancun, Mexico in 2004. As he warmed to his usual theme of criticizing the press for trivializing politics, Richard Littlejohn asked him how he squared that with his story about John Major's underpants. And the *Sun* political editor Trevor Kavanagh waded in: 'You didn't even bother to write the underpants story, you gave it to someone on another paper.' Campbell was left floundering.

He gave his first post-Number 10 interview to *The Times*, in which he described Paul Dacre, editor of the *Daily Mail*, as the 'most poisonous man in British public life'.9 The special phone which linked him direct to the Downing Street switchboard was said to remain in regular use. He claimed he still spoke to the Prime Minister 'at least twice a week'.10

The end

Based on Lord Hutton's interpretation of events, Campbell's moment of pure vindication was justified. Campbell had some reason to see Hutton as the final, apocalyptic victory in the long battle against the culture of British political journalism which he had joined in the spring of 1986, when as a young *Daily Mirror* reporter he had accompanied Neil Kinnock on his visit to President Reagan. He turned his back on the lobby then. For eight years he had worked against it from within. Then for three years, as Tony Blair's press secretary in opposition, he had connived with it to bring about the downfall of the Tories. Once installed in Downing Street, he had systematically set out to use the apparatus of power, and all that it meant in terms of patronage and threat, to attack it. In 2002, through the attack on lobby practice and the

Black Rod affair, he had confronted the press and lost. With Hutton he had won. But Campbell was not satisfied with vindication: he wanted BBC heads put on pikes and paraded through the streets of London as traitors. He got what he wanted. But his gloating triumphalism helped to stimulate a backlash against the scale of punishment inflicted on the BBC. Blair was livid. Six months earlier Campbell had defied him by singlehandedly declaring war on the BBC; now he wrecked Blair's own plan to use Hutton to make peace with the BBC. Inside or outside Downing Street, Campbell was out of Blair's control. When Greg Dyke left his office, he was greeted by hundreds of cheering BBC employees. Polls showed that a majority of the public simply refused to accept Hutton's conclusion that the government was completely innocent, while the BBC was guilty on all counts.

The Hutton report was a victory for sure, but a curious kind of victory. New Labour had never understood truth, or for that matter falsehood, in the manner of a philosopher or an historian. Truth is sometimes complex, often subversive and always difficult. Campbell was only interested in simplicity. Campbell understood truth in the most brutal kind of way: as an instrument of power. Truth was something that the ruling party owned, controlled, and used as a weapon, just as it owned and controlled jobs and patronage. In the 1980s Campbell perceived, and this insight was by no means without merit, that truth had been appropriated by a rancid press, propagating its prejudices free of facts and argument, on behalf of a Conservative government. Ownership of the truth was being used as a tool to destroy the Labour party and lift up Thatcher. In the late 1980s Campbell learnt these lessons of defeat. He could hardly avoid doing so. At the *Daily Mirror* these were banged into him again and again. He drew two conclusions during this unhappy time. The first was that the British press was fetid, partial and venal. There was nothing original in this perception: it was shared with all activists and politicians on the left.

It was Campbell's second insight that was so original and potent. He concluded that Labour could use the press, evil though he and his allies thought it was, for its own purposes. This accounts for much of Campbell's subsequent political importance: he was the first figure to find a solution to an intractable problem that had baffled the finest minds on the democratic left for a generation. The genius of Campbell, and there really is no other word for it, was to grasp that the monster could be turned. He saw this opportunity far earlier than any of his contemporaries either on the left or the right, and then he worked out its consequences with a clear-sighted ruthlessness that still takes the breath away. And so once Campbell came into Downing Street he used every technique that Mrs Thatcher had used in her pomp, and added a few of his own. She had wooed proprietors and feted a select band of editors and favoured writers, and Campbell helped Blair to do the same, only with far greater intensity than anything attempted by the Conservatives. The central objective was clear. Campbell was utterly determined to get his message across in his own way under his own terms. He sought to destroy anybody or any institution which stood in his way.

Campbell was no intellectual, never read his Marx or his Gramsci. Nevertheless, without knowing it, he entertained the Marxist insight that facts were not a neutral commodity, and that all institutions were value-laden. Having once obtained power, Campbell and his ally Peter Mandelson, who perhaps understood more deeply the nature of the project upon which they were both embarking, set about converting the state into an agent of New Labour rule. They turned their attention, as we have seen, to the government information service, dismissing nearly all departmental heads of information within two years. They greatly expanded the number of special advisers and turned them into a system of political commissars, there to enforce New Labour writ through Whitehall. Campbell refused to work closely with government officials unless they became cheerleaders for the New Labour project. Once again Margaret Thatcher had pioneered this route.[11] But once again Campbell was much more systematic and brutal than she ever was. Thatcher had had a great deal of vestigial admiration for the traditional forms of the British state. Campbell had none, except in so far they could be adapted to suit New Labour in power.

The real importance of Alastair Campbell is not as a colourful and interesting individual, though historians are certain to regard him as one of the most intriguing figures ever to operate from the heart of Downing Street. He was really the dominant personal manifestation of Tony Blair's attempt to govern Britain in an entirely new and different way. Previous governments, whether Labour, Liberal or Conservative, had all respected the institutions of representative democracy:

parliament, cabinet government, both backed by an independent civil service motivated by a disinterested ethic of public service rather than a feverish loyalty to the government of the day. The unique feature of New Labour is that it did not even pretend. Tony Blair and Alastair Campbell disliked and were contemptuous of cabinet government. Campbell in particular was quite openly derisive. 'When they had big cabinets,' Campbell once remarked, 'they spent their day doing one of two things: tearing lumps out of each other or writing diaries.'[12] This contempt for strong cabinets, like New Labour's angry obsession with the press, was a by-product of its anguished past. Labour's internal battle in the 1980s had taught New Labour the virtues of discipline, centralized control and the elimination of public debate. Tony Blair could not see the point of cabinets. He governed as a benevolent dictator, tempered by character assassination.

Campbell was Blair's vizier or grand chamberlain. Since he had such complete authority he was greatly feared by Cabinet ministers, capable of poisoning or favouring their careers. Though technically no more than a press adviser he carried more mystique and authority than they did. Campbell was the most senior and powerful representative of a new political class: the political adviser who carried more clout than politicians. Campbell was fighting an age-old battle, for the elite against an unruly democracy. But he was operating in a new environment, on behalf of a renewed ruling class, and using novel techniques. In the words of the commentator Anthony Barnett, he was seeking 'a strategy for preserving and renewing traditional rule from above in the era of a vermin press'.[13] He was among other things, a sharp symbol of the decline of representative democracy. He had invented instead a form of manipulative populism, bypassing parliament and Cabinet in an attempt to communicate directly with the voters. Margaret Thatcher had enjoyed certain insights into how such a system might work, Alastair Campbell turned it into a methodology.[14]

The events leading up to the death of David Kelly, as laid bare by Lord Hutton's investigation, showed very clearly this novel method of government in operation. Theoretically all matters to do with the government scientist David Kelly should have been a matter for the Ministry of Defence. Indeed, in a piece of touching reverence for old forms and protocols, Downing Street spokesmen insisted right up to the end that the MoD was the 'lead department' when it came to handling Kelly. In practice all decisions were made through a cabal of officials within Downing Street, much of the time without reference to the Secretary of State Geoff Hoon, a hapless figure.

The Hutton inquiry illustrated the collapse of traditional dividing lines between civil servant and politician. Campbell had a powerful role in the hardening of the language, and changing the substance, in the infamous intelligence dossier of September 2002. His comments were acted on with alacrity by John Scarlett, chairman of the Joint Intelligence Committee. Protestations from the Defence Intelligence Staff were ignored. It emerged that Campbell had been allowed to chair an intelligence meeting, in an extraordinary breach of procedure. Meanwhile Scarlett himself seemed to take on some of the functions of a spin-doctor, clustering round the word processor of a Number 10 press officer to help draft a press release. Campbell jauntily referred to Scarlett as his 'mate'. This was another New Labour innovation. Under the old constitution, intelligence information, in all of its uncertainty and confusion, had been well beyond the reach of press aides, however eminent. Now it was suddenly malleable, capable of being shaped by spin-doctors to suit the exigencies of daily political combat. Campbell and New Labour had reached a settlement with the British state which it could hardly have dreamt of seven years before.

Nor were the civil service and then intelligence services the only institutions to see their traditional independence from government challenged. Central to the project was the establishment of a domesticated press and the broadcasting media. From the moment he entered Downing Street, Campbell sought ceaselessly to bring this about. Some organizations he could capture, like News International. Others he tamed. Those he could neither tame nor capture he ruthlessly targeted, like Associated Newspapers. From the very start he launched a long, attritional attack on the BBC, and the independence of its news judgement. When the BBC came under all-out assault from the government over the Kelly affair, after six years of hand-to-hand fighting with Campbell, it tried to repel the attack. But it lost. Campbell's deepest and most equivocal legacy is that he changed the culture of parliament, the intelligence services, Whitehall and the BBC.

So his forced resignation in the late summer of 2003 did not merely mark the passing of an individual. More importantly, it marked the end of an experiment in government. It was decided that the special powers, granted through Orders in Council, which enabled Campbell to tell civil servants what to do, should not be passed on to his successor. Cabinet ministers started to show, for the first time since 1997, some sense of legal and constitutional importance – one might say that they recovered their self-respect. The length of Cabinet meetings has started to increase. A new generation of Cabinet ministers set out their own agendas rather than tamely parrot the line set of the 10 Downing Street morning meeting. When, as in April 2004, Blair did a U-turn on a referendum on the EU constitution without first discussing it formally at a Cabinet meeting, ministers were confident enough to stage an open revolt. Parliament started to assert itself, and a series of back-bench rebellions reminded 10 Downing Street of the value of a powerful Chief Whip.

The mood in Downing Street changed. It became less exciting, but calmer, more measured, less intense. In a remarkable departure Tony Blair started to talk of public-service reform not as a matter of months, but over a period of ten or fifteen years. 'There are no fits going on, no one is saying, "Is Alastair in a good mood or a bad mood today?" It is much less emotional,' remarked one Downing Street adviser. 'Tony can breathe fresh air at last,' said a friend of the Prime Minister. 'Now that Alastair is gone it has enabled him to think things through more clearly in depth. And Cherie is much more content.'

Campbell's all-powerful twin role as Blair's chief spin-doctor and head of the government information service was divided in two in an attempt to prevent anyone wielding such far-reaching influence again. His job as Blair's chief spin-doctor was given to David Hill, an old-fashioned figure likely neither to covet nor to acquire the extraordinary influence over Blair that Campbell had exercised for nearly ten years. Crucially, Hill did not inherit Campbell's power to give orders to civil servants. Peter Mandelson, of course, sought to fill the huge vacuum left by Campbell's departure, causing resentment at Number 11 by chairing meetings for the Prime Minister. But there will never be another Alastair Campbell.

appendix one

The Grid

18-24 Aug	Mon 18	Tues 19	Weds 20	Thur 21	Fri 22	Sat-Sun 23-24
			WEEK 34			**PRINT: 15 AUG 2003**
Main News	Hutton inq: Teare, Powell & Manning	Hutton inq: Manning & Campbell	Hutton inq: Tebbit, Smith & Kelly	Hutton inq: Anderson (FAC) & print journos 00.01 GCSE results US/UK Iraq update rept to UN		Jowell: speech at Edinburgh TV Festival plus Q&A (23)
DURING THE WEEK Sun asylum week ✓ Colombia IRA trial verdict (tbc)						
Statistics	00.01 Tomlinson rept on 2003 exams process	Milliband: key stage test results for 7, 11 & 14 yr olds	Public sector finances (June) CML mortgage lending survey (July) Comparison of indep economic forecasts	Retail sales (July) ONS health quarterly; CBI monthly trends; invest-ment (Q2); life expectancy 91-01; regional GDP 01/02; light rail 02/03	UK output, income & exp	
Other Government News	Blears: action on hooliganism Inc latest stats Hutton: more cash for cataract ops Morley: Darwin biodiversity grants Hope: con doc on building regs re sound proof Lewis: new adult skills adverts DTI: briefing re Smart 1 mission to Moon HSE rept on incidents at BP Grangemouth	DPM: planning item Good Hope hosp Birmingham franchise Milliband: rept on teaching reading DPM to coalfields regeneration site, Doncaster NHS grant fraud item DH: Nurses Pay Review Body rept re Agenda for Change PM public e-mail goes live (no launch) (tbc)	00.01 HMIProb rept on London probation Jowell: foundation stone for Diana Fountain Hope: arson control grants Blears: visit to Haringey police re drug testing MPC minutes	00.01 Blunkett asylum interview in Sun (tbc) ONS Health Quarterly rept inc Shipman stats & deaths of young people DPM visit to Bristol (New Deal for Communities) National Archives monthly release (1700) inc Poulson files Ofwat rept on water companies financial performance 02/03	Ofsted rept on early yrs progress Law Comm annual rept	Jowell: plan for BBC On Line review (23) Central London buses all pay before you enter (23)
Europe		Lockerbie draft UN resolution (tbc)	UN Sec Coun debate on Middle East EU emergency protection for cold water reef	ECB Gov Coun		Schroeder & Berlusconi meet in Verona (23)
General	Lakhani appears in NY Court re missile charge Soham police officer on trial for child porn (reporting restrictions)	Bio Weapons Convn mtg, Geneva (Kelly 1 min silence)	Football: England v Croatia friendly, Ipswich ✓ Postcont: end of consultation on liberalisation	CWU start post office strike ballot (result on 11 Sept) (tbc) USUNICEF/Iraq Gov Coun vaccination day	Edinburgh TV Festival (22-24) Indonesian Foreign Minister in Australia for terror talks Lee Ryan of Blue (team of popular musicians) in court re drink-driving Cricket: England v South Africa, Headingly	New directory enquiries 118 line starts (24) Major rail closures begin for works (23) Notting Hill Carnival (24-25) World Athletics Championships, Paris (23-31)

Black Rod's Letter to the PCC

Lieutenant General Sir Michael Willcocks KCB

Draft

8th May 2002

Thank you for your letter of 7th May 2002 which invites me to comment on the complaint from Alastair Campbell about newspaper and magazine articles concerning the Prime Minister's role in the funeral of HM Queen Elizabeth the Queen Mother. I am of course only too willing to help, but I should make it clear from the outset that I have absolutely no knowledge of the Prime Minister's personal involvement in any of the events being investigated, nor of any of his dealings with his staff. What I think therefore would be of most help to yourselves is that, first, I should explain the circumstances as they affected myself and my team. Then, rather than attempt to pick out and deal with elements of the No.10 submission and the articles to which it relates, give you our recollections of what was, for us at least, a hectic period of planning, preparation, rehearsal and execution of a complex event. I will deal with your more specific questions at the end, as I believe it is necessary to understand the context before it is possible to make a considered judgement on the articles.

I received the news of the Queen Mother's death in the late afternoon of Saturday 30th March and quickly established with Buckingham Palace that I could give the order to "execute" the plan for the lying-in-state immediately. The first Palace co-ordination meeting was set for 11.00 am on Monday 1st April and I therefore called my initial meeting for all the Palace of Westminster staff on Sunday afternoon 31st March. It was on my way to that meeting from my house in Oxfordshire that I received the first of many telephone calls from the staff at No.10 Downing Street.

The substance of this call was to query the role of the Prime Minister in the coming ceremonials. Phrases such as "doesn't the PM greet the Queen", "doesn't he meet the coffin" and finally "well, what is his role?" were used. However, on that first occasion, it was what I would have expected of such a call. I answered all such questions by pointing out firmly, there being no latitude in the planning, that the PM had no such roles but would merely lead the tributes of the House of Commons and if possible be present with the House in Westminster Hall for the arrival of the coffin on Friday 5th April. I explained how, on Parliamentary, as opposed to Government, occasions such roles are undertaken by the triumvirate of the Lord Great Chamberlain, the Lord Chancellor and the Speaker. There was no mention at this stage of the "internal guidance on the role of the PM, written in 1994" which it was later claimed was the reason behind these queries. This is a document of which we have had no sight and have no knowledge. None of our many iterations of the plan for the Queen Mother's lying-in-state ever included a central role for the PM.

However, after this initial contact, and throughout the next 5 days, my staff and myself were telephoned, at times it seemed constantly, by staff at No.10 repeating these questions on the role of the PM, but also exerting rather more pressure along the lines of: "don't you think the PM ought to be at the North Door? (of Westminster Hall)"..........; "he must have more of a role surely......."; "Don't you think that he ought to be given a role?" etc. Although, because of the demands of the circumstances, we could not keep a complete telephone log, the records that we do have show at least a dozen or so of such calls and a personal visit by a member of No.10's staff, all of which followed the pattern above. The feeling we all had was one of sustained pressure from that quarter and, although it is true that at that stage, I was never asked to change the arrangements, the clear impression was one of being made to feel that we should. This was reinforced by being told that if there were to be any variation we could always get back to Ms Claire Sumner at No.10.

My outer office, where three of my secretaries were working full time, was set up as an operations room for this period and a constant flow of people passed through it at all hours. It is therefore possible that many of these gained the sense of our frustration at the constant querying of No.10 and some would have heard the exchanges and subsequent staff discussions. Hence there may indeed have been collateral sources who may have spoken to journalists.

At one stage on the telephone I had to take a No.10 official through the entire ceremonial for the arrival of the coffin, minute by minute, and person by person. It was largely because of this experience that I proposed that the two Houses of Parliament should, once the Royal Family had taken its leave, file past each side of the coffin to exit via the North Door led by the PM and the Leader of the House of Lords respectively. There were also the practical considerations of how to get the number of Peers and MPs out of the Hall in a dignified fashion. I was thus able to give the PM a role and show him on the plan for the ceremonial, which was subsequently collected by No.10.

I come now to the events on the day of the reception of the Queen Mother's coffin at Westminster Hall. Shortly before the arrival of HM the Queen at the North Door, and when the reception party of the triumvirate and the Archbishop of Canterbury and myself were lined up to greet Her, I received an urgent message from No.10, via the Co-ordinating Officer for the Police Protection Officers, saying that the PM intended to walk to the Palace from Downing Street and wished to know if he could enter via the North Door. I had a fairly public discussion on the merits of such a walk, with among others the Lord Chancellor, and sent back a message to say that I didn't advise it. By return I received a more insistent request that in any case the PM be allowed to enter through the North Door. I said that I didn't think it was a good idea so close to HM the Queen's arrival but also that "he is the PM so of course he can if he really wants to". In the event, he arrived by car and not via the North Door.

Let me now turn to the publication of the various articles. I was unaware of the Peter Oborne's article in the Spectator until alerted to it by Ms Sumner of No.10 who asked if I would provide a refutation of the first two paragraphs which related to events involving me. I said that I would do so because the statement that I (presumably the official mentioned) was told that the PM was unhappy and that he wanted the arrangements changed was not factually correct insofar as it affected me. I therefore produced the following statement on the record which I read to No.10, and gave to our own Information Officer and to my team of my Deputy and my secretaries for use in any further Press enquiries:

> "In the immediate aftermath of the news of the death of HM
> the Queen Mother, I was contacted by the staff at No.10 to
> brief them on the PM's role in the events that would take
> place in Westminster Hall. I did so and explained the
> ceremonial. At no stage was I ever asked to change these
> arrangements".

This statement was in my handwriting and not issued as a press statement.

Later, in a further telephone conversation with Ms Sumner I told her that I had made the statement, that I had not been asked to change the arrangements, because it was true. However, I went on to say that I did not feel I should be drawn into any further dealings with the Press because, as No.10 was aware, there was some substance underlying the bald facts of the Spectator paragraphs and I could not lie about the events.

The second article to appear was that of the Evening Standard on Friday 12th April. Once again I had no contact with the paper either before or subsequent to its publication.

Finally, we come to the Mail on Sunday articles. Here, I did have contact with their author, Simon Walters, before publication. He came to see me on 11th April to research a story on the costs of the lying-in-state operation. At the end of the interview he made it clear that he had sources which in effect substantiated the underlying thrust of the Spectator's original article. Although I repeated my on the record statement, I was surprised by the quality of his information because I could not in truth deny the main force of his contentions.

Perhaps I could end by observing on the central question you posed me on whether the publications published inaccurate material. I start, of course, by reiterating that I have no knowledge of the PM's involvement in all this or of his dealings with his staff.

You may feel that, by making my on the record statement, I have already answered the question with respect to the Spectator article. I do not believe that to be so as it could be argued that my denial was a very narrow and very precise interpretation of what Oborne had written and it was based only on the early contact between myself and No. 10. Given this and the full circumstances of what followed my interpretation might be seen as making a distinction without a difference. Had the contacts with No. 10 merely been limited to a proper and understandable exploration of the PM's role at that early stage, then Oborne's article would have been without foundation. However, given the way in which pressure was subsequently applied, had Oborne chosen to express the essence of his allegations in a different way, they could not have been denied.

The Standard article, insofar as it affects me, merely casts doubt on the veracity of my denial. I believe I have covered my views on this above and I do not need to comment further.

I find it rather difficult to fault the Mail on Sunday, insofar as its articles dealt with my experiences, as they capture events reasonably well. There may be matters of exaggerated tone but these are more a matter of journalistic style and interpretation; in all other respects their reporting, on events that concerned me, is broadly accurate.

I hope you find the above useful in your deliberations, but do not hesitate to come back to me if you require clarification, or you need anything further.

GENTLEMAN USHER OF THE BLACK ROD

Notes

Prologue
1   *Independent*, 31 January 2004.
2   *Radio Times*, 9 February 2004.
3   Private information.

Chapter 1
1   *The Times*, 2 March 2004.

Chapter 3
1   Interview with author.
2   *Sunday Telegraph*, 6 January 2002.
3   ibid.
4   ibid.
5   ibid.
6   *Daily Mirror*, 7 March 2003.
7   Private information.

Chapter 4
1   Interview with authors.
2   Private information.
3   *Sunday Mirror*, 23 April 1989.
4   *Sunday Mirror*, 30 April 1989.
5   *Guardian*, 4 April 1998.
6   *Daily Mirror*, 27 May and 2 June 1992.
    I am indebted to Colin Brown, John
    Prescott's biographer, for pointing
    out that Campbell was responsible
    for both articles.
7   Andy McSmith, *Forces of Labour*
    (1997), p. 262.
8   Nearly a decade later Campbell, as
    the Prime Minister's press secretary,
    was accused of attempting to have
    Hernon thrown out of the parliamen-
    tary lobby.

Chapter 5
1   *Today*, 9 May 1994.

2   *Today*, 30 May 1994.
3   *Today*, 17 February 1994.
4   Private information.
5   *Guardian*, 1 February 1991.

Chapter 6
1   Private information.
2   *Sunday Express*, 19 July 1992. See also
    John Rentoul, *Tony Blair*, Little,
    Brown (2001) for Campbell's role as
    'proto-press secretary'.
3   Private information.
4   South Shields Custom House, 30
    January 2004.
5   *Newsnight*, 12 May 1994.
6   *Today*, 16 May 1994.
7   Private information.
8   *The Unfinished Revolution* (1998).
9   *Today*, 6 October 1994.

Chapter 7
1   Private information.
2   Private information.
3   See Rentoul, op. cit. p. 257.
4   Private information.
5   *Sunday Telegraph*, 26 September
    1999.
6   The term White Commonwealth
    was first used to describe the select
    group of mainly Labour-supporting
    lobby journalists cultivated by Joe
    Haines.
7   Private information.

Part 2
1   Private information.
2   Accompanied by fellow Labour press
    officer Hilary Coffman, partner of

David Hill, who was to succeed Campbell six years later.

3   Private information. Asked two years later if he had made comments to civil servants about ministers' private lives, Campbell said: 'I wouldn't do that.' Pressed to say if the report of his conduct, provided by an official who witnessed it, was a fabrication, he said: 'No. I'm giving you the answer and I know what the game is and I'll just have to answer the questions as best I can.' He repeatedly said he had made no such remarks to 'a meeting of civil servants'. There was no suggestion the comments were made at a formal meeting; they occurred when he wandered into a room where officials were chatting. He added: 'What I can't deny is that in all the time I've spoken to different people, that I've said things about people of a personal nature. I can't deny that because I have conversations with people. Sometimes I have had to because of the nature of the job.' See *Mail on Sunday*, 29 August 1999.

4   Private information.

5   Private information. The quotes from the Cabinet meeting are taken from a contemporary record.

Chapter 8

1   Interviews with authors.

2   He meant the Sunday papers.

3   Interviews with authors.

4   Paul Linford, 'North MP Puts Labour In A Spin', *Newcastle Journal*, 4 July 2000.

5   Linda McDougall, 'Blair's Fallen Star', *The Times*, Friday 5 May 2000.

6   *Sunday Telegraph*, 6 April 1997.

7   Private information.

8   The authors are grateful to lobby journalists for this anecdote.

9   Private information.

10   Private information.

11   Private information.

12   *News of the World*, 3 August 1997.

13   Andrew Rawnsley, *Servants of the People*, Hamish Hamilton (2000), p. 57.

14   Private information.

15   *Daily Telegraph*, 30 January 2001.

16   *News of the World*, 8 November 1998.

17   Press Association, 8 November 1998.

18   Private information.

19   *Guardian*, 16 November 1998.

20   Interview with author.

21   *Sun*, 10 November 1998.

22   Private information.

23   6 January 2003.

24   Campbell memo to Field and Harman 15 January 1998.

25   ibid, 26 February 1998.

26   *Daily Express*, 22 June 2000, 'Why Blair Knows The Truth About Europe'.

Chapter 9

1   *The Times*, 18 October 1997.

2   Asked whether Campbell had briefed him on Brown's alleged 'psychological flaws', he replied: 'I remember that one week in January 1998 I wrote a column about the relationship between Gordon Brown and Tony Blair which I thought was rather a good and well-informed column and which was not used by the *Mirror*. It was one of the reasons I ended up leaving.'

3   *Observer*, 18 January 1998.

Chapter 10

1   Private information.

2   Private information.

3   Hardy, interview with authors.

4   Private information.

5   Press Association, 3 August 1999.

6   *Sunday Express*, 26 November 2000.

7   Family reasons prevented Desmond from taking it up.

8   Private information.

9   *Guardian*, 30 May 2002.

10   *Sunday Express*, 26 November 2000.

11   Private information.

12   Private information.

13   For instance Campbell drafted the Blair prospectus *Principle, Purpose, Power*.

14   See Matthew Parris, Another Voice, *Spectator*, 26 October 2002. Parris generously concludes: 'I do not think Alastair threatened me dishonestly. I expect he had no recollection of our in-car conversation, realized this was

long before Euan went to the Oratory and concluded I must have made it up.'

15   *Daily Express*, 21 June 1994. 'Blair wants to send son to Tory flagship opt-out school.'

16   Quoted on *Guardian Unlimited* website.

17   ibid.

18   ibid.

19   By the time that the Mittal scandal occurred Campbell no longer personally briefed the lobby. The job had been taken over by two spokesmen, Tom Kelly and Godric Smith, while Campbell took on a more strategic role as Director of Communications. The quotes are taken from the Downing Street website, from which it is impossible to tell whether they were actually uttered by Smith or Kelly.

20   Lobby briefing, 11 a.m., 11 February 2002, No. 10 website.

21   Lobby briefing, 4 p.m., 11 February 2002, No. 10 website. 'FCO officials would then have drawn up the draft which would then have been submitted to the Prime Minister for signature. In this case, the Prime Minister had signed it and sent it back unchanged.'

22   See, for instance, Marie West and John Lichfield, 'Blair Comes Under New Pressure on Garbagegate,' *Independent*, 14 February 2002.

23   Lobby briefing: 4 p.m., 11 February 2002.

24   Lobby briefing: 11 a.m., 11 February 2002.

25   As reported in the *Daily Mail*, 14 February 2002.

26   *Bucharest Business Week*, 23 July 2001, Vol. 5, No. 28.

27   David Hughes, 'Four Lies of No. 10', 14 February 2002.

28   See for example Philip Smucker, Sarah Womack and David Graves, 'Sphinx Reveals Secret of Blair Family Break', *Daily Telegraph*, 28 December 2001.

29   Nicholas Watt, 'Blair Faces Tax Bill For Holiday at Egypt's Expense', *Guardian*, 6 April 2002.

30   BBC seminar, Nuffield College, Oxford, 23 January 1998.

31   BBC *Today*, 23 January 1998.

32   *Observer*, 17 August 1997.

33   Private information.

Chapter 11

1   *Daily Mail*, 24 December 1998.

2   For Campbell's official version of events see *The Times* on 24 December. It read: 'The minister telephoned Mr Blair at about 10 p.m. and, in an emotional exchange, said that he was angry with himself for landing the Government in trouble. He then told the Prime Minister that he intended to resign. In another conversation at around 10 a.m. he confirmed his decision and Mr Blair did not attempt to dissuade him, agreeing with him that he should go because of what Mr Blair himself saw as a serious lapse of judgment.'

3   Private information.

4   Private information.

5   Peter Mandelson and Roger Liddle, *The Blair Revolution*, Faber (1996).

6   Later on, towards the very end of his period in No. 10, Campbell went into training for the London marathon and would jog into work.

7   *Daily Mail*, 30 August 2003.

8   See for example 'Halt the Asylum Tide Now', *Sun,* 18 August; 'Our Heritage is Crumbling', *Sun,* 19 August; 'Health', *Sun,* 20 August 2003.

9   The story was leaked to the Labour-supporting *Daily Record*, which rejected it, believing it to be a smear, and then to the *Sun* which published it.

10   Private information.

11   Andrew Rawnsley, *Servants of the People*, op. cit., p. 68.

12   Private information.

13   Private information.

14   Private information.

15   See analysis in the *Spectator*, 5 June 2002.

16   Private information.

17   Private information.

18   Private information.

19   See 'Heseltine and Blair in Secret

Euro Plot', *Sunday Express*, 28 February 1999.

20   Goodlad was induced to abandoned his safe Conservative seat of Eddisbury to become High Commissioner in Australia. Patten took a number of posts, ending up as a European Commissioner.

21   Friends of Portillo did not discourage suggestions that he might be a candidate for NATO secretary general, a job which in due course went to the former cabinet minister George Robertson.

22   Conversation with Alan Clark. See also Alan Clark, *The Last Diaries*, ed. Ion Trewin, p. 281, 'Gratifyingly Alastair C came on the phone for 35 minutes on Friday night twice offering me a peerage, incidentally.' Campbell later denied that he had ever offered Clark a peerage. See *The Times*, 7 October 2002.

Chapter 12

1   Michael Crick, *The Boss*, p. 457.
2   See *The Times*, 17 January 2004.
3   Private information.
4   *The Times*, 17 January 2004.
5   See Crick, op. cit., p. 456.
6   *Sun*, 26 May 1999.
7   Private information.
8   Interview with authors.
9   Private information.
10   *The Times*, 16 April 1999.
11   Private information.
12   *Sunday Telegraph*, 6 July 2003.
13   New Labour spin-doctors were reportedly present along with President Clinton at the June 1999 meeting in Florida where Hillary Clinton finally decided to run for Senate.
14   Interview with authors.
15   Campbell letter to Jones, 27 March 2000.
16   In the end the Hindujas' cash donation to the Dome amounted to just £365,000.
17   Private information.
18   Private information.
19   Andrew Rawnsley, *Servants of the People*, revised edition, Penguin (2001), p. 450.
20   *Observer*, 28 January 2001.

21   *Guardian*, 30 January 2001.

Chapter 13

1   Private information.
2   Private information.
3   Private information.
4   Private information.
5   Lobby note, Friday 8 June 2001, No. 10 website.
6   Private information.
7   Private information.
8   Marathon runner Campbell said he would try, but never got the chance.
9   Private information.
10   Private information.
11   *Tony Blair: The Making of a World Leader*, Philip Stephens, Politico's (2004).
12   South Shields, 30 January 2004.
13   Private information.
14   *Sunday Times*, 3 March 2002.
15   Interview with authors.
16   *Daily Mail*, 30 August 2003.
17   Private information.
18   See Professor Peter Hennessey's lucid account in the RSA Journal, December 2002, pp. 42–45.
19   Hennessey, op. cit.
20   Hennessey, op. cit.
21   *The Times*, 23 February 2004.
22   *The Times*, 25 February 2004.

Chapter 14

1   Fabian Society pamphlet, March 1999. The analysis that follows is partly drawn from Peter Oborne, 'A Flea in the Government's Ear', *British Journalism Review*, vol. 13, no. 4, 2002.
2   Jonathan Freedland and Roy Greenslade in the *Guardian*, John Lloyd in the *Financial Times*, David Aaronovitch in the *Independent* and Alice Miles in *The Times* were all important and articulate advocates.
3   *Political Quarterly*, Autumn 2002; *Prospect Magazine*, October 2002.
4   The articles in the *Spectator* and *Evening Standard* were written by Peter Oborne. The article in the *Mail on Sunday* was written by Simon Walters.
5   The briefing from the Prime Minister's Official Spokesman on the offi-

cial Downing Street website for Thursday, 11 April 2002 can still be read today. The PMOS states that the *Spectator* story 'was a lie and simply malicious gossip which was being written as fact'.

6   *Guardian*, 22 April 2002. In an article on the Guardian Unlimited website, he accused the *Spectator* of a 'gross distortion of journalistic ethics'.

7   Campbell's letter to PCC, 24 April 2002.

8   Simon Walters.

9   Black Rod's 'killer memo' to the PCC, 8 May 2002.

10 Interview with authors.

11 Private information.

12 Private information.

13 Private information.

14 Private information.

15 Private information.

16 See for example *The Times*, 13 December 2002.

17 Private information.

18 Private information.

19 Private information.

20 *The Times*, 6 December 2002.

21 Private information.

22 Private information.

23 Private information.

24 *News of the World*, 8 December 2002.

25 ibid.

26 Private information.

Chapter 15

1   Private information.

2   'How Saddam Hides Illegal Weapons Sites: Blair to reveal spy dossier of video and phone taps,' *Observer*, 2 February 2003. 'Blair: Iraq's Dirty Tricks Foiled (Hans) Blix', *Sunday Mirror*, 2 February 2003.

3   HC Debate, 3 February 2003, Col 25.

4   Even the Labour-controlled Foreign Affairs committee concluded that Tony Blair, by referring to the report in the way he did, 'misrepresented its status'.

5   Although he did say the information was 'unreliable' and had been 'misinterpreted.'

6   At no stage did Campbell ever complain about the *Mail on Sunday* story to the paper.

7   The first, sent a week later, merely challenged Gilligan's knowledge of the JIC and wrongly denied the forty-five-minute claim was based on one uncorroborated source. In fact Defence Minister Adam Ingram had already confirmed it came from a single source. In the second, sent on 12 June, Campbell changed tack, claiming the BBC had broken its own guidelines by relying on a single source. And he attacked them for repeating an allegation in the *Sunday Telegraph* that he had written a letter of apology to the head of MI6, Sir Richard Dearlove. This was disingenuous, since it later emerged that Campbell did apologize to Dearlove, though by phone, not in writing. The letters can be seen on the Hutton Inquiry website, CAB/1/0244 and CAB/1/0250.

8   Private information.

9   *Today* programme, 25 June 2003.

10 *Guardian*, 28 June 2003.

11 On some sections of Burnley FC's terraces, Blackburn Rovers are referred to as 'Bastard Rovers.'

12 See the GICS media monitoring unit transcript of the interview on the Hutton inquiry website, CAB/1/0368.

13 Private information.

14 Private information.

15 Private information.

16 *Guardian*, 4 July 2003.

17 Private information.

18 Private information.

19 At the Hutton inquiry, Gilligan produced the £4.15 drinks bill, showing he and Kelly had had a bottle of Coca-Cola and a £1.95 bottle of Appletise, which the reporter claimed back on BBC expenses. Lobby journalists in the inquiry room blushed at the thought of their own expense claims.

20 Richard Sambrook also wrongly said Kelly was a 'senior and credible source in the intelligence services' when he gave a *Today* programme interview to answer Campbell's attack on 26 June. Afterwards he claimed that he felt unable to correct

this mistake because of fears that might help identify Kelly.

21　Hutton inquiry evidence CAB/39/0001.

22　ibid.

23　John Scarlett, chairman of the Joint Intelligence Committee.

24　Sir Kevin Tebbit, permanent secretary at the MoD, was quite clear about this sequence of events when he came in front of the Hutton inquiry on 13 October: 'A policy decision on the matter had not been taken until the Prime Minister's meeting on Tuesday [8 July]. And it was only after that that any of the press people had an authoritative basis on which to proceed.'

25　*The Times*, 8 July 2004.

26　Interview with authors.

27　Interview with authors.

28　*The Times*, 10 July 2003.

29　See Hutton inquiry September, p. 39, exchange between James Dingemans and Mrs Kelly. Mrs Kelly: 'Jack Straw had said he was upset at the technical support at that Committee meeting, he had been accompanied by somebody so junior.' Dingemans: 'How had Dr Kelly taken that?' Mrs Kelly: 'He laughed. It was a kind of hysterical laugh in a way. He was deeply, deeply hurt.'

30　*Independent*, 4 August 2003.

31　Shortly after Waugh's story, Campbell was jogging in Hampstead and saw the slight figure of Waugh walking towards him near the Royal Free Hospital. 'Paul!' he boomed, veering towards his prey. 'No, it's Mark actually,' came the startled reply. Paul Waugh's identical twin brother, Mark had come from visiting his wife in the Royal Free, where she had just given birth. 'Oh my God,' said the horrified Campbell, who apologized profusely.

32　*Today* programme, 16 July 2003.

33　See Report of the Inquiry into the Circumstances Surrounding the Death of Dr David Kelly CMG, HC 247, 2004, p. 44.

34　Report of the Inquiry, p. 303.

35　ibid, p. 303.

Chapter 16

1　Official Transcript, 22 July 2003.

2　'The issuing of the statement authorized by the Prime Minister did give rise to the questions by the press as to the identity of the civil servant, and these questions led onto the MoD confirming Dr Kelly's name …' Report of the Inquiry, p. 286.

3　Smith contradicted Campbell's evidence to the inquiry by revealing that on 7 July Campbell had floated the idea of leaking to a friendly newspaper the fact that Gilligan's source had come forward. Smith said he talked Campbell out of it.

4　Private information.

5　Private information.

6　Private information.

7　Private information.

8　*Daily Telegraph*, 31 January 2004.

9　*The Times*, 10 January 2004.

10　ibid.

11　Charles Powell and Bernard Ingham were close to abandoning even the pretence of civil service impartiality by the end.

12　Private information.

13　Anthony Barnett, 'The Campbell Code', www.opendemocracy.net

14　See David Marquand, 'Tony Blair and Iraq: a public tragedy', www.opendemocracy.net

Index